*f*P

THE
BOY KINGS

A JOURNEY INTO THE HEART

OF THE SOCIAL NETWORK

KATHERINE LOSSE

Free Press
New York   London   Toronto   Sydney   New Delhi

A Note to Readers
Names and identifying details of some of the people portrayed in this book have
been changed.

Free Press
A Division of Simon & Schuster, Inc.
1230 Avenue of the Americas
New York, NY 10020

First Free Press hardcover edition June 2012

FREE PRESS and colophon are trademarks of Simon & Schuster, Inc.

For information about special discounts for bulk purchases, please contact Simon
& Schuster Special Sales at 1-866-506-1949 or business@simonandschuster.com.

The Simon & Schuster Speakers Bureau can bring authors to your live event. For
more information or to book an event, contact the Simon & Schuster Speakers
Bureau at 1-866-248-3049 or visit our website at www.simonspeakers.com.

Designed by Carla Jayne Jones

Manufactured in the United States of America

10 9 8 7 6 5 4 3 2 1

ISBN 978-1-4516-6825-4
ISBN 978-1-4516-6827-8 (ebook)

To <3

"Shall I project a world?"
—*Thomas Pynchon*

CONTENTS

INTRODUCTION

At the sputtering beginning of this new century we were all, perpetually, waiting for something to happen. After the sudden, unexpectedly fiery morning of 9/11, we developed a new, nonspecific vigilance: a demand to know that some critical event, somewhere, was occurring, however distant. Most things that the cable news reported on after 9/11 seemed irrelevant: a toothless bomb scare here, a prop-plane crash there. We clung to televised surveillance because it was the one thing we could count on: distant wars and threats. To assist our indiscriminate monitoring, cable news created a news ticker that ran underneath the newscast to assure us hourly that yes, somewhere, something terrible had occurred. And, perhaps, because war, unlike understanding and diplomacy, seemed clear and defined, our president started a war, but that didn't work; so he started another war, and that didn't work either. Suddenly, nothing was really working.

I spent the early 2000s nursing a nervous anxiety that reflected the nation's, fed by a general sense of foreboding and by outsized ambition and aimless anticipation—the impulse to do something or be someone at all cost that characterizes one's early twenties. Having graduated from Wesleyan with a degree in English, I found myself in a graduate program at Johns Hopkins that was, I soon discovered, as spectacularly failure-ridden as the new century. My Ph.D. program began golden and full of promise, with the assurance that we would enter easily into the ranks of the elite and tenured professors produced by the top-rated English department. However, constant and sundry department shakeups and scandals left us uneasy and uncertain, and my bright future seemed doomed. Jobs in English departments were dwindling and most Ph.D. students were finding themselves in decade-long holding patterns, waiting for jobs that would never come.

To add to my sense of anxiety, Johns Hopkins was perched atop a hill in Baltimore, which is a bizarre and barren city, especially for someone from Arizona, unfamiliar with the advanced state of America's postindustrial urban decay. Hopkins, we were told proudly in orientation, was the largest employer in the city. The unacknowledged second was the drug trade, supported by the steady stream of heroin flowing through the port. The streets just beyond the campus were full of mayhem, opaque and unreal to the outsider, with men on street corners wearing long white T-shirts whose daily work I would only come to grasp after *The Wire* began airing. As the show's Omar explained, capturing Baltimore city's prescient, postapocalyptic logic perfectly: "It's all in the game." He was right: If we went to Hopkins hoping to indulge in the endless play of academic discourse, what we got instead was a cold education in the hard facts of twenty-first-century American life: wealthy institutions pitted against students, individuals against one another, rampant poverty and violence. No one—not the Hopkins students who were occasionally murdered, nor the grad students whose promised jobs didn't actually exist—was safe anymore.

In response, students I knew at Hopkins developed a streetwise approach to life. "You have to fight crazy with crazy," we told each other before we ventured out on the empty, dangerous streets at night. It was this mode of watchfulness, alert to the sinister and absurd, rather than the lessons of literary theory, that I would end up taking from Baltimore when I left. Literary theory, after all, had begun to seem not so much like a profession as a luxury. As my thesis advisor often said, "I am rich, millions are not," quoting *American Psycho,* but he could just as well have been describing Johns Hopkins, an island of money in the midst of an alternately warring and desolate city that wasn't so much a twentieth-century relic as a window onto the twenty-first century.

As if to occupy us while we all waited for news that something had happened somewhere, in 2004, Mark Zuckerberg released a technology that hit Hopkins and spread quickly across campus like iPods had the year before. It was called The Facebook then and I discovered it while sipping coffee at the campus cafe above the underground library. A couple of students sitting at the table next to me, who sported the Hopkins uniform of North Face jacket and sweatpants, spoke excitedly of the new network and what they were able to see on the site. "Everyone's on it," they said, "you can see where they're from, where they live, and who their friends are. I don't know if it's creepy or cool."

I opened my clunky white iBook, typed www.thefacebook .com in the browser address bar, and created an account with my university email address. (This was required to log into Facebook then; one had to be a student at an Ivy or near–Ivy League school to use it.) It was true, you could see everything: all the students on campus, their pictures, their interests, their friends. And, in being able to see everything, I saw that The Facebook had miraculously solved the biggest social problem that plagued Hopkins and had led to its low rankings in student satisfaction. The campus had no public space aside from the library, which is why that afternoon, like most, I was sitting in the sunlit cafe with my laptop, taking a break from the dungeonlike stacks below. In an instant, Facebook had created a public space, albeit a virtual one, that was accessible at any time, from anywhere.

In 2004, other online social networks, like Friendster, already existed. However, most college students had spent their high school years on AOL, and knew that having a public, guileless, and unprotected Internet presence was little more than an invitation to be spammed by sexual solicitations from faraway men. Before social networks, AOL Instant Messenger and similar chat services were the only truly interactive, in-real-time forms of communication on the Web. In those days, I was always somewhat dismissive of boys who asked me if I had AIM, because it was obvious that they wanted to communicate in instant message form to avoid all the social challenges and filters of real life and, say, ask me out without having to look me in the eye, or look at me at all. So, the idea of creating a profile on an open, national social network felt like an unnecessary risk, another way of making yourself available to millions of distant strangers for the benefit of only a few friends. Who needed that? The lonely, maybe, or the exhibitionist, but most people weren't enough of either to make a public online profile listing all your private details that compelling. However, by building a virtual agora made up only of people you might actually know in real life, Facebook had suddenly created a good reason for everyone, not just the Internet-obsessed boy in his bedroom, to be identifiably on the Internet.

As one such boy who attended a class for which I served as a teaching assistant protested, pre-Facebook, and after Googling me without success, "You're not on the Internet!" (Because for the boy in his bedroom, and eventually for everyone else on the Internet, gathering data about people using Google felt like a god-given right). "Good," I replied, with satisfaction.

It wasn't like I didn't use the Internet, to the contrary. In the 1990s, when the Internet was in its infancy, I had an email account that I could only access using a no frills program that had no buttons like those currently seen on the Web; to send an email, I had to type a command like "send." Teenage hacker friends that I met at punk rock shows in Arizona used the Internet primarily to trade information about what were then high-tech hacks: a tone dialer cobbled together from Radio Shack gadgets that allowed you to make free phone calls from pay phones, or a breakdown of how credit-card numbers are generated that allowed you to crack credit cards. It almost seemed, then, that this was what the Internet was for: an anarchistic sphere devoted to wielding technology against corporations. I thought it was cool, but in the absence of sites targeted to more general interests there wasn't much for me to do online except write emails and visit bulletin boards, all green text on black screens.

A hacker once taught me that, in Pine, the email software used before AOL came along, you could type commands like "finger" to see when someone had last checked their email. This was when I realized that, online, there was always a way to get more data: You just had to know how to go deeper into the code and know more than the average user about its obscure loopholes and commands.

After the boom of the late 1990s ushered in the consumer Internet, I became a regular on forums devoted to fashion and style, such as Makeup Alley, where women traded beauty and fashion information. Under pseudonyms, we discussed our lives, always protecting our personal details from prying eyes or search-engine crawlers. The overriding rule of the Internet was simple then: You could say whatever you wanted as long as you didn't say who you were. I also took care to avoid all the cheap-seeming websites, like the fledgling MySpace, which appeared to be founded on the idea of empty exhibitionism and populated by predatory men looking for pictures of women to devour and discard. I was on the Internet enough to know that in the few short years that broadband had been available, it had become easy for men to find images of women to use as a shallow substitute for sex or love. For women, there was no value—there was even potential harm—in putting yourself online and offering yourself up to strangers, to have your image distributed infinitely across the Web. As the boys of the Internet often said on the troll-filled message board called the Daily Jolt, the only community discussion forum at Hopkins before Facebook landed, "There are no girls on the Internet." It was true; there weren't. If we were there, we were as protected by pseudonyms and secrecy as the guys who were searching for us.

Now, in the fall of 2004, with my newly created Facebook account, here I was: on the Internet under my real name. Visiting Facebook's rudimentary privacy page, which had just a few drop-downs that offered options to make your profile visible either only to your school or only to your friends, I realized that it was possible, for the first time on the Internet, to protect my profile from being visible to anyone outside of my immediate group of acquaintances. I breathed an elated sigh of relief. *Now, we can all finally use the Internet!* I thought. No more dealing with creepy guys assuming that just because I was on the Internet, I was available to be virtually stalked and harassed with pictures of penises, followed by a barrage of insults if I didn't respond. The privacy protections of the restricted network (people outside of Hopkins couldn't see my profile or even that I had one) made it feel, surprisingly, okay.

Facebook made it easy for the Internet-wary to be comfortable, because, in addition to the privacy protections, the initial layout of the site was minimalist to the extreme. It was strikingly clean, and novel in its simplicity, lacking the gaudy advertisements and spammy content that were inevitable elsewhere on the Internet. The profile consisted only of a modestly sized photo and a set of profile fields that the user could fill out or not, according to their own comfort level. It seemed fun, literary almost, like a newly published, frequently updating book that was more interesting to peruse than the dry, archaic texts I studied in the library. The first interest I listed on my profile was the *gold standard*, because I had always been interested in the idea of things that don't change form, that hold value, that aren't subject entirely to the whims of an economy in which nearly everything is disposable, temporary. The other interests I listed on my profile were flirtier and less abstract: *praias* ("beaches," in Portuguese), braiding my hair. This was the trick with Facebook, like the way you present yourself at a party: to say something without saying too much, to appear interesting without trying too hard, to be true to yourself without telling everyone everything. "Never apologize, never explain," Roland Barthes wrote in *The Pleasure of the Text*, which we studied in class. This seemed like the right way to approach a prying technology that, I could already sense, would never be satisfied by just a few bits of data. Much later, Facebook would seem to whisper, "Tell us everything." Even though in the beginning it was less inquisitive and shared your information less far afield, I already sensed that I had to remain its boss: I had to be able to tell it *no*.

Facebook was entertaining and engaging precisely because, unlike most technical applications at the time, it didn't seem like a sterile bunch of lines of code. Just as at the other prestigious universities that had Facebook networks, the Johns Hopkins University Facebook network was a delightful web of in-jokes about campus culture—such as the "I Check

Myself Out In The Mattin Center Windows" group devoted to the vanity-provoking windows of the Arts Center, or the "Hopkins 500," devoted to the approximately five hundred students who could be seen at parties interspersed with profile photos of artificially tanned sorority girls, intense medical students, and Hopkins' requisite lacrosse players. It was the first Internet site I had ever used that mirrored a real-life community. The cliques on Facebook were the same ones I ran into at the library and campus bar, and the things people said to each other on their walls—water polo team slang, hints at the past weekend's conquests, jabs at Hopkins' lacrosse archrival Duke—were similar to what you heard them saying at study tables or around pitchers of beer. The virtual space mapped the human space, and it had all happened virally in weeks.

Logging on to Facebook that first day, in retrospect, was the second, and to date the last, time that any technology has captured my imagination. The first was when Apple advertised the first laptop, the PowerBook, in the 1990s—with the words, "What's on your PowerBook?"

"World domination," my teenaged self answered instinctively. That's what these devices were made for, I thought: so small and yet so powerful, so capable of linking quickly to and between everything else in the world. I had a sudden fantasy of me, in ponytail and sweatshirt, remotely manipulating the world from a laptop, armed with ideas about how the world should be and the new ability to distribute them. From the laptop, I could write and distribute information faster than ever before. It was intoxicating to imagine, and Facebook's sudden, faithful rendering in 2004 of the physical world into the virtual felt the same. What could you do, now that you could see and connect to everyone and everything, instantly?

But what, also, could be diminished by such quick access? In the realm of ideas, it seemed easy: Who wouldn't want to distribute and discuss ideas widely? However, in the realm of the personal, it seemed more complicated. What was the benefit of doing everything in public? Were there types of information that made sense to distribute person to person and mouth to mouth, rather than digital page to digital page? Is information itself neutral, or do different types of information have different values, different levels of expectation of privacy, different implications for distribution and consumption? Did I *want* or *need* to know, passively and without asking or being told, who went out and what they wore and who hooked up the weekend before? Should all information be shared equally quickly and without regard to my relationship to it? And, finally, and most important, as we ask whenever we begin a new relationship with anything, would this be good for me?

Whether Facebook would be good for me in the long term was an open question, but in the immediate term it was, and rather quickly, to my surprise. It happened while I was perusing Facebook Groups, which I loved for their wealth of humorously delivered anthropological data. Reading them was much like being anthropologist Margaret Mead, but online, sitting on the couch in the comfort of pajamas and slippers. You could skip from the world of the lacrosse team to that of the small set of black Hopkins students, each with their own concerns and jokes and slang, in a span of seconds.

In this, Facebook Groups seemed more fun and less creepy than reading people's personal walls, which from the start had a slight, unseemly quality of eavesdropping on semiprivate, out-of-context, easy-to-misinterpret, conversations. The interjection of distant voices on friends' walls was always vaguely unreadable, unpredictable, illicit. "Let's play this weekend," a girl would post on the wall of a guy I knew, suggestively, and it felt weird to read, not because I didn't think girls liked him but because the utterance didn't actually reveal anything that was particularly relevant or useful. A girl wants him, I now knew, but I already knew that. Lots of girls did. The technology invited me to speculate about whether he wanted this girl back and whether they would go out and what would happen next, offline, all of which was really, in the end, irrelevant to be speculating on in advance. If two people like each other, they'll hook up, if not, they won't. All this noise was just noise, but a very present noise, a noise that we all, now, needed to consume, whether we cared to or not. In those cold November days, with the winter quickly coming on, there wasn't much else to do but watch and attend, curiously, to this new system that was just beginning, with a vengeance, to bring us online and publish the slightest social vicissitudes of our lives—the fact that someone likes us, the fact that we may be attending an event—to the world, for everyone to wonder about.

One such November day I discovered a group called "We're going to Brazil and you're not, bitches," referring to a Hopkins-led trip to Brazil that was happening a few weeks later. The group, like most Facebook statements that are about trumpeting some aspect of a person or group's identity, had no other purpose than to state that this group of students was going to Brazil and everyone else was not, bitches. My first thought was "Why didn't I know about this trip?" and then I recalled that without a public space outside of classrooms and the stacks, it was nearly impossible for Hopkins to distribute information about extracurricular activities. My second thought was, "I, too, am going on this trip, bitches." I mean, why not? I had nothing else to do.

I went straight to the campus study abroad office and asked them to put me on the Brazil trip, though it was only weeks away and they'd already processed everyone's visas and itineraries. Miraculously they did, and two weeks later I was on a flight to Rio de Janeiro, away from the academic dramas of the English department and into another, more vivacious society.

"You two are so California," our trip leader said one night in an outdoor bar in Brazil about me and a boy from Malibu wearing fluorescent sunglasses. He was a true California surfer kid, with a permanent tan and ocean-colored green eyes, and, in conversation, we discovered that we both dreamed idly of revolutions we wanted to play a part in someday. While the students from the East Coast gossiped about who had hooked up the night before, we talked about South American revolutionary movements that no one else on the trip had even heard of. This prompted them to perk up and listen. In the status hierarchy of the trip, we were California, and California was cool, and therefore revolutions were cool. "American culture starts in southern California and moves east," I always told people on the East Coast who wanted to know why I knew about something they didn't. This was before culture moved at lightning speed through the Internet, spreading from one coast to the other in minutes. I'm not sure now how anyone lays claim to cool anymore.

I wasn't actually from California, but people often made that mistake. I dressed with a casual beachiness and spoke with a slight Valley girl lilt that I never tried to lose. It was a hallmark that said (I hoped) that I didn't take myself too seriously. It took too much time to explain to people that before the real estate boom of the 2000s and its influx of midwesterners looking for a warm-weather McMansion, my home state of Arizona was like a bedroom community of San Diego, like southern California without the beach.

Being so close, and yet still a half-day's drive away from us, California was exciting, exotic, a dream of American perfection that we could actually touch. When school was out, my best friend Dana and I would drive the long desert highway to San Diego, entertaining ourselves by searching for the Hotel California, which legend said existed somewhere on the highway. "Is that it?" one of us would ask, upon seeing a white building silhouetted against the sky. "I don't know," the other would say, and we would drive on, searching. I think that we almost prayed that we would never find it, so that we could keep searching, forever.

When I returned to Hopkins I began the semester-long transition from my life as a graduate student to whatever would come next, which I didn't know yet. All I knew was that I had to leave the decaying east and find my way back west, to the place I belonged and where I had to believe, if only to ward off depression at my failed grad school career, that dreams still came true.

To this day, when I say "California," I usually mean the beach cities of the south, replete with surfers and sunshine, not the quasi-cosmopolitan north. Northern California is somewhere else, a California that was familiar to me in 2005 only from the Joan Didion essays that I devoured in my late teens, in search of life advice. "Q: In what way does the Holy Land resemble the Sacramento Valley? A: In the type and diversity of its agricultural products." Didion repeats, like her own accidental childhood mantra, and this always stuck in my head, a perfectly meaningless set of lines to someone who had never been to Sacramento, but suggestive of abundant riches tucked away somewhere north of Santa Barbara. It is perhaps because of this quote, and that I was broke, that I decided to move to northern California.

I ended up in Berkeley, which, with its large student population, was all I could afford. It was close enough to Silicon Valley, where I knew the money was, and was a much cheaper place to live than Palo Alto, where a one-bedroom apartment couldn't be had for less than $2000 a month. Through Craigslist, the 2005 unemployed person's best friend, I found an apartment near the university and a temporary job as a copywriter at a design firm in San Francisco. My job was to write copy for a line of skin-care products that were being manufactured as a house brand for Target. My initial enthusiasm quickly submerged by tedium, I wrote descriptions of cucumber-scented lotions and cleansers that I had never actually used. There were only so many ways to describe a face wash—invigorating, refreshing, cooling—and by the end of the month I felt like I had written all of them.

I was relieved at lunchtime when I could walk out of the office to San Francisco's long piers, enveloped by a perpetual fog that felt more like Oregon than California. Lunches at the aggressively artisanal cafes in the Ferry Building were too expensive for me, so I bought tacos from the Mexican food trucks that served the downtown's working class who commuted in, like me, from the East Bay.

Back in the design office, bored with the endless lines of copy that had all begun to sound the same, I would take to surfing Facebook. With very few features beyond profiles and messaging, Facebook was like a richer, more playful form of email, with the option to post public messages on people's walls. Since there weren't many fields, friends' posts occasionally had a deliberation and clarity that were entrancing, like you were reading little glimpses into the soul of the person—the thing they wanted most deeply to communicate to the world. Facebook was also a quick if not particularly satisfying salve for loneliness: In the Bay I knew no one, but online there were faces I knew, updating their pictures and profiles regularly, making familiar jokes.

In late July 2005, I had been working as a copywriter for a month when my boss, a micromanaging type with bleached teeth that glowed fluorescent, caught me looking at Facebook and chastised me. I felt indignant, given that in my view she was getting the most compelling descriptions of moisturizing cream that she could ask for from a random Craigslist hire. I even paid attention to alliteration and redundancy in my writing and fact-checked my work to make sure I wasn't making any overtly untrue claims about the ability of the products to make you more beautiful (and after doing this job I learned never to take any claims on a beauty product label seriously). But, as with many contract jobs, my work went largely unappreciated.

While I was illicitly perusing Facebook at work a few weeks later I noticed a bulletin on the normally blank homepage that said, "Do you want to work at Facebook? Send us your resume." That night I emailed my resume to the address listed, not knowing what they were looking for or what a job at Facebook might entail. I felt intrigued by the prospect, though. As new and strange a product as Facebook was, I sensed in it a power, the allure of a new social institution that had no limits and that might never end.

CHAPTER 1

WELCOME TO THE FACEBOOK

I don't know why Phil Rochester, who was engineering royalty in the valley and had been installed by venture capitalists to help with scaling up the tiny Facebook team, selected my resume from what must have been many that appeared in his inbox. I suspect that his choosing me had to do with the fact that Johns Hopkins featured prominently on my resume. He was a Vanderbilt alum, and I had learned in Baltimore that upper-crust southern elitism, conscious or not, runs deep. When I left Johns Hopkins, despite all its academic drama, my matriculation there faded immediately into a simple signifier of the elite. This is what an American private university is, not an education so much as a pedigree, a mark of distinction.

When Rochester called me he was at Costco buying tires,

multitasking with his BlackBerry in typical Silicon Valley fashion. He couldn't be bothered to conduct a proper interview. He assumed, efficiently, that as an English major from an elite school I was capable of answering user-support emails. "Come in Tuesday," he said. "You can try it for a few days. If you don't like it, you can leave. It pays twenty dollars an hour. That's pretty good, right?" he asked. "Uh, okay," I said. Neither the job nor the pay being offered was very good, but short of learning how to program, I knew couldn't compete for a real job in Silicon Valley. My only choice, if I was going to try to make my fortune there with all the others, was to find a way to make my lack of technical skill my strength.

Driving my scuffed white 1994 Camry into Palo Alto for the first time in early September 2005, I noticed instantly how perfectly bland and ordered the town was. The sidewalks off the main street were nearly as clean and prim as at Disneyland, or maybe, more aptly, *The Truman Show*. I had trouble finding the Facebook office at first ("It's up the stairs, at Emerson and University," Rochester had told me) and walked up the wrong set of stairs into a halfway house that operated in an old motel left over from the city's preboom days. That encounter with seediness would be my last in Palo Alto (the halfway house closed soon after and is now most likely a startup office).

"I don't even know what a quail looks like. . . . Facebook is hiring" was scrawled in chalk on a sandwich board at the foot of the stairs of the building next door, as if this was someone's boardwalk pizza parlor hiring for summer employees. I didn't know why they were talking about quails (I never did quite understand the reverence for quails or the fact that they showed

up everywhere, on custom Facebook T-shirts and office whiteboards, except that this was a private club and like any club it
needed in-jokes), but the sign's irreverence was a relief: I might
fit in here, I thought, in a way that I never had done in the hu-
morless atmosphere of graduate school, which regarded all jokes
as a suspect diversion from criticism.

As I entered through the office's glass doors I looked
around for Mark Zuckerberg, whose name I knew only from
the bottom of Facebook's pages, all of which read "A Mark
Zuckerberg production." I imagined someone ghostly, dark
haired, not unlike the half-blurry figure with mussed hair in
the first Facebook logo (which turned out, disappointingly, to
be a slightly modified piece of Microsoft clip art). He had to
be dark to make something like this, I assumed. Facebook had
too much gravitas already as a useful but slightly unnerving
social experiment not to be created by someone with a streak
of darkness.

It turned out that Mark preferred to work at night, I was
told, when he had a home-court advantage over VCs and other
businesspeople used to keeping regular daytime hours. I was
surprised and not a little disappointed to find out when Mark
finally came into the office later that day, preoccupied as always
with taking calls and holding meetings behind the glass door of
the video game room, that he was sandy blond, and not particularly tall. I imagined someone reedier, wilder looking, more dark
genius in the basement than light-haired goofball in shorts and a
Harvard hoodie, shuffling around in athletic shorts and Adidas
sandals. We didn't actually meet on my first day: He reserved his
hearty welcomes for the engineers, prodigal sons prized for their

ability to convert life into lines of code. Customer support was barely on Mark's radar.

When I was finally introduced to Mark the following week, he smiled, seeming to like me well enough, although he soon moved brusquely to something else. He always seemed to be on a different plane when talking to nontechnical employees, distant and detached, reserving his attention for those who were directly important to him: VCs or his fellow founders, and then, gradually, the engineers that he took a liking to. It would take years for one of those people to be me. By then, people assumed that we were friends and had known each other forever. And I guess whether or not we were in fact lifelong friends was irrelevant, because, in the world we were making, all it took to establish a friendship was a few lines of code and a click of the friend button. I received a friend request from Mark a few days after our first meeting, and I clicked accept, though nothing particularly friendly had thus far transpired between us. But I was starting to see that, here, it didn't matter: The world of relationships, as far as Facebook is concerned, is simple.

At eleven in the morning on my first day at Facebook, the office was an empty warren of desks, about forty feet by forty, cluttered with open drink bottles, half-unwrapped snacks, and video games. A few desks were occupied by young, plain-looking guys in T-shirts, gazing at their screens. They looked barely awake, having not yet consumed their daily quota of bottled Starbucks coffee drinks and Red Bull and seemed startled, if not displeased, to see a strange new woman in the office. The only other woman in the office—an administrative assistant—was more animated, smiling toothily as she welcomed me in. She sat in front of a large piece of graffiti art featuring a cartoonish, heavy-breasted woman with green hair floating above an ominous cityscape, like an adolescent version of the eyeglasses over Gatsby's East Egg. Many of the pieces of graffiti in the room featured stylized women with large breasts bursting from small tops that tapered down to tiny waists, mimicking the proportions of female video game characters. It seemed juvenile, but I wasn't very bothered—it just seemed like the kind of thing suburban boys from Harvard would think was urban and cool.

"We had to move the really graphic painting to the men's bathroom because someone complained," an engineer told me as he gave me a tour of the tiny office. He said this with the slight mocking disapproval that was my new colleagues' default tone in response to anything that resisted their power. I got it: Just because a few women might be let into their Palo Alto clubhouse, we weren't supposed to complain about things like sexy images of women on the walls. This was their kingdom and their idea of cool, and we shouldn't mess with it. I could see that it was, in a sense, a test: If you couldn't handle the graffiti, or the unrepentantly boyish company culture it represented, the job wasn't going to work out. Easy, I thought, and anyway, given the absence of women around, I figured they would need me for something. You can't run a successful company with boys alone. The office was small but the stakes, I could tell, were already high. The cold, outsized confidence in the air—a sense of grim determination that accompanied the graffiti and the graphs and the scrawled in-jokes about quails on the whiteboards—said that they wanted to win it all.

Rochester eventually emerged from taking a phone call in

the kitchen. He was an august man with gray hair and an untucked faded polo, whose gaze would only ever seem to fully focus when he was talking animatedly to other engineers in the office about *scaling*, or keeping the site up in the face of increasing users and page views. Scaling, I would soon find out, was the fetish of the valley, something that engineers could and did talk about for hours. Things were either *scalable*, which meant they could help the site grow fast indefinitely, or *unscalable*, which meant that the offending feature had to be quickly excised or cancelled, because it would not lead to great, automated speed and size. Unscalable usually meant something, like personal contact with customers, that couldn't be automated, a dim reminder of the pre-industrial era, of human labor that couldn't be programmed away.

Though I didn't quite realize it on this first day at Facebook, I was in possession of a skill set—that of the English major—that was woefully unscalable as far as Facebook was concerned, more of a liability than an asset. When I perused Mark's profile on Facebook after we had become virtual friends, I noticed that in the Favorite Books field he wrote, "I don't read." Okay, I thought, gearing up for a long battle to be appreciated in my new role, this job *might* work out in the end but it is not going to be as easy as I had first thought.

Rochester's mature appearance made me think that perhaps this wasn't just the nerdiest fraternity house in Silicon Valley and that there might be some adults at the helm who understood the importance of having employees with different skill sets. He gathered me and Oliver, a blond Stanford poly-sci grad, into the conference room to give us a polite but rushed description of our new position. "You'll basically be answering emails from users. Jake will teach you how to do everything," he said, handing us off to Jake, another Stanford grad who had started as the first customer-support rep three weeks before. Now that we were here, he was our de facto manager, at least until the official customer support manager could be hired. I sensed from the glowing, familiar way that Rochester said Jake's name that they already considered him an old hand. When Jake walked into the room a few minutes later wearing a Stanford T-shirt and cargo shorts over a wiry, athletic frame, I guessed that their acceptance of him had to do with his classically preppy looks, like an Abercrombie model come to life. Facebook, it seemed, wanted to have it all: to be the new and scrappy kid on the block and also have the feel of an old boys' club that had been around forever.

"What email address do you want?" said a blond IT guy with a goofy smile that put me at ease, as he set me up on my new, work-supplied iBook. "Kate@facebook.com," I said immediately. He pushed the laptop over me so I could set my password. "It has to be strong," he said with a French accent, "that means it can't be an obvious word, and it needs special characters." I typed in a strong version of the word "Salvador," after my favorite city in Brazil, with a dollar sign instead of an "S." Maybe this technology will save us from something (loneliness, alienation, boredom—I wasn't sure), I thought, and if it doesn't, maybe it will at least save me, by making me some money and relieving me from the fate of having to start over from scratch, somewhere else, again. I was tired of starting over.

Launching my email program and seeing that "kate@face book.com" was my address was a heady feeling, like starting a new country in which I was the only Kate there, queen of a world in which every other Kate would be derived from my archetype. Facebook still had fewer than 5 million users, but I was sitting at the top of what would become a very large virtual land mass. Facebook's name alone gave me gut confidence in the site: It was a real-life term that represented the website's function exactly. In choosing this name, Mark had announced his intention not to create some type of Internet fad but to replicate a real world need for a basic human directory. Internet fads come and go, but directories—like phone books before everyone went mobile—satisfy the basic human need to find and stay in contact with people.

Jake, Oliver, and I huddled around the conference table with our laptops and some Cokes from the fridge, which Rochester had showed us proudly was stacked full with every caffeinated soda we could desire. The lights in the conference room were turned off, as Rochester assumed that, like the engineers, we would want the room to be as dark as possible. I always liked working in darkness; it made things feel more exciting, less like an office and more like we were peering out at the world on our screens from inside a cave. Jake introduced us to the janky application through which users' emails to Facebook flowed. Once we learned how the software worked, Jake taught us, without batting an eyelid, the master password by which we could log in as any Facebook user and access all their messages and data. "You can't write it down," he said, and so we committed it to memory, just the first of many secrets and customs we would learn as we became indoctrinated into our new lives as Internet social administrators.

I experienced a brief moment of stunned disbelief: They just hand over the password with no background check to make sure I am not a crazed stalker? I kept checking Jake's face to see if he would test or caution me in any way about how and how not to use the password, but he didn't. I worried I would be like a bull stepping into the proverbial china shop: What if I accidentally perform the data equivalent of knocking something over, accidentally changing someone's password or forgetting to log out of their account, posting on their profile when I meant to post on mine? As surprising as it was, in a way, it was also reassuring, a vote of confidence in me as I stepped into a vast sea of personal data.

Security measures would later be implemented that made it impossible for anyone to use the master password without authenticating themselves as an employee, and a year after that, the password would disappear entirely in favor of other, more secure forms of logging in to repair accounts. But, at the beginning, there was only one password, and like all the boys in the office, I now had the keys to the kingdom. The dummy account we logged into to administer each school network, equipped with a pixelated photo of Mark wearing an Oxford button-down and a slight smirk, was called "The Creator," and it did feel a bit like being a kind of omnipotent, all-seeing god.

After an hour's instruction from Jake, we were set loose on the emails flowing in from colleges across the United States. They ranged from the briefest request for a password to long expositions on the social phenomenon that was Facebook and the way it had already changed social interaction on campuses for better or for worse, depending on the author's viewpoint.

The most glowing fan letters to Facebook betrayed the author's new sense of power while using this technology: even the shyest person could now glean information and participate virtually in social worlds that formerly seemed restricted or off limits.

There were also complaints about the usual stalker types familiar from the rest of the Internet, voraciously devouring images of women, seeking the most flesh-baring photographs, and spamming women with requests for sex. Jake, Oliver, and I played the police of the virtual college campus, issuing warnings and adjudicating arguments, and were also its tour guides, explaining how poking and tagging and blocking worked to people who were just learning to conceive their social lives in virtual terms.

"What does poking mean?" was a question asked hundreds of times a day, sometimes by people who really didn't know and other times by people who relished the sexual frisson of writing to Facebook to ask about "poking" and its many interpretations. We always responded innocently, "It's just a way to get someone's attention," knowing full well the range of childish and sexual connotations in play. Being coy, not admitting the libidinal urges driving so much of the site's usage, was professionally necessary, a way to differentiate Facebook from the cheap and overtly sexual vibes of MySpace. Being coy was also part of the fun, part of the illusion we as a company were constructing that life on Facebook, unlike in reality, was always safe, easy, playful, free, void of cost or obligation. As Dustin Moskovitz, Mark's Harvard roommate and Facebook co-founder, said over lunch in the office that fall, with his dry, practical intelligence, "Everything on Facebook is flirty." He was right. Facebook, like flirting, was a fun way to present yourself lightly and attractively to the world, with no downside, and no commitment.

A few weeks later, just as I was beginning to worry that I would be one of the only women working at Facebook, Maryann and Emma joined the customer support team. They were close friends of Jake and Oliver's from Stanford, pleasant in appearance, also nontechnical in major, and we got along as well as needed to perform our duties. At night they disappeared to parties full of former Stanford students and the requisite ping-pong balls and beer-laden Beirut (beer pong) tables that were their university's preferred nighttime sport.

This particular social clique preferred to discuss parties to more personal or intellectual topics, so we didn't go beyond casual pleasantries, but that was fitting for our mission of superficially connecting everyone in the world. We had Facebook as a topic of conversation. If we wanted to know more about each other we could visit each other's profiles and read the details we put there, and if we wanted to get closer than that, we could IM each other privately. From my first day onward, it was like my coworkers and I were connected always, virtually at least, chatting and emailing and posting on each other's Facebook walls. The first thing Dustin said to me after I had been taught my initial Facebook duties was to get on AIM. "We are on it all the time," he said, and it was true, for better or worse, we were.

Since a formal coolness was how our team interacted— smiling nods followed by fast descent into our screens and the emails and Facebook pages contained therein—users were my most emotionally expressive correspondents that fall. Thousands of emails flooded our system each day asking us for everything from just letting them in because they didn't have a college email address to solving their messiest social problems, asking if we could delete a regretted message before someone read it or let them see the account of someone who had blocked them. The angst that flowed through onto my screen was overwhelming, sometimes. I felt a bit like the advice columnist Dear Abby for a digital age, counseling people on various online social minefields and talking them down from ledges. Facebook made it so easy to say things that people said things they regretted, and as I read the distraught emails I started to feel an apprehension. What happens to society when you promise people they can have whatever they want: instant contact, hundreds of photographs of people you barely know, endless digital validation? Real life has limits, but the Internet, where everything seems free for the taking, has none. What will this do to our relationships, I wondered, or even more intimately, our souls?

For us, as administrators, everything on Facebook really was there for the seeing, as we were not subjected to the privacy barriers that existed for regular users. Our tools displayed everything that happened on the network: last logins, location of login, and deleted posts. We even had an internal tool, called appropriately, Facebook Stalker, that showed who had looked at our profile, which revealed fascinating insights. For one, my female friends studied my profile more often and for longer periods of time than my male friends, which suggests a digital version of the old dictum that women dress for each other, not for men. With access to every piece of data that existed on the system, working at Facebook was like playing the game from the hacker's side, despite the fact that I wasn't a hacker: The users gave us data freely and we consumed it, delighting in the new facts that came in by the hour.

As exhausting as answering emails for eight hours a day could get, there was something rich and fertile about Facebook as both company and product that was seductive, enticing. This is something that could go on forever, I thought, not like a business but like a family, like royalty, like the Dallas oil scene of Silicon Valley, crowning its own kings and queens and generating its own society. Who wouldn't want to be a part of that?

On Friday afternoons we got together for All Hands meetings. I looked forward to them because they were the one time we discussed things as a company, and the only meetings when everyone at the company was included. Mark would stand somewhere in the office, his posture unusually straight for someone dressed casually in a joke T-shirt (around this time he preferred one that said "I love Sloths") and sandals. Everyone would gather round, sitting on desks with flip-flops dangling or on the floor with legs crossed, watching and listening while Mark discussed the week's business: deals made, products launched, technical issues experienced and resolved. Occasionally, Matt Cohler, a Yale guy with a VC background, would chime in on financial things or Dustin would comment on site growth and health and any major down time that week. Everyone watched in rapt attention, smiling, as there was much to smile about: We had so much to do, together, and the All Hands were where we got our motivation for the next week and months.

As we worked steadily in October 2005 to prepare for the launch of the Facebook Photos feature, where users would finally be able to upload photo albums to their profiles (prior to the launch of Photos, the only photo a user could post was their profile photo), Mark referred to all of us in an All Hands meeting as a "Facebook family," and even though most of us had just met, the kinship was palpable. It also would be profitable for us to get along; if we liked and cared for each other, it would be easier to accomplish the high goals Mark was setting out for us: more Facebook networks, more Facebook features, an ever-faster flow of information.

I liked to listen to Mark's discussion of the product philosophy and goals at these meetings, which were to me the most fascinating part of the job: what were we trying to do, with this fledgling Internet identity registration system? "I just want to create information flow," he said in his still nearly adolescent voice, lips pursed forward as if jumping to the next word, and everyone would nod, all cogitating in their own way about what this meant. Mark's idea of information flow, though vague, was also too vague to be disagreed with, and even if we came up with counter-instances to a model of pure information efficiency (for example, I wondered, do I want my Social Security number to flow freely?), we knew that we weren't supposed to disagree. Mark was our leader, for better or worse. When the meetings ended he would say either "domination" or "revolution," with a joking flourish of a fist, and everyone would laugh, nervously, but with a warm and almost chilling excitement. It was like we were being given a charter, by a boy younger than most of us, to take over the world and get paid to do it.

Aside from the general questions that I started to ponder, questions such as what were we were doing, and what did it all mean, and that I kept to myself, there was one area of our work in Customer Support that required us to have philosophical discussion and debate. Facebook, like the Internet in general, made it so easy for people to post and gain visibility for content that people with extreme and often unpopular views went wild on the new platform, creating groups devoted to whatever cause they espoused. Most of these groups were devoted to bullying of some kind, from petty harassment of a classmate to hatred of a marginalized group.

In the Customer Support Team's daily discussions of what behavior would be permitted on Facebook, we decided that any attack on an individual person would be against our Terms of Service, since we had no interest in or ability to track down the validity of any bullying claims. How were we to know why some woman on campus was being called "a slut" or "whore"—the common bullying claims made against female Facebook users— and why would we care to investigate such invidious claims? Further, individuals were the core users of the service, so to allow for the bullying of individuals would hurt the product's growth, and for us, growth was paramount. People had to have a basic sense of safety while using Facebook if they were going to use it at all.

Attacks on groups of people were harder to interpret and

police, since it was difficult to tell when something was hate speech, free speech, a political disagreement or some combination thereof. (Was the group "I hate people who wear Crocs" hate speech? We had to consider it, along with the more serious hate groups aimed at blacks and gays.) Many Facebook groups made it easy for us to decide: They posted pictures of dead and gored bodies and were covered in swastikas and death threats. In the odd logic of our work, it was almost a relief to see blatant death threats because they meant that we didn't have to comb the group looking for indications of the creator's intent (people on the Internet are rarely subtle in their hatred). Thus, after long discussion we decided that if a group contained any threat of violence against a person or persons, it would be removed. One aspect of our jobs, then, became scanning group descriptions for evidence of death threats, and searching for pictures of dead people. This was the dark side of the social network, the opposite of the party photos with smiling college kids and their plastic cups of beer, and we saw it every day.

One afternoon, as I sat on the couch in the office reading emails, a user at a school in the Midwest wrote in to report a group that was devoted to gay bashing. Upon investigating the group I found that it indeed violated the Facebook terms of "no death threats," as the words "kill gays" were all over the page. With a click of a button in my administrative tool, the group was deleted. I also wrote an email to let the offending group creator know that his hate speech wouldn't be tolerated. This commenced a long correspondence between me and this unfortunate soul in the heartland who insisted, virulently, upon his right to say anything he chose about gays. He also baited me by creating new groups with increasingly violent slogans and images of beheaded bodies, which I continued to delete, responding as calmly as I could. Finally, just as I was fearing that this stalemate would go on forever, I happened to glance at his password, which in the early days was displayed next to a user's name in our admin tool. "Ilovejason," it said. Pitying him more than feeling angry, I wrote back and told him that this case was closed and if he created one more hate group I would disable his Facebook account forever. He stopped writing after that.

Between the alternately dull and dramatic emails from users, the highlight of the work week was Friday afternoon happy hour, when at around five o'clock, our caterer would wheel a table laden with snacks, wine, and beer directly into the grid of desks where we sat. Engineers would emerge from behind their screens for a few minutes to grab a beer and return as quickly as possible to their screens. Customer support employees, who were hourly rather than salaried workers, would continue to dash off emails to users, sometimes with a beer in hand, before clocking out and grabbing another beer and gathering on the gray, modern mass-market couches in an alcove near the office entrance to talk.

By six or seven o'clock, after a few beers, people grew chattier, engineers and admins and customer support reps mingled, and we began to get to know one another in person. It felt like that early moment in any social circle when you're not sure what will happen: Who will be friends with whom, what cliques will form, who will be most popular? It all still felt protean, unformed, like the first months of freshman year. All that was clear was that Mark was in charge, supported by a small group of deputies from Harvard and Yale—Dustin, Matt—and it was up to the rest of us to figure out what our roles would be and where we would fit.

Mark rarely drank or socialized at the happy hours with the rest of us. Occasionally I heard stories, sometimes from Mark himself, about parties and high jinks at the house in Palo Alto that he had lived in with Dustin and a few other engineers the year before—something about a drunken flight on a zip line and another story about blown circuitry in the middle of a beer-fueled coding session. There were whispers that they used Facebook to stalk Stanford girls and invite them to parties, but that made them no different than most guys on the network. But, by fall 2005, when I started working there, Mark's demeanor in the office, if it had ever been particularly relaxed, was already developing into that of the intent executive preoccupied with larger things than company happy hours, despite the fact that he wore shorts and T-shirts and often padded around the office barefoot.

The most relaxed I ever saw Mark was when my dad, a math professor, came to visit the office one happy hour that fall. Suddenly every engineer in the office, including a suddenly smiling and talkative Mark, gathered around my dad to talk about calculus and graphs. I hadn't even told anyone that my dad taught math; it was like they sensed a kindred, elder spirit, someone who understood with them that graphs were the most beautiful and inspiring things in the world. Mark was so at ease and unassuming in that conversation that when I asked my dad as we left the office, "What did you think of Mark?" he answered, "Which one was Mark?" I had the thought then, as we walked to dinner at the Italian place down the street, that it was my dad, and not me, who should be working at Facebook: Unlike me, he would instantly fit in, and everyone could talk about graphs happily ever after. But my dad didn't need a job, and I did, so my dad flew back to Phoenix and I stayed in Silicon Valley with the engineers and the graphs.

In the small office of twenty engineers and a smattering of support reps and admins who were rapidly becoming friends, Mark's presence tended to be more aloof than the others. He walked with his chest puffed out, Napoleon-style, his curly hair jumping forward from his forehead as if to announce him in advance. My general sense of camaraderie with most of the engineers, with whom I had exchanged at least a few words around the kitchen fridge or over a beer at happy hour, felt cooler in relation to Mark. Someone has to be the boss, and no one likes the boss (do they?) and so it seemed natural that I felt nothing more than a slight wariness around him, born of his Silicon Valley status as an anointed boy wonder. He seemed more of a necessary evil. I was almost relieved that he was so distant, so preoccupied—like a father you know won't be overly concerned about what you were up to.

Three weeks after I started working there, Facebook celebrated its five-millionth user by throwing a party in a dimly lit space below a swank new restaurant in San Francisco. It was the first and last company party I attended that was made up mostly of people—adults—who didn't work there. (As we grew bigger, we turned inward, populating parties mainly with Facebook employees, until it felt like we were our own island.) The five-millionth-user party was attended mostly by venture capitalists, curious or invested in this new, already buzzing upstart of a company. The name Peter Thiel, PayPal's infamous founder and billionaire, was on everyone's lips, but I couldn't identify him because all the men at the party looked like a version of him: dirty blond, excessively fit, with drinks held casually against their unbuttoned blazers as they discussed investment business and tried hard to impress one another. My customer support teammates and I stuck mostly to ourselves in the corner, having nothing to offer the investors, watching while they swarmed over the mussy-haired engineers standing around clutching barely touched drinks.

As I sat on a couch watching all this in my cocktail dress, holding a melting gin and tonic, I wondered at the VCs' obvious predilection for boys who looked like younger versions of themselves. I could see that as a woman I would automatically appear alien in this context. An engineer came by to take photographs and I posed, smiling, with my female teammates. One always had to smile and appear happy for Facebook. The photographer moved on to another group and I went back to musing.

It often felt like this at Facebook, like I was the only one who was watching, seeing what was happening not as a privileged participant but as an observer. Dustin, the most critically astute of the Facebook founders, did not fail to notice. A year after I started working there, we were talking at a smoke-filled party somewhere in the Stanford hills when he said to me, matter-of-factly, "You're going to write a book about us," as we descended the stairs into a crowded den to watch a band that had just begun to play.

CHAPTER 2

IN HACK WE TRUST

That first winter, to go along with the perks of meals, laundry, and gym memberships that Facebook provided, the company rented a house in Tahoe for employees to use on the weekends. Mark is serious about wanting us to have fun, I thought. The prospect of escaping my queue of Facebook user emails to frolic for a couple of days in the woods sounded ideal, but the three-hour drive to Tahoe and sixty-dollar-per-day ski resort tickets were more than I could afford on my customer support salary. I felt lucky and relieved every month just to make my thousand-dollar rent and my four-hundred-dollar student loan payment. Anything else was a rare, luxurious extra.

But Facebook, maybe more than any other company, was a social scene, and I knew that it would be important to take part in company social events whenever possible. When Luke, an engineer who had recently quit grad school at Stanford to work at Facebook, invited me and my customer support team-mate Maryann to go to the Tahoe house in January with him, Dustin, and Mark, I was excited. It was a good crew, I thought. Luke surfed ocean waves in his spare time in addition to surfing the Internet at work, and was chiller than the typical engineer. He reminded me of someone you might chat with over beers at a beach bonfire while on vacation. Dustin, who, like Luke, was from Florida, was also fun and sociable when he wasn't sleepless and stressed from his responsibility of making sure that the site stayed up at all hours of the day and night. Maryann was a tall, beautiful woman from Stanford by way of Marin County, San Francisco's wealthy northern suburb. She had a perfect smile and never seemed to complain, and in this, she was, some of our colleagues remarked longingly, their ideal woman, whole-some and girlish. Maryann would eventually become the literal face of the company: her beatifically smiling picture appears to this day in the sample "Jane Smith" account that is used in Facebook's new feature announcements. Back then, however, Maryann and I were just among a few token female employees, similarly dressed in jeans, T-shirts, and long ponytails, recently embarked on what would be for both of us a long journey with the company.

After the drive to Tahoe, we threw our things on bunks, then gathered around the table to drink cheap Trader Joe's wine and listen to music. As the night proceeded and we be-came steadily more drunk, we played mp3s on someone's iPod louder and louder, screaming the lyrics to Green Day and

Sublime so loudly that we were essentially doing karaoke, the singers' voices drowned out. Sensing that this moment called for more entertainment, I donned the bearskin, complete with head, that adorned the banister on the stairs leading to Mark's and Dustin's rooms (like all companies, ours functioned according to status hierarchy; the important people got the best rooms while the rest of us slept on bunk beds downstairs). Mark thought this was hilarious and insisted that I continue to wear the bearskin around my shoulders. Luke, who built the wildly successful Facebook Photos product that had launched months before, naturally took pictures all night of our shenanigans to post to Facebook in an album he titled "Opening Night," so the rest of the company could see how much fun we were having.

In one of the last photos Luke took, Mark is gesturing at me haughtily like an emperor as I stand doubled over in laughter with the bear suit draped over me. It was all innocent fun; everyone was laughing and enjoying themselves, but when I saw the photograph appear in a Facebook album on Monday I was struck by the loaded nature of the image, ripe for interpretation, in which Mark appeared to be commanding an employee, female, to submit. If I were his PR person, I thought, I would tell Luke to take it down. Whether to protect the company, or Mark, or myself, I wasn't sure. In this take-no-prisoners company, where you were either willing to devote your whole young life to it or not, it was starting to be hard to tell the difference. I felt certain that some gossip writer was going to find the photo and post it in an article about Facebook someday. In fact, the photograph appeared in Gawker four years later, with the caption, "This one *also* might lead the confused and bewildered to conclude that Mark Zuckerberg got drunk in Lake Tahoe and taunted a co-worker."

Perhaps more interesting than the fact that the photo was taken and posted on Facebook is that it didn't occur to anyone in the office that there was anything wrong with it, or that the picture revealed something about the culture of Facebook that it shouldn't. Mark was too busy programming to get to the part of a liberal arts education where you study social inequality. As he wrote on his business card with boyish hubris, "I'm CEO, bitch." That image was saying that power wasn't something to be questioned; it was something to collect and brandish. This—not the anarchist ethos I knew from my punk-rock hacker friends— was Facebook's new world order.

As the months passed, moments like these occurred with unsettling regularity. When a female employee reported being told by a male coworker in the lunch line that her backside looked tasty—"I want to put my teeth in your ass," was what the coworker said—Mark asked at an All Hands (it was hard to tell whether it was with faux or genuine naiveté), "What does that even mean?" I went to Mark at the open office hour he kept after the meeting and told him that it was unacceptable to blow off sexual harassment in the office. He listened to me, which I appreciated, but understanding of the crux of the matter; that is, that women by virtue of our low rank and small numbers were already in a vulnerable situation in the office, did not seem to register.

Confronting him that day simply had the effect, I think, not of making him more sympathetic to women's plight at Facebook, but of making him realize that I was a force he would have to reckon with. Employees weren't supposed to challenge his power, but when we did we became, paradoxically, the thing we were supposed to be in the action-hero logic of the company: a rule-breaker, a threat, and, therefore, someone of interest to be courted and co-opted.

Mark's tendency to mock or disregard everything that wasn't a technical issue triggered a sinking feeling that accompanied the heady glee we all began to feel over the early months and years as the Web site soared higher and higher, gaining more users and more rounds of funding and more celebrity. Sometimes my head spun just thinking about it—the wealth, the power, the eventual fame for all these people, I could see it all happening. This is the American dream, I thought, wide-eyed, for who even believed in the American dream anymore? In grad school we invoked the Horatio Alger myth to discredit any ideological move that was designed to distract the masses by suggesting that anyone could be rich, anyone could succeed. The irony of being a critic of the Horatio Alger myth only to end up in my own Horatio Alger narrative was almost too much.

I was a student of the humanities, including histories of colonialism and revolutions and, despite Mark's talk in All Hands, I knew that the war that Facebook was waging, if it continued the way it was going, wasn't exactly revolutionary. The company's entire human-resources architecture (and, conveniently, Facebook had no actual HR department to correct any of this for a long time) was constructed on the reactionary model of an office from the 1950s, in which men with so-called masculine qualities (being technical, breaking things, moving fast) were idealized as brilliant and visionary while everyone else (particularly the nontechnical employees on the customer-support team, who were mostly female and sometimes, unlike the white and Asian engineering team, black) were assumed to be duller, incapable of quick and intelligent thought. It was like *Mad Men* but real and happening in the current moment, as if in repudiation of fifty years of social progress.

For example, on Mark's birthday, in May 2006, I received an email from his administrative assistant telling me that it would be my job that day, along with all the other women in the office, to wear a T-shirt with Mark's picture on it. Wait, what? I thought, *he's not my god or my president; I just work here.* The men in the office were told that they would be wearing Adidas sandals that day, also in homage to Mark. The gender coding was clear: women were to declare allegiance to Mark, and men were to become Mark, or to at least dress like him. I decided that this was more than I could stomach and stayed home to play sick that day. I was the only one. The other women in the office, including Mark's girlfriend, who did not work at Facebook, but had come to the office to celebrate his birthday, happily posed for pictures wearing identical shirts printed with Mark's picture, like teenage girls at an *NSYNC concert or more disturbingly, like so many polygamous wives in a cult. These pictures also appeared in Gawker years later, making me relieved that I had stayed home so that I wasn't immortalized forever online in such a strange, *Stepford-Wives*-like pose. I wondered if any of the women had been secretly troubled by the request that they pay homage to Mark or if, as often seemed the case, everyone was just happy to belong to something.

My customer-support teammates, like Maryann, were always cheerful and pleasant, but having been friends since their freshman year, they were naturally much closer to one another than they were to me. Maryann and Jake soon seemed to be dating, though, being cagey as Facebook employees often were, they didn't make it Facebook official for years (they would eventually, like many of our colleagues, become engaged). I wondered if I would ever have my own clique at the company. It seemed important: people to post on your wall, to invite you to events, to pose with you in photographs at company parties.

In January 2006, a new engineer showed up. We struck up a conversation at happy hour that, to my delight and surprise, veered away from the usual topics of Facebook administrative duties and programming issues. "In my interview, Luke told me I could work on studying gender dynamics on Facebook by looking at the data sets," Sam said, "and that's one of my main interests, so I decided to come to work here." (Once hired, he was assigned to product development rather than, as had been advertised, to research.) He wore an old, tattered D.A.R.E T-shirt from the 1990s, baggy, unpretentious jeans like a skateboarder, had alert eyes and an impish smile. In other words, he was exactly the type of guy I was friends with—a little indie, cute, not obsessed with polish—but also, openly gay. This was unusual at Facebook and, I realized as we chattered on about topics of great interest to both of us, like gender studies and the futility of grad school (he had been contemplating grad school prior to being offered the Facebook job), a welcome development. By the end of the night, after most customer support team members had gone home and Mark and a few engineers were still staring at their screens in the back of the office, Sam and I were trading quotes from the movie *Heathers*. "Lunchtime poll," one of us said, and we both delivered the line from the movie in unison. "Aliens land on the earth and say they are going to blow it up in three days. But the same day you get a call from Publishers Clearing House saying you've won five million dollars. What do you do?" we recited with mock *Heathers*-like haughtiness that dissolved in laughter. That night when I left the office, for the first time since setting foot there, I felt elated, like everything was going to be okay, because I finally had a real friend at Facebook.

Sam and I weren't the only ones obsessed with movies. Mark and Dustin kept quoting from their favorite action flicks, like *Top Gun,* on the footers of pages of the site, such as "Too close for missiles, I'm switching to guns." This wasn't just a job or a website or even a social network, the quotes seemed to be saying that it was war, and it needed to feel and look like one, complete with battles waged and won, soldiers bloodied and triumphant, camaraderie formed, just like in the movies.

Perhaps this really was what Mark was thinking. He seemed not so much to be on a mission for programmers, but for heroes, protagonists, leading men. That spring, Mark brought in five engineers from Harvard who became known as the Microsoft Five, after the old-guard software company in Seattle where some had previously worked. The Microsoft Five sounded like some kind of cowboy band who rides into town and shoots up a saloon in a Western.

As the Silicon Valley legend goes, the Five received their Facebook job offers while at a party. Their first reaction, allegedly, was to reject the offer. They assumed that the upstart Facebook couldn't pay them enough or treat them as seriously as they were accustomed to being treated. The Five's initial disinterest gave Facebook the drive to wage one of the first of many oedipal raids on an older company's talent, in which Mark could prove that despite the company's youth and scrappiness it could win the brawl for status. It seemed sometimes that, to Mark, battling a bigger competitor was almost as exciting as winning the war, as I would see again when, three years later, we turned our attention to the valley's biggest behemoth, Google.

Once the Five had been convinced to come to Palo Alto, they immediately wore, without flinching, the new label *star programmer,* not just a coder but a personality, a social leader, a celebrity center around which the valley's attention can swirl. Jamie, who, unlike the other four, came from Amazon but was included in the Five, was the clear prize for this new celebrity model of Silicon Valley; he was tall, dark blond, handsome, and of very old money. He looked like a gentleman in the nineteenth-century portraits that hung on the wall in my seminar room at Hopkins. The other four guys weren't as portrait-perfect as Jamie; they looked less like movie stars and unlike him, had not been the presidents of painfully elite Harvard final clubs, replete with invitation-only parties and secret rituals. However, in the race for status that Facebook was mounting, they had enough: They were from Harvard and they were programmers, which made them the valley's version of good old boys. The Microsoft Five quickly established themselves as a new, explicit kind of fraternity: They called themselves Tau Phi Beta, or TFB for The Facebook Fraternity, complete with Greek letters, custom T-shirts, and weekly keg parties at the house they rented together.

Sitting there in the office in my usual uniform of worn jeans and cardigan, watching this new social order unfold, I felt that, as they say in Internet speak, we were doing it wrong. While having an office social scene was necessary, nobody really likes fraternities, with their macho attitude, hazing rituals, and beer-soaked party aftermaths. If we were supposed to be cool and California, calmly convincing people that it was okay to pass us their most private data on a daily basis, we would have to come across as less aggravatingly aggressive than a fraternity house.

Bringing employees together, in the life-as-work-and-work-as-life culture of late 2000s Silicon Valley, was a core business mission of any startup. It wasn't enough to work there, you had to devote as much of your life to it as possible. At Facebook, being a startup devoted to virtual socializing, we couldn't just work all the time. We had to have some kind of scene in which human stories could unfold, if only in the first instance to have something to document on Facebook. We needed to entertain each other.

This seemed to be part of the motivation behind the company's various social perks, such as the happy hours, catered lunches and dinners, regularly occurring company parties (in which employees were bused to a venue, provided copious amounts of liquor, and photographed by professionals hired for the occasion), and the houses that had sprung up, such as TFB (the Facebook fraternity) and the house in Tahoe.

As the site's user base nearly doubled throughout that spring, from 5.5 million users to ten, and everyone's sense of responsibility magnified by the week, I had the idea, selfishly perhaps, that a pool house would be a better way to lighten up and bring us closer than a frat house. After all, what better way to establish good cheer and team spirit than around a pool, drinks in hand, sun shimmering off the water? "We should get a house with a pool," I said to Mark one night that spring during the Friday happy hour. He flashed his characteristic look of askance approval, smiling, but looking half-away, as if to retain his sense of executive control. "That's a good idea," he said, pulling out his BlackBerry (huge by today's standards) to dash off an email with the request.

I was stoked about the pool house. At that point in my life, I was in need of two things: an outlet for my revolutionary energy and a new career that would work out in a way that grad school had not. Throwing my entire lot in with Facebook (to the point, even, of moving in with my coworkers at a company pool house) could turn out to be perfect. My interest in the Hotel California had not faded a bit since the days when my friend Dana and I drove the highway to San Diego searching for it. What more perfect metaphor for American society, and its obsession with belonging, with scenes of darkness and excess, with cults that you fall into and find it hard to leave? It felt like America was right there with me, ripe for a new experiment in community spirit. And the pool house would be my Hotel California.

As we were moving into the summer house in Menlo Park, I placed a Hotel California LP on the mantel in the empty living room. I smiled to myself as I regarded it sitting there, with its picture of a classic Los Angeles hotel illuminated golden behind palms, unnoticed by my colleagues milling around the house. In addition to the record and my clothes, all I brought to the house that day were a few books that I'd packed to help me make sense of this new scene about which I knew little. Joan Didion's famous words from *Slouching Towards Bethlehem* were on my mind that afternoon as the sun set on our new house and I settled my things into my room. "California is a place in which a boom mentality and a sense of Chekhovian loss meet in uneasy suspension; in which the mind is troubled by some buried but ineradicable suspicion that things better work here, because here, beneath the immense bleached sky, is where we run out of continent." We, I felt that day, was me, a conglomerate of one, at the end of a line and the beginning of another, staking a claim to what I suspected would be a new gold rush.

Unlike the office with its domineering male energy, the house felt relaxed and cool, I thought with satisfaction, as I toured it in a denim skirt and flip-flops. A seventies ranch home of no architectural value, the house was solid—a little better, as most things are, for the wear and tear. The front yard sported *Edward Scissorhands*-like topiary bushes and a perfectly green lawn. As is typical in suburbia, the front living room sat in shadow behind closed drapes and went largely unused. The back den with the requisite seventies-porn-movie-style wet bar, stone fireplace, and sliding glass door to the pool, was where we would socialize. It was a little like being in *The Brady Bunch,* without parents.

Mark's room was across from mine, small and bare, but he didn't stay there. He had a famously minimalist apartment nearby (he claimed to own no furniture and have only a mattress on the floor for a bed) but he kept the room as a social placeholder, coming over with his friends or his girlfriend on the evenings and weekends to hang out. When he was at the house he invariably took up position under a Roman-looking tent by the pool, pacing back and forth while he mulled over the day's business. In his sandals and shorts, with his hand sometimes raised to his chin while he mused, he looked every bit the part of a little emperor.

I remarked on this to Sam as we lay in our bathing suits on the pool deck that first weekend, surveying the scene. Since meeting at happy hour, we had quickly formed something of an alliance. Alone, we might just have been the odd employees interested in something besides accumulating mountains of data and power but, together, we were the weird kids who occupied the far edge of Facebook's cultural map, composed mainly of Harvard fraternity boys, preppy Stanford kids, and other engineers of similar provenance. Sam and I claimed the pool as our de facto territory, given that we were more comfortable in swimsuits and in the sun than most of the engineers, and set up our towels on the deck in the afternoons to watch the goings on around the house.

Lucy, a petite, good-natured Stanford ex-cheerleader who had recently been added to the customer-support team, lived at the house and often worked on answering emails from the pool, her laptop perched precariously on the edge of the deck. Fiercely competitive (she made sure to win all sports competitions held at Facebook, like the yearly Game Day, which wasn't very hard to do, considering that most employees weren't particularly athletic), she made it a point to answer more emails than anyone else, even while half submersed in the pool in a bikini and turning a deep tan.

Maryann also often came to the pool in her bikini and set up her towel nearby, tanning quietly behind big sunglasses, pleasant and reserved as always. She was unequivocally considered hot at the company. But, I sensed, the last thing you wanted at Facebook was to be the hot girl, especially if you weren't protected, as Maryann was, by a close group of college friends who also worked there.

One day, one of the sales guys told me pointedly that I was hot, reminding me that I was surrounded by men who were in the habit of sorting women into hot or not-hot categories. Facemash, Mark's first website at Harvard, was designed to allow viewers to rank the attractiveness of Harvard students' photos. I wanted to be the cool girl, not the hot girl. The cool girl always has a chance of winning, because she has something beyond looks. As Stevie Nicks once said about her trip through the male-dominated music business, "I never wanted to be too pretty."

At another summer barbecue, I overheard Mark talking with some engineers about whether it was better to date a girl for looks or intelligence. "I dated a model once who was really hot, but my girlfriend is actually smart," he said, as if they were mutually exclusive categories. "Why can't a girl be pretty and smart?" I asked him in front of everyone. "Why does it have to be one or the other?" The group went quiet for a second, seeming confused. I knew then that if you had to pick one in order to succeed at Facebook, smart, not hot, was the thing to be.

On weekend afternoons, there were usually some boys milling about the pool house with laptops or beers drawn from a keg that was kept under Mark's tent. Occasionally someone important—usually an exec or VC, who would pull up to the house in a blaze of Audi exhaust—came over to talk to Mark in hushed tones under the tent. "It feels like we are in ancient Greece," I observed to Sam. There was not much for us to do at the pool house, though I found out later that, while he was pacing and we were sunning, one of the things Mark was mulling was whether to sell the company to Yahoo! for one billion dollars. I had a vague sense from the intense vibes during those days that something very serious was under consideration, but I didn't think for a minute that Mark might sell the company and we'd all cash out and go home so soon: We had a pool house, a gathering mass of enthusiastic boys (and a few equally energetic girls), and the future to dominate.

One newcomer, who claimed a room on the opposite end of the shag-carpeted hall from mine, struck me as another kindred spirit like Sam, though at first I had no idea why. Tall and lanky, he didn't have any visible muscle, just long boyish limbs. His face was pale and his hair paler, his eyes close together and set far back, hidden by a coy bowl of dishwater blond hair. I felt strangely, incongruously sure of him, having the unbidden thought as we talked by the pool on our first night in the house that he had a good heart.

My sense was that he brought a mysterious form of light, some spirit that we were all seeking, to the house. His name was Thrax.

A few months earlier, I was working at the office when someone sitting at a nearby desk said, "We've been hacked." I looked over his shoulder at a Facebook account they were eyeing. It looked like a MySpace page. That is, all the profile owner's information was perfectly arrayed as they had entered it on Facebook, but the formatting had been tricked into rendering like MySpace, with shouting features of gaudy colors, floating text, and smarmy profile fields like "Mood" and "Who I'd Like to Meet."

Dustin worked quickly to trace the hack to its source while the rest of us looked on at our screens in puzzlement. When he found the hack, or perhaps when it had found him (the whole point of hacking is not so much to break something as to get attention for breaking something, and so a hacker is not likely to rest long without telling someone, often the hacked, about the exploit), he told us the hacker's name. Curious, I looked up his profile.

My first reaction to Thrax's profile picture, of a bony college kid in an American Apparel T-shirt and a mop of emo hair, with red paint Photoshopped over his lips for effect, was that this kid wants attention so bad it's painful. He looked like the kind of wiseass who wants to make you pay. For what, it didn't matter.

At the time of the hack, Thrax lived in Georgia, attending a Southern college most of us had never heard of. However, he wouldn't live in obscurity for much longer: Dustin hired him a few weeks later, on the theory that you want to keep your enemies close, especially when they can break your site. So, a few days later, Thrax showed up in the office, wearing the same skinny T-shirt and baggy jeans he had worn on his Facebook profile.

From the minute he arrived, despite or maybe in part because of his cagey, impudent gaze beneath his long bangs, there was an almost preternatural aura of celebrity and inevitability about Thrax: The Harvard guys, who had made careers doing everything by the book, had been looking for this boy, long before they knew that this hacker savant from Georgia actually existed. At happy hour on Thrax's first day in the office, everyone swarmed him, asking questions about the hack and about his strange provenance in a state far from all of our own. A few of the Harvard engineers, perhaps miffed that they would now have to share the spotlight, wondered if Thrax was just a *script kiddie,* a derogatory term for an unschooled kid who copies code from the Internet rather than composing it himself. From my vantage point in the office, watching, I felt a sense of bemused relief. Things are finally going to get interesting. The Harvard boys have some competition, and Thrax seemed to understand, if nothing else, how to create a mysterious, compelling character out of the bits of the Internet that he mastered with his oddly long, ghostly white fingers.

Facebook was waiting for Thrax and brethren to arrive because, unlike startups that build computer chips or enterprise software, the network is about two things: personality and stories. People and stories are what keep us coming to the site. Whether out of an instinctive need to keep tabs on our surroundings or as a way of fostering social bonds, it is human nature to want to know what is happening to the people in our circle and, with Facebook, we don't have to bother to ask them. But, like any novel or film, a story requires characters and drama.

The Harvard boys couldn't satisfy this need alone. Their knowledge of the Internet derived from books and computer science coursework, not the trolling, rule-free websites where kids from the middle of nowhere honed their understanding of Internet warfare and developed well-known online profiles and networks of like-minded hacker friends. One of these friends, Emile, had worked with Thrax remotely (they lived in different states at the time) on the hack and, after Thrax arrived and was a hit at Facebook, the Harvard engineers tracked him down in Louisiana and asked him down to the office. When Emile showed up for his interview, it was the first time that Thrax, along with everyone else, had met him in real life. After some hand-wringing by the Harvard guys about whether any or all of these unschooled hacker boys from the middle of nowhere were just script kiddies, Emile was hired on, too. I liked Emile: Underneath all his trolling and half-shaved, half-long metal haircut, he too, I sensed, had a good heart.

Indeed, the hacker's appeal for the valley's legions of software engineers, business development execs, and money guys is not in what he makes (most hacks are by definition, technically shoddy, because they are executed quickly) but in the fact that you never know what he is going to do, what boundaries he will transgress. Silicon Valley imagines that the hacker's moves are sylphlike, quick, and made under the cover of night, while rule-abiding citizens, powerless, are asleep. In short, the hacker is sexy, a dangerous, bad-boy version of the plain programmer at work in his cubicle. The hacker's capacity to surprise—or in Silicon Valley parlance, *disrupt*—is fetishized in the valley as a source of power and profit for tech companies, Facebook among them, which considers its stated ability to "move fast and break things" a core company value. As Paul Graham, the valley's revered hacker guru and founder of the prestigious seed-capital firm YCombinator, put it while lecturing to valley entrepreneurs at what is called *Startup School,* "We don't want people who do what they are told." Or, as the startup enthusiasts on Graham's Hacker News board counsel each other, "It is better to ask for forgiveness than permission."

As Facebook matured, the staff came to encompass three distinct types of guys. Skilled, dependable programmers, often Asian-American or foreign born, who were hired to code and keep the site running. Supervising them, the Harvard and Stanford boys, mostly white, who wrote code, while they acted as the reassuringly familiar white faces of the company and ascended the ranks into leadership positions. Finally, the elusive, heavily video recorded, highly sought-after hackers, whose job was as much to act the part of the fresh-faced rogue impresario as to write code. Facebook needed these three types because while all could code, the hacker was what the quiet programmers and by-the-books college boys couldn't be: the classic, renegade American hero that we all know from books and movies.

It was a hot July afternoon in the office and I was being barraged with IM's from colleagues asking me if I was dating Sam. These were people who didn't usually IM me; they were the office social hubs, usually Harvard and Stanford guys, who felt it was their job to stay on top of all relevant office gossip that may affect the company social scene. There were lots of office couples developing, and so they wanted to make sure they stayed up to date on the latest romantic news.

"Huh?" I typed back to the many queries. "Sam is gay. Didn't you know that?"

"Yeah, but it says on Facebook that you guys are complicated."

"What?"

I went to Facebook and saw that on my profile I was suddenly "in a complicated relationship with Samuel Henley," and there was even a story to that effect: "July 23, 2 AM: Kate Losse and Samuel Henley are in a complicated relationship." Oh, I thought, I get it. Sam was testing the new product, News Feed, which would launch weeks later. Engineers and customer support were always testing as part of our preparation for product launches, trying to find the bugs in a feature before launch, and around the office testing was a good occasion for a joke on everyone else. We could get away with anything if we said it was a test.

Still, I was taken aback by the fact that the site had literally written a story about us and distributed it to our friends, illustrated with a photograph that had been posted to Facebook a few weeks earlier, of Sam and me in the pool at the summer house. This fully articulated story, written and illustrated by a machine, meant that authorship was no longer human but algorithmic; we didn't write our own stories anymore. In the photograph the algorithm chose to illustrate our new relationship (to provide visuals for a relationship story, News Feed finds a photo in which both parties to the new relationship have been tagged), we were dangling over the edge of the summer-house pool, our bodies trailing off into the water, and Sam was smiling straight into the camera, while I look slightly off center, quizzical. The water was a beautiful green, pacific, surrounded by darkness. It was an entrancing picture and I could see why everyone, regardless of the fact that Sam and I were just friends, wanted the story to be true. Everyone loves love stories, even if they are just the byproduct of a quality assurance test.

This new product was intended, as all engineering innovations are, to produce efficiency, allowing us to consume content about our friends more easily and automatically than before. However, the publicity provided by News Feed, the way it functioned like a newspaper, did more than just feed information more efficiently. It established a world in which anything that happened to us became food for a narrative, in which we became like characters in a novel that Facebook and its algorithms were writing, whether we wanted to be in it or not.

As was the case with all new features, we had already been using News Feed for months before it launched. As I lay around the pool house with my laptop, watching people play, I was also reading the newspaper-style updates that would appear in my feed. They were usually photo albums from fellow coworkers—pictures of parties at the summer house and elsewhere around Palo Alto.

The general concept of News Feed was simple: An algorithm was now surfacing content that it believed, based on your activity on the site (what you looked at), you would find interesting. But like all technology, the social news generated by a computer lacked some of the nuance of the real-life gossip channels it replicated. Information that would have gotten to you via human contact and conversation now surfaced as impersonally as if you were reading the *New York Times* (or more aptly, *People*).

As News Feed was nearing completion in August 2006, I was sitting on the gray modern couches in a sunny alcove on the engineering floor, testing the feature, when Pasha, the product manager in charge of News Feed and the only woman with an engineering background at Facebook, asked me to review some of the stories for wording. "I'm not good at this," she said, "You are. Help me." I supposed that she had turned to me because at that point I had already developed a reputation as the literary one, due to my status updates composed of music and literary quotes and my general disinterest in saying anything absolutely literal.

Pasha handed me a printout of the News Feed stories the team had prepared. At first glance they were, technically, neat: pulling profile photos and updates from the story's characters to create an algorithmically generated story. However, as I read through them I cringed a bit—they were not about telling a meaningful story, they were about delivering news in as hard and fast a way as possible. "So and so is no longer in a relationship," the story said, illustrating the news with an icon of a broken heart, one not unlike the icon of a broken hard drive that signals doom on an old Macintosh. Building the algorithm was one thing, I realized, but delivering stories that felt like they had been delivered by a human was another. I tried to intuit what model of the social world the stories assumed, and if it was one I recognized. Some of the stories didn't seem like anything I would be instantly apprised of in real life: For example, that some acquaintances were having a party I wasn't invited to, or that an old ex-boyfriend was now in a new relationship. While in real life I might find out about these things later, they just weren't things that I needed or wanted to know immediately, as they happened.

I shared my concerns about the bluntness of News Feed with Pasha—that it wasn't just telling me things quickly but telling me things I typically wouldn't know about—and she said that she would take them back to the engineers. None of the stories were removed. I wondered, then, if News Feed and the future of Facebook would be built on the model of how social cohesion works—what is comfortable and relevant to you and what isn't—or if it would be indifferent to etiquette and sensitivity. It turned out to be the latter, and I'm not sure Mark knew the difference. To him and many of the engineers, it seemed, more data is always good, regardless of how you get it. Social graces—and privacy and psychological well-being, for that matter—are just obstacles in the way of having more information.

As I worked with my fellow Customer Support Team members to help engineers test News Feed and work out the bugs, I began to see that we were trafficking in a new kind of programmed, automatic gossip, in which the mere act of updating your profile (or in this case, of Sam updating his profile and linking to me) becomes a story—online and off. The machine becomes the wandering bard, telling stories, real or something other. As Jean Baudrillard wrote, "The map becomes the territory."

When Sam was done testing a few days later, he removed our relationship from the site and we went back to being single, to the disappointment of our coworkers. And in the meantime, News Feed slowly became the core of the Facebook product, occupying the center of the homepage and, increasingly, the center of our social lives.

In a sense, Thrax's Facebook hack in spring 2006, which, in addition to making Facebook look like MySpace, also generated innocuous conversation posted to unsuspecting users' walls (e.g., "Hey, nice shoes," or, "This wall is now about trains.") was the first to elide our speech, motivated by individual intention, with that of a machine's. Unlike the usual viruses that create spammy posts that are trying to sell something, Thrax's Facebook worm created conversational messages that sounded like posts a friend might have written. "The whole point of them was that they could have been real," Thrax explained, describing the hack later to an adoring tech blogger. I doubt, however, that making a philosophical point was the hack's main goal, as Thrax and the other hacker boys that came to Facebook rarely trafficked in philosophical arguments. They preferred instead to use the Internet to create and distribute as many "lulz," or jokes, as possible. Lulz, on the Internet, were a goal in themselves, a new way of creating a scene and attracting attention from people waiting patiently to be entertained in front of their screens.

Thrax's Facebook hack was just the latest in a long sequence of virtual scenes that he had made. He told me about them as we hung around the pool house that summer, tapping away on our laptops at the kitchen table or strumming on guitars in the dark on the living room couches. As a child, his mother arranged for him to have headshots taken and shopped him around at audi-tions for child actors. When that didn't pan out, he took to the online world, where he and his friends created online personas and held LAN parties (in which people network some computers together in a room and play games) late into the night.

In high school, Thrax built a website (ready-made blog sites like Tumblr and WordPress didn't exist yet) where he blogged about the parties he went to each weekend. "Everyone at my school read it," he recalled. "There was always drama on Monday about what I had written and everyone would talk about it all week." By college, he was an active participant in the Something Awful forums, a site where people who are essentially professional Internet users (though they were often only thirteen years old) stay abreast of every meme and Internet in-joke cresting through the online world.

People in forums like Something Awful and the infamous 4Chan—an anonymous message board with a no-rules policy that results in an endless contest by users to shock one another with the disturbing or merely absurd—don't use the Internet the same way average Internet users do. They play the Internet like a war. The goal is to win every battle—a comment war, an attack against a Web page, or a contest to create the funniest memes. Battle is waged by an often passive-aggressive, often humorous Internet kind of fighting called *trolling,* and the best troll wins. The trick of trolling is to prove that you know more than your opponent—via wit, argument, or sometimes, silence—to show that they don't control you. In Internet culture, everyone is either the king or the pawn—or what, in Internet culture circa 2006, was "the pwned," a combination of "pawned" and "owned" that means both.

One Saturday afternoon that summer, as we lounged on couches in the pool house, half surfing our laptops and half talking, sometimes sending AIM messages though we were sitting three feet away from each other, Thrax told me a story from his precollege years. One day, Something Awful's moderators decided that, finally, he'd gone too far with his trolling and banished him from the site. To Thrax, this was worse than a very public high-school breakup. "That's when I realized how much of an asshole I was," he recalled, with a seriousness that verged on what almost seemed like tears, "It really affected me and I felt devastated." As I listened to Thrax talk about the dark days of his ban, slightly confused by the amount of emotion he felt for his banished Internet profile, I perceived a new, strange kind of existential crisis that affected these young men: a failure to exist virtually.

That summer, I dismissed this insight. Thrax was simply an interesting kind of freak and there would never be a mainstream market for his brand of obsessive online self-documentation and attention-seeking. I was wrong.

It was ten o'clock on a weeknight in July and the streets of Menlo Park were, as usual, dark and empty. Thrax and I were driving to Safeway to buy groceries. The radio in his car, a used BMW that he had bought off of Craigslist a few weeks earlier for six thousand in cash, worked intermittently, and received just one signal from an old-timey jazz station that only played at night. These technical limitations, rare in a world where engineers could deploy technology to get whatever they wanted, already felt like they fostered a kind of luxury, a rare form of value. Instead of choosing from ten GBs of pirated, curated, and sorted mp3s, we were grasping to pull one radio signal from the air, and it would play what it chose, in analog.

There were two Safeways in Menlo Park. A new one, with soft tones and Whole Foods–like stage lighting, and an old one, with seventies signage and the harsh glare of fluorescents. The old one was scheduled to be torn down but, for the time being, it stayed open twenty-four hours, so we always ended up there. We went grocery shopping in the middle of the night because it was the only time that we were both awake. In the morning, Thrax was sleeping and I would be at work. After midnight, he was working (or at least he was at the office, where he alternately coded, watched, or filmed videos, and managed his Internet presence across multiple forums and sites) and I would be asleep. Our schedules overlapped only between ten and midnight, and this is when we became friends.

In the empty Safeway lot, Thrax parked his car, letting the jazz station that we fought so hard to find trail on for a few seconds before turning off the engine. As we walked toward the fluorescence of the grocery store, I noticed that we were both wearing thrift store T-shirts and old jeans: the suburban indie uniform, though we both come from places the other has never been. I was surprised that we had anything in common at all, not just our clothes, but music, our dry humor. Georgia seemed too far to be familiar. I'd read too many stories about the South in my literature classes to think of it as anything but other: a place where all the American themes of racial darkness twist into something even darker, stranger, more impenetrable than in the American states like California and Connecticut, which are seemingly without accent. Yet here we were in the parking lot in the middle of the night, two young Americans on a mission to buy groceries in matching outfits.

Though we were in California, Thrax's grocery list read like it was definitely from somewhere else. Bologna, white bread, Miracle Whip. We wandered the overly bright, unkempt deli side of the decaying Safeway for fifteen minutes looking for sale bologna, meaning that it cost ten cents less than the one that wasn't. Thrax explained that in Georgia he was able to eat for twenty dollars a week just by buying the right bologna. This confused me, because he was earning at least twice what I was, and even I couldn't imagine that the five or ten cents' difference mattered. But he was strangely resolute about buying the cheapest sandwich ingredients.

As I followed him around the aisles, I found this to be equal parts cute, as if he were introducing me to his former life as a scrappy, d.i.y. Georgia teenager, and equal parts a sign of the telltale deployment of power that marks the powerful. Driving a used BMW to Safeway to buy the cheapest sandwich ingredients to save the pennies, the constantly weighing pleasure versus cost, was all part of the game, of the calculation required to organize the resources to build the things that would remake the world the way it should be.

Eventually we found the cheapest bologna, bread, and spread. Thrax was incensed that even the budget bologna was at least thirty cents more than it was in Georgia and complained about it all the way to the produce section. Once we were there, he forgot all about the bologna and started making fun of me for looking for organic fruit. I could see why the idea of organic produce was ridiculous to him; he didn't eat it, as it was never on sale at whatever Georgia supermarkets he bought his bologna from in college. He couldn't know that it tasted better than the genetically manipulated fruit sold at Walmart, and so, of course, the whole idea of organic seemed like some kind of Ponzi scheme that only a naive California girl would fall for.

This is the classic position of the nineteen-year-old boy hacker: He thinks that, by having nothing and being from nowhere, he can outsmart everyone and build an empire without anyone taking notice. He thinks everyone is by definition an easy mark, comparatively weak, because he assumes they have it better than him. He thinks he will know, unlike the naive masses, when he's being taken for a ride. His job—which is also his identity, an identity he chose at around age thirteen when he first began searching the Internet for evidence of how it worked, of how it could be broken—is to find the holes, whether in a website or in someone's logic, that he can exploit.

That night in the grocery store I could have tried to explain to Thrax, but didn't, that I bought organic food because it makes me feel better, and that this was my hack: to live as richly as possible with next to nothing, with few reliable career prospects as of yet, in a place that didn't have as ready and profitable a place for me as it did for him. I invested in what made me feel sharpest, most lithe, most radiant for the long term, because I knew that if I was going to pull off this hack, it was going to take a while. In that sense, perhaps it wasn't a hack, but then neither would his be. We were both going to use Facebook to get what we wanted. We loved Facebook—it had already given us information, power—and we knew it would use us, too, so we felt that it was fair. Hackers, like everyone else, have a morality of sorts.

Most of the men in the office, at twenty-three or twenty-four, were too old and too formally educated to qualify as authentic, self-made hackers, but everyone wanted to imagine himself as one. So, that summer, Mark ensured that the new office—now at 156 University Avenue, after we outgrew the first one—was decorated as a kind of shrine to the boy king. The top floor, which was allocated to nonengineers because it was too sunny to suit the tastes of engineers, was plain and relatively clean, lit by large windows that revealed the perennially blue Palo Alto sky.

The engineering floor below was dim, with blinds drawn, and decorated in cool tones of gray under all the empty drink bottles, shipping boxes, and candy wrappers that collected amid twenty-four-hour coding sessions. Desks were squeezed in like a battalion, from the entrance hallway all the way to the back of the room, where Mark's desk sat clean and bare, furnished only with his laptop. The other engineers' desks were piled high with toys and gadgets and screens: At least one thirty-inch monitor and several extra smaller screens just in case (we customer-support reps were each given one twenty-four-inch monitor). A set of TV screens mounted all along one wall displayed graphs depicting various site statistics: egress and active users and the current load on the servers. Occasionally, like in any fraternity house or other place where young men gather, the men on the engineering floor would play pranks on one another by putting embarrassing photographs of each other on the screens for all to view.

The floor wasn't all young men: By the summer of 2006, three women held product manager positions in engineering. All had been friends with at least one of the early engineers before they were hired. To become a product manager, it seemed, you had to be vetted as much for your ability to get along with the guys as for your product management skills, so no women were ever hired cold into this role. The PMs were a welcome, necessary presence on the floor, providing a warmer reception when customer-support employees occasionally went down to the E-floor, as the engineering floor was called, to discuss preparations for upcoming Facebook features. The men were friendly on an individual basis, too, but the overall atmosphere of the engineering floor tended toward the tense and aggressive. One of the Harvard guys was always jokingly threatening other engineers that he would punch them in the face if they displeased him, until even the most combative engineers had had enough of his violent banter and asked him to cut it out. Regardless, humor around the office usually had a warring, masculine bent, which came from the top: "Domination," Mark was always saying, joking in a way that was also, you knew, serious.

There were also often moments of levity during the workday in those early months. One afternoon, as we sat on the third floor answering emails, Maryann got an IM from the floor below that said that we needed to come downstairs quickly to see something. "What's happening," I wondered, as we got up from our desks and walked down to E. The boys—nineteen-year-old designer Justin, who had been recently convinced to drop out of college and come to work at Facebook, Thrax, and anyone else with hair that was long enough to flip out of his face at the end of a faux runway—were in the midst of doing a fashion walkoff, starting at one end of the office and walking like runway models to the other side as engineers and customer-support team members cheered them on. They pretended to flip blazers over their shoulders like so many *GQ* models.

At the far end of the engineering floor were two small rooms that served as the war rooms, where engineers could work intensely together on developing new products. To the left was Mark's office, a spare white room straight out of a mafia interrogation scene. The room to the right was where the boys would hide out and sometimes build things they weren't supposed to: It was piled with screens and blankets, as if they were living and sleeping inside the screen. Large letters spelling "Lockdown" hung on the door, declaring a state of product emergency even when there wasn't one. The engineers seemed to like the idea of a perpetual lockdown because, on such occasions, they were expected to spend all their time in the office, focused fully on the mission. Between the rooms was a couch piled with more blankets, oddly cozy and comfortable, from which one could survey the whole floor. When I walked the gantlet of desks to get to the end of the office, which I had to do occasionally when I came down from the top floor for meetings, I was relieved to get to the couch, away from the prying eyes following me and to a place where I could turn my gaze on them. In its architecture, both virtual and physical, Facebook was like one big battle to retain control of the gaze.

The mere fact that we worked in an office presented a structural issue to overcome: Real hackers don't work in offices. They work at home, in their parents' basements, or anywhere but an established work environment. After the move to the new office, Thrax told me about a time in college when he and a friend drove to New York City to visit their Internet forum friends and ran low on cash. In order to afford the gas to drive back to Georgia, he pulled over to the side of the road, his friend took out his laptop, found an open wifi signal, and hacked into the AAA Web site to get a discount for gas in order to get them home. Hacking, like any other rogue American pursuit, abhors the corporate in favor of the casual or even slightly illicit, which is why Mark hired graffiti artist David Choe to paint the walls of Facebook offices with scheming figures holding their fists high.

To make sure the engineering floor felt as playful and casual as possible, it was decorated with toys of all kinds: scooters, deejay equipment, Lego sets, puzzles. Every once in a while, Dustin would order a particularly interesting and expensive toy online to entertain the engineers and have it delivered to the office. One day that summer, a lifelike dinosaur that somehow grows arrived in the mail. Everyone cooed over the new robot pet and took photos of it to upload to Facebook. Another day, a king's crown—replete with fake jewels and red velvet—materialized, and the boys took turns trying it on. It settled, finally, on Thrax, who by virtue of his age and unschooled pedigree was the true boy king. The crown eventually became the prototype for one of the first virtual gifts that Facebook would sell, and naturally the gifts' first buyers were the engineers, who took turns buying each other virtual crowns to post on each other's walls.

Looking like you are playing, even when you are working, was a key part of the aesthetic, a way for Facebook to differentiate itself from the companies it wants to divert young employees from and a way to make everything seem, always, like a game. In the ideology of the new Silicon Valley, work was for the owned. Play was for the owners. There was a fundamental capitalism at work: While they abhorred the idea of being a wage slave, the young men of Silicon Valley were not trying to tear down the capitalist system. They were trying to become its new masters.

Without anything academic to study in Palo Alto, I kept myself entertained by studying people. By day, I studied the profiles of the people whose Facebook accounts I had to log in to and fix or investigate. I developed a taxonomy of all the different types of college users. There were surprisingly few types: the fraternity kids, the artsy alternative kids, the middle-of-the-road boys and girls who play soccer and study political science. My favorite profiles, more often than not, were those of black students, who tended to use Facebook more socially and conversationally than white students. It reminded me of a difference I had observed in Baltimore between the anxious, solitary white grad students and friendlier, more talkative local Baltimoreans, making me wonder if black culture, or maybe just southern culture, placed more emphasis on community and conversation, whereas white culture was focused more on the idea of every man for him or herself.

Around this period, we discovered a bug that affected the inboxes of people with over five hundred messages. They would suddenly see a so-called ghost message hovering in their inbox. As soon as someone wrote in to report the bug, I knew that, most likely, they were black. White people, I discovered by reading people's messages and walls, tended to lurk and judge more than they communicated, so their accounts rarely generated that bug. It was almost as if the system itself was designed for lurking instead of direct communication and broke under any different mode of use.

By night, in Menlo Park, I studied the engineers as they came over to the pool house to grill, swim, and socialize. They were always a little anxious and awkward, working to remain calm and in control in situations where their programs weren't at hand to do that for them. When all else failed, we could always talk about the site, because it consumed our days, transacting almost all of our activities and experiences. It seemed like we wrote on each other's walls as much as we saw each other in person. And also, we each had a life-changing financial interest in making the site as addictive and ubiquitous as possible.

It felt somehow life-affirming to be away from the computer, to see people in person instead of reading their intensely crafted profiles on Facebook. I had already started to wonder whether the fact that I was more comfortable offline than on, unlike the engineers, would mean that I would have to be the bearer of the human—the one who feels where others couldn't or wouldn't.

I kept a running tally in my head of the things and activities in the summer house that seemed human and normal, looking for reassuring evidence that, despite Facebook's fascination with the cool, technical mediation of our lives we were just warm, social animals after all. I used what I knew of life from Baltimore as my gauge. Baltimore is maybe the least technically advanced, most tragically human place in America. Kids in Baltimore didn't hack or have computers; hacking for them meant hanging wires from window to window to poach electricity from the house across the way. I kept Baltimore's poverty in mind as the baseline against which all this Silicon Valley technology and all the real-life fantasy it enables could be measured.

On weekends, the house's dining room table was converted to a Beirut (beer pong) table for parties, and I counted this as a positive: Beirut was clearly active, social, real. At Hopkins we played it in dirty row-house fraternity basements that were the privileged mirror of the dirty row houses that the poor squatted in only streets away. I gave the Beirut table extra points for being a little messy, a little loud, a little burly (involving cheap beer rather than smooth, pricey liquor), and because laptops weren't safe there amid the flying ping-pong balls and splashing beer. Anything that got engineers off their computers must be healthy.

People brought instruments to the house and played them, and this too seemed like a reassuring sign. Mark had a guitar and on occasion he played Green Day songs while we all sang. Pictures of these sing-alongs also made their way to Gawker three years later, but the bloggers didn't find the video on Facebook of us singing "Wonderwall" and its rousing chorus of "Mayyyybe, you're gonna be the one that saves meeeeeeeee." I sang extra loud on the chorus, perhaps aware of the lyrics' special resonance. Watching the video again on Facebook today, I noticed that we seemed much happier here than in later videos, brimming with energies that have long since been focused and contained.

I suppose that that summer, nothing was certain; it all could have turned out to be an odd camp that we attended and then disbanded, instead of an early moment of youthful alacrity in a company's inexorable rise to power.

Thrax kept a stock of musical instruments in the den that he played whenever there was anyone to listen, and he had a crowd-pleasing ability to instantly play any song he had ever heard. At parties, he entertained guests by playing songs on the keyboard long into the night. Thrax's total lyrical recall intrigued me from the first, seeming like the musical expression of all the autistic savant tendencies of Silicon Valley, a way of turning all their obsessive, numerical perfectionism into music. Eventually it came to seem, like the emerging social Internet itself, to be just another way of grabbing and keeping attention, of saying, "Look at me." But, for a while, it was entertaining, even charming, a gift of song in a sterile valley.

One night, at two in the morning, as people gathered with their beers around Thrax's electric piano, I asked him to play "Hotel California." For once, he didn't know the words, so I had to sing them. The boys in the office preferred Daft Punk and the song "Robot Rock" as an anthem, speaking excitedly and without irony of wanting to become robots one day. That made me wonder: Why? What's the pull of being a robot? I imagined that being a robot sounded as unnatural to me as my obsession with Hotel California must have seemed to them. No one ever asked about the Hotel California record on the mantel or why I'd put it there. The record, like all of this, and like the viral memes we would be in the business of distributing, seemed to have just happened, part of an odd conglomeration of things and people that have convened here, now, to be grouped together for a while, only to later disperse.

"The site broke," someone yelled from the den after Thrax's off-key version of "Hotel California" had trailed off. The boys happily retreated to their laptops to log in and start fixing bugs. They always brought their MacBook Pros with them to parties, and they seemed happy to have an excuse to have their familiar screens in front of them, networked to the system and to distant friends on instant message. When the evening would take its usual, inevitable turn and morph into a laptop party (you could always count on something breaking back then— breaking and bringing the site back up at two in the morning was part of the glory), I would just shrug and go outside to the pool, alone. It wouldn't be my way to confront the boys about their antisocial-seeming commitment to technology, at least at first. In those early years, my stance toward the company and the new world we were creating remained anthropological and cautiously optimistic. I had some notion that a writer doesn't intervene in her subject until she feels she understands it. That summer, there were still a lot of unknowns to be reckoned with.

When the house wasn't swarmed by engineers and their laptops, it was cool, open, empty, mine. I liked to pad around the carpeted rooms, reflecting mostly on the fact that I was happy to be here, now. I was entranced by the deep stillness of Menlo Park, the light, fir-scented breeze that entered through the open windows at nightfall, the way the cool darkness seemed to aid both looking back and looking forward. I felt lucky to have the rich privilege of starting my life anew, with fifty or so smart people, in very fertile circumstances, though the payoff we were working for wouldn't manifest itself for a while. For now, the stillness—the absence of the sirens of Baltimore, the cool peace, the warm sense of limitless potential and profit—was enough.

CHAPTER 3

PIRATES OF THE RIVIERA

> You run, I con. A tiger don't change its stripes.—thrax96
> Huh?—k8che
> That's from *Lost*. I think I'm going to put that on my
> Facebook business card.—thrax96

When I first began working at Facebook and Dustin said, "Get on AIM, we're on it all the time," he wasn't joking. Most conversations in the office, from the driest work-related exchange to the most overt flirtation, happened on AIM. At times, this led to confusion—an engineering manager might send you an AIM asking you to go get coffee during work hours but it would be unclear whether this was for professional or personal reasons. At that moment he could be interested in befriending you, just as later he might be arranging your promotion. When you were online, with your Adium (our preferred AIM client) status set to available, it was open season in terms of what you might get in the way of messages: Because we were sitting at different desks and often in different rooms, separated and protected by technology, anything could happen and often did.

"Can you introduce me to that Japanese girl you are working with?" was one AIM message I received from an older database engineer who was known to exclusively date Japanese women. Having read Edward Said's *Orientalism,* like any liberal arts student, it was hard for me not to find this somewhat suspect. "Not right now, we're working," I thought, but simply pretended I didn't get the message. AIM, like the social Internet generally, was more about your desires than it was about social graces. Any messages you didn't want to answer, you could just pretend not to have seen it on your screen. Conversations faded in and out, rising and falling in intensity depending on the participants' interest, with an impunity that would be considered rude in real life.

I quickly learned to ignore most of the random messages from guys in the office—they were just sending out a quick ping to see if I was clueless enough to accept a date from someone who could easily be asking the same thing of twenty other girls at the same time. I paid attention to instant messages from Thrax, though, because we were friends. "I just saw that there's a shower room on the third floor that has shampoo and towels; it's well-equipped," I typed to Thrax at work one day and he answered, with a suggestive non sequitur, "Yes, yes, I am," and I thought, "Did he just say that at work? Are we awkward, hormonal teenagers or coworkers?" I guessed that, symbolically at least, we were both. Instant messaging, like everything we were building, was a way to play without consequences, the adult-proof playground of the digital age.

At the end of that first summer, the office was a focused hum of work, punctuated by the usual happy hours and periods of playtime. Engineers were preparing to launch News Feed in September, and in customer support we were doing our routine work of answering emails while also helping out with feedback and testing for the new feature. I had received a tiny promotion to senior customer-support rep and an even tinier raise, at fifty cents more than my previous hourly wage.

As we were getting ready to move out of the pool house, Thrax instant messaged me that he and Sam were going to Las Vegas for the yearly hacking convention called Defcon. "You can come if you want," he typed, and I did. Not just because I liked them and our indie-ish little crew but because, as fun as working at Facebook was, there was a freedom in being somewhere else. When we arrived in Las Vegas, despite the fact that we were in the fakest city in the world, at a convention dedicated to being so far inside a computer that you can break it and everything it is linked to, for three days everything felt real.

It was Sam and Thrax's first visit, but I had fallen in love with Vegas years ago. In high school, my youth orchestra had done an exchange with the Las Vegas youth orchestra and we spent three days touring the hot Nevada desert, staring big-eyed at the towering houses of money and sex that dot the landscape. On the last day, we finally toured the famous Strip, which was less populated in the 1990s but no less grand. Perhaps it was grander then for being less dense, with casinos spaced widely apart, rising from the desert like Arabian castles. From where I sat on our orchestra's tour bus, I saw nothing against the horizon but a perfectly sun bleached, gold-accented acropolis with pillars as staunch and august as those in Rome, only brighter, bone-white against the nuclear blue sky. Our bus driver told us over the PA that Caesars Palace lacks an apostrophe because, "At Caesars, everyone is king." Taking in that man-made immensity from my shaded perch on the bus as a teenager, I had a sudden, chilling feeling that I, too, could be king.

Perhaps this is the feeling Las Vegas is designed to inspire; against the backdrop of the strip's perfect strangeness anything you could imagine seemed possible. This is its, and America's, promise. This is what makes it all okay. "This is America, you live in it, you let it happen," Thomas Pynchon wrote in a novel about the creation of a revolutionary underground mail system. "Let it unfurl."

On this second trip, at the height of the real-estate bubble, it felt like America was unfurling grandly: I was at an underground hacker convention with a gay programmer from M.I.T. and a glorified college dropout from Georgia. And we were having fun. Under the neon, away from the fishbowl of the Facebook office, where, at any time, twenty Harvard computer bros were gossiping on AIM, imagining they could track everyone's every move, we were free. Las Vegas was too big, too fake, too glittering to let anyone in it be tracked by the cool blue frame of Facebook.

"We should have stayed at the Wynn," I told Thrax and Sam when I noticed that the administrative assistant had booked them a room at the Riviera, one of the oldest casinos on the strip, with the thin, quilted, flower-print bedspreads to prove it. As soon as I mentioned the Wynn, though, I almost wished I hadn't. It would be the last time any of us ever stayed in a cheap hotel together on Facebook's dime. From what I had read of the first dot com boom six years earlier, when programmers went from working in nondescript cubicles to throwing money around on bottle service in downtown Manhattan like they were bankers in *American Psycho,* it seemed only a matter of time before we would all realize the full extent of privilege that comes with working for the next big thing on the Internet. Not just a good salary and bragging rights over your friends but the right to expect to stay in five-star hotels and sleep on 400-thread-count sheets every night.

We couldn't use our computers anywhere near the convention; the security of anything with a circuit was most probably compromised. In order to go online at all and remain in contact with Palo Alto, we had to connect via an elaborate system the boys wired in our room, draping cables over the headboard and across the floor. While the boys were at Home Depot buying cables to rig the room, I parted the faded chintz curtains to enjoy the vertiginous view of the backside of the Strip, concrete parking garages and hotel towers reminiscent of Eastern bloc buildings. I reveled in the cracked, gold-speckled Formica sink and the smoke-stained walls of our room. "Let it unfurl," felt like a goad to some grand experiment, bigger than any of us, and it was already happening.

Downstairs, the Riviera casino was at once garish and dim, thronged with pale hacker types wearing black T-shirts, shorts, and tall boots. Some had ponytails and beer guts, others were skinny punks. All were busy hacking or going to talks about hacking. The entire convention was a contest to see who could outhack the hackers, war games for people who didn't feel comfortable in sunlight. Las Vegas was the perfect host, since in the August swelter it was too hot to leave the hotel during the day.

In the elevator on our way to the conference, a *goon*, as the Defcon staffers are called, told us that the elevators had been hacked to go twice as fast as usual, and we laughed nervously as we sped the thirty floors down to the casino.

As we walked across the casino floor to a talk on hacking forms of identification (which, fittingly, I got into by wearing Sam's badge, since Sam had decided to go to the pool instead), Thrax asked passersby rhetorically, in an exaggeratedly pretentious voice reminiscent of a BBC announcer, "Are you the wheat, or are you the chaff?" The young men scurrying across the floor in their oversized T-shirts printed with the names of obscure Web sites didn't notice him, intent on winning their next hacking competition. Though the diffuse hacker community was connected twenty-four hours a day via IM and Internet Relay Chat throughout the year, Defcon is the one time where they get to come together with their people, their tribe; there are tests, levels, judgments. It felt, appropriately, a bit like being in a video game, finding our way down long hallways and bypassing the goons who guarded certain rooms.

I didn't know what Thrax considered wheat or why he was posing the question to the room, but at that moment I felt like I was the perfect actor for my role there, as girl to these boys: I knew to be graceful where the boys were gawky, savvy where they were clueless, sociable where they were awkward. I also felt, in my own way, that I was a hacker, too; I had found a side route into a technical world at Facebook where otherwise I wouldn't really belong. In computer hacking, gaining ground-floor access to a system is called *getting root,* or having the security key to the entire system, meaning you can change things or delete data at will. "If you have root, you can do anything," Dustin said sometimes as an admonition to engineers, warning them never to give up root access to Facebook to an outsider. And I was getting root.

As we were lounging on the beds in our room at the Riviera later that afternoon, avoiding the 110-degree heat outside, Thrax announced, with an air of finality, "I am going to make a reservation at the most expensive restaurant in town," as if this was a sport and finding not just any expensive restaurant but the most expensive one would score us the most points. And why not? Facebook was paying. Thrax had figured out that much about his position of privilege: that he had an expense account and that we should use it. Sam and I said nothing, continuing to stare up at the Riviera's yellowed ceiling. Though younger than us and with fewer diplomas, Thrax was the man on this trip: He was keeping the receipts, he had the company credit card, he was Facebook's green-eyed, adolescent hacker, leading man. We were just along for the ride.

Sam and I spent the afternoon at the pool at Caesars Palace, opting for the iconic hotel's opulence over the Riviera's seedy ambience. We were always looking for reasons to lie on chaises in the sun, or in the sauna in Thrax's apartment building in winter. "Oh, you guys are getting naked again," Thrax would observe matter-of-factly whenever, on social occasions, Sam and I would inevitably find the closest pool, beach, or sauna in the area and strip to our swimsuits.

Sam, unlike the rest of the engineers, adopted a wry tone in relation to all of this: the site and the company. He was a military kid whose mother was in the Air Force and acted as the family breadwinner, toting Sam and his sister around to various military bases in America and in Europe. He didn't have particular attachments to places or even to particular social milieus that the rest of us did. He knew this scene would pass and that there would be another. "You look pale," we would often say to Sam's fellow engineers in the office with affectionate sarcasm, quoting *Less Than Zero,* because it was true, and because it was funny. Everyone in the office looked pale—not because they had been away from California, like Clay in the novel, but because they lived indoors. "You look pale," Emile would sometimes say back to us, trolling, since by the end of the summer Sam and I were well-bronzed.

Thrax called us at three in the afternoon after waking up from a nap or the night before, we weren't sure. His sleeping schedule was erratic, consisting of twenty-hour days on the computer followed by sleep, from which I imagined him waking only to put his fingers back on the keypad and resume the line of code or AIM chat that he was writing when he passed out. The mere thought of this completely unregulated, unnatural sleep cycle made me imagine a sensation akin to being plugged into an electric socket at all times, minus fresh air, circadian rhythms, or exercise. His apparent lack of the need to exercise or be in nature fuelled my only mistrust of him at the time: Can he be entirely human? Most boys need to be outside sometimes, to tackle the open street, on a skateboard or a bike. I had never met anyone who could be indoors all the time, who drove everywhere, who didn't need to burn off energy outdoors. I wondered how Thrax didn't get rickets, how even his young bones could stay firm without sun.

Eventually Thrax made his way to Caesars to join us at the pool, dressed in shorts and a T-shirt that was slightly too big. Shorts on most grown-ups are automatically funny, and he must have realized that because he told us immediately that he didn't want to wear them anymore.

"I want us to go shopping to buy clothes for tonight," he declared, having made reservations at a steakhouse at The Palms, then the most expensive restaurant in Vegas (according to his extensive research). He said he could charge the new outfit to Facebook and, when I thought about it, I figured he could. A one-hundred-dollar shirt was nothing compared to $25 million or whatever our latest round of funding was (at this point, I was losing track).

Facebook was not going to buy me an outfit to wear that night, and I wasn't even going to try to slip it onto the company credit card. I'd have to wear the same American Apparel tank dress from grad school that I'd been wearing all weekend, while Thrax would don the new outfit that I would help him find. It felt ludicrous, to be shopping for VC-funded clothes for a kid who made more money than I did, but then there was nothing about the entire experience—the hacking convention, my new crew of friends, our Facebook business cards with whatever snippets of pop culture we chose to put on them, like Mark's "CEO, bitch" or Thrax's "You run, I con"—that was not, from some angle, ridiculous.

"I think we should go to Marc Jacobs," I suggested, because at the time it was my favorite store, and the idea of putting a skinny boy in a pair of skinny pants sounded like a good way to spend an hour.

"Who's that?" he asked.

I almost laughed. For all his obscure, self-taught knowledge of technology and Internet culture, he really was straight out of Georgia. "His stuff is cool, kind of mod," I explained. "You'll like it." I wasn't even sure if he knew what "mod" meant but he didn't ask.

Sam and I continued to lie on the chaises for a while, letting the glittering Vegas sun gradually slip behind the Ionic columns that circle the pool. Thrax didn't relax, leaning forward on the pool chaise, drumming his fingers against his knees. He looked at Sam and then back to me, and asked, "Is Sam coming with us?"

"Uh, yeah." I mean, I had assumed so. Sam was sitting right beside us and looked as confused as I was that this was even in question.

"I think it should be just us," Thrax said, affectlessly, flipping his hair out of his eyes with a flourish. "It's time for Sam to be the left-out one." His flinty eyes looked directly at me, as if challenging me to make a choice. What? I thought. Who is this kid? Why do we need to leave Sam out?

Despite Thrax's wish to leave Sam out and occupy the center of attention for a while, all three of us walked away from the pool and towards the Caesars Forum shops together, racing through the casino's deliberate labyrinth on a mission for what Thrax thought would be fashionable clothes. I led the boys past Agent Provocateur with a tinge of longing that told me that in my heart what I really wanted was a boyfriend who would take me to Vegas and buy me a lingerie set that I could wear because I would know he loved me, and it would be okay to be naked, vulnerable in front of him. But I, we, were not there yet. Our scrappiness was exquisite in its own way, but not yet safe, not something I could make myself completely vulnerable to. We were at a hacking convention that was about breaking things, not making them secure. Despite this, I felt better with these boys than I did with the standard, preppy engineers we had left at the office. I thought this was why I sought out the hackers rather than the Harvard bros as friends: If I had to succeed the normal way, I wouldn't make it. We had this in common.

While I felt comfortable in the hackers' company, there was also an intense opacity to them. Who were these people that the company adored, and were they people at all, or were they some kind of channel through which an American alpha masculinity was in process of remaking itself? Why else would you want a friend to be left out except to even the score in a game that you're inventing so you'll have something to win? In college and at grad school, there was a notion of politics, of some kind of larger human goal to one's work. Here, in the valley, it seemed that life was a game and the goal was just to win.

But what did it mean to win? At the time, I thought it meant that we got to be everything we imagined for ourselves, that we got to write the script to get exactly what we wanted. But what we wanted and how we would get there was not yet clear, quite.

It was a strange feeling knowing you are supposed to want to win when you aren't sure what it is you are winning.

That evening, the three of us were sitting at a table at the Palms, Thrax in a Lacoste button-down I had picked out after we spent two hours in Caesars Forum, rejecting everything else for being wrong in some way—too trendy, too fratty, too try-hard. There were celebrities in the restaurant but we barely turned our heads. We were at the center of things, even if no one else knew it yet. Thrax ordered a $175 bottle of wine that only Sam and I were old enough to drink. We poured him thimblefuls while the waiter wasn't looking, and cut zestily into our steaks, feeling more sophisticated than usual in the sleek atmosphere created by the room's mirrored columns, modern furniture, and soft lighting filtered by palm fronds. It felt, suddenly and intensely, that we had arrived.

That night, back in the hotel room, I really did have to choose between them, unlike earlier that day by the pool, since there were two lumpy Riviera beds and three of us. I didn't hesitate—it seemed right to sleep in Thrax's bed, and so I did, and the three of us talked ourselves to sleep. Thrax's hand and mine stretched near each other instinctively and I woke up later with my arm slightly touching his. His skin felt cold, almost inhuman, but I didn't pull away.

For several years, we slept this way on work trips or social ones—they were one and the same: connected, but not quite, like the physical enactment of the AIM messages we tossed back and forth just to show each other that we are here, online, simultaneously together and apart. In retrospect it seems that this, a tangential state of connection, never total, never lost, always there at midnight when you are bored or lonely and need a slight, subtle reminder that you are loved, was one of the things Facebook was about, and it was our job as employees to embody it. Thrax's and my insistence on a noncommittal proximity was the perfect manifestation of what we were creating for the whole world: a system devoted to potential connection, a way of being always near but never with the ones you love, a technology of forestalling choice in favor of the endless option, forever.

At the time, nobody, maybe not even us, quite understood this. One day, as we were driving to a pinball convention in San Jose, the song "Face to Face" by Facebook engineers' favorite band, Daft Punk, was playing on the radio: "It really didn't make sense, just to leave this unresolved." Sam blurted out in pent-up frustration, "This song is about Kate and Thrax! Why doesn't Kate just go over to Thrax's house?!" I instantly thought, but didn't say, "Because that would be too real," and I meant it—the thought of showing up at Thrax's house, looking him in the eye, and admitting that in some weird circumstantial way we liked each other seemed impossible. Because, at some point, around that time, in the little society we were constructing out of bits of code, it seemed that privacy—true intimacy—had become too scary.

CHAPTER 4

WITHIN THE MILE

*D*o you live within the mile?" employees asked often in the fall of 2006, as if testing each other's commitment to the company cause. At an All Hands meeting that April, after listing the company's latest news, such as the $25 million round of funding (at a company valuation of $525 million) that Facebook had recently received from several venture capital firms in the valley, Mark had announced, "We've decided to offer a six-hundred-dollar-a-month subsidy to employees who live within a mile of the office." The company asked engineers to be on call and able to rush to attend to site crashes or other technical crises at any moment. Engineers were issued company BlackBerrys that they kept turned on at all hours, grabbing their phones instantly upon waking to scroll through the night's engineering-related emails. Customer-support employees were hourly rather than salaried workers and thus could not legally be called on twenty-four hours a day, but we were nonetheless expected to remain alert to any critical emails and available to drop other plans and help with any last-minute testing or crisis response.

We didn't have a nonwork life: Life was work and work was life. We did this because we expected that we would be rewarded accordingly—any short-term losses, such as the option to date casually and devote energy to nonwork pastimes, would be more than compensated by long-term gain in the form of stock options we hoped would one day be worth millions of dollars. Facebook, we understood implicitly, was looking for soldiers, not journeymen. But keeping us close to our work and ready to jump into it at any time wasn't the explicit purpose of that six-hundred-dollar-per-month housing subsidy. "The reason for the subsidy is that I've heard statistics saying that people who live within a mile of their workplace are happier, and I want people to be happier," Mark explained. My immediate feeling in response to his announcement was indeed happiness, and slight surprise; he didn't usually mention mood-related words like "making people happy" at All Hands meetings, preferring to discuss technical goals like scaling and growth. But my goal for Facebook, when I thought about it, was to make people happier, and so it seemed important that we, its employees, be happy, too.

However, what we customer-support employees didn't realize when he made the announcement, was that by "people," Mark was referring to engineers, as an email that was sent out that evening to clarify the announcement explained. Engineers were the only ones covered by the subsidy, which struck all the support employees as shocking since we, with our $30,000 a year instead of their $80,000-and-up salaries, most needed it. But this privileging of technical people wasn't an anomaly. As a young designer explained to me bluntly, "Everyone upstairs is dumb," referring to the floor above the engineering lair at the 156 University office where customer support, administrators, and salespeople sat. My impulse was first to laugh at his ridiculous, blithe dismissiveness, until I realized that it wasn't very funny. The way that things were going, these guys might actually rule the world some day. And, being that I was nontechnical and, also, I believed, not dumb, I wasn't sure what this preference for engineers over anyone with a different type of skill set would mean for me.

The fact that support employees were not, in Mark's view, "people" at the company sparked a revolution. Surely, what we couldn't contribute to the company in technical skill, we contributed in social skill and compassion for users. "We thought we were all in this together," we complained among ourselves, and then in emails to executives, like Chris Kelly, Facebook's general counsel, who occupied the rare position of being both nontechnical and also somewhat important, due to his law degree and political connections to Washington. The few executives, like Chris, who understood the cost to company spirit of leaving customer-support employees out, eventually sided with us. In an announcement that Mark made just slightly apologetically at the next All Hands, the subsidy was extended to everyone. After that, almost everyone, if they hadn't already, moved within a mile of the office. It was, in retrospect, the only time employees mounted significant internal resistance to a decision Mark had made.

With everyone living nearby and our rent subsidized and food catered and even our clothes washed for free by Facebook's designated laundry service (which would also develop film, shine shoes, and mend purses if you simply dropped them off in the laundry bag every week with your clothes), we now had the makings of a self-sustaining compound from which we might never have to leave: If not a fully fledged compound, at least the perfect cast of characters and lifestyle to richly populate the pages of Facebook for our and others' entertainment. Bringing us nearer to work, in small apartments instead of gathered around a pool, was a necessary move by the company: The summer house, though only three miles away from the office, was a bit too far, a bit too fun, a bit too much of an escape from our burgeoning digital reality. There, people gathered and talked and played in real life. This next phase of the company's growth would be about making our Hotel California a virtual rather than actual reality, and this would require an absolute commitment to cause and digital country: this is where we would make the Facebook nation real.

"Are you still having fun?" Mark would ask me over the course of that year. I sometimes wondered for a second, out of curiosity, what he would say if I said *no*. He didn't speak to me much around the office except to ask this question, as if he was silently and casually monitoring the mood of nontechnical employees, wanting to check in briefly about whether we were having fun or not. I suspect he knew that if we were having fun, we would keep going, even if we weren't particularly important or well paid. So I always said *yes,* to which he always answered, "Good," and then wandered off, eyes downcast to his BlackBerry. I think he asked me if I was having fun because, on balance, I was. The whole Facebook enterprise was too strange and sudden and golden, rich with potential, not to be fascinating. How wouldn't such a wealth of ambition, boyish antics, and global potential be fun? No matter how broke and in debt I was because of my student loan, I was now indexed to an intensely wealthy venture-capital apparatus that could save us all from ever struggling with money or recognition again.

While resetting users' passwords and explaining how to re- solve browser cache issues wasn't particularly exciting, odd and novel forms of Facebook usage occurred frequently that were fun to figure out. "I can't tell if this group is real or not," another customer support rep said to me from across the desk where we were all jumbled together on the third floor of the 156 Univer- sity building, as the office was getting crowded with new em- ployees. Since the previous fall, when I started, the Customer Support Team had grown from the original five people (Jake, Oliver, Maryann, Emma, and me) to over twenty employees, many of whom were Stanford humanities graduates, with gradu- ates from a few other private colleges mixed in. He showed me a group called "If this group reaches 100,000 people my girl- friend will have a threesome." We clicked over to the profile of the group's creator and he looked real enough, with a profile photo and friends and flirtatious wall posts from girls, standard stuff for a college guy on Facebook. The group he created was growing at an absurdly fast rate, with friends seeing that another friend joined the group and joining it as well. Most of the people joining were guys.

I wondered vaguely if his girlfriend was okay with having their sex life plastered all over Facebook, but I thought it possible that she might be. American college women, after all, are known to kiss each other at parties for male attention, so this group was kind of like the virtual version of that, except that her boyfriend was the one running the show. Just another day at Facebook with another set of peculiarly Facebook problems, like discerning whether someone really wants to have a threesome, or if they are simply, in grand advertising tradition, selling sex to get publicity. It turned out, after we monitored it for a while, that this Facebook group was the first purposely designed as a viral marketing scheme—once the group had 100,000 members, its creator used it to promote a new music Web site. This scheme worked because, while what Facebook was offering users was a connection to their friends, what it offers marketers is the greatest viral distribution mechanism yet invented. In real life, you had to talk to someone to tell them you liked something: Here you could simply click a button, "join group," and Facebook would tell everyone you know.

Some college kids in the group saw that Facebook employees had joined it to monitor them, and started asking us questions on the group wall. They wanted to know what it was like to be us, employees of the site they spent all their free time on. Thrax, naturally, was glad to trumpet our riches for them: "This bacon-wrapped shrimp tastes delicious, doesn't it, Kate?" he posted on the group's wall, and then a few minutes later, "I'm going to come up to your floor for another piece of steak." The college students visibly salivated in their comments after Thrax's posts. I felt a tinge of guilt, recalling my mother saying, "You should never brag," but that sentiment seemed archaic, out of place.

The new product that we had been testing all summer and that would launch soon that fall, the News Feed, would become the most efficient way yet of distributing evidence of one's good fortune—pictures of how much fun you were having or some new thing you had bought—to all your friends. So, as we monitored the group, I could imagine the students' envy as they regarded us, these extravagant Silicon Valley clowns eating catered meats while supporting the site they used to flirt and procrastinate. In truth, the shrimp wasn't that tasty—in the early days, the caterer always overcooked and oversalted everything for the tastes of boys used to fast food—but the people watching us didn't know that. On Facebook it all sounded, and was, impossibly rich, like we were having the time of our lives and, sometimes, I think we were.

Living within the mile meant you were all-in, willing to compromise all other aspects of your life in order to remain fully available to Facebook. Some employees still chose to live in San Francisco, which gave them the option of spending time with non-Facebook employees, but that seemed like a suspect choice to those of us within the mile, whose lives revolved around the company.

While I had begun my job at Facebook with a wait-and-see, month-by-month attitude, the increasing fun and excitement encouraged me to deepen my personal investment in the company. Now that the summer house was coming to an end, I decided to go all-in and move within the mile.

I found a room in a rambling, tree-shaded house full of Stanford graduate students that felt a bit like an army barracks for academics, with thin carpet and nothing in the way of luxuries. The shower, to my unhappiness, was shared by five people. At eight hundred dollars, it wasn't cheap, but after taxes, the subsidy made it a bearable three hundred dollars per month. By this time, I was getting used to the unreal economics of Palo Alto, and my time in Baltimore had made me an expert at hacking my way through poverty: Pay rent and loan payments first, eat as cheaply as possible, preferably home-cooked meals, buy practical clothing on deep discount at Loehmann's or Neiman Marcus Last Call. There wasn't money for much else.

So, by necessity, instead of, as in Mark's case, by choice, my room was furnished with just a mattress on the floor and a laptop. It felt almost good to live a spartan existence in the midst of Palo Alto's sunny plenty, undistracted by anything but our digital mission. There was a masculine, military purity in this lifestyle that wasn't natural to me but that, like almost anything, I could play at for a while. Next to our project of connecting everyone in the world via what felt like an email system on steroids, enhanced by photographs and auto-fed updates, everything else was expendable, frivolous. And since Mark's minimalist aesthetic, expressed on his Facebook profile as a wish to "Eliminate desire for all which doesn't really matter," coincided with my financial means, I decided I would adopt a minimalist lifestyle, for lack of other options.

The role model for what it meant to be fully committed

to the mission was Dustin, who had been working tirelessly to keep the site up for over two years, never complaining, always on call, always, improbably, keeping his cool (Dustin's hard work paid off: He is now, famously, the world's youngest billionaire). I joked with him that he was the Bodie—the hard-working, street-wise young thug on *The Wire*—of the founders, hoodie up, working around the clock from his desk to secure our digital *corners,* which, in this case, meant launching new networks, monitoring traffic flow, identifying issues, fixing bugs. "Dustin a soldier," I said, echoing the voices from *The Wire,* whose accents I remembered from Baltimore. Dustin, ever modest, didn't answer, but the dark circles under his eyes some days did. As exhausted as he often looked, I admired his wholehearted dedication and thought that if they would only let me, I would be a soldier, too. I trusted Dustin, because of his dry wit and warm humility, honed no doubt by having worked at a burger stand in high school, more than Mark, whose blankness verging on haughtiness inspired only curiosity in me, so I never doubted that soldiering for the cause of Facebook, if not for Mark himself, was just.

Despite my energy and ambition to help the cause, there was no way to be a true, 'round-the-clock soldier on the customer-support team. We clocked hours on a time sheet and suffered the power trips of our recently hired head of customer support, Andreas. He was an oily, artificially tanned man who had made a career in the insincere world of corporate customer service, which made him a surprising hire, given Facebook's ideals of youthful, modern efficiency. He seemed to have been hired because the powers that be—VCs and executives—wanted a mature adult to manage customer support, rather than the twentysomethings we were (they trusted youthful nontechnical employees much less than youthful engineers). Andreas didn't understand how Facebook worked or the byzantine site rules that we were charged with enforcing, but that wasn't really his job: His job was simply to be the person assigned to be in charge of the hourly workers, like Foucault's baby in the panopticon. His power was simply in the fact that he was there, watching, even if that simply meant playing around on Facebook all day while Jake, Maryann, and I managed the Customer Support Team in practice.

Andreas hadn't attended college and seemed threatened by the fact that the team was composed mostly of newly minted Stanford grads. As customer support grew, he began pressuring us to hire the least educated people he could find. One day he asked me to interview someone who hadn't gone to college, whose resume was heavily misspelled, and whose only previous experience was working at Pizza Hut, and seemed disappointed when the person turned out to be far too unskilled in typing and writing to hire.

Customer-support employees had the least amount of power in the company, so if we wanted to escape our lowly and maligned position, we had to hack our way through and around Facebook's hierarchy one way or another. Anyone with a shred of hustle did this. There was a handsome Italian boy on our team who did next to nothing, clocking in hours he never worked, but showed up at the office just enough to smile, dark-eyed and long-lashed, at Andreas, who let his shiftlessness slide. None of us blamed the kid. It was all in the game, and in some way, everyone was playing.

The game of building kingdoms that executives from Mark down seemed to be playing reminded me of a quote from *The Wire*, "The king stay the king, unless he a smart-ass pawn." I grew more obsessed with *The Wire,* the deeper I found myself falling into Facebook's game (on weekends, I would sometimes watch an entire season and try to use it as inspiration to game Facebook's system and better my career). Someone suggested that Thrax could be Omar, the stickup artist in *The Wire* who robs drug dealers (because his MySpace hack was kind of the Internet equivalent of a stickup) but that didn't seem quite right to me. Omar had a Robin Hood politics to his piracy. He stole partly to redistribute the drug dealers' wealth to the neighborhoods they fed on. In high school, Thrax had been a pirate for piracy's sake: He had wanted to transfer media (movies, music, episodes of *I Love Lucy,* a show he openly adored) over to his servers just to have it, in the event that he might want to watch it someday and also, because having gigabytes of data at hand was part of how hackers proved their status to one another. The more media he could pirate and store on his copious hard drives, like digital stash houses, guarded by firewalls instead of guns, the better. "I'm kind of obsessed with piracy," he would say to me, later, as if even he knew this drive to accumulate data was a slightly odd, excessive pastime, a new kind of drug.

The minimalism that Mark espoused extended in my case to a minimalism of people. Without money to go out in Palo Alto (and with very little to do there if I went), I had to be selective about what I did and with whom. The Harvard guys were less careful with money, because they didn't need to be. While not typically flashy, they liked to take limos to party in the city or go wine tasting in Napa. Photo albums of these trips would always show up on Facebook afterward, full of pictures of engineers in dress shirts and ties lifting champagne glasses and rolling around on the floor of the limo, smiling with glee. I went on one Napa limo trip and, a week later, upon receiving my three-hundred-dollar share of the bill from one of the Harvard engineers, I realized that I would I have to find other ways to have fun.

So I was lucky to have Sam and Thrax as friends; their less fancy upbringings made them frugal by habit. Sam rode his bike and the bus everywhere; his apartment was furnished with a couch and the dartboard that he brought from Massachusetts in homage to the bar games of his family's working-class hometown. That fall, his sister Micaela, a clever bioscientist who dressed for the beach in short shorts and flip-flops regardless of the weather, moved from Massachusetts to live with him while she looked for work. Her social hallmark was that she proudly carried a six-pack of beer in her purse at parties, just in case the hosts hadn't supplied enough, and the Facebook engineers whose parties we went to were duly impressed and chastened: Micaela had outmanned them.

So it was that our social life in Palo Alto consisted of hanging around at our apartments playing games, like Scrabble or darts, or watching movies and, because our Facebook friends were always there, the office. When there was nothing else to do, we could always run around the empty office after midnight, tinkering with the toys and games the boys had accrued and lolling around on the body-sized bean bags that are Silicon Valley's furniture of choice. In many ways, the atmosphere of our lives that year was like an oversized preschool.

One night, after drinking on the office roof, Sam, Thrax, Justin, and another self-taught engineer, Isaac, who had been hired over a year earlier to help Mark and Dustin code until he was let go a few months later, played hide and seek happily in the dark office, amid the desks and monitors and warren-like rooms filled with blankets and video screens. During our game, I hid under the catering table obscured by the folds of a tablecloth, like Eloise at The Plaza. Thrax eventually found me because, as you do when playing hide-and-seek in childhood, I gave myself away by giggling when he came near. But, given the circumstances, how could we not laugh? We were, technically at least, adults, crawling around on the floor under computers in some of the most expensive square footage in America, waiting until our boy emperor decided it was our turn to be king. This sense that we were part of a developing royal court was bizarre, and I think accounted for the mirth everyone often felt around that time. In pictures from this period, tagged for posterity, we are almost always laughing, our faces contorted as if we can't believe our absurd good fortune. Mark never took part in these games, preferring to sit at his desk in the deep corner of the office, face illuminated by the glow of the screen. He was playing a bigger game.

Despite the financial limits of my life, I didn't feel like I was missing out. On adulthood, yes, but then, if I had been chasing the trappings of adulthood I wouldn't have been at Facebook. Adulthood meant commitments, mortgages, marriage. In the

youth-fixated world of Silicon Valley, where VCs fought over
the teenage boys that they wanted to hire or invest in, all of that
seemed almost unimaginable, beyond reach. For one thing, the
only way to afford a mortgage in the valley is to have already
made your millions, and, for another, there were no men there.
There were many kinds of boys, yes, but in the course of my day-
to-day existence I couldn't say that anyone I interacted with, of
any age, really seemed like a mature, sophisticated man. With
the exception of the gray-haired Rochester, who hailed from an
earlier period in the valley that seemed to be less about youthful,
social glitz and more about the nuts and bolts of building software (Rochester joked about how after working at Facebook he
began to wear more fashionable clothing), the oldest men there,
in their thirties and forties, seemed as disinterested in anything
except business victory as anyone else.

The older men in the office could be as unbridled in their
wide-ranging desires for sex and attention as the younger ones.
One of the few married engineers on the team was known by his
female colleagues (after he had made several unwelcome propo-
sitions to them) to invite lower-ranking women at the company
to have threesomes with his wife, all while trolling and starting
bullying flame wars on online forums. ("Pics or it didn't happen," he retorted like any teenage Internet troll when someone
sent an email to the company's social list saying that women
wearing nursing bras had assembled outside the office to protest
Facebook's ban on breastfeeding photos.) Like any sexual preda-
tor, he groomed people by sending them emails with innocuous,
friendly banter, gradually moving in to make a sexual proposition. When I received an email from him calling me "my lady"

and asking me to lunch, I quit responding to any but his most professional emails.

Within the mile, I rarely socialized with anyone who wasn't a Facebook employee. Among colleagues, we already had a scene, filled with rapt faces waiting to consume our activities and personalities both online and in the office. We also knew too much about Facebook—what features would be released and what shocking transformations of the social world would be attempted next—to let down our guard around other people, especially in the valley. It was impossible to meet anyone new at a bar or coffee shop in Palo Alto or San Francisco without the conversation turning to Facebook as soon as I mentioned where I worked. It was becoming a national obsession, and even nonemployees could, and would, talk about it for hours, as if they worked there, too. Everyone wanted to know what we were doing and what would happen next. So, given the choice between having to answer endless questions that I couldn't really answer (like what features we were going to launch or whether I could read people's messages, to which the answer was an unsayable *yes*), or staying inside our social bubble, it was easier simply not to hang out with anyone outside Facebook.

Until everyone in the world was using Facebook, anything else felt like a distraction. The unspoken goal was clear: to bring everyone on board the social network and make their lives as clean and technically efficient as our own in Palo Alto. We were so convinced that Facebook was something everyone should have that when the product team created an experimental feature called *dark profiles* in fall 2006, nobody even flinched. This product created hidden profiles for people who were not yet Facebook users but whose photographs had been tagged on the site. It reminds me now of the way members of the Mormon church convert dead people, following the logic that if they had known about Mormonism when they were alive, they would have been believers. Facebook was our religion and we believed everyone should be a member, even if they hadn't consented yet.

At the time, the fact that these profiles were called *dark* gave me slight pause. Chase, a perpetually grinning senior project manager by way of Stanford, who was in charge of keeping engineers on task, explained the project further at one of our weekly product meetings, where he explained the latest developments to the customer support team. Chase was slight in stature but carried himself something like an athletic coach, always carrying and consulting a clipboard with notes and product schedules. He had a quick, musical way of speaking that made any announcement he made sound perfectly reasonable. "You see, Mark always had this idea for a kind of Wikipedia for people, or what he called a 'dark Facebook,' where each person would have a wall and people could write anything about them on it. That was actually what he was going to make first at Harvard. But he realized that people wouldn't use something that didn't allow them to erase bad things people said about them, so he made Facebook instead." Thus, the product they had now built was a kind of compromise. People would still be added to the network whether they wanted to be or not, but at least now, should they decide to activate a Facebook account, they would have a chance to control their profiles. In a way, I had to admit that it was a bit of genius: We were using every technical means at our disposal to create a database of all the people in the world. It was the kind of information that every organization that wanted to expand its membership, including the Mormon church, would wish that they had.

While I don't think anyone came to work at Facebook precisely to have *super access,* as we called our ability to view anything and anyone on the site, regardless of the user's privacy settings, once we had that power, no one wanted to lose it. The whole product, in a sense, was a means of obtaining knowledge about other people, and as Facebook employees we had a leg up on everyone else. Another employee in engineering, a designer, was blunt about his personal motives for working at Facebook. "I built this to find you," said a quote he inserted as an *Easter egg* (a programming term for an intentional hidden message in a Web site or video game) on the search page. The designer's words perfectly captured the intent that drives much of people's Internet usage: to search for partners, whether sexual or romantic, in the easiest and quickest way possible.

Social network usage statistics indicate that men and women have different online viewing habits: Two-thirds of the photos viewed on social networks, Harvard researcher Mikolaj Piskorski found, are of women. "Men prefer looking at women they don't know, followed by looking at women they do know. And women prefer looking at other women they know." Consumption of men's photos is proportionally the smallest segment of viewing behavior, suggesting that women are less interested in consuming men's photos than heterosexual men are interested in viewing photos of women they've never met. In the end, no matter how much we tried, we couldn't use technology to produce love. Because love, unlike technology and its uses, requires commitment to one, instead of the broadcast and consumption of many bits of distant, digital content. Love doesn't scale.

At the time, however, the knowledge and the power and the wealth we were developing would be too intoxicating for us to care about something as unquantifiable as an intimate feeling. We were all, I think, lonely on some level, but the answer wasn't to find love and another life away from Facebook: The answer was to work harder, scale faster, and get bigger, and love would be waiting for us somewhere at the end. Everyone wanted to be king, first, myself included. The rest could follow.

On September 5, 2006, after we had been testing it all summer, Facebook finally released its first and perhaps, to date, most controversial new product: News Feed. Before News Feed, Facebook had been a comparatively discreet book of profiles, maintained and updated individually by each profile owner. News Feed introduced a new homepage where any and all updates to a friend's profile might appear as a broadcast story, with a headline and accompanying photographs. Your friends' activities on Facebook were now news, and your homepage was a kind of social newspaper.

However controversial, the News Feed was new, and whatever is new or new-seeming (because most so-called innovations in Silicon Valley are combinations of other products and ideas) must be built, launched, and used by as many people as can be convinced to use it. So, News Feed was launched to all users, in one fell swoop. I stayed up until midnight the night before the launch, lying on my bed in my bare room, to watch as the product was pushed out. Back then, we always pushed at midnight, since that was when traffic was lowest and all engineers were awake. One minute the homepage was blank, boring, harmless, safe. The next minute it was full of stories, of what someone was doing now, of a new friendship made, of a relationship ended. The automated literature of our lives had begun.

If my early response to the product that summer was one of unease, users reacted with an entirely different magnitude of distress. The day we launched News Feed felt, without exaggeration, like a minor Vietnam, complete with helicopters and reporters circling the office to videotape the protesters who threatened to appear in our courtyard. I arrived at the office feeling jittery and gun-shy, having lain awake all night wondering what the reaction would be when college students on the East Coast woke up to find that their lives had been serialized overnight.

Email after email of the thousands we received that day told graphically of the betrayal and evisceration the users felt. Phrases like "I feel violated," and "You've ruined my life" were common, and the emails were long and passionate, filled with all the personal details and drama that they felt Facebook had exposed without warning. "I just broke up with my girlfriend yesterday and thanks to your 'News Feed' everyone on campus saw a story about it this morning! How would you like it if people started publishing stories about your life without telling you?" one user howled.

I did nothing all day but sit at my desk reading the agonized emails and responding to them with a stock, impassive answer along these lines: "This information was already available to your friends on Facebook; we're just delivering it more efficiently." Sometimes, I modified the stock response with an acknowledgment of the user's story and feelings, just to sound a bit more human, like I cared, which I did, because at some basic, human level, I sympathized with their feelings. If I hadn't known the News Feed was coming, I would have been shocked and upset, too.

As the day progressed and the email continued to flood in, I started to feel brutalized myself: The pain, anger, confusion, and shock expressed by the users was real, even if the product itself meant no harm. By midnight, there were still thousands of emails in the queue, and it became clear that we were never going to get through them all. As always, there was a technical solution: With the click of a button, Jake blasted the stock News Feed response email to everyone who had written in that day, whether their query had to do with News Feed or not. I left the office and wandered home down Palo Alto's empty Hamilton Street, bleary-eyed and emotionally battered, looking forward to losing consciousness in sleep.

I suppose that the users' shock at News Feed stemmed, in addition to the feeling of being suddenly exposed, from a sense that, overnight, without warning, their online presences had gone from static profiles to live-updating digital characters, put in narrative form for others' enjoyment. Were they ready to be characters dancing perpetually in the virtual courtyard of Facebook's Hotel California for our friends' entertainment? Whether or not they were ready, it had happened.

This was always the case with social-media technology: It meant no harm, but that did not mean that it would not cause it. This is how technology is pure, and this is why people love it so much. Ascribing intentionality or an emotional impact to a piece of technology or what it does is impossible, and the product that is built mediates between the intentions of its creators and its users. Technology is the perfect alibi. Facebook doesn't hurt people: People hurt people. This is true. But just as Facebook makes it possible to do things faster, more efficiently, more cheaply, it makes it possible to hurt people faster, more efficiently, with less cost to themselves. It removes any sense of direct responsibility for our behavior, for how what we do makes others feel. With Facebook, you can act and be seen acting without ever having to look anyone who is watching you in the eye, or look at them at all.

In a tense All Hands meeting a day after the News Feed launch, Mark, responding to employee fears that we had badly alienated users to the point of fleeing the site, predicted that the controversy would settle. Four days later, it became clear that he was right. To mollify users and perhaps also anxious employees, executives, and VCs, Mark consented to the addition of privacy controls that allowed users control over what profile updates could appear in a News Feed story.

But, in this, as in future cases, the users got over it. They had to; they had no choice, and we knew it. The only competitor of Facebook in 2006 was MySpace, and MySpace didn't even count, with its hard-to-read, glittery fonts, wildly decorated pages, and absence of technical advancement. When people asked us, "How are you going to beat MySpace?" we acted as if we didn't even hear the question, looking off into the distance in the manner of Mark, who was asked to answer this question often by press and investors. "They are doing something different," he would say, and, by that, it sounded like he meant, "They don't even matter to us." MySpace's focus on individual self-expression in a clunky, technically primitive interface was not where the Internet was going, in Mark's parlance. The Internet was heading in the direction of replicating not just individual identities but the relationships between individuals—or maybe, ambitiously, the entire social world as such—and Facebook was already doing that better and more comprehensively than any other service.

As if they knew that employees desperately needed a release after our week of doing battle in the social-media trenches, the company obtained tickets for all of us to go to a Dave Matthews concert. I didn't even like Dave Matthews that much, but it was with relief that I left the office early that Friday to dress for the concert and put accusations of technological "rape" and "betrayal" out of my mind. I picked out one of my old college-style outfits, as if willing myself back on campus studying literature, instead of serving as an accidental private in a social-networking war.

In keeping with the camp-cum-college atmosphere of the company, our party planners always arranged for buses to transport us directly from the office to company parties and back. In a small gesture of resistance, Sam and I would always go to the dive bar across the street (it was divey by Palo Alto standards, at least, with plain décor, lower prices, and an Erotic Photo Hunt machine that we played often on breaks from work) for a grown-up Manhattan, dark with whiskey and bitters, before boarding the bus like so many teenagers headed to prom night. Like everything anyone at the company did, our archaic preference for whiskey over vodka would be immortalized in a Facebook group, called the "Society for Anachronistic Alcohol," which was created by Harry, a saxophone-playing engineer whom Rochester brought in from his former company. The group name itself became anachronistic, because in two years everyone would be drinking whiskey, thanks to *Mad Men* and the emergent pop culture of vintage masculinity.

Facebook had rented a VIP area for us at Shoreline Amphitheater, Silicon Valley's concert venue, which sits in a stale-smelling bog across from Google headquarters. This was the first such designation for most of us, and it felt exciting. VIP-ness was something that someone else, more important and with more money, always had, but now we were skipping the lines and walking directly to our own private area, where we could observe regular concertgoers from behind a fence and, in turn, be observed. The whole point of VIP treatment, it seems, is to speak to our universal human desire to feel special, valuable, desired: And to have something that others don't. When we were VIPs, as Thrax might have put it, it is time for everyone else to be the left-out ones.

In the VIP section, we milled about, talking to each other while drinking wine or beer from the open bar and, mostly, feeling relieved that we were no longer in the throes of the News Feed tumult. It had only been days since the feature launched, but days in Internet time are like weeks in regular time: Even twenty-four hours is enough to put distance between you and an Internet phenomenon. Harry seemed already to have intuited this—that anything that happens online will pass—as he looked placid at the party, just as he had all week while employees were biting their fingernails and attempting to remain calm. Or, perhaps, he simply didn't care how users felt about News Feed as much as I and some other employees, judging from the strained, worried looks on their faces all week, did.

Regardless of our feelings about the new technology we had just unleashed on the world, the traumatic events of the week brought us closer to each other, as a battalion must feel after a skirmish, and we huddled in circles chatting, feeling united against our users mobbing us from across the Internet.

As the sun set on the lawn, we moved to our seats close to the stage. Our VIP treatment enhanced the de facto sense of entitlement that we, as Facebook employees, were beginning to feel. We felt entitled because we had just built a device—News Feed—that replaced the organic word of mouth and socially networked communities that made bands like Dave Matthews popular. A band's fame spreads when people discover them and start telling friends, but News Feed now made it possible for people to spread their taste in music instantly by listing favorite bands on their profiles. We knew that there would be much power in this. The only thing more powerful than celebrity is to own the tool that makes it.

However, the Dave Matthews band was of a previous, predigitized time: all guitars and instruments, instead of the electronic music that looped constantly in the office. The music was real, and the night felt more palpable and present than anything else since those days in August when we had escaped the virtual unreality of Palo Alto for the authentic unreality of Las Vegas. My heart sang a little at the music, at the way everything felt, at the flick of Thrax's pale hair on my nose as he talked into my ear. It was nice to feel things, rather than watch text and images scroll by. At one point I looked behind us and saw that Rochester, old-time computer geek and valley billionaire twice over, was dancing.

On the bus back to the office, Thrax and I sat curled up companionably, holding hands, watching the dark Peninsula sky pass by outside the window, but we stopped short of a kiss. "I can't have a relationship story show up in News Feed," he explained, and I filed that away in my groggy, battle-scarred head as a perfect statement to summarize what had happened that week. The narratives Facebook wanted to tell about us already had the upper hand, and News Feed had only launched three days ago.

As the winter came and the engineers were consumed by work, racing to build the next wave of features, I retreated into my own hobbies—writing, painting, taking long walks to Stanford's Lake Lagunita and back—almost forgetting about technology for a while. I left my computer at the office when I went home, and since the company didn't give customer-support staff BlackBerrys, at the time the smart phone of choice, I still had an old Samsung flip phone that delivered nothing in the way of data. When I was away from the office, I was effectively off the grid, though I was still in the heart of it.

I watched our lives overlap with technology at an ever-increasing pace, as News Feed quickly grew central to people's sense of their social worlds and smartphones became everyone's favorite toy, and grew almost nostalgic for the rough edges and unprogrammed contrasts of Baltimore. The whole city of Baltimore is a patchwork of rich and poor, green and gray, black and white, and I missed it. I worried that I was getting soft in the medium sheltered tones of Palo Alto, where no one seemed aware of how dark or how light and beautiful the outside world can be. In Baltimore, the view of all of it—and the corresponding awareness that the world was full of people with different circumstances and experiences, particularly ones less fortunate than your own—was inescapable. In Palo Alto, there were houses, shops, a few offices, and many computers all talking to one another, each pretty much the same as the other. But I knew that the rest of the world was full of people poorer, darker, and less technologically provided for than the engineers were in Palo Alto, and this lack of awareness on their part was draining. Here, it was like we were living in a fantasy of perfect wealth, where everyone was the same and everyone was equal, but *everyone* was defined as young engineers competing for the same crown.

CHAPTER 5

VIDEO NATION

*B*y Facebook's third birthday in February 2007, the site had 15 million users and the company had at least 150 employees. We had bypassed the famous Dunbar's number that Mark cited often as an archaic, real-world social limit that Facebook had to succeed in making obsolete. Anthropologist Robin Dunbar proposed in a 1992 article that approximately 150 is the maximum number of people that any individual was able to know and keep up with at a given time. So, as the company sailed past 150 employees, our internal society would be a test of how well Facebook can help us manage social contacts and, in Mark's words, stay connected, despite our growing number.

On this February afternoon, the sun flooded the third floor of the office, where administrative assistants were rushing hurriedly to prepare for the party. By three o'clock, the room was festooned with blue balloons, blue cakes, and kegs. Employees in navy-blue hoodies that said *Facebook* across the front—the first of our many unofficial company uniforms, which change whenever the designers concoct a new riff on the Facebook logo, were drinking and playing Beirut on tables set up for the occasion. As at all our parties, professional photographers roamed the room taking pictures of employees practicing their most flattering poses—hand on hip, smile wide, like we were the happiest people in the world. And, at parties like this, we were happy, because we got to do what Facebook did best: enacting and documenting a uniform, unspecific glee, a moment with no larger concerns, in which everyone smiles on command, with nothing to fear from the ever-present cameras and their incessant need to document us.

I had a specific reason for my happiness, beyond Facebook's birthday and the almost parental relief I felt that the enterprise we had all been working tirelessly on was entering its third year. Whatever this toddler network was, and intended to be, it was going to be huge, I was sure. I was also ecstatic because in four hours I would be taking my first long vacation since I began working at Facebook. I would be boarding a flight to Rio de Janeiro, back to Ipanema and its glorious beaches, and away from all of the digitally prompted smiling and poking and constant virtual coddling. For the past four Spartan months of work, I was completely dedicated to Facebook's cause, but also saving every penny in order to spend three weeks away. At some atavistic level, I missed a world where everything wasn't planned for me, where things weren't always new and gray and clean, where I was forced to be present in the flesh, confronted with situations I couldn't preview and manage remotely.

I bought the cheapest ticket to Brazil I could find, a five-hundred-thirty-dollar round-trip ticket on Taca Airlines, on a Southwest-sized 737 that was too small to make the full journey to the southern hemisphere and had to stop in Panama to refuel. As we winged out of SFO and onward toward the tropics that night, the flight became turbulent and children on the plane screamed in Portuguese for hours. I remembered the story Micaela told one night at a Palo Alto bar about when she and Sam were children and flew between Army bases on planes with nothing but seatbelts tethering them to the floor, and that they cheered whenever there was an exciting patch of turbulence and wished for more. While I wasn't afraid of flying to Brazil by myself, I wasn't fearless enough to cheer on this roller-coaster ride far above the Amazon. It's funny how we choose what we are going to be afraid of. I can wander the streets of any city alone, but quiver at the thought of jumping blithely off rainforest waterfalls like the Hopkins surfer boys did on my previous trip to Brazil. It made me think of the computer hackers, who fear nothing when it comes to waging war on other people's virtual property, but cringe at the idea of exploring unfamiliar urban climes.

"Why aren't you going to Brazil with Kate?" Sam asked Thrax, vaguely accusingly, over IM, as I watched. Sam, Thrax, Justin, and Emile were all freaked out that I was going to Brazil alone, without friends or Facebook people (which was basically the same thing), but didn't want to betray they cared by actually saying so. "I don't have the balls," Thrax answered ruefully. I could see him picturing kidnappings and beheadings, as if all of Rio de Janeiro were like the deadly, warring *City of God*. Just the thought of a suburban American hacker suddenly immersed in

Rio's cacophonies of carnival music and street dancing seemed almost impossible, as if the sensory overload would instantly overwhelm the circuitry of someone used to sitting alone in the dark, behind a screen. I realized this was why I was going back to Brazil, because despite the fact that I had found friendship and fun at Facebook, there was another side of me—one that loved discussing romance languages rather than programming them—that felt neglected and in need of sun. If no one from work wanted to go with me, it was fine. It was time for me to go on an adventure of my own, and for them to be the left-out ones.

Landing in Rio de Janeiro after the long flight over the tropics was almost more of a relief than it was two years earlier. At the time, I was running from the ascetic world of academia; now I was running from an intense focus on administering a growing digital world. Comfortingly, Rio de Janeiro was unchanged, awash in golden light and lightly dressed bodies and the constant sound of samba. After checking in at the fifteen-dollar-per-night hostel on Rio's hostel row, I ran directly to my beloved Ipanema beach, where the sands were alive with light and the play of bodies. People tossed soccer balls back and forth and played in the surf as hawkers called out, "Agua de coco, cerveja," almost as though they were singing. There was too much to look at to focus on anything in particular, so I just took in the colors and the way it all felt: soft sand, the green of palms, the whitest light. Without a second thought, I lost track of time and the accumulated anxiety of living in a world where I was expected to be focused on a screen and be virtually available all the time.

I hung out on the beach during the day and ventured out

into the samba clubs at night with new friends made on the stoop of the hostel, all visiting from somewhere, all going somewhere else next. It made me realize that, socially, the *now* of travelling, which consists of whoever is there, in whatever place you've all happened to end up at the same time, is more natural for me to inhabit than the *now* of the Internet, a disembodied world which includes everyone, everywhere, all somewhere else, behind some other screen.

Some nights later, I was in the southern Brazilian beach town of Florianopolis, and my local hostel crew ventured to an outdoor reggae bar on a sea of sand dunes. While waiting for the band to start, a few of us walked far up into the dunes until we could see nothing but sand and sky in every direction. Someone tried to take a picture, but the moonlike stillness couldn't be captured; the light was too diffuse to make sense to the camera. I thought of my colleagues back in California and how they would be awed by this dark sublimity in the midst of a strange and wild continent, so raw and far from anything they had experienced. I wanted them to see it, or better experience it, since the moment was so much bigger than the view: It was the velvet vastness, the utter quiet, the slight wind brushing sand against our skin, the far-off glow of the bar we'd left behind. I left the dunes feeling certain that life was still meant to be lived, not continuously filmed, mediated, and watched from afar.

On my return to Palo Alto three weeks later, I rediscovered that, in the new world we were building, living life without technological mediation would be a luxury. At work, we usually approached each other with a swift efficiency, anxious to rush off to some online business, but now I lingered and smiled when I ran into coworkers in the hallway, still basking in the memories of my vacation. When in conversation at happy hour with Chris Kelly, Facebook's general counsel, whom I regaled with stories of my Brazilian adventures, I saw his face register a surprise and slight confusion that my Brazil-influenced personality was different, my presence calmer and more open to conversation. I had a brief panic that perhaps I should mask my joy at being present instead of a mere vessel from which controlled Facebook posts and comments flowed. Within a week, though, my behavior readjusted to the Palo Alto norm and my Brazilian warmth was gone: I conducted myself blank-faced, keeping conversations at work to a cold minimum, saving the information transmission for email, IM, and Facebook. I was back.

Still, having been away from it, I was more unnerved now by the office's intense devotion to the screen, so I lay low, finding a shallow substitute for the Brazilian sea by moving to a new apartment building with a pool, still within the mile. I could barely afford it but I felt, after Brazil, that a pool was necessary, as though it could fix things, if only because the splashing water wasn't safe for technology. The apartment was in a 1920s Mission-style building called the *Casa Real* whose Craigslist listing promised that it was once the home of the rich and famous of Palo Alto, though at the time it was a poorly maintained, overpriced money factory like all the other apartment complexes in town. The fact that I lived at the *Casa Real* is an irony that is not lost on me. *Real* in this case meant "royal," but in the heart of the city that aims to digitize our lives, I interpreted it differently.

That spring, I noticed that one of the designers, Ariston, a soccer-playing Duke graduate who was fanatical about movies and talked about wanting to make feature films one day after his Facebook millions were secured, was frequently updating his status on Facebook with the word *motion*. He was telling us all something, virtually, loudly, but in code. *Motion,* I found out late one night at the office while talking to Emile and Thrax, was the code name for what would be known as *Video,* a project that Ariston and Thrax were developing on their own, without Mark's direction or consent. Typically, in order for a Facebook feature to be developed, it had to be part of the product roadmap, which was a six-months-out plan that was overseen and approved by Mark and that determined what products would be built and when and who would work on them. In this case, Thrax and Ariston didn't care to wait for the roadmap to catch up to them: They wanted Video, and they wanted it as soon as possible, so late at night they sneaked into the screen- and blanket-laden room off the engineering floor and built Video.

Years later, the building of Video would be described in a Facebook recruiting advertisement as a "brilliant hack" that proved how maverick and self-directed the engineers were. But, in truth, making Facebook Video was not a radical disruption so much as it was, like most of Silicon Valley's products, an evolution and combination of various existing products, an obvious next step for the company's suite of technologies. After all, video already existed on YouTube, which was founded by a former Facebook employee who had left a month before I started, and on the streaming video site that Thrax had already built in college. The fact that Facebook later used the story of Video's maverick origins as a recruiting tool shows how the making of Video was a culturally vital act of rebellion for Facebook; you can't claim the identity of a hacker company if your engineers aren't breaking any rules.

So, while Thrax and Ariston did not invent video, they were compelled to bring it to the company and claim it as Facebook's own (like all of Facebook's products, such as Photos, the product was simply and grandly called Video, as if it were the one and only). Their compulsion wasn't just to disobey orders and build something they weren't supposed to, but, in the spirit of the company, to strive toward a monopoly. The would-be kings did not come to Facebook to only half digitize the world, to own a record of text and still images. They wanted to own moving images. They wanted to see everything. They wanted to film everything. They wanted no limitation on the documentation and distribution of our lives, or the degree to which they could access the lives of others. And finally, perhaps, they wanted to be stars, by building the technology so that they could make the movies that would make them and everyone around them stars. As if to drive this home, the Facebook Video frame was fashioned in the form of a movie screen: wide and black, as though we were watching ourselves in a theater. If there was anything prescient about this in 2007, it was that the world wasn't yet in a place where everyone wanted to use technology to make them a star.

In fact, the idea that building this technology could make you visible to the world like a celebrity, or even turn you into a celebrity, didn't really occur to me then. In 2007, Facebook still seemed as though it was gaining value precisely by being private, by showing you what you would have seen anyway offline: the intimate lives of people you were already intimate with, private moments that you had participated in. Mass fame seemed like the confused pursuit of actors in another medium: reality television. At the time, the only people I was connected to on Facebook were people that I knew and with whom I shared real-life social experiences. I couldn't fathom yet why you would want everyone, even people you've never really known, to know you.

To me, Facebook Video was just another gadget to play with, but a little gratuitous at that point, technology for technology's sake. The test videos Thrax uploaded overnight as he built the product seemed to make this point over and over: They were scenes from an empty, dark office, scenes of faces flickering at the camera, saying nothing, fiddling with their floppy hair. Nothing happened in them and I wondered what impulse caused him to click record. Why this moment and not the one five minutes later? I always wondered that when I saw that a new video had been posted.

The lack of action or purpose in the test videos perfectly represented the motivation behind these projects: to technologize everything, just to say that we did. The televising and digitization of private life was the new colonialism: without any continents left to explore and own, private life had become the last frontier. "Television Rules the Nation," a hidden quote that Thrax and Ariston inserted in the header of the Facebook Video page, was visible only to those who knew to highlight it with their cursors. When everyone would be using Facebook, the technologists would have captured life itself, all the moments in our lives that used to be belong only to the people who lived them. To own not the physical map of the world but the map of human life was, I began to think, the goal.

As a woman and a customer support employee I was expected, for the most part, to follow the engineers' leads, because we were a technical company and this implied that what we were doing required technical skills. The trouble was that I also embodied Facebook's ethos of rebellion all too well, and there was no role available, at the time, for a woman who broke the rules. I did my job and accomplished my goals, but beyond that I didn't feel compelled to fall in line. I knew that if I simply did everything I was told, I would not be of any interest to Mark, who preferred employees who were slightly dangerous, like the cyberpunk characters in the 1990s movie *Hackers* that he and many other engineers referenced often. I decided I would develop my own project, off the grid, and in a nontechnical capacity.

While Thrax was building Motion/Video, Sam and I stayed up late some nights to prepare and launch Facebook networks in other countries. First, I would have to gather all the metadata about university networks abroad (like the names of schools, their locations, and their web domains, which we would use to authenticate students as legitimate members of their school's Facebook network). Then, Sam would run a script he had written that would build the networks and check for any issues before declaring them live and ready for registrations. Once the networks had been launched on a given night, usually around midnight or one o'clock in the morning, we would toast to our new territories. On the Watch Page, a page Dustin developed that allowed us to see how many Facebook users were registered in any given Facebook network, we would observe as users instantly began signing up for the new networks we had created. Next to the name of each network, a count depicting its number of users would steadily mount upward, first in the single digits, then growing into the hundreds. If we were doing really well, it could reach into the thousands overnight.

Building new networks abroad was fun and independently motivated, a very Facebook thing to do in the company's developing corporate mythos of the self-starting employee, and good for the site's growth. As such, our work was to be rewarded. However, as in any corporate hierarchy, any time people went around the rules at Facebook, it unsettled middle management. "You are doing an excellent job in customer support, but I've noticed that you are working outside the department," Andreas told me in a performance review that spring, his eyes narrowing, wanting me to be afraid. He was more concerned with maintaining company hierarchy than, as the rest of us were, getting critical work done by any means necessary. It's possible he didn't stop to think that the networks abroad needed to be launched in order to build momentum for Facebook's growth outside the United States. While Andreas didn't understand this, Dustin did: One night, when I was hanging out with Sam at his desk on the engineering floor, Dustin tacitly encouraged us to launch more networks. "He's your boy," Dustin said to me, gesturing to Sam. He knew that the company had lucked out with us: We were doing work without his even having to ask. This, like Thrax making Video, was the startup dream: that the product you are making is so compelling that your employees will advance it in their sleep, or at least in the time when they should be sleeping.

So, I nodded and pretended to listen while my manager chastised me, and then, late at night, continued to launch new networks with Sam anyway. This dissonance between upper and middle management is what happens when you work for a company like Facebook, which is simultaneously about control and the dismantling of control. Facebook wanted to disrupt the market without having its own order disrupted, to perpetually change and break things without allowing its users the same privilege. Internally, it was the same: Engineers were tacitly encouraged to break rules while the rest of the company had to follow them, unless they had some tricks of their own. The people in the company who could get around this paradox were the ones who could *social* it (the short term for *social engineering*, or hacking one's way around something using social means) by breaking the right rules and, above all, remaining popular, and in doing so riding all the inherent corporate contradictions as far as they would take them. Facebook's work environment, like much of Silicon Valley, and even like the Internet itself, was always about power: about maximizing your own power while conceding as little of it to others as you could.

Maybe as reward for my labor or maybe because he just happened to have an extra ticket, in April 2007 Dustin bestowed a ticket to the Coachella music festival on me. All of my friends at the company were going, but at three hundred dollars per ticket plus three days of lodging expenses, sadly, I didn't have the money to go. So, when Dustin gave me the ticket I felt like Cinderella with the glass slipper: I could go to the ball in the desert. I hadn't left Palo Alto since my trip to Brazil two months earlier and I was, as always, anxious to leave—light and heat and live music were as essential to me as coding and Python (the preferred programming language in the valley) were to my coworkers.

As the sun was going down over Palo Alto, Justin, Emile, and Thrax picked me up in Justin's Honda (later, everyone drove Audis, but no one had that kind of money yet, so mostly we drove practical Japanese sedans) at my apartment for the long drive to Coachella. We always did everything at night, since everything in the valley was cooler and more vital in the dark, and driving was no exception. We would be in the car for six hours, traveling past garlic-scented Gilroy and onward to the flat dreariness of the I-5 and, finally, outward to Palm Springs. I assumed that we would sit and talk and listen to music like my friends and I always did on the drives to Los Angeles from Phoenix, but this was a different time and a different kind of road trip. As we drove into the darkness of the I-5, computers and gadgets started to come out of custom-made Facebook messenger bags and were turned on.

While I was resting against the headrest in the backseat, trying to sleep, I saw the telltale glow through my eyelids of the laptop screen bobbing in front of me. "Noooo, not again, not here," I thought. I understood the constant presence of photos and video at parties but in the car? While I was sleeping? "Kate's going to hate me forever," Thrax said to the screen, turning it on me, "Talk." The video camera on his MacBook Pro was recording my nap, which was now over. It was my job to perform. So, I talked about nothing into the camera, addressing Jamie, who was sitting at home watching us on Facebook from his sandbox. Sandboxes were testing areas that occupied what was called the *developer tier* of the site, which only engineers and other employees could access. Engineers would play in their sandbox as they developed new code for the site, and only when the code was fully developed would they migrate the code to the live site at one of the weekly midnight pushes. While I talked to the camera, Thrax narrated the scenery passing by. "Buses welcome," and "Daylight headlight section," he read off the highway signs. "I think we're in the middle of nowhere." We were indeed in the middle of nowhere, but I kept talking to our distant audience, and Emile did too. Then we signed off, "We love you, Jamie," we said, and at that moment it sounded like we did, although it wasn't something we'd say to him in person. I think we could tell him we love him because he was so far away, and to love him is to love the technology that allows us to speak to him anyway, safely, intimately, from afar. Our technology, ourselves: For us, at the heart of this revolution, they were ever increasingly the same.

From the minute Thrax's project began to be built, forcing each other to perform in videos became a kind of a company ritual: Video was most often used by Facebook employees for practical jokes. At a party, someone would turn a camera on and pretend to be setting up for a photo, but after everyone was posed and moue-ing, they would reveal that it was a video all along. The subjects of the video would shriek when they realized what had happened, everyone would collapse into laughter, and the video would always be posted to Facebook for everyone to watch and laugh at. The joke never seemed to get old.

After we all finished speaking dutifully into the camera, Thrax posted the video to his sandbox in the development tier for other Facebook employees to view. Employees often loaded Facebook from this tier because it gave us access to new things that weren't available on the site yet (one caveat about using a development version of Facebook was that things were often broken and buggy there, so one never knew whether a wall post would go through or a photo would appear). Other employees, who were sitting at their desks in Palo Alto, posted comments on Thrax's video to say they saw me sleeping in the video five minutes before. This is bizarre, I thought. We are still in the car, locked in a glass bubble in the middle of Joan Didion's beloved Central Valley with farm-land on either side, and already people have been able to watch our carbound activities. Why is this kind of immediate sharing of our most mundane moments with distant friends even a thing that is happening? The answer to this question, as with all the things that Facebook made over the years, was that the sharing was happening because it could. If it could be built, it must be, and we must be, if not the first, then the biggest builders of this and every other thing. This was the code of the valley.

Thrax and Emile entertained themselves by filming more videos and sending them back to Facebook, and reading the comments on the videos that were posted immediately by our colleagues in Palo Alto. It was a perfect, near-live feedback loop: We couldn't be alone for a second, even in a moving car. And, apparently, our activities in the car were more interesting than whatever the people back home were doing, because they couldn't resist watching and commenting on them. It is an odd logic, this, but it is the logic the social net depends on: That because something or someone you know was filmed, it becomes interesting, worthy of watching. Technology and distance make us more fascinating to each other.

Midway to Palm Springs, we stopped at a truck stop to buy drinks and stretch. There was a store next to the convenience mart full of fake guns and firecrackers, and Emile, Thrax, and Justin bought them, playing cowboys in the parking lot at three in the morning. This made more sense to me as a thing to do with friends on a highway in the middle of the night. Of course, Thrax was making a video of this activity that he would post to the site as quickly as was technically possible. However, because we were in Bakersfield in the center of absolutely nowhere, his Sprint data card didn't work and we had to return to a strictly analog existence for the last hours of the drive. The boys' fingers itched with nervousness, drumming loudly against their knees in the dark, unmediated hush of the car. When technology failed, they had nothing to do.

It was too early to show up at the house we had rented, so we stopped at the Cabazon outlet mall on an Indian reservation, where every retail brand has an outlet and where the winds from the desert sweep unrelentingly across the asphalt, like a Sahara in a strip mall. I felt better when we were shopping because, unlike hacking, it was familiar territory. This was the one activity where my companions would consent to follow my lead. "I think you should wear linen shorts," I told them, since we were going to the Empire Polo Field, where Coachella is held.

The name Empire Polo Field struck me as appropriate for

us because, in a way, we were like colonists, but for the social Internet instead of land. When other people saw the crowds at Coachella, they saw faces; we saw profiles on new Facebook accounts. We knew they would all have a Facebook profile one day.

At the mall, we went to Ralph Lauren and searched the aisles full of fake palm trees and golf shirts for linen, which they, of course, had. As we were leaving, one of Thrax's friends called from Georgia, and we stood around in the windy parking lot while they talked in Southern accents so strong I could hear a drawl oozing through the phone. I leaned closer to absorb the accent: It was so thick and real, from a place I could barely imagine. His friend wanted to come to Coachella but couldn't afford it, and I was reminded how lucky I was that Dustin gave me his ticket.

We left the mall for the vacation house, where Chase and his crew of Stanford graduates were already ensconced. I made Brazilian caipirinhas out of copious limes and lemons for everyone, and pretended in all the stark sunshine that I was in Brazil again, even though I was surrounded by my pale coworkers of Silicon Valley. Thrax wandered around with his video camera, as always taping everything and nothing: the kitchen countertop strewn with booze and bags of chips, the pool, the people lying on chaises. They waved idly at the camera when it was pointed at them, saying *hello*. "You shouldn't film for so long as you are walking into the room," Chase said, "It makes the video look like a porno." I suppose that Chase was right in a way: The taping of everything made it feel like we were in a porn movie, without the sex, but with all the weird, awkward exposure of our private presences to an audience we couldn't see. Thrax agreed, but nothing changed. The camera was always on.

Each morning at Coachella we parked the car in the dusty lot of the Polo Field and walked across acres of horse-soiled dirt to get to the entrance. (Years later, everyone would be rich enough to buy VIP passes and bypass the dusty march, but for now this was a long, dreaded, communal part of the Coachella ritual.) We made lazy commentary on the long walk in for the camera, MTV VJ style, about the fashions of Coachella: As usual, there were moccasin boots and American Apparel shorts that year, as if everyone were living a three-day Western desert fantasy, like *Casablanca* for Palm Desert. I was reminded of my favorite writing professor's injunction that we "Make up movies for ourselves to star in; write the lines." Life was exactly like that, everything was a line and a scene, except that these movies were really being filmed, and we had to invent our characters on the spot.

Once we got through security we raced to see Ratatat, whose metallic chords and looping beats were, along with Facebook's musical heroes, Daft Punk, one of the soundtracks of 2007, introspective and masculine and hazy, like a long desert drive or a programmer's long code session. After the set we stood around on the lawn, forming a small island in a sea of people all racing to find something to see. The cell towers on the polo field were overloaded by phones grasping for signals, and we lost all the bars of connectivity on our devices. Rendered inconsolable by the loss of connection, Justin stared at the screen of his Black-Berry, changing position every few minutes to see if he could find a signal. His new BlackBerry Pearl had just been released that week and, even though it was signalless, as we stood on the grass illuminated by the setting sun, he proclaimed it beautiful, touching its curved lines with love. It was as if this new smart phone carried all the secrets of the world, like the conch shell in *Lord of the Flies*.

Back at the house that night, we collapsed on the living room floor in exhaustion, too tired to continue the party into the early hours of the morning, as many Coachella concertgoers do. There weren't enough bedrooms for all of us, and Chase's group had done the work of renting the house, so they got the rooms and Emile, Thrax, Justin, and I slept on blankets on the floor. As we were nodding off to sleep at around two in the morning, Sean Parker, the Napster co-founder and early Facebook employee, who had left the company weeks after I got there but was still friends with Chase, knocked at the door with what Chase later told me was a doctor's bag full of drugs, which everyone politely declined. Standard methods of being bad, like doing drugs, seemed inefficient and superfluous to us. The real drama was in the way we were changing everything, the way the whole world would relate to one another, so fast, without anyone knowing it yet. This, not actual drugs, was what got us high. For the rest of the night, I drifted in and out of sleep on the scratchy Persian rug, my feet occasionally accidentally kicking Justin or Emile, while Chase and Sean talked on and on.

On a hot May afternoon, a few weeks later, I was sitting in the back seat of Thrax's BMW, waiting for him to emerge from his apartment. Ariston, Thrax, and I were driving to San Francisco to see a band. Thrax finally came out of his building and walked to the car, slowly, because he was, of course, filming. He opened the car door and settled the camera on Ariston, whose beatifically wide smile stretched an inch wider for the camera. "Heyyy, Thrax," he said, almost flirtatiously. "Glad you brought that thing," referring to the camera. "Ha ha, of course, dude, of course," Thrax replied.

I noticed that when they were filming they spoke more intimately with one another. Perhaps it was because they were speaking not just to each other but to an audience that must be seduced. Technology was, as always, the alibi. But the camera didn't really protect them: It picked up every lilt in their voice, every tinge of desire. I suppose we must seduce our viewing audience because nobody came to Facebook to be unknown, uncelebrated, alone. They came to build something that would make them larger versions of themselves that would create fame and propagate it to everyone, everywhere. This was a new fame factory, and we were flirting not just with each other but with fame, with the idea that, someday, if we played our cards right, everyone would be watching.

Thrax turned the camera on me where I sat in the backseat. I was wearing my favorite terrycloth hoodie, which was almost a piece of armor at that point, a thin form of resistance to our new, constant state of video surveillance. My face was in shadow but my smile is bright, teeth gleaming digitally on the video that will live online forever. I declared to the camera, "Video nation," because that is what we were going to become. Facebook's user numbers were mounting quickly that April, reaching 20 million, our international networks were beginning to grow, and video would soon be launched. Thrax laughed with delight. "Video nation," he concurred, and cut the scene.

CHAPTER 6

THE MIRAGE

Facebook is a technical company," Mark began saying with increasing frequency at All Hands meetings in the spring of 2007, as we prepared for a new wave of product launches. It was a mantra that he wanted us all to memorize and repeat as often as possible to anyone who would listen. At first, I wondered what the force of this insistence was: why *technical,* and not *social*? If the product was about people, why was it important to say *technical* over and over?

Talking to various engineers about this, I discovered that Mark's point was to differentiate Facebook from other web companies for purposes of recruiting. "Good engineers will only work at a company that grants privileges to the technical people," they explained. "They need to know that their ideas and decisions will be considered primary, and not those of marketing or business guys." The unmentioned competitor in this conversation was MySpace, which, in March 2007, had more than one hundred million users to Facebook's 20 million but, nevertheless, remained an object of scorn. In the technical world, MySpace was considered a mere shell for spam, a skeleton social network built by an email marketing company rather than an engineering company. Because its parent company, Intermix Media, was based in Los Angeles, MySpace initially gained traction among aspiring Hollywood actors and musicians, thus cloaking it temporarily in an aura of artistic cool, but it did very little to develop itself as a product after that point. Thus, MySpace was not technical, and Facebook was. As far as Mark was concerned, Facebook was the first social network devoted to technology first, and he wanted to stake this claim within the tech community. Thus, Facebook planned and arranged its first F8 conference in downtown San Francisco, which was where Facebook would publicly announce its commitment to technology.

As May 2007 approached, the company prepared furiously for F8. The proof of the company's technical nature, which would be unveiled at F8, was the Facebook Platform, a new product or set of tools that would permit a Web application like Facebook to interface with external code written by outside developers. This would enable engineers who were not employees to build applications that run on the site. Users could then interact with friends on the site in a wide range of applications beyond the ones, like Photos and Groups, which were created by Facebook. We were all so aligned in our sense that Facebook would dominate the world that none of us really questioned the hubris involved in naming our conference "Fate." Platforms are the ultimate technology for a Web site with global ambitions because they are a way of bringing every developer to play on your turf, even if they aren't playing on your company's team, and we were the first social network to build one. Moreover, as far as Facebook was concerned, we were the first social network committed to technical innovation at all.

However, because I was not technical, I was not actually invited to attend F8, despite being employee number fifty-one at a company that now had over two hundred employees. In the push for technical dominance, Mark had been engaged throughout spring 2007 in a shift that a few women in the company began referring to as the "technical purge," in which everyone without a technical background suddenly found their positions in question. Mark began to insist that new positions be occupied by technical people. I wasn't particularly surprised, since, as customer-support employees, we always had questionable status anyway.

The customer-support reps who wanted to go to F8 could only attend on the condition that they serve as coat checkers. Perhaps I was as guilty as the engineers of feeling starworthy and VIP, but I wouldn't accept being treated like the second-class help, and this would serve me well. While the engineers were huddled in a room at San Francisco's W Hotel, where they could concentrate away from the crowds of press and developers swarming the conference, furiously preparing for F8, I left the Bay Area to spend the weekend with my parents in Huntington Beach. At the beach house my parents rented, I had to sleep on the couch, but it was better than checking coats at a conference called "Fate."

The following weekend, I was lying on a futon in Thrax's apartment late one night, listening to Sam, Justin, and Emile rehash F8. Thrax told a story about the night of the conference, hours before the Facebook platform was announced. The engineers were all holed up at the W, coding as quickly as their fingers could type. The problem was that the revolutionary platform, which Mark had announced in his keynote with the words, "Today, together, we're gonna start a movement," wasn't ready. The boys were still writing code and patching bugs to make it work at all.

Even though Thrax and Ariston began building Facebook Video in defiance of Mark's orders (as Video gained traction in the company and all employees were using it, Mark came to accept it) it turned out to be a boon, as it gave him a Facebook application built on the platform to announce as part of the launch. But at the eleventh hour, the platform and video were still unfinished, so even as Mark announced them, Thrax was writing furiously to code. As he told us the story, he had been coding for three days, and his body and vision were starting to fail. When he fixed the last bug to make video work, he left his laptop on the bed and went to the bathroom to get a glass of water. He didn't make it to the sink. He collapsed on the marble floor, exhausted, and fell asleep. Later he woke up and, in a half-dreaming state, tried to move but couldn't. His exhaustion was so extreme that his limbs couldn't register his thoughts. "It was scary," he remembered, "it was like my body wouldn't ever work again."

As the guys reminisced excitedly about the heroics of F8, congratulating themselves on their latest victory in the march to take over the world, I thought about Thrax's story. It was as if, in the process of building out his technology, he had reached the technologists' desired state in which he no longer had a human body. If the scene had been a video—and, for once, it was not, for there was no one there to record Thrax's fall—Daft Punk's "Robot Rock" would have been playing. This, maybe, was Facebook's primal scene: The moment when technology consumed the body, reality, and what was left of the physical realm.

Bored with F8 and Platform chatter, which was all anyone at work had talked about for months, I suggested watching *The Wire*. Sam agreed and Thrax quickly downloaded the first episodes of season one from one of his many pirated media sites. A few minutes later, Mark and a few friends arrived at the apartment to hang out. Mark said that he wanted to play video games and, since even at that late hour of the night he was still the boss, we let him commandeer the television in the living room for video games while Sam, Thrax, and I retreated to Thrax's bedroom to talk. Eventually, Mark left and we wandered back out to the living room to make up songs on the electric piano.

It was close to three in the morning when I left the living room and went to the kitchen in search of eggs. Thrax always had eggs, if nothing else, in the fridge, and it seemed like a comforting sign of a domesticity that couldn't be coded away. I made sandwiches out of eggs and stale bread, as Thrax and Sam tinkered in the dark on the piano. It was just us here, now, without the crowds and Mark and the blogs and the excited worship of influential Silicon Valley tech bloggers like Robert Scoble, for whom the Facebook Platform was the next great technical revolution, at least until the next exciting new application or platform came along. The only reason I knew who Scoble was, and that he had been raving about the platform, was because I was accidentally there, watching and listening to the boys that occupied the center of it. As I buttered the bread slices and slid the fried eggs onto them I wondered if the world would ever care as much about any of this—being technical, building applications, making platforms, owning platforms—as Mark and Scoble and the rest of the Valley did, and where all of this was going to lead.

"Are you coming to Thrax's birthday party in Las Vegas?" Sam asked me over IM while we were both at work.

"I can't . . . it's going to be like five hundred dollars for one night with airfare and the club and hotel," I typed back.

"Jamie says that you have to go. We need you," Sam returned.

"I know, but I can't afford it. I make a third of what you guys make. If they want me to go, they're going to have to help."

"Okay, I'll talk to Jamie and see what he says," Sam said, switching to a different AIM window to talk to Jamie.

Later that day Sam messaged me with an answer.

"Jamie says they'll pay for the club. He doesn't seem to get why, though."

"Ugh, I don't get how they don't get how rich they are compared to everyone else. It's like they think everyone is a rich guy from Harvard."

"Well, what they don't realize is that you'll remember this." Sam was right, just as he usually was when it came to reading the idiosyncrasies of the social world we inhabited. While I tended to observe things quietly, Sam unabashedly posted mocking witticisms on the other boys' walls, making loving jokes of everything they held dear. This was Sam's brand, and he could get away with it because, as an engineer, he knew they needed him. He was also gay, and cute, and being both made him an asset to others rather than a source of competition for female attention.

"They want us around to spice things up," Sam once said to me at a party, as if we occupied the position of some kind of self-aware court jesters. Sometimes, when we made fun of the more staid engineers, they liked it because mockery was another form of attention. Other times, they didn't realize we were poking fun. For example, rather than remembering the names of all the latest smart-phone models that were released every week, we began calling smartphones "technologies," refusing to differentiate between all the different versions like the Bold, the Pearl, and the Curve, that were being released as fast as RIM (and, very soon, Apple, with its iPhone, which first went on sale in late June 2007) could make them. "Use your technology," we would say when we needed to call someone or get driving directions. Soon some of the other engineers were calling their phones "technologies," too, either not realizing or not caring that we were gently mocking their and the company's obsessions.

While I made no secret of the fact that I found technology

to be as silly as it sometimes could be useful, I knew that I was still expendable, especially in the age of the technical company and the purge. My thoughts about Sam's conversation about the upcoming Vegas trip with Jamie, which I kept to myself, had to do with the Harvard guys' paradoxical cluelessness about the very things that they claimed to know most about: money and power. Their success in life, achieved in their teens or earlier, blinded them, I suppose. They assumed everyone had the same chances in life, the same easy path to wealth, where knowing just a little more about gadgetry than everyone else went a very long way.

Despite the fact that I was the poorest guest invited to the birthday party (everyone else was an engineer) by millions of dollars, I agreed to buy a two-hundred-dollar, round-trip Southwest ticket to Las Vegas for one day of partying. I figured that I'd just drink cocktails beforehand at the hotel instead of throwing hundreds of dollars at bottle service. Not going to Vegas for Thrax's birthday wasn't really an option. I was the only girl who was considered one of the boys. They needed me there, a female presence, an anchor around which they could keep oriented and keep things from spinning wildly out of balance. I felt like we were always in danger of that, as if with a little nudge, the entire enterprise, social and business, could veer out of control, fast. We had too much power, and very few checks on that power.

One day, at around this time, one of the Harvard guys posted a screenshot in News Feed of a new application that he, Thrax, and Emile were developing. It was not an official Facebook application. It was intended to be released as a platform application, meaning that users could add the application to their profiles if they wanted to, but that they didn't have to. I could see from the screenshot that the application was called "Judgebook," and that its purpose was for Facebook users to rate female users on their appearance. The screenshot showed two women's Facebook profile pictures, set side by side, with a space for the viewer to input a score for each. The tagline of the app was, "Judgebook .com: never judge a {face}book by her cover," which hardly made any sense, but the photos side by side made clear what the words couldn't: This was a way for men on Facebook to explicitly judge women's looks and assign them a score. For what? I thought, but then I remembered that Mark's Facemash application, which predated Facebook as his first popular Harvard site, was based on the same concept. The difference was that to make Facemash Mark had to steal students' photographs from the Harvard servers (for which he was famously disciplined by the university administration), but in Judgebook's case, the photos were already there on Facebook, submitted by users themselves.

In another screenshot in the same album, the Harvard engineer posted a screenshot of the domain names he had purchased to host the application: Judgebook.com and Prettyorwitty.com. It was like Mark's comment at the barbecue about having to choose between a girl who looks like a model or is smart, all over again, only in web application form. You could either be pretty or you could be witty and, in either case, you would definitely be judged and scored and rated. It was at moments like these that I realized it was the great and twisted genius of Facebook for anyone who was interested in rating things constantly, as Mark and the engineers who made these types of applications seemed to love doing. Facebook made it possible for men to have endless photographs of women available for judging, and women simply by being on Facebook became fodder for the judging, like so many swimsuit models at a Miss America pageant. Because, with Judgebook, like all Facebook platform applications, women did not have to consent to have their photographs used by the application. The application would alight upon your data and feed it into its database whether you wanted to be judged or not.

Sometimes, that year, I got a sick feeling in my stomach that I didn't want this world in which we are all ranked virtually, by virtual strangers, on the basis of popularity and appearance. Even worse, I felt like I might not have a choice in the matter. I didn't want it to be like this: I wanted us to make things better, not worse, for humanity and, especially, for women. I thought that more information would be helpful, not realizing that *information* as defined by these engineers was not value free. There were different kinds of information that we could be exchanging and receiving but, instead, we were learning about how pretty people were and whether people liked them, and how much. The world the boys were building was as weighted against the less powerful as much as the analog one they seemed to want to disrupt and leave behind.

On a flat, dry Friday in July I boarded a Southwest flight to Las Vegas for Thrax's birthday, happy as always to escape Palo Alto, if only for one night. I didn't care that I was about to spend my last five hundred dollars for what was basically a bachelor party without the wedding. I had been teetering financially for so long that this kind of budgetary risk just seemed normal. Besides, the cult of money and power that we belonged to was only getting deeper and bigger. I may have only had five hundred dollars in the bank, but there was an iceberg of money building under us all in the form of the stock options that we were all vesting month by month. The stock options still had very little value, as there was no public market for them yet, but, by May 2007, the site had grown past 24 million users, had 40 billion page views per month, and was already the sixth-most-trafficked site in the United States. As Facebook's potential to IPO became steadily more secure, though we knew it would be years off, it felt a little like we were all fronts for something else, faces of some future that hadn't yet been realized.

The year before, when Thrax and Sam and I had played at being high rollers at the dinner table at the Palms, it all felt adorable and twee, a grand lark, like we were Silicon Valley's version of starlets about to get discovered. Now I wasn't sure; things were more serious, less playful, heavier than before. Facebook was growing steadily bigger, but my doubts about the new digital world we were all beginning to live in were growing too. But, regardless of how I felt about the big picture, I had been at Facebook long enough, almost two years, that I knew I too had to win, regardless of what it cost.

A man sitting next to me on the plane took my mind off my brooding by buying me a gin and tonic from the always cheerful Southwest flight attendants, whose jokes on the PA system became bawdier the closer we got to Las Vegas. We toasted to the fact that in an hour we'd land at McCarran Airport, the gateway for so many unrepentant sinners longing for release into Las Vegas's bacchanalian excess. As we sipped our drinks and watched the red desert pass by underneath us, he told me about his job at a company in San Jose, which manufactured the security keys that we used to authenticate ourselves when we administered Facebook. In a way, we were in the same business: His job was to authenticate my employee identity, and my job was to authenticate his social identity. In the Internet's turn from anarchy to being a proxy version of real life, authentication was becoming big business.

The plane landed and we were released into the temple of tackiness that is the mirrored McCarran airport and the city it serves. The first blast of heat on leaving the terminal was liberating, soaking into my skin with an intensity that both awakened and calmed me. In the taxi line, I ran into a business development guy from Facebook whose movie-star good looks were widely considered to be the reason that he was hired, perhaps in addition to his Stanford MBA and whatever actual smarts he had. He was also there for the party, so we shared a cab to the Mirage Hotel and Casino. While he checked us in at the hotel desk, I stood on the busy carpet and watched enormous fish swim in the floor-to-ceiling tanks that line the lobby. As the fish watched me from the water I was not sure if I could tell the difference between observer and observed.

The view of the strip as we entered the penthouse suite the engineers had reserved for the party was breathtakingly bright and dark at the same time. Floor-to-ceiling windows gave onto an endless desert night punctuated by glittering signs that barely penetrated the blackness. The penthouse was entirely covered in marble, so it was like walking in a mausoleum. Sam and I retreated to the bathroom and took photographs of ourselves splayed suggestively against the tub. When we would get back to Palo Alto we would post them to the Facebook group we had made devoted to homegrown Erotic Photo Hunt pictures, as in the bar game where you look at two pictures of a lightly clothed person and try to find five differences. We created pictures for the group by first posing for a picture, then taking another picture in the exact same pose, but with a piece of fabric slightly moved, making a game of teasing the viewer. These tame Erotic Photo Hunt pictures were the premeditated, ironic version of the suggestive party photos that our colleagues posted on Facebook at the end of every weekend.

The mirrors lining all the walls of the bathroom multiplied everything, extending us to infinity, adding to the hallucinatory feeling that all of Las Vegas is designed to trigger. When we emerged from the bathroom, the penthouse had filled with friends, or rather coworkers, preparing for the party, dressed uniformly in collared shirts and skinny blazers. People brought bottles of liquor and lined them on the bar, like a movie about a birthday party in a suite in Las Vegas.

Everyone left for dinner except Sam and me, who remained in the suite like kids at an emptied-out grown-ups' party. The boys were going someplace expensive that I couldn't afford and, like the good friend he is, Sam skipped dinner and stayed behind with me. We turned the radio up loud and blasted the Cure, singing aloud to the sky and the lights twinkling for miles in the distance. "Love cats," we sang, tiptoeing around on the marble, spinning in circles until we were dizzy and collapsed on the lacquered sofas with a view to the Mirage's pools thirty floors below.

Eventually we descended the elevators to the casino with the intention of finding the boys, but were distracted by everything else: the lights, the tinkling of coins in the slots, the crowds thronging the casino, going to and fro as if orchestrated by machines. Disoriented, we walked outside to breathe in the arid desert air, and kept walking, down the strip, farther and farther from the Mirage. We came to a towering old-time neon sign for the New Frontier Casino. "Closing night, July 14" it read. That was the next night. We had to go in.

The New Frontier was in a sorry state, barely hanging on until its slated demolition. The slot machines continued their relentless beat, tinkling and singing with the sound of fake coins, but the air was heavy with smoke and dread. We toured the casino floor and put a few dollars in the machines. A waitress, soon to be unemployed, brought us white Russians made of the harshest of vodkas. We chatted with a few security guards near the cage, where all the money was dispensed, who told us the casino would be demolished in a few days. I decided that I already missed the place even though it wasn't gone yet. As we were leaving to walk back toward the Mirage, I took a picture of the New Frontier's neon sign, which read, "Thanks for the good times."

By the time we got close to Caesars' Pure nightclub, where the others were, we could barely walk, not because we were half drunk, but because our feet were worn out from trekking down a few miles of Las Vegas concrete. I checked my phone and realized that the others had been texting us all night. Their texts grew less grammatical as, I imagine, they grew increasingly drunk. "Where are you?" they asked, and Sam and I texted back that we were outside Caesars, collapsed on a patch of grass next to a barely clothed Roman statue that gazed seductively at the Imperial Palace casino across the street. "Come, we need you" they texted, over and over. What did they mean, they need us? I wondered. They never said that. They had never needed us so badly before. They never needed anyone. As far as I could tell, our entire lives at Facebook and within the site itself were being reconstructed so that no one ever really needed each other, as all our needs for attention could be satisfied by whomever was on-line, chatting with us or viewing our updates and making comments. "Should we go?" Sam asked. "I don't want to," I replied, "they only want us because we aren't there."

We lay back on the grass for a while and let the twinkling sky descend upon us, bathing us in uneven light, bright for nighttime. When we tired of the outdoors, we returned to the penthouse. None of the guys had returned from the club so we realized with glee that the one bed in the suite was ours. We jumped in, and I picked up the phone to call room service to deliver us a large plate of grilled cheese sandwiches, charged to Jamie's room tab. After eating the sandwiches, we fell asleep under the crisp white comforter, our fingers still oily with grilled cheese. Later, as the light was dawning over the strip through the floor to ceiling windows, all the guys tromped in, in various stages of drunkenness, and fought for space on the bed and on every available soft surface. Realizing that we wouldn't be able to continue our luxurious sleep, Sam and I got up and walked down to the pool, where people were already starting to gather in bikinis and swim trunks. We lay out on the chaises and tanned, half asleep, until it was time to catch a cab back to McCarran and fly home.

That Sunday, after I'd slept off our long night, I logged in to Facebook to see an endless stream of videos that the boys had filmed at the club. In them, the boys were not chatting up or kissing girls they had met, as I had expected. Instead, they were performing an elaborate ritual only they would have the strange, cold vanity to invent, in which they would methodically chat up and reject girls that the bouncers had brought to their table. "Leave! You're not pretty enough!" one of them seemed to say over the din of the club as he shooed the girls away in succession like so many servants.

Even though I had been living in this boys' world for almost two years, I was still a bit shocked. Their products ultimately reflected their real-life behavior. Instead of making a technology of understanding, we seemed sometimes to be making a technology of the opposite: pure, dehumanizing objectification. We were optimizing ways to judge and use and dispose of people, without having to consider their feelings, or that they had feelings at all.

What would happen to me? I wondered. Was I pretty enough to make it past the bouncers? Was that, in the end, what this was about? Was it even possible to be pretty enough? Were my colleagues ever satisfied with reality, or was reality always deficient in comparison to the perfected digital image? Did I even care? Did it matter if I was trying to win a war I didn't believe in? I wasn't sure, any more, what I believed in, but I knew that I didn't want to live in a world where I appeared only for a bunch of engineers to judge me and shoo me away.

In their minds, perhaps, the way this worked was that everyone who wasn't them was deficient. They were architecting a system that placed them on top. "I was born perfect," Thrax would say to me, in all honesty, the following year at Coachella, gazing down at his body as we lay around in bed, chastely as always. When he said it I, as I usually did upon hearing one of the boys' preposterous statements, laughed at the absurdity of his claim. What does being born perfect even mean? I didn't know, but perhaps your own perfection is what you would have to believe in if everyone else in the world isn't good enough. And that's why you'd want to reinvent a world in which everything had to appear perfect, all the time, as if forcing everyone else to believe in being perfect, too, or at least try. With my instinctive desire for authenticity and the slightly worn-out thing—the soon-to-close New Frontier—I didn't even know what perfection looked like. Perfect, to me, was the not perfect, the unfinished, the thing you loved because it had depth and edges and idiosyncrasies.

As I sat at my kitchen table in the Casa Real reading my News Feed and its exaltation of a boyishly cold, digitally perfected ego, I realized that I was furious at all this. I hate Judgebook, I hate rankings, I hate algorithms, I thought, in a moment of total rage at everything—the company, these boys—that was near, but also far beyond my control. I just wanted to be happy and loved for who I was and I wasn't sure all the algorithms or fame in the world could produce that.

CHAPTER 7

I'D RATHER BE CONQUERING

The Facebook Platform that was launched at F8 was, already within weeks and months of launch, winning. In fact, the platform grew exponentially overnight, to Mark's and many of the engineers' surprise and satisfaction. Application developers signed up by the thousands and built applications like Farmville and Scrabulous, as users' increasingly cluttered walls showed, soon gained wide distribution. By November 2007, over seven thousand applications had been created and each day a hundred new ones were being launched. In Mark's and some engineers' views, the rapid and unrestricted growth of the platform was good because it proved that at Facebook, technical development, not the desires of marketers or users, was king.

Not everyone was convinced that the rapid growth of the

platform was such a good thing: for the company, maybe; for the users, not necessarily. As customer-support reps, our job had always been to keep the site clean, monitoring for spam and aggression from individual users, doing our best to keep the virtual neighborhood tidy, and, we hoped, meaningful—a true "place for friends." We painstakingly and manually deleted accounts that we thought were fake, and warned people whom we thought were contacting users en masse, rather than communicating in a personal way. Though paid very little compared to the engineers, we were in a sense the defenders of authenticity on Facebook, at least until engineers could figure out a way to approximate our labor with algorithms, which they eventually did, to some user consternation as accounts came to be easily erroneously flagged and deleted.

But now, developers, who could sign up to develop on the Facebook Platform from all over the world, were pumping thousands of apps and millions of formulaic News Feed stories into our carefully walled and defended network. As far as external developers were concerned, the sole purpose of the platform was to generate more users for their app and, therefore, more money for themselves. In a sense, they were simply mirroring the engineering ideology of Facebook itself: Scaling and growth are everything, individuals and their experiences are secondary to what is necessary to maximize the system. Facebook, as we learned early in the case of the group titled "If this group gets 100,000 members my girlfriend will have a threesome," is the world's most efficient viral marketing platform, a way to turn automated word of mouth into gold.

The idea of providing developers with a massive platform for application promotion didn't exactly accord, I thought, with the site's stated mission of connecting people. To me, connection with another person required intention: They have to personally signal that they want to talk to me, and vice versa. Platform developers, though, went at human connection from a more automated angle: They churned out applications that promised to tell you who had a crush on you if you would just send an invitation to the application to all of your friends. The idea was that, after the application had a list of your contacts, it would begin the automated work of inquiring about people's interests and matching people who were interested in each other.

Soon, developers didn't even ask you if you wanted to send invitations to your friends. Simply adding the application would automatically notify all of your Facebook friends that you had added it and invite them to add it, too, using each user as a vessel through which invitations would flow, virally, without the user's consent. In this way, users' need for friendship and connection became a powerful engine of spam, as it already was with email and on the Internet long before Facebook. The same "We'll tell you who has a crush on you if you just send this email to your address book" ploys were familiar to me from Hopkins, when spammers could blanket the entire email server with such emails in a matter of hours, spread virally by students gullibly entering the names of their crushes and their crushes' email addresses.

When I first started working at Facebook, I wanted to believe that my experience there could have been a love story. That is, I thought, in some sense, that Facebook could be what we all—the employees, the users—sometimes wanted: A network through which we could connect and love each other more readily and more easily and with more permanence, a place in which we could feel more authentically ourselves, together, like every new model of social organization has attempted to engender since history can remember. However, as I gradually started to ascend the ranks that year, living in its virtual reality, I began to wonder whether to make a love story out of Facebook might be, despite our desire that it be so, impossible.

In some ways, Facebook's early years had all the makings of a bright, shimmering tale: an odd assortment of smart and dedicated people thrown together to try and figure out the parameters of a new platform, a better way for people to communicate. I wanted what I assumed everyone wanted: to bring people closer, to share important information faster, and to make everyone feel less alone. And, because most celebrated people at Facebook were, technically, if not intuitively, smart, and we all seemed to believe in the same things—in making something new—I thought it might work. I wanted the world to be better than before. I wanted to help people. If there was a big paycheck waiting for you at the end, I wanted it to be an incidental outcome of the revolutionary work we did together.

Now, two years in, I wasn't sure what was really happening with the burgeoning social media craze and its associated new forms of instant, distant interaction. What I was seeing was that social websites were playing upon the biggest open and unsolved wound in our society: the need to be known, the need to be loved. It was unclear if they were meeting this need. This need is so naked, so huge: In a society in which we are wage workers and paying customers more than we are members of a community, we yearn to be understood and loved for who we really are. We want people to see us, to care, to need us as we need them, to be there. But, more often than not, in our scattered communities of strip malls and subdivisions, they don't and they aren't. We move too much, and even when we are near, we are easily estranged, whether by work or leisure or now, technology, making it ever more possible to communicate without laying eyes on each other.

As Facebook and the social Internet grew ever bigger, I wondered whether what we were building was fixing our loneliness, or just becoming another addiction, like the social games that would soon begin to be pumped out by Zynga and others, that dull or distract us from deeper feeling. I was not sure if we were enabling love or its illusion.

In summer 2007, the launch and overnight success of the Facebook Platform, and the influx of cheap, viral applications it created, wasn't the only thing that was changing. By this point, the company had grown to almost three hundred employees. Most of these were engineers, in keeping with the site's philosophy of technical primacy, along with larger and larger numbers of customer-support employees hired to keep up with user growth. In June 2007, I was promoted to a customer-support training and quality manager, which meant that I was responsible for bringing new employees on board and teaching them all the ways of Facebook site administration. My promotion yielded me a raise to a salary that was about half what engineers were making on average, and a shiny new Facebook-purchased BlackBerry, which Andreas brought into my one-on-one meeting and pushed dramatically toward me across the desk, as if bestowing upon me some mystical, valuable gift direct from the king himself. I tried to act appropriately excited about the BlackBerry, but Andreas didn't know that Sam and I had been making skeptical fun of technologies and their talismanic quality in Silicon Valley for months. Skeptical or not, I would now have my own technology to consult at any moment.

Being on salary meant that I could be asked to work longer hours, so Andreas began scheduling me to come in on Saturdays to conduct intense training sessions with rookie customer-support representatives. At one of these Saturday morning sessions that summer, I was teaching the reps how to repair a Facebook account problem and I had my laptop projected onto the wall so everyone could see what I was doing on my screen. My instant-message client was on, and Thrax began a conversation, which, as they often tended to do, veered toward the topic of his penis. This was one of his favorite topics, in addition to anything digital, to discuss on Facebook and off with friends and coworkers. I quickly minimized the chat window and, after letting the reps out on a scheduled break, typed to Thrax, "I can't talk right now. I'm at work and this conversation is being projected." Only at Facebook, I thought, hoping the rookie reps hadn't read the conversation, but not feeling that bad about it if they did. They would get used to the work environment's weird and seamless mixing of personal and professional soon enough, I figured. At Facebook, to repurpose the old feminist saying, the personal was professional: You were neither expected nor allowed to leave your personal life at the door.

While I had become inured to (and sometimes enjoyed)

the antics that went on at work, I was still worried about what would become of me at the company. Teaching customer support wasn't the worst job, but it was far from a passion, and it continued to be frustrating to watch the engineers celebrate themselves and their increasing stature in the valley when I was still part of the lower caste, barely making ends meet. The dissonance that I felt daily flew in the face of what Silicon Valley says about itself—that it is a meritocracy, that it values intelligence and creativity, that everyone has a fair shot if they just work hard enough. This was true only if you were technical, and even that may not always be enough: In the age of the social network, who you knew and who your friends were became increasingly important, too. I decided to give myself a late August deadline: If there wasn't any movement in my career by that point, I would take my vested Facebook stock and strike a new path elsewhere, however difficult that might be.

I said as much to Thrax as we sat in the parking lot of Fry's Electronics on a Sunday morning. We had stayed up all night watching movies at Sam's house and then, after a walk around Palo Alto where we passed a church and toyed with the idea of going inside for the service (we decided against it, since we were dressed in jeans), decided to drive around. Driving around with engineers in Palo Alto almost always involved a trip to Fry's Electronics, so they could check out any new technical products that might have been released in the past week. I never minded going, because the store itself is a strange and fantastic monument to the Wild West. The aisles are decorated with bales of hay and statues of figures like Annie Oakley, who poses with a gun on a bale piled with Linux manuals. I could entertain myself for a good hour observing the Western decor while engineers poked around at newly released televisions and video games.

Back in the car, a Justin Timberlake song came on the radio and Thrax confessed that he liked it. Pale indie guys weren't supposed to like Justin Timberlake in 2007. "That's cool, I like Justin Timberlake, too," I said. In the same confessional spirit after our sleepless night, I added, "I applied to new jobs this week. I can't keep going in CS forever."

"Oh, no," Thrax said gravely, going silent for a minute as the Timberlake song finished on the radio. "You should be a product manager," he mused.

"Yeah, I know, but Mark doesn't want anyone who isn't technical to be in engineering anymore."

"Oh, right," he replied, knowing as I did that this decision, like anything else at Facebook, was only really up to Mark. In that sense, we were all just along for the ride.

"Whatever, let's go to In-N-Out," I said. When all else failed, in California, you could count on a good animal-style, protein-style grilled cheese (my usual In-N-Out order) to make things feel, at least momentarily, better.

"I tell everyone I meet that I can read their entire lives in one minute," Chamath Palihapitaya said by way of introducing himself to Facebook employees when he was hired as vice president of product marketing and operations in July 2007. He was a high-stakes poker player and ex-AOL Instant Message executive Mark was bringing on board, it was surmised by the tech press, to inject some much-needed business savvy into the organization. Chamath was young, brash, and masculine in style but, unlike most Facebook engineers, he had experience managing a company.

For his first couple of months, Chamath observed operations and interviewed employees to find out how things worked. My meeting with him came in early August. We met at Coupa Café on Palo Alto's Emerson Street, where laptops sat on every table and startups were the topic of most every conversation. Over cappuccino, Chamath asked me to tell him everything about my department. I told him who I thought did the bulk of the management work (certain members of the staff), and who didn't (our boss), and what I thought the issues in the department and the company were.

"We need to get you out of the department as soon as possible," he told me. "I think I have an idea of where you will fit," he said, but he didn't tell me where. I was elated; perhaps the technical purge was ending and Mark was finally open to the idea of creating meaningful roles for nontechnical employees.

The next week, Chamath asked me and my management colleagues in customer support to do an evaluation exercise in which we ranked everyone on the Customer Support Team from highest to lowest. Sitting up late that night in the office, I assigned a score to each person on the team. Some were easy to score: They were either spectacularly hard workers or rather lazy, preferring to play company-sponsored Beirut games to the alternately hard and tedious work of solving user problems, but for most it was a queasy and difficult process of comparing apples to oranges, which, in this case, might be one person's quickness at answering emails versus another's thoroughness and accuracy.

When the results were in, Chamath came back to deliver a speech. "Look around you," he told us. "In a few weeks, some of the people in this room won't be here. They will be moved to other departments, because they've worked hard and have made themselves valuable to the company. Other people in this room won't be here, because they haven't worked hard enough. I'm telling you this because you need to understand that this is how it works: You are always being ranked, and it's your job to perform. How you do here is up to you, but no one's going to let you get away with not pulling your weight."

One of the subtexts of Chamath's speech was that he and the powers that be had finally figured out that Andreas wasn't doing much at all and, though it took some months, he was eventually let go, to most of the customer-support employees' great relief. By then, I was no longer a member of customer support, so Andreas' departure was of only symbolic consequence.

Chamath had created a small platform product marketing team to promote the Facebook Platform to developers. The team was headed by Dave, a marketing guy who had come to Facebook in late 2006 from Apple, and a classmate of the early Harvard engineers, Eila, who had worked with some of them at Microsoft. She had a stunning command of business jargon: "Leverage, fire drill, best practices, deliverables" were a few of the words she used often and that I had to learn quickly. I was assigned to work with her on various projects, like redesigning the developer site (where external developers obtained technical updates about the platform) and reaching out to developers and encouraging them to build Facebook applications.

My first week in the job I was working at my new desk in

a cramped wing on the third floor of the 156 University office, where a jumble of database engineers and platform-marketing people sat, when I received an AIM from Thrax.

"Do you want to go to a show in Berkeley with us?"

"I can't, I have to work on a sketch for what the new developer site will look like," I typed back.

"Huh? Why? That's not part of CS," came his quick response.

"Chamath is my new boss," I typed.

"Chamath is? What happened to Andreas? Are you still going to deal with CS?"

"No."

"Oh, man. So you finally got what you wanted."

"Yes."

"Without resorting to quitting."

"Uh huh," I replied, waiting to be congratulated on my promotion.

"So, you're going to sit on our floor now? Lame."

"You're lame."

"Well nobody likes u so . . ." he typed, trolling. One of the engineering managers had once said to me, apropos of nothing, "Everyone likes you," with a kind of curious envy, as if this was the *ne plus ultra* of life for the Facebook employee. Facebook did not have the like button yet, but given that we soon would, being liked by everyone was maybe a form of ultimate Facebook victory. I was nonplussed by all this, still accustomed to the academic world in which being liked was suspect: It meant you might be pandering to people for their affection. But I figured that if being liked by everyone was an asset at Facebook, I might as well claim it.

Thrax and Sam and Justin drove off to Berkeley while I sat at work with my computer and a design program that I barely knew how to use, but I was in good spirits. Now that I had what Silicon Valley considered to be a real job, I thought, I could turn my attention away from simply getting along at the company to accomplishing something important.

As a member of the tiny platform-marketing team that Chamath assembled, I attended hours-long meetings about marketing strategy and slaved over my sketches for the developer site. The site deployed robotic, techno-style fonts and spoke exclusively in the language of growth and speed, the language of developers, unlike the user support pages that spoke of connecting to friends. The change from serving users to serving developers was interesting: Suddenly, I had switched from telling users what they couldn't do to telling developers that they could do anything they wanted. Facebook engineers considered the developers to be peers, so they were keen to make sure that we were communicating and on good terms with them, a concern they had never had with the users.

My career upgrade from dungeon department to quasi-technical role meant, along with a better salary and more respect from the technical echelon of the company, that I was now on engineering time. This meant that while I could come to work later, as late as lunchtime, I was expected to stay up until all hours answering emails and devoting myself even more monastically to our new enterprise. However, even as the respect and pay were higher, which was a huge relief, genuflecting to external application developers, even if I didn't agree with what they were doing, felt a lot like the eternal reverence we nontechnical employees were all expected to exhibit for Mark and the engineering department.

We arranged parties for developers on a frequent basis, arranged contests for them to compete with one another, and most important, looked away from the fact that almost all of Facebook users' data was available to them through the platform. Technically, they were supposed to scrub their servers of the data every twenty-four hours but, if they didn't, we had no way of knowing. Mark implicitly trusted developers, external and internal, as if programming web applications was a global fraternity to which one gained membership by writing code.

That December, after I had worked for four straight months without a break on the Developer site, an engineering manager, Kai, asked me in an email, "Would you rather work on Platform or help with the internationalization process?" Kai was an engineering manager who had previously held a pre-IPO position at PayPal and relished his role as Silicon Valley elder, though he was still young, barely thirty. He prided himself as much on his personality as his technical skills, trolling often on the company's social email list and generally behaving like as much of a character as possible. He had steeped himself in Internet culture since college. When he and his wife began to have children, they nicknamed them after Internet memes like the lolcat holiday, Caturday.

"Hmm, I'll have to think for a moment," I replied.

"As the Taoist philosopher Lao-Tse said, all decisions can be made in the span of one breath," Kai wrote back.

I knew immediately what I wanted to do, but I held back for a day or two just to gut-check my feelings. After thinking it through, the answer was as obvious as on first consideration: I loved traveling, I loved languages, and I had already taken the initiative with Sam to extend Facebook networks to foreign countries before site translation was even a twinkle in Mark's eye. Internationalization—the process of translating the Facebook site interface into different languages so that anyone in any country could use the site as easily as English speakers currently did—was what a recruiter might call a core competency of mine, even if I didn't know exactly what the translation process would entail.

I told Kai that I was game to transfer to the internationalization team and, when I returned from the holiday break in January 2008, I began the process of moving to the brand-new engineering office that had just opened in a building down the street from 156 University. The "i18n Team," as it was called ("i18n" was shorthand for "internationalization"), was assembled quietly, behind the scenes, by Kai. He embraced the brewing celebritization of Silicon Valley with gusto. Sometimes he would refer to himself and his wife as the "Brangelina of Silicon Valley." His passion for Hollywoodizing things extended to work issues: When presented with conflicts between team members, he cheerfully cited his wife's lesson in screenwriting class that all screenplays have a beginning, a fall, and a resolution. He would declare that the conflict was the fall and that we simply needed to work toward the narrative resolution in which all was resolved.

"Just do whatever you think would help get things started," Kai told me in one of our first meetings, with the relaxed management style that he made into a hallmark of his brand. His zen approach reflected the cherished valley idea that we, the employees of a successful startup, were all so brilliant that we already knew what to do and if we didn't, we knew how to figure it out.

In order to put me, a nonengineer, finally, in the coveted, unscripted position of doing whatever I think needs to be done, it was necessary to create a position for me on the engineering team, the site of all creativity in Silicon Valley. The newly created position didn't even have a name. "What would you like to be called?" asked my newly hired manager, a distinguished-looking older man with friendly, twinkling eyes, Hassin, who reported to Kai. He was a localization ringer from eBay, who had been in the translation business a long time. *Localization* is the industry term for internationalization and is thought to be more sensitive to non-US countries, since, unlike *internationalization,* it doesn't imply that the United States is the center. Alas, the term never seemed to stick at Facebook, as our team had already called itself the i18n team. I decided on internationalization product manager, since product manager seemed to be the term that, for the few women in engineering, was both authorizing (working with product was the highest status role Facebook had) and nonthreatening (it made no claim to actually engineer anything, so the engineers' technical sovereignty remained untouched).

I was finally in the driver's seat, in the engineering office, the place where the boys raced around on ripstiks and ran the entire show: Facebook, social networking, and the new social media industry. The freewheeling, fecund world of engineering was kind of its own self-fulfilling prophecy: When you were an engineer, you could make things be any way you wanted them to be.

"Welcome to engineering!" Mark's admin instant messaged me as I was getting set up at my new desk, with a smiley face tacked on. It did feel a bit like being handed the keys to the kingdom.

Getting Facebook translated into languages other than English was an obvious move, and the need to extend the network to the world was something I always believed in. The best and most natural use of the product's virtual scrapbooking had always seemed to me to be keeping up with good friends who lived in distant places. When you were living near your friends, seeing them seemed like a better option for keeping in touch than posting on a social network but, when you were living far apart, a social network could always help you stay up to date.

Unlike the Platform management role with its schmoozy developer politics, I felt no qualms about working on translation. For one thing, I was finally able to work on the real Facebook product for the purposes of serving all of the users, as opposed to serving only developers. Developing the Facebook product, which, by January 2008, 60 million people were using, was what engineers lived for. When you advanced or created a feature and launched it, one minute there would be nothing, and the next minute there would be something, a new Facebook interface ready to receive new users, their data, and their relationships to each other. I had spent too much time with engineers, seeing their excitement and thrill at launching new features, not to want my own taste of the creation moment. Thrax had joked one night to Sam and me as we prepared to launch international school networks in the fall of 2006, "Are you excited to spread your seed?" I guess we were. Each new network did feel like a product of our loins, there for our decision to lend it life, that night.

The best moments at Facebook always had this intensely potent feel to them: the power to create a world. I knew that feeling of power because, in launching schools, I felt it too. Once a new network was live, I would log in as "The Creator," the name of our omnipotent test account, to survey our new territory and poke around at the profiles of people joining it. Sometimes, when we logged in, we would update The Creator's status in words that we imagined the god of Facebook might post. One night I saw that The Creator's status had been set to "conquering," and I mentioned it to Thrax over IM. "Is The Creator's status still set to 'conquering'?" Thrax, who had posted the status, asked. "The Creator's status is always set to conquering," I answered. "Ha ha," he typed back.

Becoming a fully fledged member of the engineering team that winter felt, as I long dreamed of doing, like going from being slave to being conqueror. Suddenly, I could arrive at work on my own time, as long as I was working late into the night, because it was assumed that I, like all the engineers, was upholding and advancing a whole new world, even if sometimes we were just sitting around in the office eating snacks and playing games. In engineering, getting to work late was cool, even necessary. It meant, in the ideology of the lone and maverick hacker, that you weren't beholden to authority, and that you might have been up late coding something brilliant and life-changing and disruptive (even if you were just trolling Facebook or watching porn).

Being in engineering wasn't an escape from the game so much as the ultimate playground.

The new engineering office we moved to in January 2008 seemed designed to physically reflect that we were hovering atop the world, manipulating it digitally from above. It occupied the top two floors of a 1960s style office building in downtown Palo Alto. The floors had been stripped and customized to the tastes of Facebook engineers. The floors were a hard bamboo, the better for ripstiking on, and the walls were a stark white accented by primary colors of blue and red. (Apparently, Facebook's original graffiti artist, David Choe, wasn't available to paint before we moved in.) The desks were arranged around the perimeter of the floor so that a de facto racetrack looped in a long, unbroken oval around the office. There was almost always someone ripstiking on the track, making for a constant sound of wheels on wood and the regular, rhythmic appearance of nearly identical-looking guys in hoodies rolling past my workspace; it was almost like working in the middle of an eighties roller rink, without the big roller skates and even bigger hair.

The kitchens occupied a large section of each floor, but they were intended for snacking, not cooking (the only cooking device was a microwave). The walls of each kitchen were stacked with bins of every conceivable candy bar and cereal. None of the food seemed like food to me; it was all cased in plastic and preserved to eternity by chemicals that I couldn't spell, so I made tea instead and snacked on treats from the Japanese pastry shop down the street. I eventually asked if we could receive weekly deliveries of fresh fruit and gourmet cheese and of course, now that I was a product manager, my wish was granted. The engineers didn't always eat the fruit and it would often go bad, but I was relieved that the fruit—something organic—was there. It was the only organic matter in an office piled high with every kind of digital device anyone could think of to buy. (Some were provided free: A cabinet on each floor contained every possible technology, from adapters to storage disks to high-end headphones, that we might need to use in our work.) As I watched the delivery men cart crates full of pears and grapes into the office, I felt like I was trolling the boys with fruit, as if in delayed response to Thrax for making fun of me for looking for organic produce in Safeway.

Amidst all the troll wars and ripstik races that went on in engineering, there was still real work to do. Our task on the internationalization team was to get the site interface translated into as many languages as possible, as quickly as possible. We began the translation process with an idea for an application (which, like most Silicon Valley ideas, was a transmogrification of existing concepts, one of which was the news discussion site Reddit's voting apparatus) through which users could translate bits of text (called *strings,* in engineering parlance) on the site into their language. The application fed strings to users and they entered the translation in a text box. Other users could vote the translation up or down. This type of crowdsourced interface is all over the Web now as a way of managing the Internet's increasingly heavy flow of content, but it was a newer interface then, exciting to engineers in its limitless possibilities for mechanization of things formerly considered subjective.

Voting on highly subjective content, such as the right way to phrase a complicated concept like poking or the wall, can pro-

duce more conflict than agreement. There was often no definitively correct answer but, instead, many different interpretations
of a given word. For example, the Spanish translators wanted to
know if *wall* meant the side of a building or something more like
a bulletin board (the answer was the latter, though then there
were an array of different words for a bulletin board for translators to vote on and choose from). Usually, the voting results
produced passable translations, but when there was a translation
impasse, I noticed that some engineers placed an almost reli-
gious faith in the voting process, and seemed to feel threatened
by the idea that the algorithmically decided results might not be
perfect. "The voting will fix it," they said, like a mantra, as the
translations rolled in and vied for victory on the page.

The engineers were beside themselves with glee when the
French version of Facebook was translated literally overnight by
local users; however, having spent a year in a French school as
a child while my mother was on academic business in France,
even I knew that the translations, while they were certainly done
marvelously quickly, were not polished and correct enough to
launch. I argued to my team that some kind of human review
of the final product was needed. I just wanted to know, for sure,
that the translations made sense and were at least a proximate
version of the quality on the English site. Some people on my
seven-person team, composed of engineers, Hassin, and a business development guy from Spain by way of Stanford, grew
frustrated with my stubborn defense of human cognition over
algorithm, but I didn't much mind. Being the odd defender of
the value of the human was something that I was used to and
was, after all, sort of my job. In more ways than one, I was like

the humanist troll to the company's obsession with technologizing everything.

Hassin, a linguist rather than an engineer by trade, agreed that some human input would be worthwhile and so I worked with professional translators to review the site in our first non-English languages, French and Spanish. Once launched, a user would view the site in French or Spanish by toggling a button on the Facebook homepage that would switch the language of the interface (user-submitted content like comments and status updates would remain in whatever language the user wrote in). I spent days with the professional translators while they read through pages of translations and made corrections as needed. They were working by the hour, clocking out at six o'clock, and thought it strange that I seemed perennially online the entire week, answering chats, reading Facebook, talking with them, answering questions, and responding to emails at all hours. When they left the office at the end of the day, they were done until the next morning. That, in turn, seemed strange to me. I couldn't remember when the last time was that I wasn't within spitting distance of my computer and smart phone. As much as I had once made fun of the Facebook boys for staring at their phones more often than they looked up, I had become one of them.

We launched the Spanish version of Facebook in February 2008 and followed with French one month later. Both Facebook interfaces launched to good press and widespread adoption, as the site was programmed to appear immediately in French or Spanish when a user signed up or logged in from a country in which one of those languages was primarily spoken. We moved on from those languages to getting the site translated into German, Japanese, and Italian. French and Spanish came first because they addressed the largest number of potential users but, after that, we translated in order of the wealthiest countries. Internationalization, like everything else, follows the money.

This was where I got lucky, and where my job began to save me from my dry, tech-saturated Palo Alto existence in a new way. Because we were striving for authenticity as well as technical accuracy in translation, it didn't make sense to hire American speakers of Japanese and Italian to translate the site. We didn't want a version of Japanese spoken by someone who hadn't been in Japan for years and wasn't current with the local idiom. Instead, two months after I started working on the team, Hassin decided that I would fly to Tokyo first, to work with Japanese translators, then fly directly from there to Rome, to work with the Italians. I was getting paid to go on a trip around the world, first class. "That's a nice gig," my dad said after I told him I'd be out of the country for a month. "Yes, it is," I concurred, relieved and excited. My commitment to blanketing the world with our technology was going to save me from it. It is neat how life works this way: No system is complete; there is always a way out if you work hard enough at it. And sometimes, as it was in this case, the escape hatch can be fun.

Flying to Tokyo in late March 2008 felt like the fulfillment of every late-2000s American girl's fantasy, since so many of us had seen *Lost in Translation,* and been entranced by its images of familiar American actors ensconced in Japan's cool, alien calm. I toyed with the idea of staying at the Park Hyatt, the hotel featured in the movie, but, in my perennial quest for authenticity, I picked the Okura hotel near the embassies, which had been renovated over the years to look exactly as it did when it was built in 1964. The Okura is a modernist Japanese wonderland full of exquisitely square, lacquered tea tables, enormous windows, and perfect stillness. When I arrived, I realized I was the only person in the hotel over five foot eight, and the only American. I felt like a huge cartoon character, with ungainly height and Technicolor blue eyes, struggling to appear restrained and petite amid the dainty Japanese women in dress suits and surgical masks having tea in the lobby.

When Facebook executives traveled, they had an administrative assistant arrange their trip for them but, in the simple, under-the-radar style of our internationalization team, I had no secretary and made all my travel arrangements myself. Not knowing how to arrange a car service in a foreign country, I took the subway to the translation office every day, finding my way via the signs in English that corresponded to the ones full of beautiful but, to me illegible Japanese characters. The train was full of young Japanese workers in accessorized outfits playing on their phones. It seemed almost weird that Facebook would be coming to Japan to bring them technology; they already had so much. They can probably do things on their phones that I won't for years, I thought. This was why winning Japan was so important to the guys in the office: not because they cared about the Japanese in particular, but because we needed to conquer the best. It was the Normandy of technology wars and, oddly enough, I, the American girl who didn't really care about beating Japan at anything, was the advance force, bringing them something they may not even need.

As it turned out, simply launching Facebook in Japanese wasn't enough to get many users beyond those with existing ties to America on board the site. Japan had a strong recent history of anonymous social networks, like the native network Mixi, and Facebook's insistence on real names flew in the face of that. In early 2010, Facebook opened a Japanese engineering office to target the Japanese market specifically but, to date, the network remains relatively unadopted (at 9 percent penetration) compared to other countries worldwide. But, back in 2008, we had high hopes that we could succeed.

At night, I went upstairs to eat in the restaurant on the roof of the hotel, fifty stories up, looking out over Tokyo. I didn't know enough Japanese to leave the hotel for dinner, and feared that I'd get lost. Gazing across the glittering city, I felt disoriented by Tokyo's size and its residents' calm acceptance that the city appears to go up and outward forever. My meals would go on for hours, with chefs preparing course after course of shrimp and exotic fish and finely cut vegetables on the gleaming grill at the bar at which I sat. As I sipped on tiny cups of sake and grew increasingly full, I would think, "I've come a long way from the Riviera," remembering the down-at-the-heels hotel in Las Vegas with a view of a parking garage that was my first Facebook-sponsored trip. When the bill came, I hardly looked at it as I signed, knowing that, like Thrax on his search for the most expensive restaurant in town, I could now, finally, charge anything I wanted to.

The 'round-the-world trip was a strange mix of power and disorientation, as if I were poised on the next great turn into the unknown of the cycle that I had signed onto almost three years before. When I left Tokyo a week later, and flew directly to Rome, it was the day before my check landed in my bank account, so I didn't have enough money to get Euros to pay for a taxi to the city. Sitting on my suitcase with my BlackBerry dying, I searched the Web until I found instructions in English for a train from Fiumicino airport to the city center. I sighed with relief when I was sitting safely on the train, its heavy steel wheels rumbling loudly into the ancient heart of civilization.

Having been traveling for almost twenty-four hours, I was so eager to get to the hotel that I accidentally got off the train a stop early and ended up walking the last blocks, trailing my suitcase along the dark cobblestoned street, exhausted and disheveled after a long flight during which the sun never set, allowing me to take photographs of Siberia that I later posted on Facebook. It was as if a part of me, childlike and overeager, still couldn't believe that I was doing this: flying around the world leading a charge for a company worth millions that would take over the world. At other times on that trip, I still felt like a kid alone in Europe with a backpack and not enough money to get to the next city.

However, once I was ensconced at what the Internet told me was the best hotel in Rome, I could relax, and took great pleasure in doing so. The room was small, as they are in Europe, but the walls were covered in baroque gold leaf and the bathroom was covered in black marble. I ordered room-service spaghetti from the Michelin-starred restaurant on the roof of the hotel and figured out how to order cars in advance to get anywhere I needed to go. It took a while to get the hang of it, but I was steadily learning how to play this business-trip game.

While Tokyo was interesting, Rome was, for me, much more comfortable, which made sense, for a million cultural reasons. There, in the musky villas of Italy, one of which housed the translation office where I worked with translators, was where the whole concept of conquering, and sociality, seemingly native to Italians, was invented (or at least that is what we were told in elementary history class). As I dressed each morning to take the car to the office, I felt like the female version of an ancient conqueror, intent on taking over Italy.

In my off hours, I ran around the city in gladiator sandals that would be perfectly in fashion when I showed up at Coachella two weeks later. Touring the Colosseum, I noticed a sign etched with a quote from Agricola that read, "The Romans, great robbers of the world, after all the lands have been devastated by their exploitation are exploiting the sea. They cannot get enough of East or West; they alone desire to possess with equal madness the richness and misery of nations." I took a picture and uploaded it to Facebook. Ironically or not—I couldn't tell anymore. At this midpoint in my career, I was on a mission to conquer the world, and the words resonated. That afternoon (which was the middle of the night in Palo Alto and prime engineering work hours), Thrax reached out to me, over AIM:

"Where in the world is Kate?"—thrax96
"I'm in Rome, conquering."—k8che
"I'm at my desk, conquering."—thrax96

I supposed then that we were both right, and whatever ear-lier misgivings I held about conquering it still felt exciting to be the bearers of this new world. That evening at Harry's Bar on Via Veneto, a luxe-styled vintage expatriate hangout with copi-ous velvet drapes and tassels, I made sure to toast to our exploits. "To conquering," I said with a slight tip of the glass towards the Colosseum, never quite sure, as one can never be sure on the Internet, in its flat tones and wide openness to interpretation, whether I was half-mocking anything, including myself.

After a week and a half in Rome, working late nights and then the next day until dusk, taking a break in the early evening to drink Americano aperitifs on the Via Veneto and watch the passersby, I was ready and happy to return to the United States. In truth, I felt a new sense of victory and accomplishment after years of struggle and a sense that nothing was ever quite whole. In the previous three weeks, I had finished the Japanese and Ital-ian Facebook, and even gotten a bit of a tan from walking around Rome. What's not to like? Facebook's cognitive dissonance was dissolving, for me at least: What they promised to the engineers, I—a woman, a nonengineer, a humanist, a writer—could have, too, and it could be fun. On my Air France flight back to Los Angeles, I thought of nothing but home: palm trees, sundresses, good Mexican food, the southwestern United States. Everything was finally coming together.

Even the fact that Air France lost my luggage on a layover at Charles de Gaulle Airport didn't ruin my bliss: It was April 24,

2008, time for Coachella again, and, as we had been saying on Facebook since 2005, I'm going to Coachella, bitches. In the only outfit I had, an ensemble that I had been wearing for at least thirty-six hours, I jumped into a rented Jeep and drove toward Palm Springs, in love with the desert dust, gritty and real, and the sun, bigger than it ever gets in northern California. The desert was my territory, prickly and warm and endlessly beautiful. Away from the thirty-inch monitors and endless nervous distraction of the Internet, I could live. I sang along to the bouncy Akon songs that played on the radio, more exuberant evidence that I was home in the United States, where our culture is hybrid and poppy, without history, perpetually new.

Since, as the logic of technology dictates, we must always be upgrading, Thrax had found a new house this year, bigger and grander than last year's, although there still weren't enough beds. It was a classic Palm Springs midcentury modern with a tennis court and a hot tub and at least three bedrooms. I hoped that I wouldn't have to sleep under the coffee table as I had the year before. But, after parking the Jeep in the driveway and entering the house, greeted by a mirrored wet bar already stocked with booze and backed by glass doors looking onto the pool and the desert, I didn't care anymore. I could sleep outside on the pool chaises if I had to: In the desert, I was home.

Later, sitting on the pool deck, taking in the huge purplish-blue sky, Thrax asked, sans camera for once, about my flight from Rome, not whether it was a good flight but what class I flew in. "Did you fly business class?" "Yep," I said. "Aw, yeah!" he cawed, "it's official!" In his eyes, my status at the company had finally been recognized. It was funny but not untrue, I guess, that flying business class, more than joining engineering, constituted proof that I had arrived. It was one thing for Facebook to ask me to get the site translated, it was another to buy me a nine-thousand-dollar plane ticket to Tokyo and another eight-thousand-dollar ticket to Rome and an eight-thousand-dollar return ticket to Los Angeles. The last month of my life—according to my travel receipts stashed away somewhere in my purse—cost Facebook more than my entire salary the year before. In Silicon Valley, you have to know that you are worth it to them, and money is the language they speak. Companies have *valuations,* as they are called, but so do employees, in the form of salary and perks and status, minute decisions made each day about where employees will sit and what they can get away with and what team they'll be on. It's simply that an employee's worth is not so explicitly stated by monetary value; it's all these things together.

As always, our days at Coachella passed like some kind of American Apparel–sponsored shaman journey that we shared with thirty thousand other people. The goal was to get from the car to the grounds to the sets we wanted to see, all without losing ourselves in the heat and the crowds. When, each night, we managed to find our way out of the trampled fields and to the car and home again we felt as if we had reached an oasis after a trek across the Sahara.

On Saturday night, we skipped the last headlining band and reached the parking lot early, having learned the year before that you have to have an escape plan. (In 2007 we didn't have one, so we had to hack our way out of the parking lot by finding a hole in the bushes big enough to drive through.) Our conversation in the car turned to how hungry we were and the fact that no one had eaten since our late breakfast at a roadside taco stand, so we turned off the highway in search of food, which is scarce in the desert at midnight. Soon, Thrax and I were in the grocery store again, only this time it was the Palm Springs Walmart instead of the Menlo Safeway. In 2008, even Walmart had an organic section, but I didn't care, because all we were doing was finding enough food to feed us after twelve hours of trekking across the Coachella lawn in search of music. I didn't argue with the hot dogs, sloppy joe mix, and white bread that Thrax dropped into the cart. My legs were wobbling with jet lag, and I was just trying to stay up and awake until we could get home.

In the checkout line, we leaned against the shopping cart, companionably close, hipbone grazing hipbone, too tired to talk. In my sun-worn and jet-lagged mind a vivid memory surfaced of us shopping family style at Safeway, two years before. Because Air France misplaced my luggage and I had yet to receive it, I was wearing Thrax's signature T-shirt, the one with a grenade on it and the name of the first streaming video Web site he made in Georgia, and madras camp shorts. "You look like Thrax," Emile had exclaimed with affectionate approval when I walked into the kitchen wearing Thrax's clothes that morning. As we walked down the checkout lane, Thrax pulled the cart behind him and I followed along with one hand on the cart, tired. "This is how my mom used to pull me along in the supermarket," he said, and in my boy's outfit I did feel a bit like the child to his parent. It wasn't the first time I felt like I was reverse aging into a pubescent boy, suffused by the postadolescent testosterone that saturates the office. "I'm just trying to make it family style,"

Thrax said, apropos of nothing, as if reading my mind, as the checkout clerk ushered us forward in line.

Oddly, Thrax often said something at the exact moment I thought it, as though our brains' synapses operated on some transparent wavelength, speaking to each other even when we weren't. Later on, when I was working directly for Mark and charged with the task of interpreting his thoughts for the world, Mark told me that his dream for Facebook was something like this, to make us all cells in a single organism, communicating automatically in spite of ourselves, perhaps without the need for intention or speech. Perhaps this connection with Thrax was some outcome of living in this new, technical Hotel California for so long, becoming attuned to each others' rhythms unconsciously, like female friends or coworkers who end up having the same menstrual cycle. Or perhaps it is something more archaic and personal. I no longer knew.

"Soul mates," Thrax said as we walked out of Walmart, speaking to himself and to me at the same time. I was so tired, still on Italian time, that it felt like I was living the line from *The Crying of Lot 49* that I picked for the "About Me" section of my profile, "Later, sometimes, she would have trouble sorting the night into real and dreamed." Was any of this real? What was I doing in a Walmart, in some boy from Georgia's grenade T-shirt, exhausted by world takeover? How could I be soul mates with a coworker that I would most often communicate with on AIM, like some disembodied voice from the Internet who only rarely appears in human form?

Soul mates seemed like such an odd word for Thrax to use that I continued to muse as we walked toward the car to meet the others, who had stayed behind. Connections, it had begun to seem, not a particular connection, are the point at Facebook and, through Silicon Valley's efforts, the thing that we are all connecting to was technology, not people. No one person, in the age of the social Internet, could provide the constant, easy attention that the technology can. As employees as well as users of Facebook, the work we did wasn't about focusing on one other person, or even on a few. Our job was to create a machine that attracted the attention of as many people as possible and allowed us to give it back in kind, and the only way it was possible to pay attention to that many people and be paid attention to is through technology. In real life, we didn't have that many inputs and outputs. We could only talk to so many people in a day. Technology, then, was our new soul mate, telling us it understands us, telling us that we are connected, that someone loves us, that we are not alone.

But then, I realized, Thrax might, as a human, have needed to identify a "soul mate" or two or three because the rest of his world was a chaos of technically enabled attention and infamy, a million races to beat others at this or that, in which a new race began as soon as the last one ended. In the constant chase after attention and fame, he might now more than ever need someone who didn't care who was winning, how many followers he had or what he had said online. Saying soul mates then, in our new world, wasn't about a real relationship but simply an assertion and desire for such a thing to exist, that there be some substrate of real beyond the screen, much like the sustenance in the form of sloppy joe mix that we had just bought at Walmart, that we must eat because, without it, regardless of how much we live in the digital world, we couldn't subsist. Perhaps one day soul mate, like friend, would be a category of Facebook relationship, content to be neither anything more, or anything less, than that.

A few weeks after my return, there were rumors of an important new hire that Mark had made to the executive team. That Friday, he convened an All Hands to introduce Sheryl Sandberg, a high-powered, multimillionaire advertising and operations executive from Google, whom Mark said he had been courting for an executive role since the Davos World Economic Forum in January. "Sheryl and I met at a party and we immediately hit it off," Mark announced. "We began talking for hours. She asked me questions about how I was running the company. I was really impressed with how smart she is." Mark spoke with an uncharacteristic smile and glow, not flirtatious exactly, perhaps a function of some kind of sense of relief, as if he had been seeking someone like Sheryl for some time. "When I met Sheryl the first thing I said was that she had really good skin," Mark continued, "and she does," he said, gesturing toward Sheryl, whose face was admittedly creamy in tone. She was smiling, and didn't flinch.

Sitting among my colleagues, I felt bemused and a bit perplexed, as I had never heard Mark comment on anyone's skin before. He obviously had never spoken about any of the engineers' skin as making them particularly suited to their role. Mark went on to say that, "Everyone should have a crush on Sheryl," and some engineers claimed in an engineering-wide email thread immediately after the meeting to have the requisite crushes. It seemed odd to me, as if all of this kneeling to worship Sheryl was some kind of compensation for the fact that no female employee had ever received such treatment before. At any rate, Sheryl had arrived, and would be occupying the role of chief operations officer. I wasn't sure what that implied at first, but it turned out to mean that she would handle everything that Mark didn't want to: essentially, all department operations outside engineering. In addition, with her Google ads background, she would have a prominent role in ads strategy.

At a one-on-one meeting with Sheryl weeks later, I found out that she had an interest in the topic of women at Facebook and in Silicon Valley generally. In her months-long process of getting to know the company, she scheduled individual meetings with all the women in engineering. (By that point, they numbered about fifteen out of hundreds of engineers, including Maryann, who had been promoted into a position as user experience lead on the engineering design team, and would eventually come to manage the user experience team, a new department that was devoted full time to testing new features and collecting user feedback.)

Sheryl and I met in a small meeting room off the mini-kitchen on the engineering floor. "I don't know if you know this, but I do a monthly women's meeting at my house that is women only, where women in the valley can gather and hear an interesting female speaker and talk with one another," she said, "so I care about this stuff." She paused for a moment. "Tell me everything," she said, directly, leaning forward on the couch where she sat. I liked her forthrightness and the way she looked at me directly, creamy skin and all.

I told her that I was generally happy in my role as internationalization PM, which I was. I also let her know that there were a few situations involving men in the department that I thought she should know about. For example, one of the engineering directors had been known to proposition women in the company for threesomes; I also had an issue with an engineer who behaved alternately dismissively and aggressively toward female product managers, but the situation had been handled ineffectively. "I was told by an engineering director to go in and talk to the guy and try to resolve the situation myself, but when I did that, the engineer somehow twisted things around and called me a bad feminist, as if to distract from the conversation at hand, and the conversation didn't go anywhere. It was pretty unpleasant," I said.

"Offense as defense, I get it," Sheryl commented.

"Yeah, exactly," I concurred. Sheryl is cool, I thought, she gets it.

"Well, thanks for talking to me, I really appreciate it," Sheryl said, winding up our conversation.

That was the last time I met privately with Sheryl, and I thought that if her conversations had gone similarly with other female employees then her arrival was definitely going to be a boon for women at the company. I didn't hear back immediately about any of the issues I had raised with her, until she stopped briefly by my desk one day a few months later and in the low, succinct office voice that she mastered, said, "I just want to know that the situations you told me about have both been handled." I had heard nothing about it. "You see, I'm so good that I make things happen and no one even knows about them," she smiled.

It was then that I noticed that the director who propositioned employees had been subtly demoted and the aggressive engineer had been transitioned to another team. Both men, of course, continued to work at the company, so in some sense I wasn't sure what exactly would be different. However, the fact that that there had been some action, after years of guys getting away with whatever behavior they wanted, was comfort enough.

Sheryl's housecleaning sweep through the department was the last transformation of our workplace that most of us saw from her, as far as our day-to-day work was concerned. Mark continued to conduct the All Hands meetings and serve as the voice and visionary of the company, which was his due, of course. However, women I talked to were disappointed that Sheryl and her voice had quickly receded to the background, leaving Mark and his vision of a brash, move fast/break things culture to define the company.

Aside from the initial excitement and activity surrounding Sheryl's arrival, as 2008 drew to a close, the office was crowded with more and more guys, in desks packed increasingly close together, but there were still very few women. Facebook had started to resemble, more than ever, a fully fledged fraternity. Sam even said so to me as he was telling me about some tournament— whether chess or ripstiking or gaming—the guys on our floor had held the night before. He liked the fraternity aspect of Facebook, to my initial surprise but, as I thought about it, I began to see why. These were the brothers he and all the boys never had, the popular techno frat that didn't exist at Harvard or Stanford. The engineers had been together so long that they knew each other inside and out, like frat boys in their senior year. They played games of chess all day on the kitchen tables, and didn't look up when I watched, as if they didn't see me, because they didn't; like any woman on the sidelines of a varsity match, I was not in the game. They raced ripstiks around the floor all day and night, keeping charts on the whiteboards of who won.

Their venture into a world of pure competition was here now, charted by points and what Facebook would soon call *credits*, a form of virtual Facebook currency that began to be tested internally as a way for Facebook users to reward each other for posting entertaining things. Winning battles for status was no longer the precocious activity of young hackers, but a codified way of life. And, just like in a real fraternity, there was an obvious hierarchy, as well as rituals, which in this case involved chess games and the occasional limo club night instead of football and pub nights. Facebook had made being a nerdy programmer cool and normal, at least within the confines of the valley.

I stopped paying attention to the social dynamics at work, since, like all frats, everything and everyone in it looked the same from the outside. I was a sorority of one, and it was getting lonely. Any hint of a new, creative, coed society that I had felt in the beginning, composed of gays and straights and men (or boys) and women, had become stratified and compartmentalized just like in the American institutions we had wanted to leave behind.

Fortunately, my job kept me traveling for the rest of the year, bringing me back to Palo Alto only long enough to get lonely again before I could pack for some new and exciting destination. I was in Dublin for work on September 29, 2008, when the stock market crashed, and I spent the night in a bar at the Four Seasons Hotel, reading news of the crash on my laptop as piano music tinkled in the background. While checking Facebook, I received an invitation to a group created by a designer called "Party like it's 1929," that bore the description "If we're going down, might as well go down in style."

That night, I also received an email that Dustin had sent to the engineering team announcing that he would soon be leaving Facebook to, as everyone always said when they left, pursue new things. Noooooooo, I broke immediately into a silent wail, my eyes tearing up, not quite realizing until that moment how much I had depended on Dustin to be the company's witty, practical, human counterpart to Mark. "Daddy Dustin," Sam and I had sometimes jokingly called him, since we all sensed that Dustin was the one most likely to listen to us if we had a problem, or needed to talk to someone in power. I ended the night by writing a Facebook message to Dustin to express my gratitude to him simply for having been there, though I had never called on him directly, then went to sleep in my hotel room as the lights of Dublin twinkled coldly in the night.

Whenever I landed in some city, fresh from business class and flush with my Facebook expense account, I had the precious experience of being anonymous, free, unlinked to a hierarchy that I didn't control. I started to revel in that freedom, purchased ironically by a site that would like to remove anonymity from everything. "In the future, when you check in to a hotel it will know what music you want to play and who your friends are, based on your Facebook profile," I used to tell people in my prior job as platform product marketing manager, to tout the possibilities of the platform and its promise that we could have our friends and our likes with us, at least virtually, all the time. But, in truth, I was almost happier escaping to places where no one knew me.

Several times, when I was not scheduled to make a business trip, I made the one-hour hop to Las Vegas for the night and checked into a hotel, in love with the glittering anonymity the city affords, the sense that no one on the Strip knows who anyone else is: There are too many people and too many nooks and crannies in all the casinos for anyone but the casinos' eyes in the sky to keep track of. Real friendship and intimacy are beautiful and necessary, I knew, but I was starting to wonder exactly who my friends were. Were they all the people on my profile, or was there some finer specification, and what was it? It was hard to tell anymore.

Back in the office, friends were an elastic, untroubled term. Many of the people on my Facebook profile were coworkers I interacted with on the site only, but, to most, there seemed to be no discrepancy in this. In the logic of our business, to comment on a friend's post was better than speaking to them, because everyone saw it. Everyone wanted to see everything. This was all justified under the company's corporate buzzword, *transparency*, though no one seemed to know exactly what it meant. The fact that it was hard to define led Mark to begin a discussion on the company's internal discussion page asking everyone to submit ideas for what *transparency* was. We discussed the word for days, and all that was decided was that no one knew. For some, like

Mark, who posted in the thread with everyone else, the word *transparency* seemed to have the ring of enforced integrity, as if in a transparent world there could be no lies, no hidden information, and that nothing bad could happen because everyone knew everything about everyone. I was not so sure. Having occupied a powerless role at Facebook, I was conscious of the way in which power affects behavior. The engineers acted; the support team and users were acted upon. This disparity was why, sometimes, revolutions had to happen, or at least percolate, anonymously and in secret.

The simplest definition of transparency that I figured applied to the context of Facebook was a sheer technical one, using technology to broadcast whatever was happening, a Big Brother by another name, but with what the company considered a positive value instead of a negative one. One Saturday in November, when I was in the office (weekends were the best time to work because it was the only time when the office was quiet and I could get anything done), I took a break to play Rock Band with Emile and Thrax in the glass-walled game room on our floor. They decided that it was not enough to simply play the game. Everyone needed to see us playing the game. They rigged a video camera that broadcast our performance onto the wall and also onto the Internet, where Emile and Thrax's legions of Internet fans were apparently waiting, ready to watch from their bedrooms in Croatia and Louisiana. They also rigged an input device so that the fans could talk to us. Their chats were broadcast onto the wall for us to see and respond to. We were as close as we could get to total transparency, a set of characters in a virtual world full of people watching and listening and talking with us from around the globe.

In the midst of banging out a version of Linkin Park's "Crawling" on our plastic instruments, a viewer typed "You are gay," at us, religiously following one of the Rules of the Internet, which is to always question someone's sexuality, for no reason. "Yes, I am gay," Thrax typed, following another rule of the Internet which is do not argue with trolls, if you do, they win. I felt a bit like Margaret Mead on Bali, watching the natives of a distant world enact their culture.

The fans watching us on the Internet were perplexed to see me there, since another rule of the Internet states that there are no girls on the Internet, and they proceeded from questioning my gender or even my existence, to telling me that they would like to fill all my holes. This was standard Internet behavior, and I barely blushed, though it seemed a bit violent, in a virtual way, much like the Internet itself. People will do and say anything online because they can. Thrax and Emile were unperturbed, barely registering the curse words flowing at us through the screens, since this was the way the Internet was. Not only were insults the Internet standard but, as Facebook grew, we were becoming the Internet, its new owners, like the rail men of 1880s America surveying their newly installed rail lines in the Wild West, kicking the iron and making sure it worked. And work, it did. Like the boys in their rooms in distant states, we were safe here five floors above Palo Alto, connected by wires to worlds we would never see.

Later that afternoon, I walked the few blocks home to my apartment. As I was cooking dinner, with my laptop open on the kitchen table, my screen was still tuned to the game room in the office, the boys were still playing, and the watchers were still watching, throwing insults and questions at the screen as Rock Band songs started and stopped, chords scrolling endlessly to infinity. I closed the laptop and drove to San Francisco to meet friends and go out, in real life.

San Francisco is a thirty-minute drive from Palo Alto, but every mile felt like it was taking me slightly closer to reality, or at the least, to some Bay Area approximation—now abuzz with Twitter and a whole new generation of social apps—of it, that I sorely needed. Like the old Facebook relationship status option that we removed some time in 2007 in order to make the site sound a bit more mature, when it came to reality, I was at a point where I would take whatever I could get.

CHAPTER 8

THE <3 ECONOMY

If, in 2006, Palo Alto felt like a shimmering, tech Disneyland, a city in circuit-board form, all tidy blocks and green lawns and the near-silent hum of every form of digital device anyone could think of, by 2009, it had started to feel like a shopping mall for venture capitalists searching for the next Facebook. New, glossy restaurants sprang up to serve unending rounds of business lunches; a Four Seasons Hotel went up at the intersection of University and the 101; all last traces of Palo Alto's scrappier preboom days were washed away, replaced by the town's brand of bland, midrange minimalism.

San Francisco, by contrast, was still a welcoming, disorderly mixture of tech wealth and street grime. When I went there on the weekends, I could only wear flat gray boots and tights under neutral skirts, because anything I wore emerged a dirty gray any-way, not unlike San Francisco's sky with its persistent fog punctu-ated by sun, and sun only on certain streets. For all the extremes of climate and class—you are as likely to be chased down the street by a bum demanding change as jostled on the sidewalk by a tech multimillionaire focused on his iPhone—San Fran-cisco retains an aura of cool authenticity, the muscle memory of having been once a gritty gold-rush city, packed with drunken miners and the women who tended to their needs. Thus, people flock there from all around the Bay Area on weekends to soak up some remnant of a hearty, physical past, made edible in the form of rustic breads at Tartine, and whiskeys neat at the many bars along Mission or Valencia Street. Whatever San Francisco lacks in leftover grit, it can afford to invent in the form of endless dives (some truly old, some decorated to seem so), handcrafted cups of coffee that take five minutes to brew, and high-end res-taurants decorated to look like 1800s homestead kitchens. How-ever stylized, San Francisco is the unpolished flip side to Silicon Valley's perfect grid.

In contrast to the hardscrabble aesthetic emerging in the Mission, Facebook remained insistent on its high-tech fantasy of a perfected, digital life, where everything was always new and inefficiency was always being outmoded. "Harder better faster stronger," Daft Punk's robot vocals still looped in the office and at company parties, perennially picturing a cleaner, faster world. But Facebook's rapid growth, at 700 employees and 150 million users, strained at its uniform ideals. New offices full of Face-book lawyers, advertising managers, and User Operations (as the customer support staff were now called, in recognition of the fact that the department served users rather than paying customers) employees sprouted up around Palo Alto, staffed with people of all types, though the engineering office remained as concentrated with young men as ever. The company did its part to maintain a young aesthetic across the departments by issuing branded American Apparel T-shirts and sweatshirts. Other companies in Palo Alto issued their own branded clothing, making for humorous scenes where, say, a team of ten Palantir (another Peter Thiel–funded startup, this one devoted to developing software for military intelligence) engineers in company-branded track jackets faced off at a crosswalk against a team of engineers in the same jackets that said Facebook on the front.

By 2009, the once cool and spacious engineering floors, where boys could ripstik around freely at top speed, were growing crowded with desks, toys, and new engineers who were being hired as fast as they could be found. As the din in the office rose I kept my headphones on and my eyes glued to my screen, monitoring the translation process, my inbox, and my Facebook feed, in which boys took turns noting the failings of some new piece of technology or posting photos of the new devices they picked up that week at Fry's Electronics.

On Mondays, the albums full of party photos from the weekend would begin their march down the News Feed. Photo albums posted by Facebook employees had more so-called weight in my News Feed because they usually contained other Facebook employees, and the News Feed algorithm assumes that if many of your Facebook friends have done something, you want to know about it. The combined algorithmic weight of friends tagged in Facebook employee party photos and the sheer number of photos that they posted turned my News Feed into an endless panorama of coworkers socializing, perpetually frozen in smiles with drinks held to their chests. Their photos increased in visibility for the next few days of the week as fellow employees liked and commented on them. The people whose photos were liked most rose further in the rankings so that, the next week, I was more likely to see their pictures, whether or not I ever hung out with them. News Feed was, to my bemusement as a *Heathers* fan, like the algorithmic version of the Heathers in the cafeteria, taking note of whose popularity was rising and falling and making sure that everyone was apprised of the popular people's movements.

My monitor pulsed with a steady flow of emails and task notifications, some urgent, some not so much. An enduring argument on the engineering social email list about the best way to optimize the temperature on the engineering floors would include exchanges like, "We should vote on what temperature everyone wants it to be," and the reply, "No, then the result would be suboptimal for at least half the office." The arguments on email could go on for hours, circling around the logic of what was essentially subjective: room temperature. Subjectivity in general tended to drive engineers crazy: They wanted there to be one answer, one solution, one optimization that worked for everything. As often happens online, these threads devolved into an argument about the communication form itself: "Stop switching the headers on the subject lines," one engineer would command icily, "it ruins the threading in my inbox." "Stop sending so many emails to e-social, you're ruining my productivity," another would say. "No way, e-social is sacred," someone else might claim. "You're supposed to be able to send anything you want there. If we lose e-social, we lose our culture." In a pattern common to online communities, the social list began as a dream of easy, fraternal companionship, followed by a rising, fractious concern that the quality of its community was being lost.

Just as in earlier days, users fretted constantly that Facebook was becoming MySpace; as we grew, we fretted constantly that we were becoming not-Facebook. By 2009, everything that happened at work seemed to prompt the feeling that, in Facebook's perpetual nostalgia for its own early culture, we were losing our utopia. It was starting to always be the "end of an era," as the boys commented often and nostalgically when looking at old photos of themselves in the office: The boys were growing older despite themselves; the office was growing bigger despite Mark's desire that it stay small and focused. "Smaller companies are always better," he would say in All Hands meetings that year to explain hiring plans and why, even though we were growing quickly, he wanted to avoid uncontrolled hiring. Size was the enemy of swiftness, and swiftness: "Moving fast and breaking things"—was the company value that Mark repeated most often. (The others, like "be bold" and "be open," were less punchy and required more effort to explain.) As the engineering team grew into the hundreds, the product teams were refashioned on the model of little startups, with their own war rooms, so that they could feel like small companies despite being part of the larger group.

Despite all these attempts to remain small in feeling if not in reality, in meetings, almost daily, someone would say, "I am worried that we are losing our culture," and everyone would look around helpless, as if they didn't know what to do, or how to save the precious essence that they felt slipping from their grasp. Sitting on a meeting room couch, listening once again to this exchange, I recalled my Hopkins advisor saying, "You are what you do. If you don't do it anymore, how can it be your culture?" He was making a point about cultural identities in America and our constant fear of losing them, even when we don't practice them anymore. I came to realize it was the identity of a nineteen-year-old boy, forever youthful and reckless, unmonitored and unstoppable, that the boys were so anxious about losing. They were worried, perhaps, about growing up. *Facebook culture,* by another name, then, might be a fear of adulthood, a desire to put off commitment, responsibility, and the difficult work of relating in real life and in real terms, forever. But how do you save your youth? How do you stay nineteen forever?

In December 2008, I was tapped again to do a job that didn't exist before and didn't have a name. "We are looking for someone to write for Mark," Facebook's Communications Director Elliot Schrage, a public policy lawyer turned PR executive who came to Facebook from Google, told me. "We're going to send out the job opening to the company so anyone can apply, but I think you would be great for it." Lols, I thought, slipping into the emoticon talk that had begun to move off my screen and into my speech. I was, after all, the only writer there, or at least the only writer who had been at Facebook long enough to justify entrée into Mark's exclusive inner circle. In the past year, Mark's circle of confidants had thinned as his original cofounders, like Dustin, cashed out in the billions, and it had to be restocked.

This shouldn't be hard, I thought. I had been listening to Mark speak about product launches for three years, and I knew all his rhetorical tics and gestures, even if I was still not entirely sure what he truly wanted for the world, or what drove him, beyond a fascination with youthful insolence, ever-expanding territory, and control. His voice is a combination of efficient shorthand (no overly big words, no overly long sentences) and imperialist confidence, always gesturing toward the next stage of the product's growth, depicted as inexorable and unlimited. Things were always being "pushed forward" in Mark-speak, as if he and the company were Atlases simultaneously shouldering and spurring the world's advancement, moving it forward with their own digital might.

Just as in the Daft Punk song, in Mark's rhetoric, Facebook's work was never over. It wasn't a Web site or a set of apps, but a platform that grows and grows, adding more users and entities (brands, places, events) and going deeper into our lives, mining that data for the benefit of the platform and, he argues, all of us. Who wouldn't want to have easy access to everything, every person and place and event around the world? he wanted to know. For a second or more, as long as it takes to log in to our Facebook accounts and survey the world before us, we all say *yes*. We too want that. Who wouldn't? As the hackers who devote themselves to pirating know, free data is seductive, enticing. There is always more and better and newer data to obtain, and new and faster ways to acquire it.

Writing a blog post in Mark's words, then, would mean formulating sentences that sounded like they were coming from the master and commander of this global platform, someone who believed in it, and assumed that you believed in it and wanted it too. If I got the job, this would be a fun puzzle, not unlike the programs the boys wrote to obtain the data they wanted: how to think like Mark, how to convince everyone that Facebook is a necessary and inevitable world-changing thing, our world's only hope for true and permanent connectedness. I knew how to do this in part because, in my more enthused moments, I believed in it too.

I worked on a sample blog post for Mark, beginning with his standard "Hey Everyone" and proceeding to describe the ways in which some new feature advanced our Facebook-connected future. The work took an evening, punctuated by exasperated moments of typing and erasing and retyping, trying to get the boyish cadence just right: just flat enough to sound like Mark, but still animated enough to be readable, compelling.

A few days later, Mark asked to meet me in his conference room. It was my first one-on-one with the boss and the first time he had ever given me his full attention, even though at this point I had worked for him for over three years. His conference room was entirely white: white plastic Saarinen table, egg-shaped chairs, white walls, whiteboards. From the glass windows I could see as far as Stanford to the west and the peninsula to the north, like a long corridor of wealth stretching to the horizon, tapering off into clouds.

Mark closed the door and stood near his whiteboard, dressed in his usual outfit of squarely cut jeans and a hoodie, looking slightly away and off into the distance. Whenever he looked at me directly, which was rare, it was either with blankness or a slight smirk, some acknowledgement that we were in on some joke that he assumed that I, as longtime Facebook employee and member of what felt by now like a virtual family, would get. I wasn't sure what the joke was, if it even existed, or if our simply being there—in command of a universe—was the joke.

"How did you know how to write like me?" he asked with disbelief, once I had situated myself at the white table, my arms folded. "When I read this I thought it was something I wrote." A slight smile appeared on his face, finally. When he smiles, you know he feels comfortable, among bros, like you're at the fraternity house and someone has said something particularly funny. I have worked hard, I suddenly realized, to hone myself into a proxy bro to these boys: nonchalant, stolid, avoiding the appearance of caring too much about anything, but especially about the wrong things, which are anything too girly or nontechnical or decorative, things that in this world do not scale. All the girls who acted like girls (and who didn't have social connections to the founders and early engineers) were still stuck down in the lower tiers of the company, largely ignored except when they appeared at company parties or in the tagged photos of them that appear on Facebook after parties.

"I don't know, I guess I've just spent a long time listening to you speak."

"Okay, well, you've got the role," he announced. Facebook tended to refer to jobs, especially the loftier and more outward-facing ones, as "roles."

"Cool," I replied, "I'm excited." I was. My interest in internationalization had been waning since we had finished translating Facebook into nearly every language. By that point, my job had segued into managing the maintenance of the translated Facebook sites, which was a more bureaucratic function than the original translation process had been. Writing for Mark, on the other hand, appealed to a stronger passion of mine: writing in English. It might be the funniest thing I had ever done, and the weirdest job I'd ever have. It seemed almost perfect that I, fascinated by the dark sides of Facebook, would become the shadow Mark Zuckerberg, there to explain what he couldn't or wouldn't.

Mark took out the sample blog post I had written and made a few stylistic notes on it with a pen. "This pretty much sounds exactly like what I would write," he said. "Except for one important thing. I never use a comma before a conjunction," he said, crossing out all the Oxford commas I had inserted as a matter of habit.

"Okay, no Oxford commas," I said. I could already see why he wouldn't like them: Oxford commas weren't efficient. His style aimed towards the quick, modern, streamlined. I reminded myself also not to use two spaces after a period.

"Have you seen *The West Wing*?" he asked.

"Some episodes, yeah, but I've never watched the whole thing," I explained.

"I want you to watch it," he said.

"Okay," I agreed. Of course, *The Wire* was the show that I believed best reflected how things really work, at Facebook and anywhere else. But, where I saw the struggle, the war on the streets that wasn't polished and clean and was waged by people who weren't in power, Mark saw the presidency and some new virtual Oval Office of his own making, as white and spotless as his fifth floor conference room.

I wondered sometimes if the very fact that I saw things in ways he didn't was what had gotten me that far. Because, for all their rabid data consumption, there was a lot the engineers didn't know. That was partly why Mark made Facebook, and why the boys of the valley were so busy turning our lives into data, as if by doing so, their algorithms could tell them something that their eyes and hearts couldn't. As Thrax announced triumphantly at his desk one day, "I just wrote an algorithm to tell me who I am closest to!" He went on to show a set of scores that, according to his algorithm's calculations, revealed how close he was to all his Facebook friends.

Two weeks later, my job in internationalization wrapped up and, in my new role as Mark's writer, I was moved to a desk near the door to his conference room. As soon as I had set up my new desk, Mark asked me to step into his office.

"I want you to write an email to the company in my voice announcing that you've moved into this position," he explained.

"Okay," I said. "Is there anything in particular that you want me to mention?" I asked.

"I think just tell the positions you've had and what you're going to be working on," he replied. "It's a good story," he added with a grin.

"Yes, it is," I thought, and smiled back. This was the inexorability of Facebook, the desire it seemed to have ever since the launch of News Feed, the desire to turn everything into a story.

Now, as I suppose we all always were on Facebook, I was the story.

Sam stopped by my new desk as I was writing the announcement to ask what I was doing there, and I told him I was going to be writing for Mark. Even Sam, who usually approached everything with deadpan irony, seemed surprised at this almost pitch-perfect, sitcom-like outcome, in which the odd literary one becomes the new power player. He recovered quickly and we laughed together as always, then he jumped on a ripstik and skated off, leaving me to my email-writing.

"Hey Everyone—" I began. "I wanted to congratulate everyone on the fact that we reached 150 million users last week. This is an important milestone and reaching it shows how well we are doing at executing on our mission of making the world more open and connected. We're really just at the beginning, though, and we have so much more to do. I also want to make a couple of announcements. One is that Kate Losse, who began in Customer Support in 2005 and has since contributed to the Platform and Internationalization teams, is going to be taking on a role as Writer . . ." This isn't hard, I thought. You just need to sound like everything is easy, like everything happens as it should. At Facebook, I remember thinking at various points along this journey, the world is simple.

When I wasn't writing for Mark, I was watching the comings and goings of executives and visitors, wondering what decisions were being made that I would have to quickly catch up on and write about. I paid particular attention whenever unfamiliar and important-looking new businessmen came to the office, as that usually meant that some deal was going down that would have to be announced to the company later, such as when a group of Russians rolled in with the vague, almost fake-sounding name Digital Sky Technologies and invested in Facebook in May 2009. Mark's days were made up of constant meetings, whether with businessmen in blazers or Facebook product engineers, streams of young men in jeans and tight T-shirts marching nervously in and out of his office on the hour, laptops in hand. I was invited to attend his weekly executive team meetings, but only to, as Elliot told me, absorb Mark's thoughts.

In the first executive meeting I attended that January, Mark, Elliot, and Sheryl discussed the Twitter threat. Mark, who was usually sanguine, was quite nervous about the speed with which Twitter was picking up users and press, beginning in 2009 with about 7 million user accounts and rapidly *hockey sticking,* as rapid growth is called in the valley (up to about 70 million users by the end of 2009). Twitter threatened to be a faster, simpler, more efficient way of posting information to a wide public. As it turned out, the hunger for social media was big enough to accommodate both Facebook and Twitter, along with a host of later apps like Instagram and Foursquare that provide slightly different variations on ways to post and distribute to an audience.

I listened to Mark and Sheryl discuss the threat and what could be done to stop it, and whether it was something to worry about. At points I wanted to chime in, and began to do so, but saw Mark and Sheryl's displeased looks and quickly realized that I wasn't really supposed to speak. This was a power and a status game, after all, and even the highest executives were playing. Everyone in their place. So, I just listened, staring out at the rooftops of Palo Alto and playing with a loose piece of rubber on my Vans. We will be fine, I thought, Twitter doesn't have any native pictures; it's just text. Facebook, as the boys taught me, was all about the faces: the pictures, the video nation, mapping a world.

Eventually, after a month or so, once I had supposedly absorbed enough of Mark's ideas and mannerisms, I wasn't invited to the executive meetings anymore, but I didn't mind. I had begun to realize that aside from the blog posts that I was occasionally called on at midnight or seven in the morning to write, I didn't have much to write. Around then, many early Facebook employees' jobs, like mine, had become mainly to serve as the trusted, familiar faces of the company, and sometimes, in the boys' case, to serve as a research and development arm for our culture, which the company was so intent on preserving.

For example, on a designer's birthday, his friends rented sumo fat suits and held wrestling matches in the yard, posting hundreds of pictures on Facebook, which showed up in all of our News Feeds due to the heavy activity of people liking them. This is what in Silicon Valley is called a *proof of concept,* proving via the metrics, which in this case are high numbers of likes, that sumo suits at parties are a cultural hit. So, at the next Facebook company party, the party planners rented the same suits and made sumo wrestling into a company party game.

By the same logic, when Thrax wore an American Apparel track jacket to work, Facebook bought one for everyone in the company to wear. For years, some people wore them every day, walking around in matching jersey track jackets like an enormous high-school sports program. In this way, Facebook (and increasingly, the valley's) fascination with what was cool could make for a certain kind of career strategy: If you had the right look and played the right games, you could play all the way to the bank.

In the late spring of 2009, we moved to a new, sprawling campus in an old Hewlett-Packard building. Mark's desk was purposefully positioned in the building's dead center, on the lower floor, nearly underground. He called the building a bunker. We were starting to dominate the social media game completely now, to Mark's sometime chagrin. While he wanted to win, he preferred us always to be in a state of emergency, on lockdown, so that we had to devote ourselves entirely to the company and its mission.

Sometimes, when people didn't feel stressed enough, he called official lockdown periods, during which employees were required to work on weekends and late into the night. Lockdown periods were often called when some new, other social product, like Foursquare or Tumblr, came on the scene and we needed to mount some serious resistance by incorporating a version of it into Facebook's feature set, like the Places product (Facebook's answer to Foursquare, which was eventually superseded by general location tagging similar to that of Google+ or Twitter). Whereas, in 2006, the social network field consisted only of MySpace and Facebook (and a dwindling Friendster), by 2009 and onward, the social application field was becoming increasingly crowded, as many more entrepreneurs and programmers and investors got into the game.

The catch for Facebook was that the more successful we became (and we were still, despite all the competition, dominant), the more likely employees were to be distracted by money and the new pastimes it enabled: fine dining, bar hopping, five-star vacations, expensive cars. In this sense, winning the game completely was a bit of a curse, because as our user numbers climbed quickly to 250 million in July 2009 and 350 million in December 2009, early employees had less incentive to work constantly, and more leeway to play games and party earlier in the night instead of waiting until the dead hours of two in the morning to socialize like we used to. New engineers were being hired all the time to take up the slack of bug fixing and code development from employees who had been there longer. The Facebook product itself made staying on task difficult: With the steady stream of pictures flowing down our pages, how could we be expected to focus on anything but planning our next photo opportunities and status updates? Looking cool, rich, and well-liked was actually our job, and that job took a lot of work.

Late that summer, employees were invited to sell up to a quarter of our stock to Digital Sky Technologies, the Russian group who had invested in the company. The Internet whispered that some of their money came from a Russian mobster with a violent past. However, when the stock sale was announced at our weekly All Hands, no one asked if the Russians' money was clean and any questions that even skirted around the topic of who they were and where they came from got what is called a *hand-wavy* answer in Silicon Valley: a brushed off nonanswer at best. Transparency may be Facebook's business, but there were some things that no one wanted or was allowed to know. One way or another, the Russians cleaned up on their investment:

Five months after we sold our stock to them the stock had tripled in price, and one of the investors had purchased a $30 million mansion in Silicon Valley.

With the new rush of money came not just new activities but increasing power and attention. Celebrities like Katy Perry and Tyra Banks stopped by regularly to take tours of the office with Mark, and employees would stop what they were doing to take pictures and post them to Facebook. All of Facebook's Hollywood dreams were coming true.

Like any power mogul, Mark's desk in the bunker was surrounded by the work stations of people he liked and had fashioned as his closest deputies. At his pod were Schrep, the engineering director, and Chris Cox, the product director, both affable white guys with friendly faces. Sheryl kept a neat desk next to mine, a few feet away from Mark's pod. Her desk, as cool and efficient as she was, held a conference phone and digital pictures of her children and husband. She spent her time either in meetings with high-powered executives or on the phone with them at her desk, which I couldn't help but overhear. I admired her firm yet dulcet phone voice, which could be both decisive and quiet at the same time. She enunciated precisely, so as to make every thought seem like a decision, like the matter was always closed and the conversation had always already reached its resolution. It was comforting to imagine the world as it sounded in Sheryl's voice: a world where every question is already answered, where efficiency is assumed, where we all, like her, are on the path toward or have already made it to the executive suite.

The floor around Sheryl's desk was piled with the endless gifts that she received from business contacts in lofty positions at Fortune 500 companies. People sent her Louboutin heels and Frette candles the diameter of dinner plates, which she unpacked while on speakerphone with some CEO or another. Sometimes, she passed them over the desk to me offhandedly, just trying to get rid of them, but usually they just sat in piles under the desk until someone cleared them away, to be replaced by new, just as superfluous, luxury gifts. Mark's desk was similarly surrounded by boxes and gifts, but they were more boyish: a sports jersey signed by a soccer star, some video game that hadn't been released yet. I didn't have any presents (other than Sheryl's castoffs), but I had a front-row view of the business lives of the extremely rich and powerful, whom I now knew spend much of their days managing the world's desire to be close to them.

Once again, six months after the move to the new office, Thrax and I were thrown together. I was informed by Chase, who came by to tell me, with the same smirk he always had when trying to get us to hook up, that Thrax was moving in to my pod. "Oh," I replied coolly, but thought to myself, "Lol, of course." Sometimes, Facebook was like the world's most well-funded preschool, as if we were all sitting around playing with our Matchbox cars and singing "So and so and so and so sitting in a tree, k-i-s-s-i-n-g." We even had ants on a log at snack time sometimes, which was funny enough to me to capture in a photo and post on Facebook. Thrax's new job was to be Mark's technical advisor, where I was Mark's writing advisor.

These were recent roles that Mark had invented, jobs that

were not so much about doing things as being something, some version of Facebook that he wanted us all to personify. It felt as if the company's drive to convert us all into characters for the world's consumption was part of what was leading to the creation of these new roles. While Mark delighted in Facebook's ability to create infinite stories and characters, he didn't want to be the only character associated with the network. He wanted company in his position as the leader of our new social media enterprise. I felt sympathetic and almost protective of him in this impulse, as I privately always had: It must be hard to be a figure that everyone expects to represent an entire paradigm shift, a new and virtual way of being. Mark, with his preternatural, abstract focus on data and systems, needed charismatic, likeable people to share in this burden. Also, perhaps, I wondered if Thrax and I had by some accident of personality personified Mark's idea of what Facebook culture was: sarcastic sponges soaking up and performing all the American culture we could find. And, most important for Mark, we shared an impish delight in conquering.

Thrax arrived in the late afternoon, as usual, and piled his new desk with games, digital components that I couldn't identify, and books. The books were a comically academic touch for someone meant to serve as the face of education's new irrelevance to success. "Hey," he said, grinning, and I returned, "Hey," as the administrative assistants watched. I felt a sudden urge to turn to my screen and resort to IM to communicate, rather than sitting here and chatting as though we were colleagues working at real desk jobs, which I wasn't sure was accurate, sandwiched as I was between Sheryl's piles of luxury gifts and Thrax's electronic toys.

Mark's office sat adjacent to our pod, with its secret back room (for especially important meetings, because the front room of his office had a glass window onto the hallway that made meetings transparent) hidden behind a wallpapered door and a single table illuminated by a *Mad Men*–style modern lamp, receiving a constant stream of celebrities and tech luminaries and wealthy Russians in silk suits.

As at the summer house years before, Thrax's and my schedules rarely overlapped, as I left the office in the late afternoon just as he was waking up and arriving at work. When he was there, he received a steady stream of engineers coming to pay their respects, to trade jokes, and to ask him to play video games or go out that weekend. The constant visitors trekking through the center of the office—executives, celebrities, endless young men in hoodies—were another reason that accomplishing any actual work was nearly impossible. We mostly just sent instant messages and read Facebook and trafficked in lulz. When Kai came by one day looking for Mark and Sheryl and they weren't there, I said in character, "They're gone, I got rid of them," like a demonic child, and he said, "Good," and we laughed. Always be trolling.

Behind our pod were circles of desks, beginning with Mark's preferred engineers, like William, a skinny Stanford grad with longish curls whom all the boys claimed to have man crushes on, due to his immaculate code. Behind him was a set of newly graduated, mostly white engineers from Stanford and Harvard who were emerging to take the places of the now departed engineers who formed the first fraternity class at Facebook. Behind them in rows were many Asian and South Asian faces working on infrastructure, mostly people I had never met, many of whom spoke to each other in languages other than English. Some of them worked so far back in the building that their desks sat in windowless rooms, invisible and far from the endless games of ripstiking and chess that went on in the center of the floor. I was thankful for their work because, without them, nothing would ever get built or fixed. The Ivy League engineers, who formed the All-American window dressing of the company, were too busy making Facebook feel like what it originally was: a youthful, half-hacker and half–Ivy League enterprise, populated with smooth white faces, native and familiar.

One aspect of my job was to post updates to Mark's Facebook fan page, which, like writing his blog posts, was a fun puzzle, an impersonation challenge. I took pictures in the office and from the travel albums on his personal Facebook page and constructed spare captions in his voice, sticking to his main themes of information flow and changing the world. Cool-sounding posts about world travel and company news were easy to write: No one can argue with a photograph of a beautiful mountain or an historic site. But, when it came to posting to my own profile, the answer to the question of what to say and how to say it was increasingly unclear. I wanted to be authentic. I wanted to say something real. Facebook tells us to share "What's on your mind?" so it should have been easy, shouldn't it, to just say what I feel? But the prompt, and the system of liking and ranking that it feeds, always gave me pause. I was not sure whether the idea of sharing was that easy.

Facebook employees tended to post about their good fortunes and their increasingly glamorous lives at the company.

They also acted as Facebook's constant cheerleaders, posting news articles about the company, photos of employees at work, and celebrating the latest user growth numbers and feature launches. They believed, or seemed to, that the smallest, luckiest details of our lives were of utmost importance to share with the world, despite the fact that, since the stock crash in 2008, the global economy was slipping further into insolvency. To read their posts about fine dining, new cars, and luxury vacations, few employees seemed very concerned or aware of the deepening financial crisis. There was only one exception to this rule of sharing: No one ever posted anything critical of the company on Facebook. It would be like committing treason, to question the thing that fed us, both with food and attention and with a continuous drip of information. Facebook wanted us, like all of its users, to depend on it.

As 2009 progressed, I learned, both offhand and in closed rooms, that there were those who shared my skepticism about our goal of transforming the world into a virtual theater of ourselves. All that spring and summer, a team of product engineers worked on a remodel of Facebook's privacy settings that, unlike previous models, made certain information, like one's profile photo and friend list, public. This meant that absolute privacy from strangers on Facebook, which was the thing that I first originally loved about the site, as compared to sites like MySpace, would finally be obsolete.

Mark's reasoning for this move was in line with his general vision of the world and where it was going, as he often put it. "We are pushing the world in the direction of making it a more open and transparent place," he would say at All Hands meetings, "this is where the world is going and at Facebook we need to lead in that direction." A guy on the PR team that I worked with sometimes mentioned this change as we stood around drinking beer at happy hour. "I don't think that I want Facebook or any site to push me to be 'more open.' What does that even mean?" he wondered. I agreed that it was an opaque and strange concept. Forcing people to be more open implied that we were all in some way closed, as though there was something wrong in the way we conducted our personal lives. How was it a Web site's place to say that we needed to reveal more about ourselves publicly? Why couldn't Facebook just let people share as much as they were comfortable with?

Most employees I talked with seemed not to be particularly bothered by the company's decision to forcibly adjust people's expectations of privacy, preferring instead to focus on the light and almost childlike-sounding goals of sharing and connecting people. "She just doesn't get it," a user support manager told me about one employee who was soon to be terminated. "She doesn't believe in the mission. She thinks that Facebook is for people without any real problems and isn't actually changing the world. Can you believe that? This afternoon I'm going to have to let her go."

I wondered who the heretic employee was. I guessed that she must have been like all of the user support team members: well-educated in the humanities at an Ivy League school, and probably unaware when hired that she had walked into a new kind of technical cult. At any rate, her awareness of issues beyond Facebook was a problem. The company wasn't paying anyone to be aware of the world beyond the screen. The only questions you were supposed to ask or ideas you were supposed to have at work, as a good citizen of the Facebook nation, were about new ways to technologize daily life, new ways to route our lives through the web.

One afternoon in his office, Mark asked me to detail his thoughts on what he deemed to be "the way the world was going." "I have a series of blog posts in mind that I'd like you to write, I'd like to you to write a post on each idea, so people can understand what we are trying to do at Facebook," he explained.

"Okay," I said. "Shoot," taking out my Facebook-branded notepad to jot everything down.

"These are the topics I'd like you to write about," Mark said, listing them off. "Revolutions and giving people the power to share; openness as a force in our generation; moving from countries to companies; everyone becoming developers and how we support that; net-native generation of companies; young people building companies; purpose-driven companies; starting Facebook as a small project and big theory."

"Uh, okay," I said, feeling a bit overwhelmed. I was not quite sure what all of this meant to Mark or what I was supposed to do with it. I thought it was interesting that he was still into "revolutions," as was I, but his list then veered into territory I wasn't sure about.

"What does 'companies over countries' mean?" I asked, starting with the first one that jumped out at me.

"It means that the best thing to do now, if you want to change the world, is to start a company. It's the best model for getting things done and bringing your vision to the world." He said this with what sounded like an interesting dismissal of the other models of changing the world. I could imagine, like he may have, that countries were archaic, small, confined to one area or charter. On the other hand, companies—in the age of globalization—can be everywhere, total, unregulated by any particular government constitution or an electorate. Companies can go where no single country has gone before. "I think we are moving to a world in which we all become cells in a single organism, where we can communicate automatically and can all work together seamlessly," he said, by way of explaining the end goal of Facebook's "big theory."

"Okay, I'll think about these and get to work," I said. A set of designers were waiting with laptops in hand outside the glass-walled room, so we wound up the meeting and I went back to my desk.

I liked the idea of constructing philosophical blog posts, but when faced with Mark's topics I felt a curious sense of displacement, like I couldn't do this even if I tried. "I may not be really sure what Mark means by this, but I know I don't believe in it," I thought to myself as I walked back to my desk. It sounded like he was arguing for a kind of nouveau totalitarianism, in which the world would become a technical, privately owned network run by young "technical" people who believe wholeheartedly in technology's and their own inherent goodness, and in which every technical advancement is heralded as a step forward for humanity. But that reasoning was deeply flawed. While technology can be useful, it is not God; it is not always neutral or beneficent. Technology carries with it all the biases of the people who make it, so simply making the world more technical was not going to save us. We still have to think for ourselves, experience the world in reality as well as online, and care about one another as people as well as nodes in a graph, if we are going to remain human. And finally, I wasn't sure I wanted to be one of many "cells in a single organism." I liked my autonomy, my privacy, the fact that I was different from everyone else—a unique individual.

These thoughts brought me as close to philosophical debate as I had been since graduate school, which was fun. But when it came to the prospect of writing for Mark on these topics, it felt close to impossible. These philosophies, while interesting and provocative, weren't the ones I could write. They presumed some kind of beneficence of technology and its makers that, having spent years at the heart of the Facebook machine, I knew not to put my entire faith in. It's not that the people making technology were bad. They were just no better than anyone else when it came to understanding humanity and what we need, and giving them the power to decide what we—you, me, people we've never met—need as humans didn't seem like the wisest choice. But then, wisdom is not what technology is about. Technology is about solving things another way; without experiencing the problems, without afterthought, without having to do much at all. Technology can do these things for you so you don't have to. Sometimes, that can be helpful. Other times, I think that by using technology to accomplish our human goals we end up missing out.

After days and weeks spent mulling over these topics and their implications, I finally came to the conclusion that if Mark believed those things are true, he was going to have to convince people of them himself. The issue wasn't one of eloquence—simply writing well, which was my task as Mark's writer. The question was what did any of these values actually mean, and why should we want them? This was something only Mark could explain. I told him that I was having trouble coming up with satisfactory essays on the topics he'd assigned, and asked him to schedule time to explain his ideas in more detail, but he was too busy or wasn't inclined to explain further—it was hard to tell. I came to the conclusion that perhaps he thought I could invent these arguments of whole cloth, or that we already were cells in a single organism and I should be attuned enough to intuit what he meant, but I couldn't, and so the essays were never written or posted.

Although I liked my new job, I was unsettled as ever by Facebook and the valley's imperative to technologize everything. Having lived in this world of endless photographs and rankings and updates for years, I had begun to notice that, whether or not there was a correlation, my real-world relationships were becoming anorexic, starved of presence. I didn't know anyone in the Bay Area—Facebook employee or not—who didn't obsessively read their social media feeds and construct real and online conversations almost entirely out of these threads. "Did you see that post on Facebook?" or "I saw your tweet," they'd say. In this way, our posts and public presence online had become the inexorable, primary topic of discussion, rather than anything private or intimate or in person. If you weren't playing in the public sphere, sporting about on the social media field while everyone watched and clapped, it was as though you didn't exist.

I knew that if tomorrow I stopped updating my social networks with the ephemera of my tastes and thoughts, no one in the Bay Area would think of me. Even in the office, where I would spend six or more hours a day, I felt more visible online than off. People were too busy reading their screens to talk to each other.

That spring, a new Facebook engineer, not yet indoctrinated into Facebook's culture of the virtual, suggested a new feature. "I have an idea," he posted on the internal discussion board, "it would be a feature that allows you to suggest to two friends who don't know each other that they should meet and hang out." A veteran Facebook engineer jumped on the thread quickly to correct him. "We already have that feature," he said, "it's called the Friend Suggestion feature, where you can suggest that two people become friends on Facebook." "No, I meant a feature where you could tell two friends to hang out in real life. . . . Oh, never mind," the new engineer said, giving up.

Incidents like these, and the contentment people at work seemed to feel as they gazed, mesmerized, at their thirty-inch monitors, made me realize finally that this—Facebook, social media, our apps and phones and screens—was never really about real social life or interaction. Social media is about bringing us online and asking us to play with one another in digital space. Social media then is the ultimate Internet game, played according to the rules and metrics created by the boys who make the games and write their algorithms.

However, it was also as if the boys who knew the Internet best also knew that there was something dark about it, about this drive to have everything while revealing nothing. This, I think, is why they trolled, for trolling in itself is a kind of admission that we can't win online as our true selves, that authenticity online makes us too vulnerable, that vulnerability (or "vulns," as the hackers say) can be exploited too easily in an online world in which information is so widely connected and distributed.

Trolling, I decided, was the native mode of the Internet, and not exactly sharing in the literal way that Facebook declares it. Sharing is complicated and private; humor is entertaining, appropriate to an audience. Neither Mark nor any of the boys said anything that particularly revealed their emotions, for the most part. In fact, it was from them that I figured out early on that serious posts were kind of beside the point, despite Facebook's business need for us to post transparently about our lives.

So, I would troll instead. However, as a girl, I knew I couldn't troll exactly like the tech boys. I didn't want to post indignantly about how some new device or code upgrade was doing it wrong. I decided that, if I were going to troll, I would have to go at it from the opposite direction. Rather than trolling with technical details, I began trolling with a fatuous, unarticulated emotion that the boys could never get away with. "<333333333333333333333," I posted as my status regularly, sometimes <3-ing particular things and people, with an exuberance that seemed infectious, for my coworkers began doing the same thing. Though I had begun posting hearts on everything as a joke, soon everyone in the office was earnestly decorating their Facebook posts with little hearts, skipping language, hardly bothering to comment anymore. It was if at some level we all intuited that "<3," whether intended earnestly or as lulz, was all anyone was looking for anyway and so, Facebook, with its ubiquitous like buttons and comments became a race to bestow and harvest as much digital love as possible.

Around this time, Facebook was testing a feature whereby users could reward each other with Facebook credits (Facebook's virtual currency, in which one credit equaled one dollar) for posting something particularly entertaining. Rather than rewarding one another by posting <3s in our comments, we could now reward each other with actual money. For the engineers who created the feature, it was as if the two were the same, and the guys in the office participated in the test happily, posting credits along with their comments. Thrax, ever shrewd, decided to take advantage. "This is a stickup, give me all your credits," he posted as his status one day. The guys in the office, realizing with delight that they had been expertly trolled, handed over their credits to Thrax in the comments under the post. As I watched the stickup transpire in my News Feed, I felt a certain awe. We had finally, literally created an economy of love, in which friendship and affection had a monetary value and a system for transacting it. However, engineers seemed more excited about trading credits to one another as a form of affection than anyone else at the company did, and the adding credits to comments feature was never launched.

"Miss u," master troll Carles of the blog Hipster Runoff said often, to and about everything, in his daily musings on Internet and popular culture that I read daily at work. Missing, I started to think, was the one true emotion of the Internet. In communicating primarily virtually we are always missing things, missing each other's points and missing out on the experiences of being with each other. So, I began to post that I missed things—

people, places, brands, states of mind—as much or more as I
<3ed them. The only thing we never missed was our screens,
staring back at us always, ready to make us feel just slightly less
alone. "Miss u, real life," I could have posted, but few people at
work would have gotten it. Real life was something everyone in
my News Feed seemed relieved to leave behind, if only for the
immediate reason that real life can't be owned and graphed and,
as such, can't make you famous and rich.

If success is measured, as it is on the Internet, by memes
spread and likes garnered, my Facebook trolling persona was
successful, but my real life in Palo Alto remained an uneventful
routine of work punctuated by runs on the Stanford campus,
which swarmed with students dreaming of their own Silicon
Valley success story. So, in early 2009, I decided to move to San
Francisco and commute daily to Palo Alto. I found a room in an
apartment at a messy end of the Mission that had been migrat-
ing from a working class to a digital class neighborhood for ten
years. I was so excited to start over in the city that I didn't mind
the fact that in the old Victorian I'd be sharing with two room-
mates the fridge door barely opened and the sills were caked
with dust so thick that it might predate the 1906 earthquake
(which the house, auspiciously for us if there were to be another
earthquake, survived).

However, it was 2009 and, unlike in bohemian times, the
past was never really behind us, just as the present was a different
place than it used to be. Technology didn't really want us to ever
leave things behind: We were expected instead to carry the past
with us, all the time, in the form of pictures and tags and the
smiling avatars of every person we have ever met, whether or not

we still cared for them and they for us. The information was just there, populating, feeding, following us around as we conducted our lives. In this way, friendship never waxed or waned, but was always present in digital space. This was the eternal now of the Internet, and this, not Palo Alto or San Francisco, was where we had all begun to live.

Some weeks after I moved and was settled into my new place, Thrax asked me on AIM, "Do you want to go out in the city tonight?" He wanted to hang out because I'd left Palo Alto, in address at least. Men never want you to leave if they think you are really leaving. In this way, men and bosses are the same. And further, at Facebook, watching out for the boys was in a way my job, whether I wanted to hang out with them that night or not. "They are your boys," Mark's administrative assistant would say to me sometimes, implying that I shouldn't leave them entirely to their own devices, even though they were always up to their own devices, trolling and playing and judging, wielding their digital might. Devices, after all, was what it was all about, as Justin knew in advance when he spent all of Coachella struggling to receive a signal on his new, now completely outdated, BlackBerry Pearl.

"I'm tired, I woke up early today," I typed back to Thrax. I was tired because that morning I had to be at work at a somewhat normal working hour—ten o'clock—to star in a video detailing Facebook's completed internationalization process, which a documentary filmmaker had been hired to produce. "You are going to be the star of the film," the filmmaker had told me, and it reminded me of an old Hollywood scene of a starlet fresh off the bus from Iowa. "Are you a producer who is going to make me a star?" I felt like asking.

The shoot that morning had been long, the lights bright, and in my interviews I kept saying the wrong things—things that weren't peppy and fawning enough—and we kept having to reshoot scenes to get things right. I was not as good an actor on film as I was on Facebook, where I could craft my lines and persona in advance. So, by seven o'clock, I was tired and, like a Hollywood diva, I was already in bed.

"I'm wearing my pajamas already," I typed to Thrax.

"So am I," he typed back. "I just woke up. Let's go out."

Oh right, I remembered—the star engineers didn't have to go to work at all if they didn't want to. At this point, Thrax went to work maybe three days a week.

"Maybe," I typed. That's the thing now, with texting, you don't have to decide what you want to do until a second before. Technology enables an intoxicating degree of freedom, endless opportunities to do something or not.

An hour later, I had time to rest and get dressed, out of my pajamas and into a pair of jeans and a sweater. I flitted through the littered streets alone to meet Thrax; Ethan, a designer who lived near my new place in San Francisco; and a newer engineer, Liakos; at The Phone Booth, a dive bar on South Van Ness Street. It was a dirty, hip place, lit all in red and purposefully seedy, the scene of many Mission love crimes, I was sure. As always, the louche aura and grime of San Francisco were comfortingly authentic. In this bar, people could even smoke due to some archaic loophole in San Francisco smoking laws, adding to its stench of authenticity. I greeted the guys at the bar and ordered Fernet—an herbal, oily black liquor from Italy, popular in San Francisco for reasons no one knows—and went to put the Cure on the jukebox. It was a simple recipe for Mission happiness, as far as I was concerned.

I decided that I had good cause to celebrate with witchy drinks in darkest Mission: Improbably, I had come to occupy the highest position I could at the biggest tech company of the decade. I had become the boss himself, or at least his ventriloquist's voice. And while I could be scared—what if I fail, what if he fires me, what if they find out I don't wholly believe in our world-bending mission—I felt mostly just relieved. Everything that could have gone wrong already had, but I was still there and, unlikely as it might seem, I was winning. My stock options were starting to be worth enough that I could leave Facebook at any time and still have a livelihood. From then on, whatever happened at work wouldn't really matter.

The bar filled with taut-muscled gay men in leather jackets, like some movie version of New York in the 1970s. Inspired by their seventies vibes I played Fleetwood Mac songs on the jukebox and danced on the sticky dance floor. Amid all this vintage authenticity I forgot myself. "Second hand news," Lindsey sang on the jukebox, not referring to News Feed or any other form of mediated information, but to a different kind of connection that never seems to die. "When times go bad, when times go rough, let me lay you down in the tall grass and let me do my stuff."

After more Fernets and a lot of talk about Facebook and our aim to create what one of the boys excitedly called a new social operating system, Thrax and I walked back to my apartment on

Valencia Street. So did Liakos, who, like many of the Facebook engineers, followed Thrax's activity closely and seemed not to be able to bear to let him out of sight for a second. Thrax was as bewitching to his coworkers as to his distant Internet fans who followed his antics online. I could never tell, with all their liking and following of him and his online presence, if they wanted to be him or they wanted him. Was he their hero or their object of desire, and are those two things all that different when it comes to boys and their icons?

Silicon Valley's culture of the boy king made gay icons and followers out of people who aren't necessarily gay. Desire is strange, and our digital world made it even stranger, for we could consume and get off on anything we wanted, in any combination of people and things. As another Rule of the Internet reads: "There is porn of it," where "it" could be whatever fetish you desire, in any digital format: "There are no exceptions." The Internet has made it so that there are no limits to what we can do to gratify ourselves. If hackers are what you want, they are there for the watching.

But, that night, for once, we weren't on the Internet. I got blankets for Liakos and put him to bed on the living-room couch, leaving Thrax and me to sit cross-legged on my bed, talking. The Internet was missing, shut out of the action on my closed laptop that lay unused on the floor of my bedroom. "Welp. Miss u," I imagined the Internet saying to us from deep within some data center somewhere, perplexed as to why it had not been made master of ceremonies, router of all human affection and friendship. Thrax was there, and we were moving perilously close, almost to the point of kissing. Something had gotten into us to bring us to the brink of a physical consummation of our long affection. Perhaps it was the Fleetwood Mac, whispering to us from the free-and-easy seventies, fueled by real drugs instead of digital ones. "Players only love you when they're playing," Stevie sings in "Dreams," and I think that the song could be updated for the Internet age to read "Players only love you when you're playing."

"We should sleep in tomorrow," Thrax said. It was Tuesday, but neither of us had to be at work until we felt like it, which in his case could be as late as seven at night or never. Maybe it was the Fernet or the fact that in San Francisco we were far away from Facebook, but I felt bolder than usual, like I might finally be able to break the fourth wall, that barrier of virtual reality that we had built. Social media instead of television was our new fourth wall, and any true connection in the world we built required you to shatter the screen once and for all. "Okay," I said, snuggling out of my jeans.

Thrax leaned in to kiss me, and I almost laughed that this was actually happening, but it was. We were indeed breaking the fourth wall, as if the iPhone's tempered Corning glass was shattering everywhere, all over my bed, against Steve Jobs's and all the other tech titans' wishes that it stay unbreakable. Then, the siren of the virtual began to sing me back to its safe, contained shores. "I don't want to have sex," I declared.

"We don't have to have sex," he said, sounding mostly relieved. We were agreed, as always, that we didn't want to have sex. Sex with each other was too real. Horribly, chillingly real. Because from sex—the true, physical, total interlacing of bodies—you cannot go back to the virtual. The virtual was what our fortunes depended on. And, as figureheads of Facebook, we had to pre-serve the distance that the company depended on. For, if everyone were connected with the ones they loved, they—we—wouldn't need Facebook and its distant promise of love always somewhere around the corner. Real intimacy is the third rail of a publicity-driven, virtual society. We must avoid it at all costs. Thrax and I had always known this instinctively. Our unerring sense of control was what helped us win the game and take our seats next to Mark.

Something had to be done, though. Our odd, enduring af-fection was still there, always available to be picked up and left when it was convenient, like secondhand news. But I wanted—I needed—to try to kill it. I felt a sudden urge to destroy this—the tension, the war, the endless battle to be loved and liked—once and for all. If I could kill it, maybe I could check out and leave it all behind. And, so, I took charge.

The perpetual competition in our working and social lives reminded me of a line from a James Baldwin novel that seemed to illuminate all of this, this war for status, "Love is a battle, love is a war, love is a growing up," he wrote. Maybe for the boys, being loved was a war, a battle we wage on social media now, instead of in real life. And, maybe, whenever they tire of this game, love will have to be a growing up, something they'll have to find somewhere else, offline, away from the screen. So, in the unmonitored darkness of that night I decided it was okay, at least momentarily, to submit, and Thrax did too.

"Just don't update your status about this," I warned, eventu-ally falling back onto my pillow.

"Hold on, I was just getting out my phone," he said, trolling.

"Not funny," I retorted, but we both laughed. It was funny.

Everything was. We were making a fortune out of broadcasting our own selves and interests to the world, and we didn't even have to go to work if we didn't want to. To punctuate this, my alarm clock began to chime errantly and we burst into more laughter. Who needs an alarm when you don't have to go to the office and when all this is over, you may never need to work again? The world was ours.

Or was it? When we did go back to work, the office and the computer screen and the crowds of virtual friends would be waiting to consume us, turning us again into totems of whatever it was they desired. For our distant audience, we always had to remain cool, in control. It was only for as long as the night held and we stayed asleep, spooned together like silver from the same set, that we could be unconscious of whatever the world was asking us to be for them. Perhaps in this world of digital surveillance and judgment, deep sleep was the only time when we were free. Maybe this was why, throughout the long climb to the top of Mark's virtual world, where winning everyone's adulation was our job, we always crawled into bed in the middle of the night, longing not for sex, but for some human presence that existed, silent and breathing, away from the screen.

CHAPTER 9

THE KING STAYS THE KING

In July 2009, Mark was in Peru on vacation, contemplating whether I should join him on his press tour around Brazil. He knew nothing about Brazil and knew from my status updates that I did, so he listened to me when I told him how to wrest Brazil from Google's Orkut social network. Orkut had grown quickly in Brazil in 2006, unlike in other countries that approached online social networking more cautiously, because Brazilians took instantly and naturally to social networking of all kinds. I told Mark that, because Brazil's culture responds to personal contact, they might take Facebook more seriously if he paid them a visit in person.

"Mark is debating whether you should be flown out to Brazil for the press tour," his admin told me in the office that afternoon, only days before the tour began. I continued eating fork-fuls of lemon tart from my lunch plate. He would want me to be there, I thought to myself. This was just Mark's way of keeping me on edge and letting me know that he was in control. If it was an important decision he would have made it earlier, and quickly. "Okay," I said to her, "whatever he wants."

When I landed in São Paulo after the long flight, I was surprised to see a security detail made up of brawny ex-military men waiting to escort me to the hotel in a bulletproof van. The security detail loaded me and my luggage into the van and told me on the ride into the city about their earlier stints guarding Dick Cheney in Iraq. One had even served as Britney Spears's private security guard, and I asked him to tell me everything he knew about her. "She is really very nice," he said, "she always made sure the whole crew was fed, and would sometimes even buy us hamburgers." I was happy to hear that Britney Spears was nice.

The men in the detail turned serious only when we passed through a tunnel. "I hate tunnels," one growled tensely. "Why?" I asked. "Everything bad happens in tunnels," he said. "We learned that in Iraq. They can block you in on both sides and do anything they want to you in the middle," he explained. He only began to relax again when we emerged safely on the tunnel's other side. "Everything bad happens in tunnels," I thought, reflecting on the past four years, Facebook's single-minded race to domination, and every strange, churlish thing that happened that I just had to shake off, because I was trapped in the middle and had to get through to the other side.

I like these security guys, I thought. It seemed healthy to be hanging out with people who had fought in real wars.

At the hotel, where an entire floor was reserved for Mark and his entourage, a member of the detail handed me a small pin to wear on my shirt. "This is in case there is an incident. We need to know who is one of ours so we can get you out of the place as soon as possible. No offense if we can't identify all the straps by face. The pin is more reliable."

"What are straps?" I asked, confused by all the security speak.

"You are the straps," they explained. "Mark is the package. He's number one, he's the guy we have to protect at all costs. Everyone else is the straps, because you're the hangers on. You're only important because he is, but we can't have you falling into the wrong hands." Lol, I thought. That was a good description of my entire job. I was only important because he is.

My room was all white, full of curved tropical modern furniture and a white marble bath with a round portal onto the São Paulo skyline. It felt, fittingly, like being in a room-sized white iPhone. I was glad that it all looked so modern, for Mark's sake. Whenever I mentioned my passion for Brazil to Americans they tended to think it is a lawless, third-world country where they will be kidnapped immediately. In reality, while violence does occur in some places, the country is rich and powerful, and Mark had to know this if Facebook was going to work at winning the country over.

We ate dinner that night at a high-end barbecue place, lush and very Brazilian, with open breezes and a beautiful tropical tree growing directly from the floor of the restaurant. I resumed a conversation that Mark and I had been having earlier about the fact that I thought it was unconscionable that we were not going to Rio on this trip. "I know São Paulo is the business capital," I said, "but Rio is the heart of Brazilian culture. Everyone knows this in Brazil, even the Paulistas who think that all people in Rio do is party and go to the beach all day. We cannot *not* go to Rio!" I was impassioned about this because my Portuguese professor at Johns Hopkins was a Carioca, or native of Rio de Janeiro, and the first thing she told us in class was that she was going to make us all Cariocas. My sudden vehemence about the Rio issue was proof that she had been successful. Even Mark seemed willing to be convinced. "Hmm, I'll think about it," he said, and actually seemed to be considering it. Well this is a first, I thought, that I could convince Mark to change his mind about anything.

I ordered us a round of caipiroskas, a national drink made of vodka mixed with fruit and sugar. Mark could barely drink his and called me crazy for drinking mine so easily. I shuddered to think what he would have thought of the nights in Brazil in 2005 when our Hopkins student group danced samba until morning, fueled by caipirinhas and the local beer. Some of us even did lines of coke in the bathroom. Mark would have passed out on sight. He hated drugs. I was told that he'd go pale at just the thought of them. At Facebook, we all knew never to even mention the word drugs near him. I made a mental note not to tell him that he was "the package," and that package means drugs in Baltimore slang.

However, there was no danger here of bumping into any drugs, samba clubs, or favelas: For the next few days, we were all business, visiting television studios and meeting with journalists on the rooftop restaurant at the hotel. One of these journalists, who, like a true, casual Carioca, wore a shirt printed with palm trees, said just as I had that we could *not* not go to Rio! Mark turned to me and said, "Whoa, you were right about this."

At one point, on a trip to the MTV Brasil studios across town, we had to stop in a park so that Mark could take an important, secret phone call. As he paced back and forth on the sidewalk, his security detail fanned out across the park, pretending to be strangers out for a walk. "They are like his 'muscle,'" I realized, as usual, entertaining myself by thinking of analogies to *The Wire*. Mark talked on the phone while his muscle tensely watched all the park's corners. The scene looked exactly like Stringer Bell taking calls in abandoned lots of Baltimore. Maybe, I thought, sitting in the van waiting for Mark to finish, he got to be Stringer after all: obsessed with business and winning, and perhaps not the one with the most heart, like Avon, but the one who got to the top.

The following day, we were sitting at lunch on the roof of the hotel with the skyline of São Paulo stretching as far as we could see when Mark declared imperially, as he gazed at the view, "We're going to write a book about Facebook together someday." That sounds fun, I thought, but then my mind reeled with questions. What would that book even be like? The book I would write about Facebook would be so different from the one Mark would write. It was weird that he assumed I thought the same way he did. My face must have betrayed my doubts and questions, because Mark looked at me with his typical coy smirk, and said, more directly than usual, "I don't know if I trust you."

You shouldn't, I thought, giving him a half-innocent look. But Mark's idea had planted a new one in my head. I could leave to write my own book, I thought. And after so many years of biting my tongue and speaking on behalf of Facebook, it would be a relief to finally speak and write as myself. After all, as *The Wire* teaches, you should never trust anyone, in business, at least. Keep your hackers close. Mark, who preferred to hire hackers, knew that. And at that moment, I felt almost, for a second, close to him, as if in the mutual ground of breaking into something—him, the business of registering the identities of everyone in the world, me, the company culture he had built—we had finally found a common bond.

And that was it. Like the security detail's van emerging from the tunnel, I felt like I wasn't locked in anymore. I could finally breathe. If Mark had figured out over lunch that I didn't believe and that I had a mind of my own, it didn't matter. Game over. And, who knows, perhaps he knew it all along.

Making the decision to leave Facebook, which, by the time I returned to Palo Alto in September, I was convinced I would do, and actually leaving Facebook, were two different things. Once one was that far into the company's tightly wound web of self-interest, in which everything we did was for the purposes of Facebook's god and country, you could not just put your security badge on your desk and walk out the door. First, there was the matter of appearances: How it would look. Facebook wanted everyone, especially its celebrated stars, to seem perpetually happy and gung-ho about the enterprise, and leaving implied that you weren't. Second, there was the matter of money: By the end of my career at Facebook, I was earning as much as a mid-to-senior-level engineer and, with that salary, had grown accustomed to luxuries that formerly were far out of reach. I had recently traded in my old Toyota Camry for a lightly used BMW 325i, which was the smallest and most entry-level BMW, but a BMW nonetheless. I liked eating Tartine pastries for breakfast and arugula salads and pasta at Beretta for dinner, none of which were cheap. I had become a card-carrying member of the San Francisco tech bourgeoisie, whether I loved technology or not, and, as I first noticed when I moved to the Bay Area in 2005 and was on the outside looking in, everything in that world—rent, smart-phone bills, restaurant meals, BMW payments, and Barneys purchases—was expensive. If I were to quit Facebook, I would need money.

Fortunately, my stock options had begun to develop significant value and, in 2009, a secondary market had sprung up in New York to trade in Facebook stock, despite the fact that the IPO was still far off. I found the number for SecondMarket on the Internet and retreated to a Facebook conference room to call them. I spoke quietly, wondering if the wires were tapped and assuming that they were, or that they at least could be listened in on if someone wanted to. At Facebook, you had to always assume surveillance, as that was our business.

The finance guys at SecondMarket were of course happy to hear from me and promised to arrange a sale. There was one caveat: In order to sell company stock prior to the IPO, one had to enter a byzantine process of paperwork, contracts, and lawyers, and one last stumbling block: Facebook had to be notified of the sale so that they could, if they chose, exercise what is called Right of First Refusal and purchase the stock back themselves.

By this point, I already knew for sure that I wanted to leave, so I said that it was fine, I would go ahead with a sale, even though Facebook would find out and I hadn't yet told them that I was leaving.

I knew that Facebook had been alerted that I was selling stock when I came to work several months later and Mark gave me a long, cold look. The friendly smirk was gone; I was no longer his bro. Sheryl gave me a similar look, not bothering to hide her disdain when we crossed paths in the bathroom later that day. I understood Mark's coldness: This company was his baby, and he had always been in control of it and, while we worked there, of us. It must be strange to see your dependents— people whose careers you have made possible, even as their long hours of work have helped your company prosper—asserting independence. However, the reactions of other executives and managers seemed strange to me. Don't they know this is just business—a huge, personal business, but business nonetheless? And, who was Sheryl, with her hundreds of millions of dollars, to begrudge a woman her first financial independence? I had worked for that stock, and now I needed it, because, unlike Mark and Sheryl, I was not already a multimillionaire. What for them was just extra, expendable wealth was, for me, money to live on. Whatever I was going to reap from my years at Facebook and my accumulated stock, Sheryl would reap more by a factor of millions. But, for them, I supposed, this really was by now all just a game, and they could afford to overlook any financial necessities, since they had bypassed the need for such considerations many millions of dollars ago. Sometimes, in the heady air of a bunker occupied by billionaires who could fund entire legacies solely on investment interest, it seemed like it was getting hard to breathe.

"I heard that you are selling stock," a manager on the PR team said to me in early 2010 after calling me into a tiny, airless conference room for a special meeting. "Yes," I replied slowly, thinking, "Are they going to stop me? Can they? Isn't the stock mine?"

"This really just makes me question your judgment," he said.

"You know, not everyone already has millions of dollars and can afford to wait years for Facebook to IPO," I explained.

"When people sell stock that means they are getting ready to leave," he countered.

Good, I thought, that means that I'm not the first person who has done this and it's a perfectly logical thing to do.

"I just don't know why you would want to leave," he continued. "Facebook has so much further to go; we're just getting started on our mission. This makes me think that you don't believe in our mission."

I began to feel like I was having flashbacks to television documentaries about church-cult indoctrination. Is he really talking about missions and not believing? I had heard this talk before (and had written some of it for Mark) but the fact that they were citing the mission and the question of believing just as I was trying to escape seemed extra creepy, as if this really were the Hotel California and even if I were running for the door, they weren't going to let me out.

To my chagrin, I burst into long-repressed tears, losing control after so many years of remaining stoic. "I can't believe that after everything I have done for this company you are treating me like this," I cried, my voice muffled by tears and mucus that were beginning to stream from my nose. "I know it's hard for you to believe, but not everyone is like you, not everyone wants to work for Facebook forever," I explained. "Some people want to leave and do something else. So, that's what I'm going to do."

"Okay, well, it seems you've made your decision," he concluded.

It was a bleary, undignified end to a long and, on balance, rewarding and exciting adventure, but at least it was finally the end. As a parting shot, Mark told his assistant to move my desk to another floor, removing me from his exalted engineering department, even though he knew my last day would only be weeks later. This was a symbolic gesture that relayed in no uncertain terms that I no longer belonged as a soldier in his technical empire, but, fortunately, I had already figured this out. I never even went to my new desk; I didn't know where Mark told his assistants to put it. In my last weeks, I came to work only to say my goodbyes, fill out exit paperwork, and eat the fine pastries prepared each day by the pastry chef. "Let them eat cake," I remembered thinking in 2006, when capital companies delivered cake to our offices, and indeed, as my last act as a member of the Facebook dynasty, that is what I did.

The day I left Facebook, in spring 2010, my life became instantly better, turning into a chillwave summer of nothing but late breakfasts at Tartine and long evenings at the park, the Phone Booth, or the Uptown, my favorite dive bars at which to talk and drink Fernet and listen to music on the jukebox. I hung out often with a new friend that I had met when he began following me on Tumblr. He listened as I talked about my recent departure from Facebook and the ideas I had about it that I wanted to write about. He had his own idea as to which television series closely corresponded to my experience. "You were like Peggy on *Mad Men,*" he said, and I realized that, yes, it was kind of like that too.

In January 2011 I said goodbye to San Francisco and moved to Marfa, Texas, to write this book. Marfa, unlike San Francisco or Palo Alto, has no great need for the connectedness that we experience now over the Internet and on our phones, and perhaps that is why I was drawn here. In Marfa, it is the land and the sky, rather than any human enterprise, which scales, extending farther than the eye can comprehend, creating nightly sunsets that seem unworldly, even in contrast to any other sunsets one has been fortunate to watch. In Marfa, the ephemera of the social web recedes; it is the land and the art, like Donald Judd's one hundred sculptures in mill aluminum, that ask you to pay attention and consider them daily.

Marfa's disinterest in the social Internet isn't just metaphorical: The phones are slow for data retrieval, so posting a tweet or reading a feed is nearly impossible, at least from the phone. AT&T's lack of investment in data infrastructure there has similar effects to the town's lack of commercial and residential development, leaving the town in a masterfully preserved condition, as if the railroad age never left. Marfa, in fact, was founded as a function of the 1880s railroad boom: It was built to be a water stop for trains to take on water to make it across the next stretch of desert. I often found similarities between the railroad boom and Facebook: The builders of each made great fortunes by connecting with great centralized lines places that hadn't previously been connected, sometimes inventing things, like photo tags or Marfa, that weren't there before.

One night in January 2012, with nothing much else to do, my friends and I walked to an old Ice Plant left over from the railroad days, now turned into an art space, where a well-known artist from New York, Rob Fischer, had assembled a glass house on a trailer and suspended it from the ceiling. He proceeded to roll and swing the house by means of a pulley back and forth from one side of the ceiling to another, sometimes smashing it against the steel beams supporting the building. At one point, as I was videotaping this (old Facebook habits die hard), the house began to swing and roll and shimmy on the pulley ever more violently. At a brief lull in the house's movement, I turned off the camera, thinking I had captured all there was to be seen. Only a few seconds later, the house shifted violently, and one of its glass panes broke loose and slid the length of the house's floor only to crash out the other side, creating a beautiful (and dangerous) cascade of broken glass that fell just feet from where I was standing. Not one of the forty people in the room with cameras had captured that exact moment on video, though it was the unintended climax of the piece.

I think that this may be the truth of these technologies that we carry around: We film and post and read social media constantly in order to capture something, some exciting moment or feeling or experience that we are afraid to miss, but the things about life that we most want to capture may not be, in the end, capturable. And, perhaps, planning and efficiency themselves, the things that technologies like Facebook want to make easy and constant, are not as easily grasped as we think. Because, in all of our newfound efficiencies, what have we lost? What, like the moment at the Ice Plant when the glass shattered, is too unplanned and ephemeral to predict and capture with our technologies? Should we keep trying, or should we take a breath, and let some things go unshared and unrecorded, realizing that this ineffability may be the essence of life itself?

POSTSCRIPT

Thrax96: Are you living in Marfa?

K8che: Yes, are you in Austin?

Thrax96: Yeah.

Thrax96: Should we go in on a yacht?

Thrax96: Like a rapper video yacht

Thrax96: Except we actually own it, unlike rappers who rent it

K8che: Haha

Thrax96: Remember the multiple times we almost had sex?

K8che: Lol

Thrax96: Lol

Thrax96: In the land of the blind, the one eyed man is king.

K8che: Not sure what you mean. Is that a metaphor about you and technology? Like the camera on your iPhone and MacBook and how you were always filming? You were the king.

Thrax96: That was a double entendre.

Thrax96: One eyed man.

K8che: Oh, I get it.

I still think that's a metaphor about technology, I mused after I had signed off. "I'm going to put that in my book."

ACKNOWLEDGMENTS

First, I want to acknowledge my family for their love and encouragement.

I would like to thank everyone on my team at Free Press, including Dominick Anfuso, Daniella Wexler, Carisa Hays, Meg Cassidy, Nicole Judge, and Claire Kelley, for their enthusiasm and support for this book. In particular, I am very grateful to my editor, Alessandra Bastagli, for her great eye, judgment, and editorial vision; and to Melissa Flashman, for being a dauntless, loyal agent and friend.

I would also like to thank all of the friends, artists, writers, and places, many but not all of whom are mentioned in this book, from whom I have drawn inspiration and with whom I have felt connected in the course of my adventures. I am especially grateful to Dana Armstrong for her friendship, to Ashley Nebelsieck for her wit, to Owen for being my true bro, to

ACKNOWLEDGMENTS

Danish Aziz for listening, to Thrax for being there even when he wasn't there, to California for always shimmering off somewhere in the distance, to Baltimore for being my school of hard knocks, to Frank Ocean for being my 2011 muse when I needed one, and to Winter 2012 Marfa for all of its art and light.

Spanish-American Short Story

Studies in the Contemporary Spanish-American Short Story

David William Foster

University of Missouri Press
Columbia & London
1979

Library of Congress Cataloging in Publication Data

Foster, David William.
    Studies in the Contemporary Spanish-American Short
Story.

    Bibliography: p. 123
    Includes index.
    1.   Short stories, Spanish American—History and criti-
cism.   I.   Title.
PQ7082.S5F6   863'.01   79-1558
ISBN 0-8262-0279-9

Chapter 2, "Toward a Characterization of *Écriture* in the Stories of Borges,"
first appeared in *Revista iberoamericana* (No. 100 [1977]); Chapter 4, "García
Márquez and the *Écriture* of Complicity," first appeared in *Studies in Short
Fiction* (16:1 [1979]); Chapter 8, "The *Écriture* of Social Protest in Mario
Benedetti's 'El cambiazo,' " first appeared in *Texto crítico* (No. 6 [1977]);
Chapter 9, "Guillermo Cabrera Infante's *Vista del amanecer en el trópico* and
the Generic Ambiguity of Narrative," first appeared as a review article in
Caribe (No. 3 [1977]).

Preface

This work deals with selected Latin-American writers of short stories and, in the case of each author, with only one or a limited number of texts. No attempt has been made to write a history of the contemporary short story in Latin America or even to deal with a canon of representative authors. Each of the texts studied has been chosen because it is indicative of a facet of the short story that parallels the so-called Latin-American new novel.

The reader may well ask to what extent the issues discussed in this study uniquely differentiate the short story from the novel, whether in universal terms or in terms of forms of Spanish-American fiction. My answer, as the student of the poetics of fiction must agree, is that they do not. No claim is made that the features identified in the chapter titles constitute a structural primer for the Spanish-American short story. It is probable that, from a theoretical point of view, any attempt to define unique structural principles for the short story beyond traditional and vague references to its length would be unsuccessful. More fruitful is to acknowledge in advance that a particular text may be considered to exemplify a particular form of literature and to proceed to detail what is noteworthy about that form or its salient aspect. Such a metatheoretical approach to the Spanish-American short story is the one adopted in this study.

Indeed, in place of an introductory chapter providing the literary historical backgrounds for the texts examined—the evolution of local-color proto-realism into the abstract structures that currently dominate—I have chosen instead to propose an explicit theoretical framework for the study of the texts selected. This framework, which dwells on the concept of narrative *écriture*, establishes a focus whereby the stories are examined as particular strategies in the production of verbal art. For if *écriture* has any one abiding sense, it is that of textual production, a phrase that implies the need to study literature as a problem in defining and evaluating the unique structuring given language and semantics within the context of the ideological postulates with which any text necessarily functions. The Latin-American short story as it is being written today is the response to particular literary traditions, both hemispheric and international. But it is also the response to metaliterary demands that define the goals and the limitations of verbal expression. What this study maintains is that the identification of a range of those metaliterary demands is just as important in terms of current literary scholarship, as the more traditional sociohistorical identification of contributions in terms of constellations of themes and techniques that define a putative intrinsic originality and an extrinsic parallel with international literature. While a historical perspective may suffer, my hope is that the particular structural strategies of the texts described will characterize the contemporary Latin-American short story in a register that, although it may be more audacious, is as equally important as the historical one.

It is easy for a preface to become an apologia for what has not been included. Although some might miss a total characterization of Rulfo's or Cortázar's or García Márquez's stories, and others may wish some other authors had been included, the choices made here have as their best defense what I hope is the reasonableness of the analyses themselves.

A good part of this monograph has grown out of seminars with graduate students, whose forbearance in the evolution of the positions that are taken is greatly appreciated. I am particularly grateful to the assistance of my two research associates, Terry Enfield and René Jara, and, above all, to Roberto Reis, whose chronic dissatisfaction with the limitations of literary criticism has goaded me into whatever precision as rational discourse this study possesses.

D. W. F.
Tempe, Arizona
December 1978

Contents

Spanish-American Short Story

Chapter I.

Introduction:
The *Écriture* of Literary Texts

Isaac Luria declara que la eterna Escritura
Tiene tantos sentidos como lectores.
Cada Versión es verdadera y ha sido prefijada
Por quien es el lector, el libro y la lectura.

(Jorge Luis Borges, "A Manuel Mujica Láinez," in La
moneda de hierro [1976] :49.)

Thus, the distinction between speech and writing becomes
the source of the fundamental paradox of literature: we are
attracted to literature because it is obviously something other than
ordinary communication; its formal and fictional qualities bespeak a strangeness, a power, an organization, a permanence
which is foreign to ordinary speech. Yet the urge to assimilate that
power and permanence or to let that formal organization work
upon us requires us to make literature into communication, to
reduce its strangeness, and to draw upon supplementary conventions which enable it, as we say, to speak to us. The difference
which seemed the source of value becomes a distance to be
bridged by the activity of reading and interpretation. The strange,
the formal, the fictional, must be recuperated or naturalized,
brought within our ken, if we do not want to remain gaping before
monumental inscriptions.

(Jonathan Culler, *Structuralist poetics*, p. 134.)

I

Mid-twentieth-century structuralism is the doctrine that symbolic
phenomena—and natural phenomena given symbolic representation—are characterized by innate and discoverable patterns of
semiotic relationships that hold between constituent elements.
Structuralism has laid claim to a privileged place in contemporary
literary studies because it seeks to establish a model of the system of
literature itself as the external reference for the individual works it
considers. The theoretician moves from the study of language to the
study of literature as a subsystem of symbolic language and seeks to
define the principles of structuralization that operate not only

1

through individual works, but through the relationships among works over the whole field of literature.

At the heart of theories of structuralism is the idea of system, a complete, self-regulating entity that evolves (that is, moves from beginning to end, by transforming or rearranging its features) within its systematic structure. Every literary unit, from the individual sentence to the whole order of words as text, can be seen in relation to the concept of system. To say that a work has structure and that its structure is intrinsic or inherent is to say more than that it has an inner logic. It is to say that the work possesses a unique architecture that both identifies it vis-à-vis all other works and serves as the basis for the integration of all of its elements into a unified systematic whole. The structuralist critic thus sees the work as an assembly of units that exist on several different levels of integration. The act of reading a literary work becomes, in turn, a sort of discovery process whereby we learn to perceive these units first in a linear fashion and then in terms of their abstract pattern of assembly. A literary work is understood when its overall structural integration is recognized.

In literature, there are clearly certain formal or structural features that are basically static, such as the division of the work into parts or the material form of the narrative voice. But as the critic takes up more and more abstract questions of structure, like the relationship between the various characters or the several potential temporal planes of the narrative, it is more difficult to speak of explicit constituents. Ironically, criticism becomes more interesting and rewarding in direct proportion to its treatment of phenomena that are not perceivable to the "ordinary" reader. If criticism is best defended as an accessory tool to the reading of literature, it cannot be satisfied to deal only with aspects of the work readily accessible to the superficial reader. Thus, "higher" criticism emerges not as the *identification* of the elements inherent to a literary structure, but as the *proposition* that certain elements or relationships between them be accepted as existing when, in fact, there is scant overt evidence that it is so. Proposition then becomes *interpretation* in the sense of a unique understanding of the literary work, accompanied by appropriate arguments designed to convince us of its priority over other legitimately possible interpretations.

II

The crucial point of departure for an intrinsic literary criticism is the *textuality* of literature: the fact that it is a text the critic can identify and study. The *texture* confronted by the reader in his initial contact with a work of literature is the most permanent quality of that work.

Texture—the materiality of the text—is, in turn, the manifestation of a series of underlying premises that may be alleged to generate the text and to be the foundation of its nature as literary textuality. *Text* is what we read; *textuality* is the irreducible nature of the literary phenomenon, that is, to say, of its very existence as text; and *texture* is the hallmark of that phenomenon.

The following concepts will be used to illustrate the structure of the contemporary Spanish-American short story.

Écriture. *Écriture* (which is the French equivalent for the more general English word *writing*) refers to the series of structural premises that underlie a literary work as a written text. These premises constitute the abstract or "deep" level of a text, and an adequate structural analysis of a literary work must involve the discovery of the conventions of rules of its underlying *écriture*. The comprehension of any symbolic phenomenon, literary or otherwise, is an abstraction to the extent that it is the abstract organization of overt elements into a code that makes understanding possible. Thus, *écriture* is identified as that abstract level of a literary text where an organizing principle is operant that enables the formulation of a structural code, recoverable by the reader, for the text.

Inscription. Inscription refers to the various material realizations in the text of the underlying principles of *écriture*, that is, their actualization as a literary text. Both text and *écriture* are static phenomena: the text that we read cannot be altered without thereby creating a different text. It is assumed that the *écriture* of a text is also unmodifiable to the extent that it is the abstract formulation that generates the specific text we read. Nevertheless, inscription involves a shifting phenomenon in that when we read a literary text we perceive a range of possible structures and multiple overlapping patterns for the overt elements of that text.

In this way, we observe different potential relationships between the inalterable materiality of the text and the equally static base that, as generating *écriture*, underlies it. Since there are no two readings of a text that are exactly identical, each successive reading, whether by one or several readers, will see the inscription of *écriture* in a different way. Yet no matter how unvarying this abstract level of an underlying text may seem to be, since it is abstract it is only partially accessible for even the most skilled reader. The purpose of the structural analysis of the text becomes then the attempt to formulate as explicitly as possible a description of its abstract generating principles. What is problematical in the process of making such an explicit description is precisely, on the one hand, the distance between multifaceted inscription and, on the other, the *écriture* to be discovered. When we find ambiguity in a literary text, we are identifying that more than one structure holds between the constituent elements of the text. Expressed simply, the primary goal of the sort of criticism proposed here is to postulate ways of seeing literary texts as organized patterns rather than as merely a flow of words with a discrete beginning and ending. Furthermore, that goal should also address itself, if only by implication, to the concern of metacommentary as to criticism's need to discover and reveal such patterns, that is, why are they not self-evident?

III

The *écriture* of a literary text then is roughly analogous to the abstract or deep level that transformational-generative linguistics identifies for languages. By this I mean that, like deep linguistic structures, *écriture*—the deep structure of a literary text—is wholly abstract and only accessible by a theoretical model of reading. This theoretical model, like linguistic analysis, is capable of organizing surface phenomena in terms of an underlying system that provides them with an interdependent order and that explains their structural function.

If the surface phenomena of linguistic utterances possess a semiological importance only in terms of an abstract system that specifies hierarchical and interdependent function, the same may be said about the higher-order discourse structures we call literary texts. Literary structuralism has discovered, along with generative linguistics, that structural units virtually cannot be said to possess independent functional meanings. Rather, this meaning is a correlative of the structural context in which they are ordered. This context can only be detailed fully in abstract terms because of the way in which surface order and relationships fail to be adequately explicit, for cognitive reasons that are not yet comprehensible to us. Thus, when we speak of the need for literary analysis to posit the existence of abstract structures, we are, like the linguist, acknowledging the need to postulate functional relationships between structural components that are not directly apparent superficially.

Nevertheless, and in contrast to colloquial communication, where we assume that the meaning-message and its transmission are primary, literary theory recognizes the premise that meaning, or meanings, is less basic and perhaps even less interesting than the way in which it is realized, structured, and inscribed in the texture of a literary work. What this means as a consequence is that in a literary work, although meaning is not trivial, the form in which it is conveyed is primary, while in colloquial communication the form of communication is relatively unimportant and its meaning is paramount. On this basis, one speaks of the "foregrounding" of the "defamiliarized" language of literary discourse.

The foregoing principles yield the hypothesis that texture—or texturalization, which is the inscription that gives form to a work's *écriture*—is a mark rather than a mirror of meaning. Meaning cannot be presumed to underlie a literary work in the sense of a semantic nucleus to which we gain access simply by peeling away the layers of textual signifiers. Such emphasis on the unavailability of underlying meaning stresses, first of all, the nature of a literary text as verbal artifact and how the uniqueness of the text makes difficult the quest for meaning when the latter is conceived of in strictly communicational terms. The attempt to arrive at a meaning presumed to underlie a text thus becomes an operation that inevitably challenges its status as a literary work, since critical theory begins with the axiom that the impossibility of reductive meaning is an inherent feature of literary texts.

The textuality of the work is what is responsible for making the meaning it seems to be conveying ambiguous or elusive, and we sense the presence of an underlying meaning while direct access to it, nevertheless, remains blocked by the special nature of the literary text. This nature stems from the fact that language functions as a counterpoint (if not, on occasion, an outright challenge) to the conventional expression of meaning via linguistic structures. Colloquial language is conventional, although literary language is not, nor can it be without losing its identity as such. (This is not the place to raise concern over whether it is valid or not that literary language enjoys such a status, an issue that is more germane to a sociopolitical discussion of literary expression.) As a result, it is acknowledged that literary language is in categorical opposition to purely communicational or conventional language. Since it is not conventional, literary language, and the texts that it embodies, breaks with normal linguistic processes such that the resulting work becomes a "difficult" communication. If a literary work is an act of communication, as it has often been called, so much so that a reading in terms of its "philosophical" or "sociopolitical" meaning is virtually inevitable in Western culture, it is a highly problematical act. It is for this reason that the text becomes a linguistic artifact that calls attention to itself as verbal text, and this nature as artifact attracts our most immediate attention as critical readers.

The following diagram portrays schematically the opposition between a model for colloquial communication and one for literary textuality:

Model for Unidirectional Colloquial Communication
Semantics ⟶ Syntax ⟶ Material Discourse

Model for Interdependent Literary Textuality
Semantics ⟷ Syntax ⟷ Material Discourse

In the colloquial model, it is emphasized that one begins with semantic meaning and that the linguistic structures, or the syntax of the language, give material form to this meaning. A material manifestation is what we perceive in the structured sentences of a discourse in a specific language. This manifest level is called the surface structure, since it is what we grasp directly in a linguistic act. In short, one can say that semantics attains, in a unidirectional process, an overt representation via the structuring rules of the syntax of a language.

In place of the model for colloquial communication, I propose a model for literary textuality in which a unidimensional relationship between underlying meaning and surface realization is inadequate for describing literary phenomena. Rather, what we have in the literary model is a circularity between the most immediate level and the most abstract one. Therefore, the constituent elements of noncolloquial discourse serve as much to propose or create meanings as merely to convey them, the latter being the case in colloquial communication. Thus, the linguistic forms of surface structure—words, morphemes, and their syntactic combinations—transmit meanings at the same time that, by virtue of the richness and the openness of linguistic structures, they suggest new meanings in an unending process.

IV

It is possible to state that the mode of texturalization as a working hypothesis of textual analysis is a result of the actualization of a series of principles that can be formulated in abstract terms. (These modes are the textual *style* in the sense of lexical-verbal selection, and *structure* in the sense of the organization of the constituent and conventional material elements of literature, such as tone, narrative person, and devices for metacommentary.) The terms of this formulation must be considered abstract, to be "discovered" by the critic's textual analysis, to the extent that they are not materially present in the work.

These principles, in turn, correspond to an ideology of literature in the sense that they involve a self-concept of the text that comments implicitly on what should or should not be done, what may or may not be done, and what is permissible and not permissible in literary discourse. We can say, therefore, that *écriture* is a point of convergence for the formulation of metatextual decisions that attain material representation in the process of textual inscription. Hence we arrive at the premise that the level of *écriture* mediates between the immediate textuality of a work and its status as an example of the literary phenomenon.

The principles of textual organization are not found on the level of surface structure nor on the level of surface texture. Therefore, a text's materiality, although a concrete manifestation, can be no more than the indirect or oblique representation of its underlying *écriture*. As a consequence, the text will appear to be unstable, fluctuating, and elusive. On the one hand, we experience its extensive richness and density of multiple meanings. On the other hand, we attempt to construct, or reconstruct, the underlying premises that generate its inscription. Reading a text must therefore become a process not of penetrating it in order to attain its alleged abstract meaning, nor of "partaking" indiscriminately of its verbal riches, but of reconstructing its *écriture*. In this way, *reading* comes to mean approaching a text as a dialectic between its *écriture* and the overt features of its inscription. Reading emerges as an ideological process also to the extent that it undertakes the identification of the value principles on which the text is based.

Thus, we have the hypothesis that the *écriture* of a text will be circumscribed by a series of potentialities and typologies that derive ultimately from literary *écriture* as a general culture and linguistic phenomenon. Such a series of principles may be identified in abstract or generic terms since they serve to define that genre of grammatological *écriture* that we call literature. Thus, we may undertake to calculate possible textual *écritures* on the basis of an abstract *écriture* underlying literature as a semiological archiphenomenon. Or we may attempt to understand literary *écriture* as part of a larger field, semiological *écriture*, which is concerned in the last instance with the use of language to generate texts as fundamental artifacts of human culture.

The way in which literary texts are produced—that is to say, the way in which a generating *écriture* motivates their material inscription—is of metaliterary importance. This is so because it indicates the adherence by the writer to a coherent plan that speaks to the issue of the text as text and to how the text is a specific example of literature in a generic sense.

V

The level of abstract *écriture* is subdivided into presuppositions and structure. The presuppositions specify the basic conditions for the generation of the text, that is, its relationship with other semiological and grammatological systems, with sociocultural values, with a general conception of literature, with other specifically linguistic systems. Structure, at least on the level of *écriture*, is the abstract configuration of surface textuality in parasyntactic terms. What this means, when seen in its most basic aspects, is that a literary text is somehow homologous to an elementary linguistic structure, to a "sentence" in the most general sense. Since a spoken utterance has an overt syntactic structure, literary texts likewise possess literary (para)syntax: the structural and hierarchical configurations that we perceive through a formal analysis of its materiality. Structure, on a deep, abstract level, stipulates as a consequence the bases of this material configuration as discourse, a discourse that is coherent to the degree that we recover and formulate—unconsciously as we read, explicitly as we practice serious criticism—these generating bases.

It is necessary that we take into account how the elements of a discourse may be linear, regressive, parallel, redundant and repetitive, antithetical, and a whole host of possibilities that emphasize the manner in which the constituent elements of a text enjoy a configuration or hierarchy of configurations that go far beyond their immediate tactic position in the chain of discourse utterance. An interrelationship characterized as simply tactic loses any real significance alongside the vast potential for abstract and fluctuating configurations that are conceivable in terms of a generating *écriture* whose very nature demands an adequate reading and an adequate criticism. Hence, the structure of a literary work, like the structure of any semiological text, cannot be understood as merely the order of its constituent elements, whether these be directly linguistic or paralinguistic (like, for example, the characters in a story, who on a higher level are as much constituent elements as the words they are seen to speak). Rather, the critical analysis of a literary text can only be valued to the degree to which it puts forth a strategy for the study of the abstract principles and the degree to which it is able to carry out that strategy and expose those principles that in the last analysis control an adequate comprehension of literary discourse.

VI

To illustrate my argument, I will now analyze the microtext "Borges y yo" by Jorge Luis Borges, who is the virtual progenitor of the microtext in contemporary Latin-American literature:

> Al otro, a Borges, es a quien le ocurren las cosas. Yo camino por Buenos Aires y me demoro, acaso ya mecánicamente, para mirar el arco de un zaguán y la puerta cancel; de Borges tengo

noticias por el correo y veo su nombre en una terna de profesores o en un diccionario biográfico. Me gustan los relojes de arena, los mapas, la tipografía del siglo XVIII, el sabor del café y la prosa de Stevenson; el otro comparte esas preferencias, pero de un modo vanidoso que las convierte en atributos de un actor. Sería exagerado afirmar que nuestra relación es hostil; yo vivo, yo me dejo vivir, para que Borges pueda tramar su literatura y esa literatura me justifica. Nada me cuesta confesar que ha logrado ciertas páginas válidas, pero esas páginas no me pueden salvar, quizá porque lo bueno ya no es de nadie, ni siquiera del otro, sino del lenguaje o la tradición. Por lo demás, yo estoy destinado a perderme, definitivamente, y sólo algún instante de mí podrá sobrevivir en el otro. Poco a poco voy cediéndole todo, aunque me consta su perversa costumbre de falsear y magnificar. Spinoza entendió que todas las cosas quieren perseverar en su ser; la piedra eternamente quiere ser piedra y el tigre un tigre. Yo he de quedar en Borges, no en mí (si es que alguien soy), pero me reconozco menos en sus libros que en muchos otros o que en el laborioso rasgueo de una guitarra. Hace años yo traté de librarme de él y pasé de las mitologías del arrabal a los juegos con el tiempo y con lo infinito, pero esos juegos son de Borges ahora y tendré que idear otras cosas. Así mi vida es una fuga y todo lo pierdo y todo es del olvido, o del otro.

No sé cuál de los dos escribe esta página.
(*El hacedor* [Buenos Aires: Emecé, 1960]:50–51.)

The following features of the text must be accounted for in any reasonable analysis:

1. The title of the text is initially misleading and ultimately ironic, for it implies the conjunction of Borges's name with an, as yet, unidentified first-person narrator. Moreover, it evokes intertextually those autobiographical writings wherein the confidant of a public person pretends to reveal to us aspects of the latter's character that he, as a bystander, has had privileged access to. As we shall see, this simultaneously is and is not quite the case with "Borges y yo."

2. The text, seen in terms of the specific verbal structures and the semantic meanings they encode, is characterized by a series of devices that contrast *el otro* (Borges) and *yo*. Stylistically the text depends on linguistic markers to categorize the features attributable to *el otro* and the feature attributable to *yo*: "Me gustan . . ." versus "el otro comparte esas preferencias, *pero* . . ." (my emphasis). Each one of the twelve sentences of the text could be rewritten schematically in terms of this A versus B relationships, and one could study the specific morpho-syntactic markers that identify first A, then B.

For example, it is possible to stress how, despite the apparent primacy given to Borges (the explicit identification by name, the first-place status in the title, the acknowledgment of his importance), the markers related to *yo* not only dominate stylistically but they are also foregrounded by being given sentence-initial placement: "*Yo* vivo, *yo* me dejo vivir, para que Borges pueda tramar su literatura y esa literatura *me* justifica"; "*Yo* he de quedar en Borges (my emphasis); and so forth. While these markers maintain the illusion of two entities, Borges versus *yo*, they are noteworthy for the overt direction of our attention toward the speaker and his "problem"; this emphasis is identifiable in a number of concrete verbal features.

3. We may carry the identification of linguistic features a step further and attempt to classify the concepts related to *el otro* and those related to the anonymous but insistent *yo*. The following is a key passage in this regard: "Me gustan los relojes de arena, los mapas, la tipografía del siglo XVIII, el sabor del café y la prosa de Stevenson; el otro comparte esas preferencias, pero de un modo vanidoso que las convierte en atributos de un actor." Clearly, the odds are against *el otro*: not only does he not have any truly unique preferences, sharing the same ones as the narrator, but his claim to them is *vanidoso* and *de un actor*. This semantic weighting occurs on two levels, both related to the fact that the first-person narrator controls the text and, therefore, our access to the truth concerning *el otro*: (1) he employs prejudicial modifiers in what is ostensibly a neutral characterization (that is, the title does not overtly announce any prejudice toward Borges, and the speaker explicitly disclaims to have any); (2) the narrator, by foregrounding himself, directs our attention away from Borges. See also in this latter regard the first two sentences of the text.

Thus, we have an intersection between, on the one hand, a stylistic patterning that apparently juxtaposes features of A versus B, and, on the other hand, a rhetoric, deriving from the intrinsic nature of the privileged first-person narration that attempts to weight our estimation of the two parties involved. This is, of course, a further intertextual echo of "him and me" narratives in that the narrator, by controlling the discourse situation, can attempt to set the record straight in his favor.

4. The bulk of the text is juxtaposed to the closing sentence, which constitutes an independent paragraph and, hence, suggests a rupture or an antiphony vis-à-vis what has gone before. And, whatever else it may be, the final sentence is an emphatic verbal gesture because it is set off graphically from the rest of the text.

However, it is important to see how this closing statement may be viewed in terms of the overall *écriture* of Borges's microtext. As I have claimed, the text is fundamentally ironic in that it maintains seriously a dichotomy between Borges and the narrator that is literally false, no matter how inviting it may be as a stratagem for self-evaluation and the romantic Doppelgängerei between the artist and the human being.

"Borges y yo" is, to put it bluntly, an ironically self-defeating text, which is one of the hallmarks of Borges's fictions, and it is in these terms that we must view the functional significance of the textual features that I have cursorily enumerated above. For what is involved is a series of false allegations: (1) there exists a person I call Borges and there exists a person I call *yo*; (2) we are to be distinguished by a series of mutually exclusive or at least incompatible features; (3) I yield to Borges, whose writings and fame dominate me, but I go on record as to the differences between us through this text, which I control as first-person narrator; (4) I affirm, if not my autonomy from Borges, my superiority by my values and by my control of the text setting forth the dichotomy "Borges y yo."

All of these allegations are brusquely set aside by the closing line of the text. By confessing that he does not know whether A or B is writing the text, the narrator both contradicts (paradoxically: can self-designated A nevertheless not know if he is A or B?) the dichotomy that he has set out to affirm and undercuts the justification and the advantage of a first-person narrative: behold me versus the other(s). What we have then is an entire textual apparatus that is fundamentally contradictory. As I have maintained, "Borges y yo" not only sets out to juxtapose *el otro* and *yo*, but ostensibly weights the case of the latter through a series of syntactic and semantic markers that constitute the concrete stylistic texture of the narrative. Yet, all of this is denied by the final statement, which so effectively vitiates the distinction the foregoing text was at pains to maintain.

From the viewpoint of my analysis, it is not enough to note the juxtaposition between A and B, between *Borges* and *yo* in the text, nor is it enough to identify the presence of certain stylistic features and a particular narrative voice (as well as other discourse features that one may want to stress). Rather, it is necessary to see the narrative in terms of a specific textual strategy and to see the features of that narrative as functional parts of that strategy, that is, to see the textual features as the reflection of a controlling strategy that we call the text's *écriture* and that those features serve to "inscribe" and give discourse form to. What could be more ironic than a first-person narrator who in the end cannot distinguish himself from his rival as a strategy for signifying the precariousness of the Western tradition's antithesis between the writer as a human being and the writer as a figure of public notoriety (*un actor*)? Or to generate a text that uses a number of rhetorical ploys to enhance A at the expense of B, only to dramatically deny the distinction?

"Borges y yo" is a clever text; it is also a text that is a key to so many aspects of Borges's writings. The sort of analysis that I have proposed focuses on overt stylistic features in order to discover an organizing principle that underlies them and justifies them from the point of view of discourse structure and coherence as functioning elements in a unique literary text.

VII

The concept of *écriture* is admittedly a flexible one, but it is not necessarily eclectic or vaguely defined. Rather than the underpinning for a methodology of textual analysis—and modern criticism is rightly skeptical of programmatic methodologies—it is a way of viewing literary phenomena that attempts to provide a principled basis for explaining the relationship between the structural components of texts. Thus, the analysis of a particular text may focus on one of those components, like plot structure or the role of the reader, that is especially prominent, with the goal of demonstrating how that component in fact achieves its prominence by virtue of its integrated role in the overall structure of the text. By interfacing the concept of *écriture* and certain highly, selectively chosen examples of the Spanish-American short story, my goal is both to validate the way of seeing texts through the concept of *écriture* and to provide some acceptable analyses of important stories. If the latter are reasonably accurate, *écriture* as a metacritical notion, although it will not have been defined in all of its ramifications, will hopefully emerge as a valuable global concept that brings together a number of important emphases in the analysis of literary texts.

Chapter II.

Toward a Characterization of *Écriture* in the Stories of Borges

No hay ejercicio intelectual que no sea finalmente inútil. Una doctrina filosófica es al principio una descripción verosímil del universo; giran los años y es un mero capítulo—cuando no un párrafo o un nombre—de la historia de la filosofía. En la literatura, esa caducidad final es aun más notoria. El Quijote—me dijo Menard—fue ante todo un libro agradable; ahora es una ocasión de brindis patrióticos, de soberbia gramatical, de obscenas ediciones de lujo. La gloria es una incomprensión y quizá la peor.[1]

I

Écriture has yet to become as widely used in Hispanic literary criticism as it has among European theorists and American adherents. Although Buenos Aires has been a focal point for the translation of structuralist writings,[2] it is curious to note the lack of any sustained application of structuralist concepts to the major works of Latin-American literature. A number of critics and journals have shown an interest in the "new criticism," but there continues to be a considerable number of essays in which the use of structuralist jargon is a substitute for the serious assimilation of structuralist models.[3]

Perhaps the foregoing circumstance—to which one might add the relative disinterest among U.S. Hispanists in paying much attention to structuralist theories—explains why a writer like Jorge Luis Borges continues to be approached from the point of view of themes

1. Jorge Luis Borges, "Pierre Menard, autor del Quijote," in *Obras completas* (Buenos Aires: Emecé Editores, 1974), pp. 449–50. All quotes from Borges's works are from this edition, and the pagination is given with the quote.
2. Particularly the materials published by *Nueva Visión* beginning in the mid-sixties.
3. See David William Foster, "La nueva narrativa vista por la nueva crítica," *Nueva narrativa hispanoamericana* 4 (1974):227–50.

and ideas in his works, rather than from the perspectives suggested by the panoply of structuralist concepts. I have written elsewhere of how Borges's stories can be studied as the realization of a structuralist poetics—the sort of program for producing literature, as opposed to studying it, implied by the basic concerns of structuralism.[4] But only a few critics have shown any interest in focusing on Borges through the lens of structuralism. Not surprisingly, the few that have done so are French critics, and Emir Rodríguez Monegal has shown how their partial knowledge of Borges's works or their deficient grasp of Spanish has resulted in some rather curious distortions.[5] Nevertheless, we must give credit to those critics for having studied Borges from perspectives with which a good many English- and Spanish-language critics still seem to be ill at ease.

Écriture is only one of the structuralist concepts that could profitably enrich Borgean criticism. To the best of my knowledge, only three papers have done so. Jaime Giordano includes a discussion of "La escritura del Dios" in a larger—and very important—study on a typology of generational *écritures* in Latin-American fiction.[6] Walter Mignolo and Jorge Aguilar Mora speak of the motif of the book as a principle of *écriture* in "Tlön, Uqbar, Orbis Tertius," although their treatment is vaguely tentative and partial (Borges criticism, even that which subscribes to specific analytical principles, has a tendency to suffer from a mimetic vagueness, a "contamination" by the texts being examined).[7] Noé Jitrik, in one of the best studies available on Borges, studies the intertextuality of *Ficciones*.[8] Although he does not base his study on the concept of *écriture*, it is clear that his interest in the underlying structures of *Ficciones* and in the implied principles concerning the production of literary texts is, in effect, the

4. David William Foster, "Borges and Structuralism: Toward an Implied Poetics," *Modern Fiction Studies* 19 (1973):341–51.

5. Emir Rodríguez Monegal, "Borges y nouvelle critique," *Revista iberoamericana* No. 80 (1972):367–90.

6. Jaime Giordano, "El nivel de la escritura en la narrativa hispanoamericana contemporánea," *Nueva narrativa hispanoamericana* 4 (1974):299–306. See also his "Forma y sentido de 'La escritura del Dios' de Jorge Luis Borges," in *Revista iberoamericana* No. 78 (1972):105–15.

7. Walter Mignolo and Jorge Aguilar Mora, "Borges, el libro y la escritura," *Caravelle* No. 17 (1971):187–94.

8. Noé Jitrik, "Escructura y significación en *Ficciones*, de Jorge Luis Borges," in *El fuego de la especie, ensayos sobre seis escritores argentinos* (Buenos Aires: Siglo XXI Argentina, 1971), pp. 129–50. Note should also be taken of the study by Nicolás Rosa, "Borges y la ficción laberíntica," in Jorge Lafforgue, *Nueva novela latinoamericana* (Buenos Aires: Editorial Paidós, 1969–1972), 2:140–73, although it is not always clear when he is speaking of *écriture* and when he is speaking of thematics.

attempt to lay bare the motivating *écriture* of a clearly unified body of texts.[9]

II

This chapter concerns itself with a partial characterization of *écriture* in a few of the major stories by Borges. No pretense will be made that a generic *écriture* has been discovered that could be used in a valid *lecture* ("reading") of his fiction as an organic whole. Nevertheless, it should be clear that the stories have been chosen for their exemplariness in the canon of Borges's writings and that, although the emphasis is on the motivating principles in individual texts, one could legitimately attempt to undercover a macro-*écriture*. Although the stories are taken from Borges's four major collections,[10] they are not treated in a chronological fashion.[11] (There is a large bulk of criticism on Borges, much of it dating from the sixties. Some of it is repetitive and superficial, while the best of the studies have dealt in excellent detail with such questions as themes, influences, philosophical matters, and, more recently, with Borges's explicit ties to the *Nueva narrativa hispanoamericana*. However, although some of the truly exceptional papers deal with issues raised in this article, to the best of my knowledge none has attempted to approach Borges in terms of a coherent *écriture*.)

The following principal characteristics of a Borgean *écriture* will be discussed:

1. Literary texts are paradoxical attempts to record accurately the vastness of the universe and the chaos of personal experience: the latter are infinite, while the literary text is finite. Thus, the text can only lapse into a partial record of the chaotic and infinite, or it can betray them by imposing a perceptual order that is merely solipsistic and convenient. In either case, the literary text is, as pragmatic

9. Although David Maldavsky does not specifically discuss *écriture*, his paper on the semiotic structure of Borges's stories follows Barthean concepts closely: "Un enfoque semiótico de la narrativa de J. L. Borges," *Nueva narrativa hispanoamericana* 3:2 (1973):105–19.

10. Jorge Luis Borges, *Ficciones* (Buenos Aires: Sur, 1944); *El aleph* (Buenos Aires: Emecé, 1949); *El informe de Brodie* (Buenos Aires: Emecé, 1970); *El libro de arena* (Buenos Aires: Emecé, 1975).

11. Ana María Barrenechea, "Borges y la narración que se autoanaliza," *Nueva revista de filología hispánica* 24 (1975):515–27, speaks of what is one essential feature of this *écriture*—the self-conscious text; see point 6 in the following description of the premises of an *écriture* for Borges's fiction. Nevertheless, Barrenechea does not avail herself of the concept of *écriture*, and the autoanalytic features she describes are attributed to a new concept of narrative rhetoric, which limits them to the superficial level of compositional strategies rather than assigning them to the level of abstract *écriture* where they belong by virtue of their text-generating nature.

message, rendered useless. In "El aleph," the pretense of synthesis unsuccessfully masks the chaotic and the unorderable, with ironies generated by a bewildered and frustrated narrator.

2. The falseness of system is inevitable. A "philosophy" imposes a perceptual order that makes the banal dreadful (the incidental and the insignificant are given a "transcendent meaning" within a vast and overwhelming interpretation of the universe) and makes the dreadful banal (the infinite and the chaotic, the contemplation of which are occasions for profound horror for finite man, are rendered banal by their reductionist assimilation to a mere man-made [para] philosophy). In "Tlön, Uqbar, Orbis Tertius," the narrator, after reviewing these complementary processes in terms of one gratu- itous attempt at the formulation of an all-encompassing system, seeks to neutralize the dreadfulness of the system and its menacing impositions on reality by retreating into a banal literary activity as gratuitous as the system itself.

3. Man inevitably flees from "alephic" truths that he believes to have discovered. Man seeks the aleph, the perfect synthesis of the infinite and chaotic universe. Although such alephs do not and cannot exist, man seeks them and, on occasion, believes to have discovered them. Philosophic systems are quasi-alephs, while liter- ary texts are pseudo-alephs). Their pseudo-ness is made apparent by the inevitable irony of the text that arises naturally from the paradox of the text—the finite versus the infinite—and predisposes the appropriate *lecture* of the text. There are, however, alephs (necessarily false) in the form of objects: a point in space ("El aleph"), a book (the one sought in "La biblioteca de Babel" and one encountered in "El libro de arena"). The contemplation of the pre- sumed aleph, because it confronts finite man with a vision of the elusive universe—a vision he may attempt to see as a synthesis, but which he discovers to be only an unordered and explosive jumble of details—compels him to flee the vision it offers to him. In "El libro de arena," the narrator is obliged to "lose" the alephic book in the Biblioteca Nacional in order to rid himself of an object that com- promises his sanity because it provides him (or so he believes) with knowledge that is more than his human limitations can handle. If the text is alephic, it too must be rejected, for it lies beyond our ability to comprehend or to assimilate it. In "La escritura del Dios," the discovery of the *écriture*—the coincidence of the word for Holy Writ in Borges's story and the critical term for underlying structur- ing principles can be taken as indicative of a homology between literary texts and other Gnostic systems—leads not to articulation, but to silence. Either the discovered truth is too profound to be spoken or it is too banal, but with the equalizing consequences of

silence that denies the text and the text on the text (that is, Borges's story on the nature of the Writ).

4. Contemplation of the infinite (because it is horrible) or its pseudo-synthesis as system (because it is trivial) may threaten the sanity of the individual and compel him to back away into an equalizing refusal to contemplate the universe and to reduce it to a distorting system. But adherence to system can trap man into believing that he is fending off the atrocity of reality by reducing it to an interpretation: the interpretating system, then, becomes a false security that leads us not away from the horror of the infinite and the chaotic, but right back to it. The system cannot avoid the chaos that it vainly pretends to reduce to ordered cosmos. In "La muerte y la brújula," the gratuitous system elaborated by the overly intellectual detective is matched by a reality equally gratuitous and transcendentally insignificant. But, rather than warding off reality by his systematic interpretation, Lönnrot abets it: in the end, the systematic solution meant to prevent a crime only results in that crime, which happens to have Lönnrot as its victim.

5. The necessary confrontation with an excess of meanings is the unavoidable result of the inadequacy of any and all ordered perceptions of experience. Thus, no event or circumstance possesses any one meaning, but rather there is a fundamental ambiguity induced by the vast range of possibilities of the infinite and the chaotic. Of course, the impossibility of unitary meaning is only a problem when man feels compelled to demand it of his own experience and of the universe that he confronts. Unfortunately, this demand is a veritable mania of man and, as a consequence, is the direct cause of his despairful frustration with meaningful systems and, on a more specific level, with literary texts. To the extent that texts aspire to be meaningful systems, they are caught in the same trap of distorting and biasing the infinite by reducing it to the finite system of the bounded text. The attempt to penetrate the mystery of meaning can, therefore, only result in a compounding rather than a resolution of the fundamental ambiguity of experience. In "El aleph," the attempts to penetrate the mystery of meaning only result in a text that oscillates between the partial and trivial detailing of the infinite (reductionist representation) and the distorting interpretation of meaning (falsificational representation). In both cases, the meaning of what is being presented remains as elusive and impenetrable—as unmeaningful, in the last analysis—as it was prior to the attempts at exegesis. In "Guayaquil," the problem of the ambiguity of meaning that underlies a number of Borges's stories becomes the major structural principle of the text, and event and text are homologized in terms of their fundamental overmeaningfulness/unmeaning-

fulness. Such too is the case with "La escritura del Dios." The literary text interprets a text that in turn interprets event and circumstance, with a regressive reduction and falsification of meaning.

6. All of the foregoing not withstanding, man's mania for interpretive systems justifies those systems and justifies literature. The proper emphasis of a concern for philosophy and literature must fall not on the adequacy of the systems/texts generated, but on their diversity and the inherently curious nature of their details. Both the diversity and curious detail make up the fabric of civilization and are worthy of study to the extent that they bespeak a fundamental "drive" of mankind. But at the same time, the richness of this fabric is, in the final analysis, only a repetition of the infinite and chaotic vastness of the universe. Once we admit the proliferation of systems and texts, we are according recognition to a process that can only have as its final outcome the exact repetition of the universe, as in "El Congreso." The result is a distracting but deliberate proliferation of both circumstantial detail and intertextual references (direct allusions to and accommodation of universal literary phenomena) in Borges's writings. [12] In "Tlön, Uqbar, Orbis Tertius" or in "El aleph," to give only two outstanding examples, there is a wealth of minutiae that threaten to choke the presentation of interpretive systems: this detail is only a partial repetition of the

12. Although Tzvetan Todorov's chronological limitations on the fantastic would seem to exclude Borges, many of his comments on that genre fit the Argentine perfectly. Moreover, the closing words of his study are directly pertinent to the aspect of Borges's *écriture* that I have been describing:

[. . .] Words are not labels pasted to things that exist as such independently of them. When we write, we do merely that—the importance of the gesture is such that it leaves room for no other experience. At the same time, if I write, I write about something, even if this something is writing. For writing to be possible, it must be born out of the death of what it speaks about; but this death makes writing itself impossible, for there is no longer anything to write. Literature can become possible only insofar as it makes itself impossible. Either what we say is actually here, in which case there is no room for literature; or else there is room for literature, in which case there is no longer anything to say. As Blanchot writes in *La Part du Feu*: "If language, and in particular literary language, were not constantly advancing toward its death, it would not be possible, for it is this movement toward its impossibility which is its condition and its basis."

The operation which consists of reconciling the possible with the impossible accurately illustrates the word "impossible" itself. And yet literature exists; that is its greatest paradox.

Tzvetan Todorov, *The Fantastic: A Structural Approach to a Literary Genre* (Ithaca, N.Y.: Cornell University Press, 1975 [originally published in French in 1970; English translation originally published in 1973]), p. 175.

infinite and chaotic features of the universe that cannot, after all, be subordinated in an ordered fashion. Thus, the pretense of order in, for example, a literary text is directly refuted by the inevitable disorder of the details it is forced to include in its commitment to systematizing them.

The foregoing principles of *écriture* in a series of Borges's stories can easily be mistaken for thematic paradigms. To a certain extent, they are aspects of theme in his texts, for they are the questions of meaning to which the texts attempt to refer. But one will note that meaning as such is not being referred to: the universe is not reduced to an interpretation, unless it is the impossibility of reducing the universe to an interpretation.[13] Rather, these paradigms that appear to be so close to thematic aspects deal with the processes of meaning, and, therefore, they have a direct bearing on the structural, textual, representation of meaning and on its limitations. In this sense, then, they deal with the principles concerning meaning with which Borges's stories operate. The stories proceed to be stories—literary texts that function in terms of the Western tradition of literature as representation, signification, and interpretation—on the basis of these principles.

Is there any principled way of distinguishing between an author's thematics and structural primes that constitute his textual *écriture*? Probably not in any absolute fashion. On the one hand, there is a merger between thematics and *écriture* when the former deals precisely with the latter. That is, when the texts of an author like Borges deal implicitly and often overtly with the question of writing and reading texts. How to deal with literature—its mysteries and its highly problematic nature—is one of the constant topics of Borges's stories. On this basis, there is a natural coming together of thematics and the principles of textual production.

But, from another point of view, one that concerns a metatheory of literary scholarship, principles such as those I have outlined belong to the domain of thematics or to the domain of *écriture*, depending on the way in which the critic views textual analysis. If texts are analyzed primarily for their content, a principle like the "opacity" of writing will be looked upon as a *topos* to be fleshed out in terms of a narrative pattern. But if texts are considered examples of structured discourse, the same concept will be considered as a problem that impinges upon the mechanics of textual production,

---

13. For a presentation of thematic, symbolic constants in Borges's work, see Emir Rodríguez Monegal, "Símbolos en la obra de Jorge Luis Borges," *Studies in Short Fiction* 8 (Winter 1971):64–77. Carter Wheelock comes closer to bridging the gap between themes and *écriture* in *The Mythmaker: A Study of Motif and Symbol in the Short Stories of Jorge Luis Borges* (Austin: University of Texas Press, 1969).

with inevitable repercussions in the way in which the narrative discourse exists as a material text. It is only in this way that the principles I have presented can be viewed to concern the very nature of narrative structure in Borges's *ficciones*.

The actual material aspects of the stories—questions of rhetoric, style, form, narrative voice (it is no accident that so many of Borges's stories contain first-person "ignorant" or "bewildered" narrators), and even to a great extent more specific issues of theme and commonplaces—are the direct reflection of the underlying structuring principles detailed above. The latter define the nature of experience upon which literature is based, and, therefore, they in turn define the nature of literature, providing the immediate parameters of accomplishment and failure as literature on which the texts must base themselves. In *The Fantastic*, Todorov distinguishes between interpretation and "poetics," which, as he uses it, is clearly a category, if not a synonym, of *écriture*:

> Two different objects, *structure* and *meaning*, are implied here by two distinct activities: *poetics* and *interpretation*. Every work possesses a structure, which is the articulation of elements derived from the different categories of literary discourse; and this structure is at the same time the locus of the meaning. In poetics, one rests content with establishing the presence of certain elements within a literary work. But it is possible to achieve a high degree of certainty, for such knowledge may be verified by a series of procedures. The interpretive critic undertakes a more ambitious task: that of specifying—or it might be said of *naming*—the work's meaning. But the result of this activity cannot claim to be either scientific or "objective." There are, of course, some interpretations that are more justified than others; but none can assert itself as the only right one. Poetics and criticism are therefore but instances of a more general opposition, between science and interpretation. This opposition, both terms of which, moreover, are equally worthy of interest, is never pure in practice; only an emphasis on one or the other activity permits us to keep them distinct. . . .
> We have therefore tried to undertake a study of themes [= semantic constants] which would place them on the same level of generality as poetic rhythms; with that end in view we have established [for the study of fantastic literature] two thematic systems without claiming thereby to give an interpretation of these themes, as they appear in each particular work.[14]

14. Todorov, *The Fantastic*, pp. 141–43.

III

"El aleph," if it is possible to accord any one of the texts of the Borges canon such a privilege, may be considered a pivotal story within the framework established in the preceding section. Perhaps more explicitly than any other story, "El aleph" addresses itself to the problems of literary composition and to the limitations on man's ability to organize, to synthesize, and to capture via the faulty medium of language knowledge and experience (which, perhaps, may be only aspects of the same phenomenon). Unquestionably, the aleph—the object in space that synthesizes all spatial and temporal points: the perfect order of the cosmic chaos—is the goal of the multiple quests to subject the universe to an objective synthesis.

In Borges's story, there are three "alephic" quests, all of which are doomed inherently to failure. All three quests are linked to an *aleph* that is understood to contain them, an *aleph* that is denounced as the mere simulacrum of a true aleph. The three quests are: the attempts by the narrator-participant—Borges the character—to describe the "essence" of his dead love, Beatriz Viterbo; the attempts by her cousin, Carlos Argentino Daneri, to compose a long poem, *La tierra*, "una descripción del planeta" (p. 619); and, finally, the attempts by Borges the narrator (that is, the character becomes author) to describe the nature of the *aleph* that is presented to him: its consequences, its falseness, and the frustration of all three attempts at possession through writing. Writing—the composition of the poem, the composition of the story *El aleph*, the composition of a satisfactory eulogy of Beatriz Viterbo—is seen as an act of possession, that is, promises, falsely to be sure, to enshrine event and knowledge in an alephic monument. This monument will withstand the erosion of both faulty memory and the annihilating qualities of the reality beyond the object that moves by indifferently as a chaotic jumble of events.

Against the three attempts at synthesis are pitted those circumstances that lead to their negation:

Reality Itself (the inevitable chaos of time and event): La candente mañana de febrero en que Beatriz Viterbo murió, después de una imperiosa agonía que no se rebajó un solo instante ni al sentimentalismo ni al miedo, noté que las carteleras de fierro de la Plaza Constitución habían renovado no sé qué aviso de cigarrillos rubios; el hecho me dolió, pues comprendí que el incesante y vasto universo ya se apartaba de ella y que ese cambio era el primero de una serie infinita (p. 617; the opening words of the text).

Individual Memory (note the irony of the following passages): Cambiará el universo pero yo no, pensé con melancólica vanidad; alguna vez, lo sé, mi vana devoción la había exasperado; muerta yo podía consagrarme a su memoria, sin esperanza, pero también sin humillación [. . .]. De nuevo aguardaría en el crepúsculo de la abarrotada salita, de nuevo estudiaría las circunstancias de sus muchos retratos. Beatriz Viterbo, de perfil, en colores; Beatriz, con antifaz, en los carnavales de 1921; la primera comunión de Beatriz; Beatriz, el día de su boda con Roberto Alessandri; Beatriz, poco después del divorcio, en un almuerzo del Club Hípico; Beatriz, en Quilmes, con Delia San Marco Porcel y Carlos Argentino; Beatriz, con el pekinés que le regaló Villegas Haedo; Beatriz, de frente y de tres cuartos, sonriendo, la mano en el mentón . . . (pp. 617–18; closing ellipsis in text. The reader, confronted with this enumeration of fragments of Beatriz, naturally wonders if the narrator has any clear image of the woman.)

. . . Nuestra mente es porosa para el olvido; yo mismo estoy falseando y perdiendo, bajo la trágica erosión de los años, los rasgos de Beatriz (p. 628; the closing words of the text).

Language-Literature as Language (the linear nature of language versus the simultaneous nature of experience and event it hopes to report): Arribo, ahora, al inefable centro de mi relato; empieza, aquí, mi desesperación de escritor. Todo lenguaje es un alfabeto de símbolos cuyo ejercicio presupone un pasado que los interlocutores comparten; ¿cómo transmitir a los otros el infinito Aleph, que mi temerosa memoria apenas abarca? Los místicos, en análogo trance, prodigan los emblemas: para significar la divinidad, un persa habla de un pájaro que de algún modo es todos los pájaros . . . [etc.]. Quizá los dioses no me negarían el hallazgo de una imagen equivalente, pero este informe quedaría contaminado de literatura, de falsedad. Por lo demás, el problema central es irresoluble: la enumeración, siquiera parcial, de un conjunto infinito . . . Lo que vieron mis ojos fue simultáneo: lo que transcribiré, sucesivo, porque el lenguaje lo es. Algo, sin embargo, recogeré (pp. 624–25; the impression is inescapable that the last sentence is spoken in vain).

Alephic Symbols (of which language and literature are specific subcategories): Yo querría saber: ¿Eligió Carlos Argentino ese nombre, o lo leyó, *aplicado a otro punto donde convergen todos los puntos*, en alguno de los textos innumerables que el Aleph de su casa le reveló? Por increíble que parezca, yo creo que hay (o que hubo) otro Aleph, yo creo que el Aleph de la calle Garay [where Argentino's house, now torn down to make way for a dairy-products store, containing the Aleph was located] era un falso Aleph (p. 627).

These quotes reveal a sense of futility in the face of the impossibility of achieving a satisfactory, alephic synthesis. Moreover, there is a pronounced irony that stresses the realization of the limitations on comprehension ("pensé con melancólica vanidad") while undermining those few assertions of partial accomplishment ("Algo, sin embargo, recogeré").[15] It is unclear whether we are to see Borges the character as consciously ironizing his own statements or whether it is a function of the *écriture* of Borges (the latter manifesting itself via rhetoric of irony). Borges's text is, therefore, its own metacommentary. As a narrative, it comments on the failure of the three attempts at controlling knowledge; but as a literary text, it enunciates clearly its own principles of *écriture* to the effect that it too is a failure in its description of failure: "este informe quedará contaminado de literatura, de falsedad" (hence, Borges's use of the word *ficción*— from the verb *fingir*, "to feign"—as the generic description of his literature), "yo mismo estoy falseando y perdiendo. . . ."

This irony—and it is often clearly an irony directed against the narrator—describes Borges's failure to retain the image of Beatriz and his failure to illustrate adequately the nature of the aleph, in which he sees one hope of experiencing a totalizing image of the woman. It is also present in his comments concerning Carlos Argentino and the cold and distrustful relationship that exists between the two men. Perhaps, in part, the narrator's irony is meant to be taken as a conscious instrument of his description of Carlos Argentino. However, that irony often serves more to characterize negatively the narrator (he communicates a marked jealousy of Argentino, both as a man and as a writer) than his antagonist. The result, then, is the impression that the narrator is describing a relationship that he is unable to control, and, as a consequence, it is difficult if not impossible for him to have the correct perspective. In other words, the relationship between Borges the character and Carlos Argentino is one more phenomenon that eludes an adequate synthesis. From the point of view of narrated action, the relationship concerns the common memory of Beatriz, a competition for literary recognition and the sharing of the aleph that Carlos Argentino shows to Borges. In all three cases, the narrative is marked by an undercurrent of incomprehension and failure: both men have lost Beatriz irremediably; Borges loses out to Argentino in a literary context; Argentino loses the aleph, partly because Borges refuses to assist him in the effort not to have the house in whose basement the aleph exists destroyed.

The aleph, by the same token that it is the structuring motif for the *écriture* of the text in the sense that it bespeaks the illusion of synthetic knowledge, is on the level of narrated action also the central point of reference for the relationship between the two men.

15. Concerning Borgean narrators, see Thomas E. Lyon, "Borges and the (Somewhat) Personal Narrator," *Modern Fiction Studies* 19 (1973):363–72.

It is introduced at first in an oblique fashion, when Borges describes the poem Argentino is composing; he learns later that the poet's "source of information" is the secret aleph. Thus, in retrospect the narrator's description of that poem becomes significant, for aside from his transparent disdain for personal reasons, it is clear that he sees the poem as a tedious miscellany:

> Otras muchas estrofas me leyó que también obtuvieron su aprobación y su comentario profuso [that is, Argentino's own]. Nada memorable había en ellas; ni siquiera las juzgué mucho peores que la anterior. En su escritura habían colaborado la aplicación, la resignación y el azar; las virtudes que Daneri les atribuía eran posteriores. Comprendí que el trabajo del poeta no estaba en la poesía; estaba en la invención de razones para que la poesía fuera admirable . . . . (pp. 619–20)

Only when we learn, along with the narrator, that Argentino Daneri is describing what he sees via the aleph do we understand that his poem is tedious because it is a verbatim record of the infinite chaos of reality. The aleph does not serve to synthesize or to abstract the universe, but only to present it in its awesome detail before our eyes. When Borges finally contemplates the aleph, his own description cannot therefore be anything more than an overwhelming jumble of unordered detail rather than the longed-for synthesis. Covering more than two pages of text in the original edition, the narrator's description concludes with the following note of near-hysteria:

> . . . vi el Aleph, desde todos los puntos, vi en el Aleph la tierra, y en la tierra otra vez el Aleph y en el Aleph la tierra, vi mi cara y mis vísceras, vi tu cara, y sentí vértigo y lloré, porque mis ojos habían visto ese objeto secreto y conjetural, cuyo nombre usurpan los hombres, pero que ningún hombre ha mirado: el inconcebible universo.
> Sentí infinita veneración, infinita lástima (p. 626; the antecedent of *tú* is not given, although it may be Beatriz Viterbo).

At issue is not the aleph itself nor, on the level of the narrated action, is it the probable deception on Argentino's part. (Therefore, we have here the *venganza* whereby the narrator refuses to cooperate in saving the house from demolition and his assertion that the aleph is false at the end of the text.) Rather, of note from the point of view of *écriture* is the flotsam and jetsam of detail. A plethora of detail is characteristic of Argentino's poem, and it is characteristic of the narrator's evocation of Beatriz and his description of the aleph and the vision it brought him. Moreover, the inevitable detail of the former aspects, necessarily embedded in the text that sets out to recall them, is complemented by the abundance of detail on the level of the text itself. That is, Borges as narrator-character embeds the detail of narrated action within the context of a description that is in itself excessively detailed (the best example of this is the ironic pedantry of the *Posdata del primero de marzo de 1943* [pp. 626–28]). The result is a form of extensive, if not infinite, regression, where the abundance of details figuratively barricades any access to a synthetic notion of what is going on. We are confronted with a morass of details that is a faithful image of the aleph; as such, we are effectively denied access to a totalizing comprehension of what is going on. To extract any sort of meaning from the text itself it is necessary to block out a major share of the details. Alternately, we can extract some vague idea of the literary feud between the two men, some idea of Beatriz and her relationship to the two, some idea of the concept of the aleph and its presence in world literature. What we are hard put to grasp is an ultimate interpretation that integrates these disparate elements and their burden of detail into a unifying meaning. It is in this sense that the aleph, rather than being a symbol for the "meaning" of text, is the organizing motif for an *écriture* that structures the very way in which we are expected to experience the text.

IV

Where "El aleph" points, in the end, to the impossibility of literature as organized and privileged knowledge, "Guayaquil"—for this reader the best of the eleven stories in *El informe de Brodie*—is structured in terms of the principle of ambiguity.

In linguistics, which has defined the concept systematically, ambiguity refers to the circumstance whereby a given linguistic utterance represents more than one abstract syntactic-semantic structure. An utterance is ambiguous if it has several discrete meanings, each of which is recoverable (that is, identifiable) once we relate concrete utterance with abstract syntax-semantics. If the discrete meanings are not recoverable, the sentence is vague rather than ambiguous. In Borges's *écriture*, reality, experience, and event are all essentially ambiguous to the extent that they have a multiplicity of meanings, which may be both complementary and contradictory. Hence, stories like "La muerte y la brújula" or "El jardín de senderos que se bifurcan" have no stable one-to-one relationship between meaning and its manifestation. In the case of the former story, the false meaning, which is the product of the rational detective's intellectual exercises, demands that reality conform to it; such a conformity becomes, in turn, the trap that assassinates the smug detective. Since every phenomenon has multiple meanings that do not fall in order of priorities, their importance and identification as meanings are denied.

As a result, the basic structure of "Guayaquil" is that of a text that describes the mystery of a mystery. On the level of narrated action, the story concerns a contest between two historians to examine and report a new document regarding the mysterious encounter between Bolívar and San Martín that led to the latter's abdication as leader of the revolutionary forces in the Andean area. On the level of text, the description fails to explain the mystery of why the native historian (once again, Borges as narrator-character) yields to the foreign historian (whom the narrator describes in the most disdainful of terms as a seedy Jew). Narrated action and text parallel each other: a mysterious encounter that evokes a past mysterious encounter, remote in time and place; and a text that fails, as the foreign historian prophesies will also be the case with the newly discovered document, to explain the fundamental mystery of the encounter. It should be noted that the document in question, like the text itself, deals with the details of the encounter. However, the document was written by Bolívar, the victor in that remote contest of personalities, while the text "Guayaquil" is narrated ("written") from the viewpoint of the vanquished Borges. On all these levels and in all these details, the *écriture* of the text permits the representation of the external configurations of event, such as language and, in the case of the narrator, unspoken thought. But significantly, what is denied is what must be the fundamental imperative for a literary text: the revelation, the disambiguation, of meaning.

This basic *écriture* of the story—the text that will provide the details of event and circumstance but not its essential meaning—is given its most direct form in the use of the bewildered first-person narrator.[16] As in "El aleph," there is a plethora of details and a paucity of meanings, and there is a first-person narrator who accumulates details but who is incapable of finding in them a satisfactory meaning. This is immediately clear from the opening of the text:

> No veré la cumbre del Higuerota duplicarse en las aguas del Golfo Plácido, no iré al Estado Occidental, no descifraré en esa biblioteca que desde Buenos Aires imagino de tantos modos y que tiene sin duda su forma exacta y sus crecientes sombras, la letra de Bolívar.
>
> Releo el párrafo anterior para redactar el siguiente y me sorprende su manera que a un tiempo es malencólica y pomposa. Acaso no se puede hablar de aquella república del

16. Concerning the narrative voices of the stories in *El informe de Brodie*, see Owen L. Kellerman, "Borges y *El informe de Brodie*: juego de voces," *Revista iberoamericana* No. 81 (1972):663–70. The story "Guayaquil" is studied by Lanin A. Gyurko, "Rivalry and the Double in Borges' 'Guayaquil,' " *Romance Notes* 15:i (1974):1–10.

Caribe sin reflejar, siquiera de lejos, el estilo monumental de
su historiador más famoso, el capitán Korzeniovski, pero en
mi caso hay otra razón. El íntimo propósito de infundir un
tono patético a un episodio un tanto penoso y más bien baladí
me dictó el párrafo inicial. Referiré con toda probidad lo que
sucedió; esto me ayudará tal vez a entenderlo. Además,
confesar un hecho es dejar de ser el actor para ser un testigo,
para ser alguien que lo mira y lo narra y ya no lo ejecutó. (p.
1062)

Of course, the narration in retrospect of the event does not lead
the narrator to the comprehension that he seeks. Indeed, the act of
narration leads to a denial of writing. Such a detail, on the level of
narrated action, is the result of having been deprived by the foreign
historian of the opportunity to examine the Bolívar letter and to
prepare a historical essay on it. But on the level of the text, the denial
is equally the result of having failed with his own document concerning the conflict with the foreign historian over the original
historical document. The historian's prophecy that Bolívar's letter
will turn out to be, if not inauthentic, at least a useless falsification of
the meeting between the two independence leaders is also implicitly
a characterization of Borges's own text concerning the nature of the
meeting between the two historians. The closing words of the text
emphasize the homology between the two documents and the two
encounters, and the sense of futility of the text and its consignment
to the fire serve as a double reinforcement of the silence of the
mystery of meaning:

Releo estas desordenadas páginas, que no tardaré en entregar
al fuego. La entrevista había sido corta.
Presiento que ya no escribiré más. *Mon siège est fait.* (p. 1067)

The role of the first-person narrator is more subtle than has been
indicated. If there is a separation of levels between narrated action
and text, between historical document and text, between a previous
encounter and a document concerning that encounter, and a recent
encounter that repeats its historical antecedent in more than one
detail (for example, the description of Zimerman, the foreign historian, recalls the details of the standard portrait of Bolívar [pp. 1063–
64]), there is also a separation of levels for the narrative voice. On
the level of the text as we have characterized it, the narrative voice
embodies the underlying *écriture* concerning the frustrating inaccessibility of meaning. But on the level of narrated action—the action
that allows the text to reflect upon the action itself and that embodies
in its structure the nature of the action (mystery, bewilderment, and
silence)—the narrator confesses to a deliberate irony and falsification of the encounter. Irony is the reward of the individual who

possesses the true meaning of an event and who underlines the ignorance or the partial knowledge of the other participants in it. The narrator mocks Zimerman's imperfect Spanish, his ludicrous dress and manners (the latter a parody of the servile Jew), and his frequent confusion concerning basic details: ("—¡Mi primer error, que no será el último! Yo me nutro de textos y me trabuco; en usted vive el interesante pasado" [p. 1064]. "—En materia bolivariana (perdón, sanmartiniana) su posición de usted, querido maestro, es harto conocida" [p. 1065]). The narrator's irony pretends to discredit Zimerman in the former's own eyes and to underscore the pathos of his having been defeated by this clearly inferior outsider. But irony too is the direct result of the use of an unreliable first-person narrator. Borges the author establishes an ironic distance between his knowledge of the pathetic self-pity of Borges the narrator and his clearly limited, self-knowledge. On both levels, irony serves to give form to the *écriture* of "epistemological" mystery and bewilderment and of textual inadequacy.

Of course, it is the ultimate realization of the inadequacy of his own knowledge that forces the narrator to confess to a deliberate pathos. He recognizes that he is, in turn, the victim of Zimerman's own irony ("Sospecho que el error fue deliberado" [p. 1064]), and that he is necessarily engaged in a falsification through the act of writing that he hoped would suffice as an explanation: "Lo sucesivo del lenguaje indebidamente exagera los hechos que indicamos, ya que cada palabra abarca un lugar en la página y un instante en la mente del lector . . ." (p. 1064).

The sum total of the characteristics of "Guayaquil" that have been described stresses a self-defeating text. Trivia abounds but meaningful substance is absent. There is an irony that as the pretense of knowledge is ironized, there is a homology between personal and historical event in which both are cloaked in the same mystery of significance, thus becoming bewildering events. Finally, the narrator's official version (which in turn is homologous with the "official" version of Bolívar contained in the pivotal document) is less of an interpretation of meaning than it is a self-justification and a record of defeat. All of these factors that make up the overall configuration of the text, and in terms of which the specific thematic and stylistic features must be understood, are in turn the direct consequence of the underlying *écriture* of "Guayaquil." This *écriture* is unquestionably the result of Borges's conception of narrative art. Part of the conversation between Borges the narrator-participant and Zimerman provides one excellent characterization of such a conception, as well as reminding us once again of the homology between the historical document and the literary text at hand, between *corresponsal* = *lector* and Bolívar = *escritor-narrador*:

> —Que sean de puño y letra de Bolívar—me contestó—no significa que toda la verdad esté en ellas. Bolívar puede haber querido engañar a su corresponsal o, simplemente, puede haberse engañado. Usted, un historiador, un meditativo, sabe mejor que yo que el misterio está en nosotros mismos, no en las palabras.
>
> Esas generalidades pomposas me fastidiaron y observé secamente que dentro del enigma que nos rodea, la entrevista de Guayaquil, en la que el general San Martín renunció a la mera ambición y dejó el destino de América en manos de Bolívar, es también un enigma que puede merecer el estudio.
>
> Zimmerman respondió:
>
> —Las explicaciones son tantas. . . . (p. 1066)

"Tlön, Uqbar, Orbis Tertius" begins by referring to a conversation between Borges and Bioy Casares regarding first-person narrators who may deceive rather than serve as reliable participant-reporters. But "La escritura del Dios" concerns the attempt to arrive at interpretive meaning, a meaning that we are told is attained but that the narrator refuses to share with the reader, thereby vitiating the rationale of his text. Such a denial simply masks the fact that a meaning has not been attained, or that it cannot be expressed in human and linguistic terms, which is the same as not having achieved it. Clearly, there is a continuity between these stories, where one moves from the inaccessibility of meaning, to the multiplicity of meaning, to the attendant inability to communicate meaning, to the subsequent denial of meaning. Although such a continuity may not constitute the one, overwhelming *écriture* in Borges's fictions, it is undeniably a ubiquitous principle for a wide variety of texts that extend from *Ficciones* to his most recent stories.

V

To study all of Borges's fictions comprehensively would result either in a superficial survey of the dozens of titles he has published or in a compendium that would unconsciously challenge the extensive pedantry of sections of "El inmortal," "El aleph," and "Pierre Menard." It is questionable whether any criticism can successfully portray the entire corpus of an author's work within a single framework. The premise of this study is that criticism can only predispose us toward an appropriate and adequate reading of an author's writings, and that a satisfactory description of a limited number of works is more valuable than brief references to many works or to a total analysis that overwhelms the works themselves. The concept of *écriture* implies a concept of *lecture*, and, as Jitrik has attempted to demonstrate, it also implies a concept of *trabajo crítico* (a term that he prefers to *crítica* because of the latter's suggestion of judgment and interpretation). In any event, there is the unmistakable understanding among contemporary practitioners of literary commentary that the one legitimate goal of criticism is to identify the rules, the principles, the premises that make literature possible. Rather than provide the reader with facile, tranquilizing interpretations of a literature that is both difficult and disturbing, the critic, in the final analysis, can only pretend to have elaborated partially on Borges's own words in the "Prólogo" to *El informe de Brodie*, They must be read as a summary characterization of his *écriture* as well as of the fundamental enigma of the very texts themselves:

> He intentado, no sé con qué fortuna, la redacción de cuentos directos. No me atrevo a afirmar que son sencillos; no hay en la tierra una sola página, una sola palabra, que lo sea, ya que todas postulan el universo, cuyo más notorio atributo es la complejidad. Sólo quiero aclarar que no soy, no he sido jamás, lo que antes se llamaba un fabulista o un predicador de parábolas y ahora un escritor comprometido. No aspiro a ser Esopo. Mis cuentos, como los de las Mil y Una Noches, quieren distraer o conmover y no persuadir. (p. 1021)

Chapter III.

Rulfo's "Luvina" and Structuring Figures of Diction

I

If one accepts Roland Barthes's and Jacques Derrida's concept of *écriture*, then we can arrive at a number of immediate consequences for the study of literature:

1. Literature is, above all else, written texts that do not have the transparency of spoken language vis-à-vis the "world/reality of reference." Moreover, written language, insofar as literature is concerned, is not simply a transcription of spoken language. Literary texts are uniquely self-conscious written artifacts whose "rhetoric" corresponds to highly structured organizing principles.

2. The proper study of literature is not interpretation, at least wherever this term refers to "getting at" a reductionist, translinguistic meaning that lies beyond the language structures themselves. Meaning, if it does exist at all, is not independent of linguistic structures, which cannot—at least in literature—be seen as arbitrary symbolizations of an absolutely accessible meaning. Furthermore, meaning must not be seen as a static object to be attained through the dissolution of linguistic-literary structures. Rather, meaning is a dynamic process, and the legitimate analysis of a literary text, instead of substituting for that text an independent, interpreted meaning, involves the study of the activities of meaning that occur within a text. Literary texts are ambiguous, polysemous, and circumscribed by the profoundly frustrating limitations of human communication. Thus, the structure of a literary text constitutes an active network of meaningful elements, rather than a veil that can be safely rended: rending the veil destroys meaning itself.

3. The elements of a literary text—form, style, rhetoric, themes, point of view, techniques, and so on—must be seen as a dialectic whole.[1] This whole, in turn, is animated by (or is the textual realization of) underlying principles that define its boundaries and limita-

---

1. Gérard Genette, *Figures*, see particularly volume 3. Genette, within a structuralist perspective, is mainly concerned with the interplay between structure and rhetoric in the novel.

tions as a literary text and that set in motion the processes of meaning that give the text its linguistic richness and engage our interest in experiencing it as literature. Those principles, abstract in nature but totalizing in the way that they account for the overall configuration of a text, are what we call *écriture*.

4. *Écriture* can be approached in one sense as the attempt to identify for a literary text a limited number of motivating, "generating," principles that can be used as points of reference in describing the dialectic wholeness of that text.

II

"Luvina," one of the principal stories—the most commented and anthologized—of *El llano en llamas* is typical of Rulfo's fiction. It entails the strange, almost eerie imprecision of place and time; the combination of an omniscient narrator with a quoted narrator who frequently remains unidentified and whose words are often introduced without any clear transition from those of the third-person narrator; the depiction of a circumstance and events (often skeletal) that remain mysterious in the absence of a clear "explanation" on the part of the narrator; the sense that somehow the story involves a "trap" for the reader to the extent that there is a major feature that he must figure out for himself if he is not to remain completely confused.

Whether or not these features constitute the much vaunted "magical realism" of the *nueva narrativa* is somewhat of a moot point. What they do constitute is a well-defined texture for the stories in which, despite the words and sentences of the text, the reader is permitted only a tenuous grasp of what is being told to him. That is, Rulfo's stories maximize the inherent ambiguities of language and of discourse (here, literary texts). Or to put it differently, the factual imprecisions and the lack of "adequate" explanations and interpretations enhance a conception of literature as the interplay of signs, while denying them the opportunity to congeal into the fixed, transparent orders of texts conceived of as messages, interpretations, and documents. Rulfo's literature reminds us so much of the traditional, hackneyed *costumbrista* literature that has remained so common in a self-consciously Mexican literature. His works include such elements as the language of the people that could almost serve the purposes of dialect studies, the evocation of specific Mexican landscapes, the narrative actions that seem to be taken from historical and sociological casebooks, thus making Rulfo's fiction distinctively and unmistakably Mexican. But despite the frequent critical emphasis on this identification, it remains a superficial one, for these thematic and stylistic constants are conjugated in narrative structures that separate them dramatically from pseudo-documentary *costumbrista* prose, with its stress on an "interpretation" of *el ser mexicano*, and turn them into the material elements of an interplay of ambiguous meaning. To this extent, the most viable approach to Rulfo's fiction must stress the productive interplay of variable meaning, rather than the reductionist interpretations that substitute for the richness of the literary text as anemic, nonliterary message.

In "Luvina," the richness of the literary text derives from two principles of *écriture* that serve as the underlying, generative basis for the story. Identification of these principles enables us to understand the text's organization and to justify individual compositional details. These two principles are (1) the juxtaposition of alternate "versions" of circumstance and event via transformations of the rhetorical formula *"no A, sino B"* and the related grammatical structure *como si fuera*, and (2) the illusion of communication through conversational dialogue.

The formula of contradiction, *"no A, sino B,"* is a venerable staple of literary rhetoric and is recognized to have enjoyed particular prominence in Renaissance poetry.[2] Yet, it is an integral part of the most colloquial of discourse, and I found it useful in characterizing *écriture* in both sections 1 and 2 at the beginning of this chapter. The following examples are some of the occurrences of the formula to be found in "Luvina."

1. Dicen los de Luvina que de aquellas barrancas suben los sueños; pero yo lo único que vi subir fue el viento. . . . (p. 94)[3]
2. Dicen que porque arrastra arena de volcán; pero lo cierto es que es un aire negro. (pp. 94–95)
3. . . . Dicen los de allí que cuando llena la luna, ven de bulto la figura del viento recorriendo las calles de Luvina, llevando a rastras una cobija negra; pero yo siempre lo que

2. Elsewhere I have studied its use as a structuring principle in a major Renaissance poem; see my article "Formulaic Structure in Garcilaso's 'A la flor de Gnido,' " *Language and Style* 4 (1971):144–52.

3. All quotes are from the 7a edition of *El llano en llamas* (México, D.F.: Fondo de Cultura Económica, 1965), where the story appears on pp. 94–101. All unbracketed ellipses in the quotes are Rulfo's. Lida Aronne Amestoy examines the text in "México. Juan Rulfo: *Luvina*," in her *América en la encrucijada de mito y razón* (Buenos Aires: Fernando García Cambeiro, 1976), pp. 138–44. Her interest in the monograph is in how myth is given shape in the contemporary Latin-American short story, and the following is her key observation concerning "Luvina": "El cuento entraña una magnífica objetivación de las profundas heridas del alma latinoamericana" (p. 142). She recognizes the use of contrasts in the story but does not focus on them from any point of view other than the thematic.

llegué a ver, cuando había luna en Luvina, fue la imagen del desconsuelo . . . siempre. (p. 97)

4. Es la costumbre. Allí le dicen la ley, pero es lo mismo. Los hijos se pasan la vida trabajando para los padres como ellos trabajaron para los suyos y como quién sabe cuántos atrás de ellos cumplieron con su ley . . . (p. 102)

5. San Juan Luvina. Me sonaba a nombre de cielo aquel nombre. Pero aquello es el purgatorio. (p. 104)

The last example is in a certain sense a synthesis of the others; it comes less than half a page before the conclusion of the text. We see that two "versions" of Luvina are being juxtaposed (A versus B). One is a false image of the town that the unidentified speaker—a drunk who is apparently addressing a man younger than himself in a small bar, the latter on his way to Luvina to assume the same position as schoolteacher that the older man had once held—rejects in favor of an image based on his own bitter, disillusioning experience. The false image consists of various claims made by the natives of Luvina (examples 1, 2, 3, and 4) and an idealization that is incorrect (example 5).

In terms of the speaker as he addresses his silent interlocutor, the image of Luvina that he acquired through suffering and despair— the loss of his illusions as a young schoolteacher, the presumed loss of his family, the physical and spiritual privations of life in Luvina— is more accurate than the image that is rejected. Regarding the meanings brought into play, Rulfo structures the drunken and broken man's anti-eulogy of Luvina around two possible images, one false and one authentic in terms of direct, human experience.

A structuring on the basis of the "no A, sino B" (for example, "no lo que ellos dicen, sino lo que yo vi/supe/sentí") establishes a larger network of meaning than if the man were simply to describe his own image of Luvina without reference to any other one. Moreover, the implied dialogue of the story suggests a juxtaposition of innocence versus experience, of youth versus maturity, of ideals versus cynicism. The man ostensibly addresses himself to a younger man who is setting out to repeat the experience of the former. The implication is that he possesses or will soon possess only the false image, but that in time he will reject the false impression and will adopt the accurate if despairful one: " 'Usted ha de pensar que le estoy dando vueltas a una misma idea. Y así es, sí señor . . . Estar sentado en el umbral de la puerta, mirando la salida y la puesta del sol, subiendo y bajando la cabeza, hasta que acaban aflojándose los resortes y entonces todo se queda quieto, sin tiempo, como si se viviera siempre en la eternidad. Eso hacen allí los viejos' " (p. 101).

III

The second rhetorical formula that serves as a principle of *écriture* in "Luvina," functioning in conjunction with the one just described, is the syntactic construction *como si fuera*. There must be at least a dozen examples of this formula in the eleven pages of the text:

1. Ya lo verá usted. Se planta en Luvina [el viento] prendiéndose de las cosas como si las mordiera. (p. 95)
2. Y sobran días en que [el viento] se lleva el techo de las casas como si se llevara un sombrero de petate, . . . (p. 95; this example follows the first one immediately)
3. Ud. verá eso: aquellos cerros apagados como si estuvieran muertos y (p. 95)
4. a Luvina en el más alto, coronándolo con su blanco caserío como si fuera una corona de muerto . . . (p. 95; this and the preceding example form a single sentence)
5. Y se fue [el arriero], dejándose caer por la cuesta de la Piedra Cruda, espoleando sus caballos como si se alejara de algún lugar endemoniado. (p. 98)
6. Pero hubo un momento en esa madrugada en que todo se quedó tranquilo, como si el cielo se hubiera juntado con la tierra, aplastando los ruidos con su peso . . . (p. 100)

This formula too expresses a contrast or juxtaposition, although it is not as explicit as in the case of "*no A, sino B*." In the latter, both possibilities are directly stated. However, in the case of *como si fuera* the contrast is between a literal or normal meaning, implied by the overall semantics of the utterance, and an alternative meaning introduced by *como si*. What is more, although the alternative meaning is meant to replace the original one as somehow more accurate or complete, it is introduced by a syntactic construction that overtly identifies it as hypothetical, contrary-to-fact or potential. If there is a contradiction, it is between a negated fact and an affirmed contrary-to-fact. Thus, in example 3, we "know" that the *cerros* are not dead, but by saying that it is as if they were does, in fact, affirm that such a hypothetical fact has a greater weight as a phenomenological reality: the reality of the mind's eye of the speaker is more important than the literal reality that others might see.

In example 1, the wind, rather than just being a natural circumstance, is seen as a wild beast. One should note that several of the examples are preceded by the phrase that stresses what the young interlocutor will see: the higher perception that will replace obvious reality. To this extent, the *como si fuera* figure is an adjunct of the "*no A, sino B*" formula. Although they may operate differently, they function homologously: *no A, sino B*/[*no es como A, sino es*] *como si fuera* B (the brackets enclose the segment of the formula that does not appear explicitly but is understood by the normal semantics of the context). Once again, we are obliged to confront an interplay of multiple meanings, to the extent that the ones that are promoted, so to speak, are metaphoric and highly personal. Instead of reality, we witness the overpowering and anguished memory of an individual for whom experience has transformed Luvina, and all that is associated with it, into a destructive hallucination of which drunkenness is the principal indicator:

> —Me parece que Ud. me preguntó cuántos años estuve en Luvina, ¿verdad . . . ? La verdad es que no lo sé. Perdí la noción del tiempo, desde que las fiebres me lo enrevesaron; pero debió haber sido una eternidad . . . Y es que allá el tiempo es muy largo. Nadie lleva la cuenta de las horas ni a nadie le preocupa cómo van amontonándose los años. Los días comienzan y se acaban. Luego viene la noche. Solamente el día y la noche hasta el día de la muerte, que para ellos es una esperanza. (p. 101)

IV

The second structuring principle of *écriture* in "Luvina" is the illusion of dialogue.[4] Not all dialogue is necessarily communicative. Some dialogue is phatic and serves more to promote human solidarity than to convey messages. But all dialogue is, by definition, an act involving the interplay of speaker(s) and hearer(s), even when the latter do not become speakers. In Rulfo's story, there is the illusion of dialogue: a man, drunk and presumably older, interacts with a young man who is about to go to Luvina to assume the duties of a schoolteacher, just as the former had done years before. The older man tells the younger one about Luvina and the disastrous effect it has had on his life. Thus, his words communicate information, advice, and, above all, a warning that prophesies a repetition of frustration and despair: "Usted lo verá ahora que vaya" (p. 103, along with similar phrases elsewhere). The following quotations indicate that a dialogue is taking place:

1. —Ya mirará usted ese viento que sopla sobre Luvina. (p. 94)
2. El hombre aquel que hablaba se quedó callado un rato mirando hacia afuera.
   Hasta ellos llegaban el sonido del río pasando . . . (p. 95)
3. Luego, dirigiéndose otra vez a la mesa, se sentó y dijo:
   —Pues sí, como le estaba diciendo. (p. 96)
4. Me parece recordar el principio. Me pongo en su lugar y pienso . . . Mire usted, cuando yo llegué por primera vez a Luvi-

---

4. Concerning the rhetoric of dialogue in Rulfo's stories, see Pilar Martínez, "Técnica del 'testigo-oyente' en los monólogos de Rulfo," *Anales de literatura hispanoamericana* Nos. 2–3 (1973–1974):555–68.

na . . . ¿Pero me permite antes que me tome su cerveza? Veo
que usted no le hace caso. Y a mí me sirve mucho. Me alivia.
(pp. 97–98)
5. " . . . Pero mire las maromas que da el mundo. Usted va para
allá ahora, dentro de pocas horas. Tal vez ya se cumplieron
quence años que me dijeron a mí lo mismo: 'Usted va a ir a San
Juan Luvina'. (p. 103)
6. "Pues sí, como le estaba diciendo. . . ." Pero no dijo nada. Se
quedó mirando un punto fijo sobre la mesa [. . .].
El hombre que miraba a los comejones se recostó sobre la mesa
y se quedó dormido. (p. 104; these are the closing words of the
text.)

Although the text is interspersed with information provided by an
omniscient narrator (for example, the closing words just cited),
there is no reason to believe that he is the drunk's interlocutor.
Rather, the *usted* of the old man remains unidentified and unspeak-
ing. As a consequence, there is every reason to believe that he does
not exist, that the old man is speaking not to a second party but to
himself as a young man about to set out for Luvina. Rather than
implying necessarily a cycle of human experience, whereby the
young follow in the footsteps of the old and are forewarned of their
impending loss of innocence and the affliction of drunken despair,
the dialogue points to the Doppelgängerei of memory that allows us
to juxtapose one level of experience and consciousness with
another. Like the A and B of the formulas discussed previously,
these two levels are set against one another, only for the former to be
rejected for its innocence and the latter accepted with bitter—and
drunken—resignation. Example 4 is perhaps the first real indication
that the man is speaking to himself, and the suspicion is only
confirmed by example 5, where the old man clearly sees the other as
himself a decade and a half ago.[5]

Thus although there is no real dialogue, there is communication:
the communication of one man's soul with itself in the attempt to
sort out and to alleviate the overpowering burden of memory. In one
sense, the interplay of meanings in "Luvina" is denied any communicational function: the speaker's words fall on no ears anxious
for the information and wisdom they pretend to convey. But as the
characterization of a soul so confused and anguished by the experience implicit in the words the old man speaks, his is indeed a

5. The identification of the nature of the old man's words is not original.
Carlos Blanco Aguinaga has already observed that "el diálogo es ya, como
siempre en Rulfo, monólogo ensimismado." See his "Realidad y estilo de
Juan Rulfo," *Revista mexicana de literatura* 1:1 (1955):59–86. My description,
rather than simply interpretive, concerns the structuring principles of the
narrative as verbal texture.

communication in which the self attempts to label and to interpret what it has experienced. The interplay of meanings, enhanced by an *écriture* based on juxtaposition and opposition, underlines the dreadful profundity of that experience: "En esa época tenía yo mis fuerzas. Estaba cargado de ideas . . . Usted sabe que a todos nosotros nos infunden ideas. Y uno va con esa plasta encima para plasmarla en todas partes. Pero en Luvina no cuajó eso. Hice el experimento y se deshizo . . . " (p. 103).

V

An interpretation of "Luvina"—the reductionist extraction of an inevitable nonliterary meaning—might stress the town as a figure of the mythic Hades from which the Orphic speaker returns to tell his tale of despair. The interpretation might stress the presence of a human cycle of youthful optimism and mature disillusionment, embodied in the narrator and to be reembodied in his shadowy interlocutor (or embodied in the two stages of the one self that speaks). It might emphasize the social implications of the story: the hundreds of Mexican hamlets forgotten by the self-congratulatory and self-perpetuating institutionalized "revolutionary" party, and the bitterness of being a schoolteacher, "one who forms the young," in such an environment. It might also stress the existential and psychoanalytic implications of the speaker as an example of Doppelgängerei. Undoubtedly, there are many interpretations for "Luvina," and attaching meaning(s) to a literary work is concomitant with the act of reading.[6] However, an analysis of the *écriture* of "Luvina" as it is reflected in a few strategic examples of textual rhetoric provides not for its interpretation but a characterization of the rules, the principles of the text that makes a sense of meaning possible and that explains the function of the concrete elements of the text itself. The latter are elements that constitute our most immediate experience in the reading of literature and the only access we have to whatever we believe the text means to us.

6. See, for example, Graciela B. Coulson, "Observación sobre la visión del mundo en los cuentos de Juan Rulfo: a propósito de *Talpa* y *No oyes ladrar los perros*," *Nueva narrative hispanoamericana* 1:2 (1971):159–66. Some of the most questionable interpretive comments on "Luvina" are to be found in Hugo Rodríguez Alcalá, *El arte de Juan Rulfo: historias de vivos y difuntos* (México, D.F.: Instituto Nacional de Bellas Artes, Departamento de Literatura, 1965), pp. 45–60; and see, in particular, his "Digresión," pp. 50–51.

Chapter IV.

García Márquez and the *Écriture* of Complicity: "La prodigiosa tarde de Baltazar"

I

García Márquez's enormous popularity has not as of yet become a controversial issue among critics. These critics, however, can be categorized into two groups: the ones who attribute García Márquez's success in both his novels and short stories to his superior manipulation of the structures of the *nueva narrativa* (structures that essentially demand an experienced reader),[1] and the ones who see the sales of García Márquez's works as directly proportional to his clever revival of some of the hoariest tricks of the old-time storyteller—what in American culture has been called the teller of tall tales.[2] Certainly, there is a world of difference between García Márquez's essentially "accessible" stories and those of Carlos Fuentes, Julio Cortázar, or Juan Carlos Onetti, where the inexperienced reader is often unaware of what is happening in the narrative. But, by the same token, novels like *Cien años de soledad* or stories like those of *Los funerales de la Mamá Grande*, despite all their surface "charm" and their apparent appeal to the tradition of the skillful raconteur, do involve complex literary structures that permit a profound appreciation of their narrative art to only a reader familiar with the features of the new novel. For example, although García Márquez's stories on "local" Latin-American themes may remind one superficially of the *costumbristic* tradition best exemplified by the Colombian Carrasquilla or the Argentine Payró, features of *Cien años de soledad* like the motif of the undeciphered manuscript are in the best tradition of the contemporary Latin-American "novelist's novel."

Nevertheless and in spite of the questions concerning García

1. Josefina Ludmer, *Cien años de soledad: una interpretación* (Buenos Aires: Editorial Tiempo Contemporáneo, 1972).

2. Ricardo Gullón, *García Márquez o el olvidado arte de contar* (Madrid: Taurus Ediciones, 1970).

Márquez's fiction that the preceding preoccupations imply, there is in reality very little actual criticism of what a proper *lecture* of his fiction should be. That is, given the concrete features of his narratives, what is the legitimate process of decipherment that they demand? The principles of a proper lecture are, it has been maintained, inherent in the textual principles of a work of literature, and lecture is the reader's proper perception of the text's *écriture*. In other words, we need to analyze the relationship of the reader to a narrative that the text implicity calls for on the basis of its *écriture*. Here, I will discuss one of García Márquez's short stories that identifies this particular relationship by characterizing it as an *"écriture* of complicity."

II

The nature of the author-reader relationship in "La prodigiosa tarde de Baltazar"[3] is immediately evident from the title of the story: the use of the adjective *prodigiosa* establishes a confidential relationship between author and reader that the character named does not enter into.[4] This is so because, in the first place, *prodigiosa* is not likely to figure in the lexicon of a provincial Colombian artisan, at least not with reference to a noun such as *tarde* (although it may occur with reference to human nouns within certain contexts). In this sense, a linguistic token is used to refer to an individual that that individual would not himself be likely to use. As we shall see, this sort of particularizing language is characteristic of the text on a larger level. In the second place, *prodigiosa* is used ironically, or at least in a way that does not quite fit the circumstances and events described. Baltazar's afternoon is prodigious in what he has accomplished artistically and the nobility with which he handles himself in the confrontation with the town's unpleasant big shot: Montiel's son asks Baltazar to build a bird cage, and Baltazar builds an elaborate one that is truly the work of a master carpenter; the town doctor offers to buy it at a handsome price, but Baltazar tells him that he promised it to Montiel's son; however, when Baltazar takes it to Montiel's house, the father, to punish his son (whom he obviously considers spoiled and effete), refuses to honor the commitment; Baltazar magnanimously gives the boy the bird cage, despite the

3. García Márquez, "La prodigiosa tarde del Baltazar," in *Los funerales de la Mamá Grande*, 6th ed. (Buenos Aires: Editorial Sudamericana, 1969), pp. 63–74.

4. The only other intrinsic study on this story is Rosa Boldori de Baldussi, "Estructura y estilo en 'La prodigiosa tarde de Baltazar,' " *Revista de literaturas hispánicas* No. 10 (1970):18–32. Boldori's study is essentially a line-by-line explication of the text, with very little in the way of synthetic structuralist commentary.

father's enraged protestations and assurances that he will not pay the man; to save face, Baltazar pretends to his friends that he has been paid magnificently and treats them all to a ruinous night on the town.

Thus, in the final analysis, Baltazar's prodigious talent has been "wasted" in that (1) he has worked so hard for no material return, so much needed by him and his hard-pressed wife (he ignores his regular work to devote himself completely to the *furor poeticus* that inspires his creation of the bird cage); (2) the bird cage becomes a symbol of his humiliation before Montiel's family: his nobility in giving the bird cage away is considerably diminished by the narrator's references to the boy's ingratitude and the fact that, after all, he has used Baltazar in the same way that his bullying father would; (3) the "party" for his friends with his presumed profit forces him to lose his watch and to have his shoes stolen as he lies on the street in a drunken stupor. The closing words of the text both underline the disaster that his work of art has brought him and stress the complicity that the narrator demands of the reader in viewing the story not from the barely self-conscious perspective of the character, but from the ironically superior one of that narrator:

> Había gastado tanto, que tuvo que dejar el reloj como garantía, con el compromiso de pagar al día siguiente. Un momento después, desparrado por la calle, se dio cuenta de que le estaban quitando los zapatos, pero no quiso abandonar el sueño más feliz de su vida. Las mujeres que pasaron para la misa de cinco no se atrevieron a mirarlo, creyendo que estaba muerto. (p. 74)

Baltazar's degradation could not be more complete. To put it in the melodramatic terms that the story seems to call for, it is all the result of his misguided artistic endeavors. Note that the text establishes three levels of perspective, only the latter one of which is that of the author and the reader-accomplice: (1) the "documentary level" of what happens in terms of undisputed fact—this would best be characterized as the perspective of Baltazar's wife; (2) the level of Baltazar's fantasy; and (3) the level of narrator's organization of the representation of circumstances and events and of the texture of his reporting. On the first level, Ursula, who like the eponymic matriarch of *Cien años de soledad*, sees the idealistic fantasies of her menfolk in terms of bedrock practicality. The second level, that of Baltazar's fantasy, includes the "sueño más féliz de su vida," induced perhaps by a combination of satisfaction over his artistic creation, the nobility of his act in the face of Montiel's meanness, pride over what the town believes to have been his success in getting money out of Montiel for an extravagant bird cage, and the drunken revery that, for the first time in his life, he indulges in. On the third level, Baltazar is depicted as a fool (albeit a noble and honest one) whose artistic pretensions lead him not to acclaim and economic success, but to the debauchery of his revery, placed in the same paragraph in effective counterpoint with his wife's thoughts: "Alguien le dijo que su marido estaba en el salón de billar, loco de felicidad, brindando cerveza a todo el mundo, pero no lo creyó porque Baltazar no se había emborrachado jamás" (p. 74).

In sum, the narrative *écriture* of the story leaves no room for ambiguity. There is a clear and effective attempt on the part of the narrator to establish several levels of perspective for the events described in the story and to weigh one of them—the one that is assignable to the narrative voice—as superior in the extent of what it is able to report and as ironic because of the counterpoint that it establishes between the others and its own, which supersedes them, as it were. Returning to the adjective *prodigiosa*, while the adjective, were they to use it, may fit both Ursula's view of the bird cage (she is proud of it and suggests shrewdly to Baltazar how to sell it) and Baltazar's own humble pride, it is used ironically by the narrator (and the title of a text may be considered the narrator's keynote) to stress the miserable level of frustrated aspirations that Baltazar more properly belongs to. (For example, Baltazar dreams of making a fortune in fantastic bird cages, only to be humiliated by Montiel's refusal to honor the commission his son gave the man.) This is nowhere more brought out than when Baltazar faces his friends after being rebuffed by Montiel. Whatever pride he had in his work of art in his magnanimity toward Pepe Montiel is dispelled by the manner in which he is unconsciously forced to accept pride for a lie, for his friends are more impressed by the sum he is supposed to have received from Montiel than by what he is personally proud of:

> En el salón de billar recibieron a Baltazar con una ovación. Hasta ese momento, pensaba que había hecho una jaula mejor que las otras, que había tenido que regalársela al hijo de José Montiel para que no siguiera llorando, y que ninguna de esas cosas tenía nada de particular. Pero luego se dio cuenta de que todo eso tenía una cierta importancia para muchas personas, y se sintió un poco excitado.
>
> —De manera que te dieron cincuenta pesos por la jaula.
>
> —Sesenta—dijo Baltazar.
>
> —Hay que hacer una raya en el cielo—dijo alguien—. Eres el único que ha logrado sacarle ese montón de plata a don Chepe Montiel. Esto hay que celebrarlo.
>
> Le ofrecieron una cerveza, y Baltazar correspondió con una tanda para todos. Como era la primera vez que bebía, al

anochecer estaba completamente borracho, y hablaba de un
fabuloso proyecto de mil jaulas de a sesenta pesos, y después
de un millón de jaulas hasta completar sesenta millones de
poses. (p. 73)

III

Turning to the specific question of how the *écriture* of complicity is
actually inscribed in the story's narrative texture, the preceding
passages exemplify the principal linguistic marker of the narrator's
involvement of the reader in a level of complicitous knowledge at
the expense of the actors in the narrative, who are barely aware of
the events in which they are involved, much less the "meaning" of
them.[5] This marker is the verbal formula "A pero B." More specifically, including the abstract performative verb (given here in brackets) that characterizes the narrator's control over the account of
event, that formula is "X creía/pensaba/decía A, *pero* [yo digo que
más bien] se trata de B." Close scrutiny of this particular structure
within the text reveals the following occurrences:

1. [Baltazar] tenía . . . una expresión general de muchacho
   asustado. Pero era una expresión falsa. (p. 65)
2. . . . [Baltazar] vivía con Úrsula desde hacía cuatro
   [años] . . . y la vida le había dado muchos motivos para estar
   alerta, pero ninguno para estar asustado. (p. 65)
3. [Pero] ni siquiera sabía que para algunas personas, la jaula
   que acababa de hacer era la más bella del mundo. Para él,

5. Note should be taken of René Jara's characterization of the narrator in
Cien años de soledad; he bases his comments on the opening sentence of the
novel:

La primera comprobación [sobre la primera frase de la novela] que salta
a la vista es que el juego de los niveles cronológicos obliga a situarse en
una superficie imaginaria, que, en vez de invitarnos a comprender, nos
exige una incorporación en un todo que es coherente desde la partida
porque está tensado desde el futuro. La visión desde arriba que adopta el
narrador implica un dominio del mundo que garantiza la existencia ar-
mónica de un totalidad en que el tiempo es un más allá del tiempo, un
presente eternizado que nos compromete porque nos incluye.
Una segunda comprobación es que el narrador posee la memoria ab-
soluta del cosmócrata omnisciente, del poseedor del conocimiento por
excelencia. El cáracter imperativo de la forma "había de recordar" revela
su complacencia en la vuelta de lo idéntico que podemos comprobar
fácilmente en una lectura rápida de la novela. Esto no significa que el
narrador sea un enemigo de la historia. Su regocijo, como puede com-
probarse por la frase final de la obra, proviene del carácter severo, ad-
monitorio, ejemplarizador que le asigna a la fabulación. . . .

In René Jara and Jaime Mejía, *Del mito en García Márquez* (Valparaíso, Chile:
Ediciones Universitarias de Valparaíso, 1972), pp. 14–15.

acostumbrado a hacer jaulas desde niño, aquel había sido apenas un trabajo más arduo que los otros. (p. 65)

4. [Ursula] estaba disgustada porque su marido había descuidado el trabajo de carpintería para dedicarse por entero a la jaula. . . . Pero el disgusto se disipó ante la jaula terminada. (p. 66)

5. En verdad, José Montiel no era tan rico como parecía, pero había sido capaz de todo por llegar a serlo. (p. 69)

6. Baltazar no era un extraño en la casa de José Montiel. En distintas ocasiones . . . había sido llamado para hacer trabajos de carpintería menor. Pero nunca se sintió bien entre los ricos. (p. 70)

7. Nada ocurrió en aquel instante, pero Baltazar se sintió como si le hubieran abierto la puerta del baño. (p. 71)

8. Hasta este momento pensaba que había hecho una jaula mejor que las otras. . . . Pero luego se dio cuenta de que todo eso tenía una cierta importancia para muchas personas. . . . (p. 73)

9. Todos brindaron por la salud de Baltazar, por su suerte y su fortuna, y por la muerte de los ricos, pero a la hora de la comida lo dejaron solo en el salón. (p. 73)

10. Alguien le dijo [a Ursula] que su marido estaba en el salón de billar, loco de felicidad, brindando cerveza a todo el mundo, pero no lo creyó porque Baltazar no se había emborrachado jamás. (p. 74)

11. Un momento después, despatarrado por la calle, se dio cuenta de que le estaban quitando los zapatos, pero no quiso abandonar el sueño más feliz de su vida. (p. 74)

It is not necessary for these examples to manifest the same identical syntactic structure. Example 3 is presented as having the *pero* clause first: other examples (although none are given) might use *sino* (a syntactic synonym of *pero*), *aunque*. Or the A/B order may be observed, but *pero* is implied (represented by a $\emptyset$ form). In example 3, not only is the order of the clauses reversed, but it is proposed that the first clause contains an implied *pero*. The following examples, along with several unmentioned ones, are discovered in the text:

12. . . . Y agregó [la mujer de Montiel]:—Montiel se está bañado. [Pero] en realidad José Montiel no había tenido tiempo de bañarse . . . . Era un hombre tan prevenido, que dormía sin ventilador eléctrico para vigilar durante el sueño los rumores de la casa. (p. 70)

13. [Baltazar] se acercó al niño, sonriendo, y le tendió la jaula. El niño se incorporó de un salto, abrazó la jaula, que era casi tan grande como él, y se quedó mirando a Baltazar a través del tejido metálico, sin saber qué decir. [Pero] no había derramado una lágrima. (p. 72).

It is important to focus on these two potential examples, because they both concern the relationship between Baltazar and the Montiel family and the way in which Baltazar is exploited by father and son (the father consciously; the son unconsciously, learning the ways of his father through constant example). Baltazar is unaware of that exploitation, but the structure of narrative enables the reader to understand more than Baltazar does, as we are told first of Montiel's wiliness in attending, even in sleep, to what is going on in his house, and second, of the calculated theatrics of Pepe's behavior. The passage makes a point of contrasting Montiel's contemplation of his son [. . . lo miraba impasible . . . (p. 71)] with that of Baltazar's view [. . . observó al niño como hubiera observado la agonía de un animal contagioso. (p. 72)]; Baltazar's act of compassion in giving the boy the bird cage is likewise, through the implied formula (example 13), contrasted with the boy's feigned hysterics. In this way, a proportion is established that signifies the relationship of conscious exploitation versus unconscious acquiescence: Montiel's contemplation:Baltazar's contemplation::Pepe's theatrics:Baltazar's generosity. Given the importance of this passage in characterizing the structural relationship between Montiel and Baltazar and the key event that will, in the end, lead to Baltazar's degradation, it is not surprising that we can find implied uses of the verbal formula that has been suggested as the dominant inscriptional marker of the underlying *écriture* of the text.

A second observation to be made concerning the recording of examples of the A/B formula is that an analysis of the text must employ a certain amount of normalization of verbal structures. That is, the inscription of the formula need not always take the same identical verbal and lexical form. We have as much as said this by indicating that example 3 may involve an inverted clausal order, and that examples 12 and 13 join example 2 in involving implied occurrences of *pero*. On the most elementary level, the syntax of a language does not lend itself, if exact repetition is to be avoided, to structures that are always identical in form. "Lo recuerdo" and "Me acuerdo de él" are semantically synonymous and could, in a certain text, be examples of the inscription of a principle of *écriture*; *recordar* is used in one example, *acordar* in another, putatively to avoid exact repetition (which is itself a principle of *écriture*; exact repetition, on the other hand, could be used to signal ritualized, incantatory and psychotic expression). However, the syntactic structure of the two synonymous verbs results in two different linguistic sequences.

Thus, we may speak of semantic identity without explicit syntactic—overt verbal—identity; there is, however, a syntactic identity that may be identified on an underlying level, that level that is defined by the Chomskian generative syntax as deep syntactic structure (as opposed to abstract or deep semantic structure in a semantically based generative model). Examination of a literary text in terms of the inscription of principles of *écriture*, or even in terms of the occurrence of the certain combinatory principles of narration, must be sensitive to the need to juxtapose structures that recur because of exact verbal identity with those that recur because of an identity that is not verbally the same but that can be discerned when the structures have been normalized on the basis of semantic and/or underlying syntactic equivalence. Todorov's study of the narrative formulas in the *Decameron* would not have been possible without the concept of normalization; normalization is treated in detail in Hendricks's work on narrative structure.[6]

In García Márquez's story, we may expand the range of explicit textual markers of the *écriture* of narrator-reader complicity by the inclusion of examples from the text of normalized structures. This becomes particularly valuable when we can show, through normalization, that the markers are present in the key passage of the text.

The third observation to be made about these markers is that not all the occurrences of *pero* structures in the text can be taken as inscriptions of the principle of *écriture* at issue (compare the following: "El doctor Octavio Giraldo, un médico viejo, contento de la vida pero cansado de la profesión, pensaba en la jaula de Baltazar . . . [p. 66]). Care must be exercised in underlining the verbal structures of a text, so as not to overestimate the value of what is said; that is what, in an earlier form of criticism, was called "over-interpretation" or "over-reading." Once a principle of *écriture* has been identified and correlated with a specific verbal marker—or series of diverse markers—that is its textual inscription, there is a natural tendency for every occurrence of the linguistic structure that the marker embodies to be given, at least tentatively, importance as an example of that marker. It is similar to what happens in the *écriture* of personification, which typically makes use of abstract feminine nouns that become in the narrative structure "persons" embodying the abstract value signified by the noun with which they are identified. At what point do we distinguish between abstract feminine nouns that are markers of the *écriture* of personification and other abstract feminine nouns that may occur simply because of the verbal style of the text or the natural frequencies of nouns in the language? It is customary to mark the personifications with initial capitals, but an ambiguous or inconsistent practice is contemplable, particularly in those narratives that may avoid the blatant personifi-

6. See William O. Hendricks, "Methodology of Narrative Structural Analysis," in his *Essays on Semiolinguistics and Verbal Art*, pp. 175–95.

cation of texts like the *Roman de la rose* or *El gran teatro del mundo*. Another example concerns symbolic names: if the names of certain characters in a text are symbolic—that is, the name is, after St. Isidore's dictum, the consequence of the thing—are all of the names equally symbolic? La Maga's name may be symbolic in *Rayuela* (particularly since it is a nickname), but Horacio Oliveira's may not be.

In the text at hand, examples 5 and 7 may not be inscriptions of the principle narrator-reader complicity, and example 4 is less clearly so than examples 10 and 11. However, examples 5 and 7 are listed because they point to the narrator's superior information and control over what is happening. Example 4, on the other hand, also ties in with proposed examples 12 and 13 as part of the complicitous characterization of Montiel and how the event that takes place leads to Baltazar's degradation. Example 4 is included for the way in which the narrator identifies implicitly Ursula's superior knowledge of the potential importance of the object Baltazar has constructed. To her—and this becomes clear when she discusses the price to be put on it—the bird cage is less an object of art, born of the *furor poeticus* that has kept Baltazar from his regular work and has caused him to ramble in his sleep, than it is a commodity to restore some sort of balance to the domestic economy. On the other hand, example 9 obviously demonstrates that Ursula, although she may see things more clearly than Baltazar on the level of their interaction, does not share the full complicity of knowledge that the narrator and reader enjoy, for at this point she is too an unknowing victim of the degradation that has been visited, without his realizing what has happened, on Baltazar.

Finally, examples 1 and 2 become, in retrospect, charged with irony, so much so that it is perhaps the clearest marker of the text's *écriture*. If Baltazar's "expresión general de muchacho asustado" (p. 65) did not originally derive from a true sense of surprise or astonishment, it will when he emerges from the stupor described in example 10. By the same token, if life had given Baltazar more reasons to be alert than astonished, the astonishment that awaits him when he realizes to what extent he lost control of a situation that was, initially, reason for extreme pride in his abilities as a craftsman diminishes necessarily the quality of his alertness (or, alternately, will reinforce the need for alertness, enhanced by the element of astonishment). Note that the use of the future tense does not mean that we are talking about what will happen after the close of the story: we are not projecting the narrative events beyond the closure of the text. Rather what is at issue is the identification of a meaning that inheres in the juxtaposition of examples 1 and 10 in the narrative itself. Again, a semantic proportion is implied: Baltazar's protective alertness:his lack of astonishment::failure of alertness [the degradation that he becomes victim of so suddenly that he is unaware of what is happening]:production of astonishment. Thus, what we understand is that the expression identified as "false" in example 1 will, by virtue of the knowledge that only we know in examples 10 and 11 but that Ursula and Baltazar can be expected to wake up to, become "true." Or, to put it in terms that exclude taking into account Ursula and Baltazar's subsequent realizations, the adjective given in example 1 is, by implication, reversed in at least the understanding of the reader at the end of the text. Since the narrator knows it will be reversed, his use of it on the first page of the text is ironic. Moreover, although it is the only time in which there is an irony at the expense of the characters that includes the reader (that is, at this point we do not know that it is going to be reversed), it does also serve to mark in passing the ultimate superiority of the narrator vis-à-vis the reader with whom he proposed to share complicitously the knowledge of events.

The importance of the markers of inscription becomes clear when we realize that they are concentrated at the three major points of the story: the initial presentation of circumstance (examples 1–4, pp. 65–66); the visit to Montiel's house, leading to Montiel's humiliation by Baltazar's generosity but, we also see, Baltazar's unknowing humiliation by Pepe's feigned hysterics (examples 5–7 and 12–13, pp. 69—71), and Baltazar's definitive and open humiliation-degradation by the lie that his "success" forces upon him to acknowledge as truth (examples 8–11, pp. 73–74). Although this may appear to be the entire story, there are several segments that are excluded (the discussion with Ursula concerning the bird cage, Baltazar's preparation to go to Montiel's house, the appearance of the doctor to buy it for his invalid wife). Within the scene involving the visit to Montiel's house, the markers are concentrated at two out of four points in the events: arrival (examples 6–7), confrontation with Montiel, Pepe's hysterics (examples 12–13), departure with Montiel's rage. The high point of the *écriture* of complicity occurs at two crucial points: the characterization of the wiliness of both Montiel and his son—the one refusing to honor his son's commitments, the latter feigning hysteria with the result of awakening Baltazar's magnanimity (examples 5–7, 12–13)—and the characterization of the way in which Baltazar falls almost unconsciously into the lie of his sale, propagated unknowingly by his admiring friends (examples 8–9). The combined result of these two high points—exploitation and lie—is the degradation of the innocent and magnanimous artist; the characterization of this degradation is underlined by the concentrated appearance once again of the markers of complicitous knowledge (examples 8–11).

IV

There are a number of directions that a discussion of the nature of this degradation could take, but they would seem to involve more of an interpretation of the story than a characterization of its *écriture*, the bases for its *significance*.[7] But let us suggest two obvious ones in a cursory manner. In the first place, the story seems to pit the innocent artist, a man from the humble sector of society for whom his artistry is not a creative gesture but for whom it vies for attention with "legitimate" means of earning a living, against the exploitive rich, Montiel the man who owns the town, which he controls with unremitting meanness (specifically, it is mean of him not to buy the bird cage from Baltazar in order not to satisfy his son's caprice, but to save Baltazar from heavy personal loss). In this way, art, which Western culture has traditionally approved of as a spiritually ennobling and liberating force, becomes the direct cause of a profound degradation: Baltazar, "como era la primera vez que bebía," is reduced to a gutter drunk on the occasion of his prodigious artistic triumph. What is more, in his drunken stupor he continues to revel in "el sueño más feliz de su vida." The abyss between this *sueño* and the narrator-reader's sense of the true dimensions of the event—with its implication concerning the exploitation of art and degradation through art—is, in turn, the complicity to which we have been referring.

The second line of interpretive analysis could concern Baltazar as an oblique Christ figure: the name, his physical appearance, and age (compare p. 65), his essential innocence, his magnanimity that arouses Montiel's philistine rage, his acquiescence in the sacrificial lie of his friend's jubilation over his presumed conquest, his degradation, the theft of his clothes (that is, his shoes), and his final

---

7. Perhaps the best interpretive comments on the story are to be found in Mario Vargas Llosa, *García Márquez, historia de un deicidio* (Barcelona-Caracas: Monte Ávila Editores, 1971), pp. 372–79. Vargas Llosa speaks directly to the issue of art for Baltazar and his "adversaries": "Baltazar . . . viene lo imaginario a través de una praxis que es tolerada dentro de cierto límites: sus productos han sido asimilados, transformados en real objetivos [*sic*]. Por vía del arte lo imaginario encuentra un acomodo en lo real objectivo. Ese acomodo, sin embargo, no resuelve una contradicción: el significado distinto que tiene la jaula para Baltazar y para los otros" (p. 378). See also Alberto J. Carlos, "Approximaciones a los cuentos de Gabriel García Márquez," in Helmy F. Giacoman, ed., *Homenaje a G. García Márquez: variaciones interpretativas en torno a su obra* (Long Island City, N.Y.: Las Américas-Anaya, 1972), pp. 213–33.

abandonment by even the *beatas* on their way to church. Baltazar's empty sacrifice occurs in the context of a presumed defeat of the rich by the humble: "—Hay que hacer muchos cosas para vendérselas a los ricos antes que se mueran—decía, ciego de la borrachera—. Todos están enfermos y se van a morir. Cómo estarán de jodidos que ya ni siquiera pueden coger rabia" (p. 73). Once again, the reader's grasp of the *écriture* of complicity leads to an understanding of the pathetic foolishness of Baltazar's sentiments. If Baltazar is a Christ figure, his truth is that of innocence and artistic accomplishment, virtues that make him, not Montiel and the rich, the one who is *jodido*.[8]

It is unquestionable that García Márquez's *écriture* of complicity excludes his characters from self-knowledge and lends an aura of woeful futility to the innocence that, at first glance, appears to be their essential charm and virtue as human beings. The ironic pathos of this circumstance is nowhere more evident than in the short novel *La increíble y triste historia de la cándida Eréndira y de su abuela desalmada* (1972): Eréndira is Baltazar and her grandmother is Montiel, and so much for the family as the true image of human solidarity. This circumstance cannot be taken to mean that García Márquez has a patronizing attitude toward his characters and their plight, or that he takes pride in the superiority of his (our) own view of them. Rather, the abyss between useful human knowledge and ingenuous charm is what is effectively highlighted by the *écriture* of complicity. Where an earlier local-color literature utilized this abyss to delimit charming but outdated customs or to denounce the ignorance of the masses, García Márquez's calculated use of it—at the expense of appearing to indulge in a cavalier disregard for the deep plight of his characters as oppressed human beings—becomes, instead, a particularly eloquent denunciation of the final degradation that these individuals are compelled to experience. It is a degradation of which they are—at least in Baltazar's case—not truly aware and, therefore, one which can be tragic and experientially useful not from their point of view, but only from that of the complicitously involved reader. In the end, it is the reader—we alone—who can make use of the knowledge in which the text is structured to have us participate. This is the true value of García Márquez's *écriture* of complicity.

8. Boldori comments briefly on the Christological symbolism of Baltazar on page 20. Reference is also made by George R. McMurray to Baltazar as a figure of the exploited artist, in *Gabriel García Márquez* (New York: Frederick Ungar, 1977), pp. 55–57: "As the story's central motif, the cage symbolizes artistic creation and illuminates the conflict between the ideal world of fantasy and imagination and that of objective reality. . . . The dichotomy between the realms of creative imagination and sordid, everyday reality are set forth, not only by the two leading characters [that is, Baltazar and Montiel], but also by the series of events that bring the story to its end."

Chapter V.

The Double Inscription of the *Narrataire* in "Los funerales de la Mamá Grande"

Por primera vez se habló de ella y se la concibió sin su mecedor de bejuco, sus sopores a las dos de la tarde y sus cataplasmas de mostaza, y se la vio pura y sin edad, destilada por la leyenda. (p. 141)[1]

I

If "La prodigiosa tarde de Baltazar" may be characterized in terms of narrative irony at the expense of the characters with a concomitant complicity between narrator and implied reader, the title story of "Los funerales de la Mamá Grande" takes a step further in developing a complex image of the *narrataire* or receiver of García Márquez's narratives. Although the story has been analyzed from many points of view—the use of exaggeration for satiric-comic effect; the distillation of the Colombian writer's denunciation of feudal society as embodied in the legendary frame of the all-powerful Mother Earth figure;[2] the use of a tone and devices that remind us of the traditional folktale, the interplay between history, legend, and

1. García Márquez, "Los funerales de la Mamá Grande," in *Los funerales de la Mamá Grande*, 6th ed. (Buenos Aires: Editorial Sudamericana, 1969), pp. 125–47. All quotes are from this edition.
2. Although the last segment of his essay deals with "la sociedad feudal," Mario Vargas Llosa places greater emphasis on the mythic-lengendary quality of the story: "Los funerales de la Mamá Grande: exageración y perspectiva mítica," in his *García Márquez: historia de un deicidio* (Barcelona: Barral Editores, 1971), pp. 398–419. The title of Vargas Llosa's monograph certainly stresses García Márquez's literature as implicitly demythificational. Judith Goetzinger, "The Emergence of Folk Myth in 'Los funerales de la Mamá Grande,' " *Revista de estudios hispánicos* 6 (1972); 237–48, despite the title of her paper, also realizes that the narrator is interested not in comic entertainment but in presenting a "powerful apocalyptical vision of total decay" (p. 248). It is, unfortunately, Ricardo Gullón's monograph that has done the most to suggest the image of García Márquez as a *narrador ameno*. See his *García Márquez o el olvidado arte de contar* (Madrid: Taurus, 1970);

fiction—no one has studied one of the most salient features of the text: the explicit projection of an image of the reader and the bifurcation of that image into two conflicting and non-complementary modes.

II

It is possible to study all narratives in terms of the structural markers that identify the implied reader—the *narrataire*, as Gerald Prince has called him. These markers may range from specific vocabulary choices that suggest a particular type of reader, perhaps one far different in sociocultural formation from the characters being described (this is, in fact, an option that we associate with naturalistic fiction, which involves its own form of narrator-reader complicity), to overt asides to or invocations of the reader. (I will use "reader" to refer to someone actually addressed, *narrataire* to refer to the implied—and therefore ideal—reader of a text; clearly, the two may be one and the same in terms of the *écriture* of a particular narrative).

In García Márquez's fiction, the *narrataire* is particularly prominent structurally, and a novel like *Cien años de soledad* can only function on the basis of an implied reader who will, in his decoding of the structurally complex novel, identify himself (if only subconsciously at first) with the many characters who undertake to decipher Melquíades's manuscript. When manuscript and novel become the same text, character and narrative become the same entity, engaged in reading the same retrospective prophecy of their sociohistorical experience.

Yet, few of García Márquez's stories are explicitly addressed to a reader, and the fact that "Los funerales" does involve an audience is perhaps why this one text has received attention in terms of the conventions of the traditional folk raconteur. Actually, the explicit address occurs only in the opening lines of the story:

> Esta es, incrédulos del mundo entero, la verídica historia de la Mamá Grande, soberana absoluta del reino de Macondo, que vivió en función de dominio durante 92 años y murió en olor de santidad un martes del setiembre pasado, y a cuyos funerales vino el Sumo Pontífice. (p. 127)

Indeed, one could argue that such a delivery to a presumed public is merely conventional and serves more to specify the self-image of the storyteller than that of the *narrataire*. In any case, what we can say is

---

María Delia Rasetti, "Análisis del 'motivo' en *Los funerales de la Mamá Grande*," *Revista de literaturas hispánicas* 10 (1970):88–98; and Robert Sims, "The Creation of Myth in García Márquez' 'Los funerales de la Mamá Grande,' " *Hispania* 61 (1978): 14–23.

that there is unquestionably the implied specification of a single kind of *narrataire*: the openmouthed ingenue who will be impressed by the verbal flourishes that accompany the marvelous, extraordinary tale the raconteur is about to unfold: his wisdom and his superior talent will provide us with an instructive entertainment. Yet, any serious reading of the story (and García Márquez's texts are just entertaining enough as farfetched yarns to threaten cunningly the serious intent of determined reader-critics) quickly reveals that the story is meaningless if the *narrataire* is left identified exclusively with the reader who is overtly addressed in the first sentence.

The *écriture* of "Los funerales" depends on the interaction of two kinds of *narrataires*. One is the receptor of the folk narrative, one of the *incrédulos* for whom the details of the story are simply too far beyond his everyday experience to be assimilated in terms other than the fantastic and the marvelous. For this reader, the legend of Mamá Grande is palpable reality because it is simply his daily experience with the feudal society in which he lives, written in the grander terms of Mamá Grande as told impressively by a raconteur with superior information. In short, the "folktale *narrataire*" comes close to the implied reader of official writings—history books, constitutions, newspapers, self-serving speeches—that is, the reader of official myths and lies that become guiding truths by virtue of their cunning rhetoric.

The second *narrataire* of García Márquez's story is the reader who is supposed to be able to gauge the distance between official history, folk legend, and demythifying literature. In short, the reader who is able implicitly to discover the ways in which the purported raconteur's tale is not the exegesis of legend, with its own particular supplements to it, but the demythification of both legend and official history and the denunciation of the way in which the two intersect to the advantage of official myths.[3] Although this *narrataire* is never spoken to explicitly, both the closing comment of the narrator's introduction and the closing remarks of his story may be taken as postulating the need for the emergence of the "critical *narrataire*" as opposed to the passive receptor of folk legends:

> Ahora que la nación sacudida en sus entrañas ha recobrado el equilibrio; ahora que los gaiteros de San Jacinto, los contrabandistas de la Guajira, los arroceros del Sinú, las prostitutas de Guacamayal, los hechiceros de la Sierpe y los bananeros de Aracataca han colgado sus toldos para restablecerse de la ex-

3. One of the major points made by René Jara in his essay on *Cien años de soledad* concerns the creation of an image of myth as a demythificational force. René Jara and Jaime Mejía, *Las claves del mito en García Márquez* (Valparaíso, Chile: Ediciones Universitarias de Valparaíso, 1972), part 1.

tenuante vigilia, y que han recuperado la serenidad y vuelto a tomar posesión de sus estados el presidente de la república y sus ministros y todos aquellos que representaron al poder público y a las potencias sobrenaturales en la más espléndida ocasión funeraria que registren los anales históricos; ahora que el Sumo Pontífice ha subido a los Cielos en cuerpo y alma, y que es impossible transitar en Macondo a causa de las botellas vacías, las colillas de cigarrillos, los huesos roídos, las latas y trapos y excrementos que dejó la muchedumbre que vino al entierro, ahora es la hora de recostar un taburete a la puerta de la calle y empezar a contar desde el principio los pormenores de esta conmoción nacional, antes de que tengan tiempo de llegar los historiadores. (p. 127)

[. . .] Ahora podía el Sumo Pontífice subir al cielo en cuerpo y alma, cumplida su misión en la tierra, y podía el presidente de la república sentarse a gobernar según su buen criterio, y podían las reinas de todo lo habido y por haber casarse y ser felices y engendrar y parir muchos hijos, y podían las muchedrumbres colgar sus toldos según su leal modo de saber y entender en los desmesurados dominios de la Mamá Grande, porque la única que podía oponerse a ello y tenía suficiente poder para hacerlo había empezado a pudrirse bajo una plataforma de plomo. Sólo faltaba entonces que alquien recostara un taburete en la puerta para contar esta historia, lección y escarmiento de las generaciones futuras, y que ninguno de los incrédulos del mundo se quedara sin conocer la noticia de la Mamá Grande, que mañana miércoles vendrán los barrenderos y barrerán la basura de sus funerales, por todo los siglos de los siglos. (pp. 146–47)

In this sense, "Los funerales" may be viewed as a metanarrative that functions on two levels, one straightforward and one that is self-ironizing and, therefore, self-critical. Since these two levels are contained within the same narrative, they cannot be easily separated and must be identified as present in the form of certain markers or features that signal the underlying tension between two *narrataires* of the same overt utterances. The insistence on the need for this text, on the need for someone to "recostar un taburete a la puerta de la calle y empezar a contar," as opposed to the already existing legend on the one hand and the oblique suggestion of what the historian will do with the material on the other, results in two strategic insistences on story versus legend-history in addition to the juxtaposition established in the opening paragraphs of the text. On the occasion of the description of the repercussions at the highest levels of government of Mamá Grande's death, the narrator notes how the event must be assimilated into official history:

Los acontecimientos de aquella noche y las siguientes serían más tarde definidos como una lección histórica. No sólo por el espíritu cristiano que inspiró a los más elevados personeros del poder público, sino por la abnegación con que se conciliaron intereses disímiles y criterios contrapuestos, en el propósito común de enterrar un cadáver ilustre. Durante muchos años la Mamá Grande había garantizado la paz social y la concordia política de su imperio, en virtud de los tres baúles de cédulas electorales falsas que formaban parte de su patrimonio secreto. (p. 139)

Indeed, it is only when the lawyers and constitutional lawmakers have succeeded in harmonizing Mamá Grande's death, which had occurred months before, with the highest purposes of the state that the funeral is allowed to proceed with all due ceremony:

[. . .] Entonces [el Presidente] adquirió plena conciencia de su destino histórico, y decretó nueve días de duelo nacional, y honores póstumos a la Mamá Grande en la categoría de heroína muerta por la patria en el campo de batalla. Como lo expresó en la dramática alocución que aquella madrugada dirigió a sus compatriotas a través de la cadena nacional de radio y televisión, el primer magistrado de la nación confiaba en que los funerales de la Mamá Grande constituyeran un nuevo ejemplo para el mundo. (p. 140)

Clearly, the event, which is part of legend on the narrative legend of the people, who live on the margin (and at the mercy of) officialdom, has been made into history to serve the demands of the latter. The text, as literature (*historia literaria* versus *historia oficial*), is able to challenge that process through the creation of a secondary, critical *narrataire*. It is the latter, of course, who is able to gauge the ironic incongruency of the following segment of narrative:

Tanto se había parlado, que los parloteos transpusieron las fronteras, transpasaron el océano y atravesaron como un presentimiento por las habitaciones pontificias de Castelgandolfo. Repuesto de la modorra del ferragosto reciente, el Sumo Pontífice estaba en la ventana, viendo en el lago sumergirse los buzos que buscaban la cabeza de la doncella decapitada. En las últimas semanas los periódicos de la tarde no se habían ocupado de otra cosa, y el Sumo Pontífice no podía ser indiferente a un enigma planteado a tan corta distancia de su residencia de verano. Pero aquella tarde, en una sustitución imprevista, los periódicos cambiaron las fotografías de las posibles víctimas, por la de una sola mujer de veinte años, señalada con una blonda de luto. ''La Mamá Grande'', exclamó el Sumo Pontífice, reconociendo al instante el borroso daguerrotipo que muchos años antes le había sido ofrendado con ocasión de su ascenso a la Silla de San Pedro. ''La Mamá Grande'', exclamaron a coro en sus habitaciones privadas los miembros del Colegio Cardenalicio, y por tercera vez en veinte siglos hubo una hora de desconciertos, sofoquines y correndillas en el imperio sin límites de la cristiandad, hasta que el Sumo Pontífice estuvo instalado en su larga góndola negra, rumbo a los fantásticos y remotos funerales de la Mamá Grande. (pp. 141–42)

The third occasion on which the narrator refers to the tension between history, legend, and story is in the closing paragraph of the text, the last lines of which have already been quoted. What has not been quoted is the long period that proceeds the sentence (itself a "majestic" period) that begins "Ahora podía el Sumo Pontífice. . . . " This period, which is structured in terms of a series of phrases beginning with *Nadie* and followed by verbs of perception (*vio, reparó, advirtió*) definitively established the juxtaposition between the receptors of legend—the masses of people who are able only to experience the sense of relief in the fact that, at last, it is all over—and the critical *narrataire* who, because he is the receptor of "esta historia, lección y escarmiento de las generaciones futuros," is able, precisely, to see how the *historia [literaria]* is, in fact, a legitimate *lección y escarmiento*. It may well be that García Márquez, like many a committed Latin-American writer who would want the audience of legend retold with the flourishes of folktale to become the critical reader able to perceive the dreadful sense of an extraordinary event, would want his literature and the image of narrative that it embodies to function as a process for the formation of the latter out of the former. Nevertheless, the text, while it does incorporate a metacommentary on the nature of narrative, does not do so regarding textual *narrataires*, and the only way in which we can speak of the interplay between the folk receptor and the critical reader is by projecting the narrative circuit suggested by what metacommentary is included in "Los funerales." To the extent that the verbal texture of García Márquez's text is stylistically bivalent—an echo of traditional, entertaining folktales versus explicit references to the story as a gesture of demythification—we may speak of the presence of dual *narrataires*, one for each level of style. To the extent that the image of narrative as demythification in the end asserts itself at the expense of innocuous popular legend (and oppressive official history), we may speak equally of the suppression of the first type of *narrataire* by the second, critical one. It is only in this sense that we can maintain that García Márquez's story, despite the presence of traits taken from the "charming" tradition of popular folk narratives, does in fact conclude by postulating the bases of its own appropriate demythifying readings and the image of the critical reader capable of undertaking the process. At the same time, both *narrataires* allow García Márquez to relate his story in terms of innocuous tales that, because they reduce historical events to legend, deprive events of the opportunity to serve as "lección y escarmiento de las generaciones futuras," a function that is alleged necessary if the people are ever to attain any significant degree of revolutionary self-knowledge. Thus, the writer both mocks a form of ineffectual narrative on significant "epic" events (in both a routine and a Brechtian sense of the word) and proposes, through the medium of his parody, what he considers to be an appropriately critical telling—and, hence, reading—of historical occurrences.

III

It remains, then, to describe the *écriture* of "Los funerales" by which the image of one type of *narrataire*—the openmouthed *incrédulo*—is supplanted by another, the critical *incrédulo*. In short, how does the story mock its own pseudo-folktale format to suggest a more appropriate level of narrative story?

There appear to be at least five rhetorical processes by which it is possible to gauge the implied rejection of one reader in favor of another: (1) exaggeration, (2) incredible circumstances, (3) remote or unusual practices, (4) ironic language, and (5) pejorative or satiric insinuations. It is notable that the most overt process is lacking: the overt address of one reader at the expense of the other. Since there is no direct address ever made to the proposed implied "appropriate" reader, it is necessary to identify him through the functional presence of the rhetorical processes listed. At the same time, it should be evident that these processes overlap in nature and presumed effect. The only reason that we are justified in speaking of different types is because we acknowledge that a literary text, for reasons of stylistic variety, is going to modulate its rhetorical pattern. Thus, rather than speaking of one basic device, we recognize several related but slightly different processes working together to accomplish an overall structural goal: the signalling of the two levels of implied *narrataires*.

Exaggeration is recognized as one of García Márquez's stock rhetorical plays, particularly when it is based on chaotic enumeration, coupled with what is essentially comic because of the inappropriateness of detail or the juxtaposition of unassociated details. Exaggeration in "Los funerales" helps to identify the alternate reader to the extent that, by distorting the details of the superficial narrative (the folktale), it suggests the absurdity of taking it at its face value. Throughout, the face value of the text is the folktale homage to the grandeur of Mamá Grande and an epic paeon to her majestic death. The implied "secret" text is the demythification of such a homage and the laying bare of how the legendary matriarch was the powerful embodiment of an oppressive social system, a woman to inspire hate rather than awe. The explicit text, when read by the implied folk *narrataire*, is marked by dignified respect. When read by the aroused *narrataire*, it is characterized by derisive ridicule. Exaggeration, like the other rhetorical processes that have been identified, functions as a key postulate of the text's *écriture* to signal the necessary, imperative transition from one reader to another. One example of exaggeration is the following passage, which speaks of the extent of Mamá Grande's domain:

> La inminencia de la muerte removió la extenuante expectativa. La voz de la moribunda, acostumbrada al homenaje y a la obediencia, no fue más sonora que un bajo de órgano en la pieza cerrada, pero resonó en los más apartados rincones de la hacienda. Nadie era indiferente a esa muerte. Durante el presente siglo, la Mamá Grande había sido el centro de gravedad de Macondo, como sus hermanos, sus padres y los padres de sus padres lo fueron en el pasado, en una hegemonía que colmaba dos siglos. La aldea se fundó alrededor de su apellido. Nadie conocía el origen, ni los límites ni el valor real del patrimonio, pero todo el mundo se había acostumbrado a creer que la Mamá Grande era dueña de las aguas corrientes y estancadas, llovidas y por llover, y de los caminos vecinales, los postes del telégrafo, los años bisiestos y el calor, y que tenía además un derecho heredado sobre vida y haciendas. Cuando se sentaba a tomar el fresco de la tarde en el balcón de su casa, con todo el peso de sus vísceras y su autoridad aplastado en su viejo mecedor de bejuco, parecía en verdad infinitamente rica y poderosa, la matrona más rica y poderosa del mundo. (pp. 129–30)

Or, in this passage, where the conjunction of details is incongruous and therefore self-mocking:

> La riqueza del subsuelo, las aguas territoriales, los colores de la bandera, la soberanía nacional, los partidos tradicionales, los derechos del hombre, las libertades ciudadanas, el primer magistrado, la segunda instancia, el tercer debate, las cartas de recomendación, las constancias históricas, las elecciones libres, las reinas de la belleza, los discursos trascendentales, las grandiosas manifestaciones, las distinguidas señoritas, los correctos caballeros, los pundonorosos militares, su señoría ilustrísima, la carta suprema de justicia, los artículos de prohibida importación, las damas liberales, el problema de la carne, la pureza del lenguaje, los ejemplos para el mundo, el orden jurídico, la prensa libre pero responsable, la Atenas sudamericana, la opinión pública, las elecciones democráticas, la moral cristiana, la escasez de divisas, el derecho de asilo, el peligro comunista, la nave del estado, la carestía de la vida, las tradiciones republicanas, las clases desfavorecidas, los mensajes de adhesión.

No alcanzó a terminar. La labriosa enumeración tronchó su último vahaje. Ahogándose en el mare mágnum de fórmulas abstractas que durante dos siglos constituyeron la justificación moral del poderío de la familia, la Mamá Grande emitió un sonoro eructo, y expiró. (p. 137)

Many other passages could be cited (for example, the physician's remedies [p. 131], the legislator's deliberations [pp. 140–41], and the funeral procession [pp. 144–46]). Since comic exaggeration is one of the Colombian writer's stock devices, one that he takes from those folktales that likewise mock what they pretend to report seriously, it is not surprising that the text is replete with strategic—and effective—examples.

By *incredible circumstance* one refers to those conjunctions of incongruous detail whereby the particular need to demythify legend—at least when that legend can be seen by the *narrataire* to deviate significantly from a civilized norm—may be stressed. For example, the attendance at Mamá Grande's funeral by both the President of the Republic (made possible by only the most lengthy of constitutional "adjustments") and by the Holy Father (made possible by only the most arduous of transatlantic crossings in his *larga góndola negra* [the Pope's traditional black Mercedes Benz 600?]) is an outrageous inflation of the honors due a local matriarch, no matter how symbolic of a feudal status quo. Hence, the description that has already been transcribed of how the Pontiff learns of the woman's death and undertakes his unheard of journey to the New World, a journey that the forewarned reader will immediately correlate with the visit by Pope Paul to Colombia in the mid-sixties, the first visit to the New World by a pope.

On the other hand, *remote or unusual practices* refers to a circumstance that, by its very nature, demands a reaction of incredulity. For example, we learn that the venerable matriarch, although endowed with the mammary attributes of a fecund Mother Earth figure, in fact, dies a virgin:

> Su hora era llegada. En su cama de lienzo, embadurnada de áloes hasta las orejas, bajo la marquesina de polvorienta espumilla, apenas se adviniaba la vida en la tenue respiración de sus tetas matriarcales. La Mamá Grande, que hasta los cincuenta años rechazó a los más apasionados pretendientes, y que fue dorada por la naturaleza para amamantar ella sola a toda su especie, agonizaba virgen y sin hijos. En el momento de la extremaunción, el padres Antonio Isabel tuvo que pedir ayuda para aplicarle los óleos en la palma de las manos, pues desde el principio de su agonía la Mamá Grande tenía los puños cerrados. De nada valió el concurso de las sobrinas. En el forcejeo, por primera vez en una semana, la moribunda apretó contra su pecho la mano constelada

de piedras: preciosas, y fijó en las sobrinas su mirada sin olor, diciendo: "Salteadoras". Luego vio al padre Antonio Isabel en indumentaria litúrgica y al monaguillo con los instrumentos sacramentales, y murmuró con una convicción apacible: "Me estoy muriendo". Entonces so quitó el anillo con el Diamante Mayor y se lo dio a Magdalena, la novicia, a quien correspondía por ser la heredera menor. Aquel era el final de una tradición: Magdalena había renunciado a su herencia en favor de la Iglesia. (pp. 133–34)

The significance to a sociologically committed reader of the self-enforced sterility of the "mother" figure and her bestowal of the symbols of her matriarchy upon a niece who, by taking the nun's veil, has also denied herself a legitimate biological role is too obvious to require belaboring. Unlike Ursula but like the bitch-woman Fernanda in *Cien años de soledad*, Mamá Grande exercises power despite an illegitimate repudiation of a productive role in society: she controls the reins of material wealth without contributing to their production as either a human being or a woman. (This is not to be taken as a sexist assignment of a predetermined role to María del Rosario Castañeda y Montero: it is her "title" and her assumed role as supreme matriarch that defines a social role that she refuses to honor. Mamá Grande is, therefore, a false mother figure, as is the Virgin Mary by the implications of Mamá Grande's endowment to her niece.)[4]

Ironic language, which unquestionably is a correlative of exaggeration and the signalling of incredible circumstances, deserves specific identification as the verbal marker of the link between the overt and the secret text. It tells us, in essence, to contradict semantically what is being explicitly signified by the verbal signs of the text. The conclusion of the story is perhaps the best example of the functional use of irony in "Los funerales," for it is here that the narrator, although reaffirming the folk nature of his tale, delineates an underlying meaning—the attainment of a structure-breaking millenium in the debt of Mamá Grande that is to be set against both innocuous legend and oppressive official history. It is this delineation that most directly evokes what I have called the "appropriate narrative" demanded by the text, and irony is a particularly effective instrument in the process. At other places in the text, like for example when the importance of Mamá Grande's death is elevated to the status of a national crisis ("El orden social había sido rozado por la muerte" [p. 138]), verbal irony is useful for marking the disjuncture between the meanness of Mamá Grande's domain and the terms in which it is

4. The best material concerning García Márquez's portrayal of a sterile feudal society is Josefina Ludmer's *Cien años de soledad: una interpretación* (Buenos Aires: Editorial Tiempo Contemporáneo, 1972).

viewed by her partners in capricious power.[5] This disjuncture is particularly emphasized by the following type of irony, based as it is on the juxtaposition of the glorious and the mundane:

Tan altos propósitos debían tropezar sin embargo con graves inconvenientes. La estructura jurídica del país, construida por remotos ascendientes de la Mamá Grande, no estaba preparada para acontecimientos como los que empezaban a producirse. Sabios doctores de la ley, probados alquimistas del derecho ahondaron en hermenéuticas y silogismos, en busca de la fórmula que permitiera al presidente de la república asistir a los funerales. Se vivieron días de sobresalto en las altas esferas de la política, el clero y las finanzas. En el vasto hemiciclo del Congreso, enrarecido por un siglo de legislación abstracta, entre óleos de próceres nacionales y bustos de pensadores griegos, la evocación de la Mamá Grande alcanzó proporciones insospechables, mientras su cadáver se llenaba de burbujas en el duro setiembre de Macondo. (pp. 140–41)

Pejorative or satiric insinuations are, in a sense, the culmination of the foregoing elements in that they overtly refer to the demand for demythification. Appropriately, they allude specifically to matters concerning the social and political order incarnate in Mamá Grande's person. The long period that is the second paragraph of the story (p. 127) is full of indirect meanings. The series of clauses introduced by *ahora que* establishes a counterpoint between a present circumstance and an absent one, alternately past and future. Whether the past is at issue (presumably the one of the secure and inalterable legend, of the belief that Mamá Grande was immortal) or the future (the order to be built out of the collapse of a feudal autocracy held together by only the allegedly eternal matriarch; compare the closing paragraph of the text) is of secondary importance. What is important is that it is not that of the present, defined in terms of streets clogged by empty bottles and the memory of a hubbub reminiscent of a raunchy medieval fair. The text sardonically defines an alternate order by virtue of its not being what is explicitly described. Against the backdrop of the interplay between the text that speaks and the secret text that is silent, the narrator undertakes to weave his story. Ostensibly framed by the present circumstance, that story, in fact, elaborates a counterpoint between what can be stated openly (legend and official history) and what can be stated in absentia (demythificational narrative). It is also, by extension, a counterpoint between the two *narrataires*, the charac-

5. For the writer's political concepts, see Gregory Lawrence, "Marx in Macondo," *Latin American Literary Review* 2:4 (1974):49–57.

terization of which has been the central concern of this study of the narrative *écriture* of "Los funerales."

IV

In closing his ecphrasis on Mamá Grande's funeral cortege, the narrator observes the following:

> En su féretro con vueltas de púrpura, separada de la realidad por ocho torniquetes de cobre, la Mamá Grande estaba entonces demasiado embebida en su eternidad de formaldehído para darse cuenta de la magnitud de su grandeza. Todo el esplendor con que ella había soñado en el balcón de su casa durante las vigilias del calor, se cumplió con aquellas cuarenta y ocho gloriosas en que todos los símbolos de la época rindieron homenaje a su memoria. El propio Sumo Pontífice, a quien ella imaginó en sus delirios suspendido en una carroza resplandeciente sobre los jardines del Vaticano, se sobrepuso al calor con un abanico de palma trenzada y honró con su dignidad suprema los funerales más grandes del mundo. (pp. 145–46)

It is clear that the series of events has been perceived in terms of two orders separated by an imbreachable abyss: on the one hand, Mamá Grande and the ego-centered legend that surrounds her and that she has in large measure created and perpetuated; on the other hand, the "reality" of the narrator, who is obliged to the series of events because of its oppressive sway as a sociopolitical occurrence, but who is committed also to exorcising its oppressive weight through the medium of his demythifying narrative. Once again, we can speak of the fundamental opposition postulated by the *écriture* of "Los funerales": the *narrataire* who accepts the legend in all of its eccentric array (for example, Mamá Grande's mighty burp as she expires, the Italian candies distributed to the children of the matriarch's fiefdom by the Holy Father) versus the *narrataire* who prevails in his understanding of the tragic absurdity of such a social order. The "shock of recognition," which reminds readers that few social orders if any are better than tragically absurd—and that Macondo's is so only to an extreme if accurate degree—is effected through the *écriture* of the dual implied *narrataires*. As I have already suggested, the use of a folktale style that validates the passive *narrataire* as the most immediate sense of the text only enhances the shock of recognition when unspoken text and the *narrataire* that it demands begin to emerge via the specific details of rhetorical inscription that have been discussed in this analysis.

Chapter VI.

The *Écriture* of Rupture and Subversion of Language in Cortázar's *Historias de cronopios y famas*

> *Apretar una cucharita entre los dedos y sentir su latido de metal, su advertencia sospechosa. Cómo duele negar una cucharita, negar una puerta, negar todo lo que el hábito lame hasta darle suavidad satisfactoria. Tanto más simple aceptar la fácil solicitud de la cuchara, emplearla para revolver el café.*[1]

I

It has been widely recognized that one of the salient characteristics of Julio Cortázar's fiction—and therefore one of his most enduring contributions to the development of the *nueva narrativa hispanoamericana*—has been his manipulation of language. This manipulation, rather than creating a special "poetic" language, involves a program for the demythification of "official" literary language and the context to which it refers. Moreover, such a foregrounding of language is the fundamental element in the creation of a self-defining literary structure. Summarizing a list of numerous features to be found in the novel *Rayuela*, Angela B. Dellepiane asserts that:

> La lista podría ser aún más detallada, pero estos son los elementos nucleares del esfuerzo lingüístico de Cortázar enderezados a obtener una *palabra prima* no ya en el plano estético sino—lo que es más primordial en Cortázar—en el ético y ontológico en el que se inscribe, por lo demás, toda su búsqueda. Pienso que esta actitud de Cortázar con respecto al lenguaje se puede calificar de poética, pero entendiendo este adjetivo en el sentido de que el lenguaje tiene no ya una "función intelectual, mediadora y nominativa" sino una función trascendente, creativa, totalizadora hasta mágica

1. Julio Cortázar, *Historias de cronopios y famas*, 3d ed. (Buenos Aires: Ediciones Minotauro, 1966), pp. 11–12. All subsequent quotes are from this edition.

63

porque impacta no sólo el intelecto sino lo intuitivo e irracional del ser. No se trata de cominucar información sino de explorar ese 'espacio' particular que es el lenguaje.

Nada hay de nuevo en los planteamientos de Cortázar excepto que él supo ver, antes que muchos otros en la Argentina y en el continente, el valor de nuevas teorías lingüísticas, estéticas y filosóficas. Teorías que le fueron particularmente atractivas dado que Cortázar percibió agudamente hasta qué punto el lenguaje de la narrativa hispanoamericana, su signo lingüístico, era cómplice de una realidad falseada y escamoteada y cómo se hacía indispensable devolver la verdad a un yo profundo sin traicionarlo. Percibió, pues, la a un yo profundo sin traicionarlo. Percibió, pues, la mitificación de la lengua literaria y se propuso acabar con ella: no más 'encubrimiento' por el lenguaje sino 'descubrimiento' por y con él. De ahí sus esfuerzos para revivir el lenguaje rechazando lo tradicional y hecho, "extrañando" (en el sentido brechtiano) la palabra para que pudiera ser capaz de instaurar esa realidad diferente que no se quería dejar ver.[2]

Critics have dealt extensively with *Rayuela*. Additionally, Cortázar's short stories have attracted considerable attention, and the extant analyses of individual stories are some of the best on *nueva narrativa* texts.[3] However, one of Cortázar's earliest and most original collections of texts has received relatively meager attention. Published in 1962, *Historias de cronopios y famas* is divided into four parts: "Manual de instrucciones," "Ocupaciones raras," "Material plástico," and the title section, "Historias de cronopios y famas." While critics have commented on thematic elements of these texts, including the often bizarre and outlandish sense of humor

2. Angela B. Dellepiane, "La novela del lenguaje," in Donald W. Bleznick, ed., *Variaciones interpretativas en torno a la nueva narrativa hispanoamericana* (Santiago de Chile: Editorial Universitaria, 1972), pp. 63–75. The quote is from pp. 64–65. See also Nélida Donni de Miranda, "Notas sobre la lengua de Cortázar," *Boletín de literaturas hispánicas* No. 6 (1966):71–83. Regarding the specific language phenomena in Cortázar, see Angela B. Dellepiane, "Algunas conclusiones acerca del lenguaje en Cortázar," *Sin nombre* 2:2 (1971):24–35. Note also the essay by Jesús Mañú Iragui, which is more descriptive than structuralist, despite the title of his monograph: "Lenguaje y rebeldía en *Rayuela*," in *Estructuralismo en cuatro tiempos* (Caracas: Equinoccio, Ediciones de la Universidad Simón Bolívar, 1974), pp. 57–104.

3. See, for example, the studies gathered together by David Lagmanovich, *Estudios sobre los cuentos de Cortázar* (Barcelona: Ediciones Hispam, 1975). However, the single best study on Cortázar's stories, one which stresses plot rupture, is Noé Jitrik, "Notas sobre la 'zona sagrada' y el mundo de los 'otros' en *Bestiario*, de Julio Cortázar," in *El fuego de la especie* (Buenos Aires: Siglo XXI Argentina, 1971), pp. 47–63. However, *Historias de cronopios y famas* is not discussed.

they reveal, the present chapter will examine "rupture" and the "subversion of language," two structural-textual features that have not been dealt with. Within a semiological context, one understands rupture to be the phenomenon whereby the established structural system of a text is "ruptured" by the intrusions of another system that, in effect, displaces the former. All texts have a unique structure that operates implicitly to organize the reader's perception of the text: whatever patterns are perceived—whether homogeneous, overlapping, complementary, antithetical—derive from the structural system that underlies the text implicitly. If at a particular point in the unfolding of a text, an abrupt or sudden shift in the interrelationships of the signs of a text occurs, we may speak of rupture: a new system emerges and installs itself, creating a pronounced rejection of the previous system.

In Virginia Woolf's *Orlando*, when the paradigmatic epic hero is suddenly transformed into a woman, we have moved from a structural system that parallels traditional epic formulas to one that mocks them outrageously. Or, in García Márquez's *Cien años de soledad* the constant movement between a structural system in which the narrative reads like a reworking of chronicles and *costumbristic* fiction and local folkloric tall tales, and one in which these elements become unified in an overall structure that demythifies accepted Latin-American reality by proposing an antiphonic literary myth— the novel as an organic vision—establishes rupture as the very basis of the novel's *écriture*. For example, Melquíades is shown not as the legendary itinerant peddler, the purveyor of useless but wonderful baubles to an ignorant provincial populace, but rather as the author of the strange manuscript that turns out to be text of the novel itself. This is only one specific instance of the pervasive use of rupture in a major work of *nueva narrativa*.

Clearly, language may—must—be a primary agent of rupture, to the extent that language is the immediate substance of a literary text, the only explicit manifestation of its underlying system. Yet, we may distinguish between a rupture that occurs on the level of the abstract system of a text and that manifests itself in terms of a shift in language, without that language itself deviating from a loosely defined general norm, and a rupture that, although it too involves a shift in the underlying structural bases of a text, requires a distortion of language itself. In this latter instance, the integrity of language is threatened to the extent that we can see undermined a communicational standard: language as a secure means of dealing with reality on a day-to-day level of social interaction, language as a ready instrument for saying what we want to say and for hanging onto our tangible world and our abstract thoughts. When Cortázar introduces the new lexical items *cronopios*, *famas*, and *esperanzas* (the latter two exist in Spanish, but not with the meaning Cortázar attaches to them nor with the morphosyntax that he gives them), we tread a fine line between easy, quotidian reality, and a challenging realm of the possibility for fantasy. On the one hand, Cortázar's rupture of the lexicon of Spanish, through the seemingly unconcerned introduction of these three new items, gives the impression that he has simply coined some new pseudo-sociological jargon to refine our perception of human types that exist among us but have not hitherto been described in quite adequate enough detail: the welcome precision of Cortázar's analysis may comfortably permit the new jargon. On the other hand, we are obliged to entertain the suspicion that Cortázar is not simply bringing our daily reality into sharper focus by identifying some assorted human types. Rather, he is challenging our perception of it by defamiliarizing it, by introducing a panoply of types and behaviors that really does not quite fit. By doing so, he is asking us to see it in a way that *breaks* with our normal, secure perception. In so doing, he ruptures the instrument most closely identified with perception, the code of social communication, language, through his introduction of elements alien to it.

Although Cortázar is known for the nonsense *glíglico* with which characters in *Rayuela* play, the sort of rupture represented by the subversion of an apparently normally meaningful code is much more effective in that it obliges the primary code to expand the fossilized boundaries of meaning; with *glíglico*, meaning is simply denied altogether. By subverting language as one form of structural rupture, Cortázar is responding implicitly to the demands of one of this century's most provocative writers on the limits of language as an instrument for communication and as a meaning for "hanging" onto a reality that we know is elusive, ephemeral. Jacques Derrida speaks of the necessity to put language and individual components of language *sous rature*, "under erasure."[4] This is particularly necessary in the case of culturally encrusted lexical items. By placing language under erasure—by foregrounding its use in even the most trivial and colloquial of contexts—we call into question its adequacy. We may, as a consequence, recognize how language must be expanded, supplemented if it is to be used as an instrument of meaning. By the same token, language must be demythified, demonumentalized as the allegedly transparent embodiment of rational man's self-deluding perception of himself and his universe.

4. See Jacques Derrida, *Of Grammatology* (Baltimore: The Johns Hopkins University Press, 1976). The structuralist concepts in this chapter are best pursued in Jonathan Culler, *Structuralist Poetics: Structuralism, Linguistics, and the Study of Literature*.

Manuel Durán, in one of the best introductory studies on *Historias*, observes the following:

> Sin prisa, mediante toques sucesivos, mediante acumulacion de pequeños detalles, de pequeños incidentes dramáticos, Cortázar nos va haciendo penetrar en el extraño mundo de cronopios, famas y esperanzas. Los personajes reaparecen una y otra vez, siempre en accion, en una serie de viñetas dramáticas: poco a poco empezamos a comprender que nos hallamos ante un mundo estable, bien definido, con relaciones sociables, con sus fórmulas para el saludo, sus alegrías y sus peligros. Quizá el mayor interés que estilísticamente presentan estos relatos reside en la utilización por parte del autor de dos estilos, diferentes—incluso opuestos—pero íntimamente enlazados y complementarios. El primero es un estilo que pudiéramos definir como "normal", "lógicocientífico", destinado a establecer la coherencia del ambiente descrito, *a ganar la confianza del lector* ante lo que está leyendo. El segundo es un conjunto de fórmulas fantásticas, irracionales, imposibles de reducción a términos de experiencia cotidiana.[5]

The purpose of the present paper is to extend Durán's statements by focusing more closely on the structural systems that underlie the texts, with particular attention to rupture and subversion of language in the terms already put forth.

II

By examining one of the four independent fragments of the text "Instrucciones-ejemplos sobre la forma de tener miedo," we arrive at a better understanding of what has been mentioned previously:

> El médico termina de examinarnos y nos tranquiliza. Su voz grave y cordial precede los medicamentos cuya receta escribe ahora, sentado ante su mesa. De cuando en cuando alza la cabeza y sonríe, alentándonos. No es de cuidado, en una semana estaremos bien. Nos arrellanamos en nuestro sillón, felices, y miramos distraídamente en torno. De pronto, en la penumbra

5. Manuel Durand (Durán) [sic], "Julio Cortázar y su pequeño mundo de cronopios y famas," in *La vuelta a Cortázar en nueve ensayos* (Buenos Aires: Carlos Pérez Editor, 1968), pp. 31–49. The quote is from p. 36. See also Antonio Pagés Larraya, "Cotidianeidad y fantasía en una obra de Cortázar," in Helmy F. Giacoman, *Homenaje a Julio Cortázar* (Long Island City, N.Y.: Las Américas-Anaya, 1972), pp. 277–87; Pagés Larraya focuses on the highlighted intersection of the mundane and the fantastic in *Historias de cronopios y famas*. Graciela Coulson stresses the foregrounding of language and certain parallelisms with modern poetry in " 'Instrucciones para matar hormigas en Roma' o la dinámica de la palabra," *Revista iberoamericana* No. 95 (1976):233–37.

debajo de la mesa vemos las piernas del médico. Se ha subido los pantalones hasta los muslos, y tiene medias de mujer. (p. 17)

Although the text is deceptively simple, a number of features should be closely scrutinized:

1. The first element of the cover title, "Instrucciones-ejemplos," presents us with a neologism in Spanish, although one that is syntactically possible in terms of current generative rules for the production of exocentric noun compounds, particularly in Argentine Spanish. Nevertheless, we might expect something more standard like "instrucciones típicas" or even "instrucciones ejemplares." While perhaps no great weight should be attached to the unusual nature of "instrucciones-ejemplos," it is only the first of a series of language deviations in the text.

2. More significant is the second principal constituent of the title, "la forma de tener miedo." In Spanish, the phrase *tener miedo* cannot be agentive, that is, it cannot take as subject a noun that instigates or carries out the action. This restriction is, of course, one of universal semantics, and the Spanish phrase simply represents a semantic structure that, in universal terms, cannot be agentive.[6] Thus, we may not expect any language to permit an agentive subject with its equivalent to *tener miedo* or "be afraid." Rather, this structure requires as subject a noun that is semantically neutral or, as a more traditional term puts it, a patient: an individual for whom the circumstance described obtains. Such structures cannot take a positive imperative—since one cannot command someone to instigate what he can only experience passively—which is why "Tenga/Ten miedo" is nonoccurring (because it is ungrammatical) in Spanish. Or why "Be afraid!" is impossible in English. Although the title does not use the imperative, it does embed *tener miedo* in a syntactic construction that, like the positive imperative, may only occur with agentive verbals. Thus, *la forma de (= cómo) escribir una novela* is possible for the same reason that *Escriba/Escribe una novela* is. Conversely, *la forma de (= cómo) ser alto* is unlikely for the same reason that *sea/Sé alto* is. Although we cannot go into a complete linguistic analysis here that would explain the obvious exceptions that one could think of to what has been stated (why, for example, is the following title possible: *Cómo ser argentino?*[7]), it does capture a basic linguistic principle that affects the title in question: "Instrucciones [a

6. For a work dealing with similar semantic questions, see George L. Dillon, *Introduction to Contemporary Linguistic Semantics* (Englewood Cliffs, N.J.: Prentice-Hall, 1977).

7. One reason is that the sentence conceives of the adjective *argentino* not as the passive one of nationality but as an active one referring to a voluntarily attainable state of mind.

noun that involves an implied imperative] sobre la forma de tener miedo" strikes us as odd because you do not [need to] explain to someone how to be afraid. One does not, normally, set out to be afraid, since fear is something that happens to one, not something one self-induces.[8] Thus, the title, while not grammatically impossible, is, if one considers it closely, semantically anomalous. This sort of anomaly is one of the elements of language rupture that abounds in *Historias*. By casually suggesting that one can and ought to self-induce fear, Cortázar is breaking with the "normal" semantic structures represented by language. These structures are sensed to be normal, and departures from them are deviant (anomalous) because we feel they correspond to the world as it is and should be. Cortázar's process of rupturing this supposition, through a localized departure from acceptable rhetoric, is one example of the sort of questioning, of putting under erasure, what we hold to be a stable and well-defined reality.

3. Turning to the text fragment in question, it should be clear that its semantic structures rest, precisely, on what we consider to be a self-evident reality. One of the reasons that the texts in *Historias* can be so brief is that basically they evoke with one or two key phrases a familiar and acceptable circumstance. To be more specific, these texts depend, at least for their initial point of departure, on a reader-shared referential or cultural code that will immediately identify a widely known experience or context.[9] That the ease of such an identification will become subsequently (and very rapidly in a text of barely one hundred words) the point of rupture only reinforces the importance of the reference to recognition in the first place: we are only able to identify the abnormal if we have a norm against which to measure it.

4. The tense forms of the fragment are unusual: since essentially a "story" is being told—a context is established and something happened within the context—we would expect past-tense verbs. However, we note immediately the use of present-tense forms. Two explanations are possible, neither of which is particularly satisfactory (the other three fragments of the text are also narrated with present-tense forms). We might say that the author has chosen the "historic present" to make his surprising tale more vivid: it is frequent for oral stories to make use of such an option. However, Cortázar's story is not oral, and one can discover no particular reason why it might want to be taken as an example of oral storytell-

8. Of course, we have an utterance like: "¿Quiere Ud. tener miedo? Vea *King Kong*." Such a structure is possible only in the (pseudo) poetic context of fear as a sought-after emotion.

9. This is one of the five codes of reading that Roland Barthes introduces in *S/Z* (New York: Hill and Wang, 1974), pp. 18–20.

ing. Alternately, we might say that the verb forms are not really indicative of either a present or a past tense, but are tenseless, as in the case of so-called durative affirmations: when we say that the sun *is* a sphere, or that two plus two *equals* four, we are not making a statement about something true in the present. Rather, these are "eternal verities" and as such are tenseless, which is why we cannot use any other tense to formulate them (when and if we do, we are practicing the same sort of sardonic rupture we might find in Cortázar: "two plus two *used to equal* four, but with the new math there is no telling what equals what!"). Western languages often use the present tense to indicate what is aspectually durative or what is customary. Compare the textbook distinction between *Juan canta* (or *Juan es cantante*) and *Juan está cantando*: only the latter is truly semantically present, for the former describes a durative quality concerning Juan and not what he is doing at the moment of the utterance.

If Cortázar's fragment is to be taken as "durative" rather than as a past action described with the historic present, then we would be obliged to say that it describes a "normal, natural, customary" event and not something bizarre that is related as having occurred but once. Perhaps the basis of the fear that the event ought to evoke resides not in its bizarre yet limited occurrence, but rather in its being (metonymically?) a generalizable circumstance. We might say, in rather puerile thematic terms, that there is always some surprise lurking in the corner of our eye that will destroy our confidence in a familiar and assuring setting. Neither of these explanations is particularly satisfactory, as has already been said. That they are unsatisfactory is perhaps another measure of the anomaly that we are able to discover in an apparently innocent text (or in the text's apparently innocent rhetoric). There is no overwhelming linguistic or stylistic deviance at issue in the use of the present tense in the fragment. But like other features, it is just another small element that does not fit. In the end, these casual anomalies coalesce into a basic pattern of structural rupture.

5. Syntactically, the narrative structure of the fragment may be represented as follows: A(a a a a a) B(b b [b' c]).[10] A represents the first five sentences of the discourse; all are basic declarative sentences and, although a more detailed description would underline differences (for example, those in which *el médico* is the subject

10. Concerning the syntactic analysis of literary discourse, see the essays in *Análisis estructural del relato* (Buenos Aires: Editorial Tiempo Contemporáneo, 1972), and Robert E. Scholes, *Structuralism in Literature: An Introduction*. For a more technical example of discourse analysis with reference to a text of Cortázar, see Francis M. Aid, "Case Grammar Applied: Spanish Language and Literature," in Don L. F. Nilsen, *Meaning: A Common Ground of Linguistics and Literature* (Cedar Falls, Iowa: 1973), pp. 90–99.

and those in which *nosotros* is), we can homologize them by the sign *a*. *B* represents the last two sentences. The connective *De pronto* in reality is a prelude to rupture to the extent that, semantically, it alludes to a detail or circumstance that stands out against the background of the larger context that has been established. In terms of what was said in section 3 above, it is at this point that a departure can be noted from the familiar context ("routine treatment by a trusted physician") that *A* establishes by deft identification with an entire referential code concerning that context: "el médico . . . nos tranquiliza"; "su voz grave y cordial"; "cuya receta escribe ahora"; "no es de cuidado"; and so on.

These phrases evoke an entire ethos associated with medical treatment in Western culture. *De pronto* marks, potentially, the initiation of a departure from the familiar. The rather complex structure given for *B*, alongside *A*, reflects the attempt to chart the working out of that departure. The fulfillment of the rupture inaugurated by *De pronto*, *B* consists of two sentences, *b b*. Although at first nothing startling is reported, what is related departs from the familiar context *A*. However, the rupture as such does not occur until the final word of the last sentence, which is thus represented in terms of a concatenation of an extended *b* structure plus the element of rupture (*c*). This element is represented by the one word *mujer*. It must be borne in mind that, in Argentine Spanish, the word *medias*, unlike in other dialects of Spanish, may mean either "men's socks" or "women's stockings"; it may, of course, also mean "women's socks." Since *medias* is unmarked for the gender of the possessor/ user in Argentine Spanish, the modifying prepositional phrase is necessary to make a distinction and thus may not be considered redundant (in standard Mexican Spanish, for example, *medias de hombre* would be anomalous, and it would be sufficient to say *El hombre llevaba medias* to elicit a broad smirk; by the same token, the latter phrase would be unnoteworthy in Buenos Aires and would simply mean that the man's feet were acceptably clothed).

All this means is that the full import of the rupture implicity foreshadowed by the introduction of the connective *De pronto* comes at the point of maximum impact, the very last words of the text. Since "silence," non-text, follows, we are left in the complete suspension that such a rupture induces. Once again, if we refer to the importance of the referential code we may understand the degree of this impact: the stereotyped image of the suave, professional physician, impeccably dressed under the white coat he presumably is wearing, suddenly turns out to be wearing women's hose. The implications of such a sartorial preference do not beg explanation. And if fear is involved as the result of the discovery of this preference, it stems from the stunning loss of faith in one of the unquestioned authorities, one of the few remaining mythic father figures in our culture. We are reminded of the visual effects Buñuel derives from the exploitation in a full-length motion picture, *The Discreet Charms of the Bourgeoisie*, of this sort of demythificational rupture (one recalls in particular the figure of the venerable village priest).

By the same token, observe what would have been the result of concluding with the phrase " . . . y tiene medias" or with the (redundant) "medias de hombre." Rather than the outrageous rupture we have jusst described—and it is again stressed that it is only comprehensible within the context of the referential code concerning contemporary Western veneration of the medical man—we would have at best a mildly amusing "rupture of the rupture" implied by the connective that shifts the text from *A* to *B*: a rupture is foreshadowed but does not occur and we seem to have a case of an anticlimactic shaggy-dog story. At worst, the text would simply be confusing, for we would be unable to grasp the point being made. This observation is an important one: the text is of interest only if it departs from the elements of the referential code that it evokes. If it simply plays out certain elements of that code, we see no point in the narrative text at all: it would be natural but insignificant that, were the doctor's pants to move a bit up his leg, we discover him to be wearing socks.

If the foregoing analysis pays excruciatingly close attention to verbal features of Cortázar's text, finding it necessary to go into a certain amount of detail concerning the nature of syntactic and semantic structures and specific lexical items, it is because the effect of the text depends on the exploitation of deviation of varying degrees from colloquial, expected linguistic patterns. Clearly, the entire point of the one fragment of "Instrucciones-ejemplos . . . " that has been examined turns on a lexical choice that dramatically ruptures the semantic norm established by the text.[11] To the extent that subversion and manipulation of language are essential vehicles for the inscription of the *écriture* of rupture in Cortázar's texts, a

11. For a survey of the issues associated with literature and norm, see the chapters in Raymond Chapman, *Linguistics and Literature* (Totowa, N.J.: Littlefield, Adams, 1973). One of the best single papers on norms and literary deviations is by Samuel R. Levin, "Internal and External Deviation in Poetry," *Word* 21 (1965): 225–37. The work of Teun A. Van Dijk on the logical structures of action narratives, of which literary narratives are an artistic subcategory, is especially important in speaking of the "expected" and the "unexpected" in discourse structures. See his "Narrative Macrostructures: Logical and Cognitive Foundations," *PTL* 1 (1976):547–68, and "Action, Action Description, and Narrative," *New Literary History* 6 (1975):273–94.

careful analysis of the full implications of his language is indispensable.[12]

III

Defamiliarization is unquestionably the basis of the *écriture* of the following text: to a certain extent it reminds one of those exercises that attempt to promote verbalization among youngsters by demanding that they explain, in logical order and in detail, the function of an everyday item that goes virtually unnoticed—and, therefore, unanalyzed—because it is so familiar.[13]

Nadie habrá dejado de observar que con frecuencia el suelo se pliega de manera tal que una parte sube en ángulo recto con el plano del suelo, y luego la parte siguiente se coloca paralela a este plano, para dar paso a una nueva perpendicular, conducta que se repite en espiral o en línea quebrada hasta alturas sumamente variables. Agachándose y poniendo la mano izquierda en una de las partes verticales, y la derecha en la horizontal correspondiente, se está en posesión momentánea de un peldaño o escalón. Cada uno de estos peldaños, formados como se ve por dos elementos, se sitúa un tanto más arriba y más adelante que el anterior, principio que da sentido a la escalera, ya que cualquier otra combinación produciría formas quizá más bellas o pintorescas, pero incapaces de trasladar de una planta baja a un primer piso.

Las escaleras se suben de frente, pues hacia atrás o de costado resultan particularmente incómodas. La actitud natural consiste en mantenerse de pie, los brazos colgando sin esfuerzo, la cabeza erguida aunque no tanto que los ojos dejen de ver los peldaños inmediatamente superiores al que se pisa, y respirando lenta y regularmente. Para subir una escalera se comienza por levantar esa parte del cuerpo situada a la derecha abajo, envuelta casi siempre en cuero o gamuza, y que salvo excepciones cabe exactamente en el escalón. Puesta en el primer peldaño dicha parte,

12. Roland Barthes speaks precisely of "abrupt movement" in his *The Pleasure of the Text* (New York: Hill and Wang, 1975) when he discusses the text that goes beyond (mere) pleasure: "Text of bliss: the text that imposes a state of loss, the text that discomfits (perhaps to the point of a certain boredom), unsettles the reader's historical, cultural, psychological assumptions, the consistency of his tastes, values, memories, brings to a crisis his relation with language" (p. 14).

13. Mireya Camurati categorizes this text and the other "Instrucciones" in *Historias de cronopios y famas* within the Bergson's concepts of *Le rire* and Vanguard art of rupture in general: "El absurdo, la risa y la invitación a la aventura: 'Instrucciones para subir una escalera'," in David Lagmanovich, *Estudios sobre los cuentos de Julio Cortázar*, pp. 73–81. However, he does not deal with any of the issues of textual rupture that have been discussed so far.

que para abreviar llamaremos pie, se recoge la parte equivalente de la izquierda (también llamada pie, pero que no ha de confundirse con el pie antes citado), y llevándola a la altura del pie, se la hace seguir hasta colocarla en el segundo peldaño, con lo cual en éste descansará el pie, y en el primero descansará el pie. (Los primeros peldaños son siempre los más difíciles, hasta adquirir la coordinación necesaria. La coincidencia de nombres entre el pie y el pie hace difícil la explicación. Cuídese especialmente de no levantar al mismo tiempo el pie y el pie.)

Llegado en esta forma al segundo peldaño, basta repetir alternadamente los movimientos hasta encontrarse con el final de la escalera. Se sale de ella fácilmente, con un ligero golpe de talón que la fija en su sitio, del que no se moverá hasta el momento del descenso. (pp. 25–26)

Hence, the term *defamiliarization* involves making the familiar unfamiliar through a (predominantly) verbal analysis that would ordinarily be considered superfluous.[14] Here it is climbing stairs, which seems so natural and familiar that it hardly deserves a second thought, much less an atomized scrutiny. As a consequence of the application of such a scrutiny—which we may describe as an ecphrasis on the simple command, *Suba Ud. la escalera*, much like the ecphrasis that we would accept as absolutely necessary were the imperative *Haga Ud. milanesas a la napolitana* directed at a non-Argentine housewife/cook—the text involves a fundamental rupture in the automatized language we associate with daily life and experience.

Automatized language, a concept originally proposed by the Prague School theoreticians of language, refers to those language forms that are unforegrounded, unnoticed in day-to-day oral communication because they are so familiar, so automatic: words, phrases, whole blocks of discourse (compare the so-called phatic speech).[15] A Spanish-speaking native automatically makes proper

14. Concerning defamiliarization (Viktor Shklovsky's *ostranenie*, a term adopted by Russian formalism), see Frederic Jameson, *The Prison-House of Language: A Critical Account of Structuralism and Russian Formalism*, pp. 50–54; and Scholes, *Structuralism in Literature*, pp. 83–85.

15. See Jan Mukařovský, "Standard Language and Poetic Language," in Paul L. Garvin, *A Prague School Reader on Esthetics, Literary Structure, and Style* (Washington, D.C.: Georgetown University Press, 1964), pp. 17–30. A more recent study of the phenomenon is R. H. Stacy, *Defamiliarization in Language and Literature* (Syracuse, N.Y.: Syracuse University Press, 1977). Ariel Dorfman has spoken of "la violencia narrativa" in modern Latin-American fiction, a term that surely captures synthetically the devices of defamiliarization, rupture, and norm-deviation, and the semiological ends they are made to serve. See his *Imaginación y violencia en América* (Santiago de Chile: Editorial Universitaria, 1970), section 4 of chapter 1, "La violencia en la novela hispanoamericana actual."

gender selection, proper noun-adjective agreement, and proper noun-verb concordance; an English-speaking native automatically gets verbs and verb particles in their proper order (for example, "Call the girl *up*" versus "Look *at* the girl"). Although these are both "difficult" processes for the speaker of another language, they are so automatic as to pass unnoticed by the native speaker, which is why we teach descriptive grammar to native speakers: to enable them to be consciously aware of what, in daily speech, they perform automatically.

This phenomenon extends, of course, to individual word choices, so much so that to call a rose by any other name does, indeed, seem strange. Hence, one might add, the seeming belief among the linguistically naive that the names for things are inherent to them, a consequence of them, as St. Isidore once claimed. And on an even higher plane, the phenomenon of automatization extends to our perception of accounting for experience via the resources of language: automatized speech aims to convey a reality that is perceived as equally automatized: climbing stairs is, like falling off a ladder, so easy, so natural, so automatic, that it suffices to express it with the automatized phrase.

Once we choose to foreground the language, we foreground equally the semantics that it represents. Or, vice versa, should we choose to foreground the semantics, we can only accomplish such a rupture verbally by foregrounding language. Simply to decide to say *para trepar una escalera*, we rupture the conditions of automatization. While *trepar* enjoys a certain semantic overlay with *subir*, it is both more specialized as to the type of action involved (that is, more careful and deliberate climbing, hazardous to one degree or another such as *subir* is not) and refers to a noun complement that customarily is not *escalera* (for example, it may be a catwalk, a ship's rigging, or any other object that combines semantically with the associated semes of deliberateness and relative hazard). Thus in *trepar . . . escalera*, both verb and object are foregrounded; the former because of the specialized nature of climbing that is not associated with *escalera*, the latter because it has "thrust upon" it the semantic range of the nouns that do combine with *trepar* in an automatized fashion.

Cortázar's text, of course, maintains the colloquial phrase *subir una escalera*. However, we can observe the following when analyzing its verbal texture:

1. By inserting the phrase in question within the context of *Instrucciones para*, attention is called to an implied necessity for such instructions. By contrast to the deviant use of *instrucciones* in the first text analyzed, deviance here is based not on the misfit between the implied jussive and a predicate that cannot colloquially take an

imperative: clearly, *subir*, as a verb taking an agentive subject, can be imperative. Rather, what is at issue is the curiousness of the so-called happiness conditions that dominate the phrase *Instrucciones para*. . . . "Happiness conditions" is one of those deliberately un-subtle terms used by generative linguists to refer to an abstract linguistic principle: in order for an item or construction to be used properly, certain conditions of the pragmatic linguistic context must be met.[16] Thus, in order for one to order a door shut, we must acknowledge tacitly that it is open, which is why "close the sealed door" is, if not ungrammatical, infelicitous. The major happiness condition that dominates *Instrucciones para* . . . (in addition to the necessary agentive-admitting property of the verb complement) requires that those instructions be in fact necessary in the real, pragmatic world in which the phrase is uttered. On this basis, *Instrucciones para subir una escalera* would appear to violate a control-ling happiness condition, which is why such a completely normal syntactic combination of modest lexical items seems to one so unusual—foregrounded in a word.

But more specifically, Cortázar's title, occurring in isolation, would be simply unusual or facetious for the reasons adduced. Occurring within the context of the texts being described and head-ing the specific text that has been quoted, what in fact transpires linguistically is double-edged. For while, on the one hand, the deautomatization of the phrase *subir una escalera*, achieved by incor-porating it into the larger context of *Instrucciones para* . . . , would seem to imply a need to defamiliarize the event signified by the phrase in question, the text proper reveals that quite the opposite is true. Semantic defamiliarization does not really take place (as it does in the following text, "Preámbulo a las instrucciones para dar cuerda al reloj": "No te regalan un reloj, tú eres el regalado, a ti te ofrecen para el cumpleaños del reloj" [p. 28]). Semantic defamiliarization leads to the expressionistic (Kafka, Borges), the surreal (Dalí), the absurd (Ionesco, Beckett), the magical real (Asturias, Guimarães Rosa), and, clearly, language or any other semiotic structure must be defamiliarized in order to convey or portray semantic defamiliariza-tion. But the opposite is not necessarily true. Although some of Cortázar's *Instrucciones* texts involve semantic defamiliarization with concomitant linguistic defamiliarization (and the passage just quoted is manifestly deviant in ways that can be quickly demon-strated through a linguistic analysis), the one at hand does not. The detailed instructions that are revealed, upon analysis, to describe in minute but unstrange terms what is in fact the totally *familiar* process

16. Dillon uses the more neutral term *pragmatic conditions*. See pp. 36–37 and chapter 7.

of climbing stairs. An apparent defamiliarization remains on the level of the linguistic sign and thus serves only to foreground what is a completely natural activity.

2. There are, of course, a few details that suggest a tentative degree of semantic defamiliarization, without actually constituting an overall semantic dislocation. Consider:

a. The use of *se pliega, sube, se coloca* is ambiguous, since it may describe either an action (*el hombre se coloca a la izquierda de la mujer*) or a circumstance (*Los precios de la carne suben de mes a mes*). While we would "expect" the description of the physical layout of a set of stairs to contain semantically nonaction verbs, the use of semantically ambiguous ones in an already overtly defamiliarized context is suggestive of a more open reading of verbs than would normally be the case. The semantically unambiguous nonactive constructions are clearly avoided, although the stylistic focus of the text may not easily lend itself to them: *la parte siguiente está colocada/se encuentra paralela a este plano* would be an acceptably unambiguous alternative.

b. Similarly, the closing phrase implies, perhaps even declares, an agentive quality for the verb *no se moverá*, as though the stairs could undertake to move themselves, or as though the fixed set of stairs were an escalator ingeniously shut off by the sharp rap of the shoe heel as it steps off the moving train onto the top, covering platform (and stepping back on them reverses their direction).

c. The conclusion of the description of a typical staircase at the end of the first paragraph establishes a contrast between what could be (semantic defamiliarization) and what in reality is (reaffirmation of the familiar). This juxtaposition is effected via the rhetorical formula "(quizás) *A*, pero (más bien) *B*": *A* is the suggestion of the unknown ("cualquier otra combinación produciría formas quizás más bellas o pintorescas"), while *B* is the insistence on the known quality of staircases ("pero incapaces de trasladar de una planta baja a un primer piso").

Although these examples threaten the implicit denial of semantic defamiliarization that underlies the text, despite repeated examples of language structure defamiliarization, they do not coalesce into a dominating pattern. Rather, they remain as semantically unstable elements within the text and constitute, one could say, a parenthetical questioning of the "familiar" semantic base that is basically at issue.

3. Textual, as opposed to semantic, defamiliarization takes many forms in the text: retardation of lexical utilization, accompanied by what in terms of an automatized standard can only be called gratuitous ecphrasis, ironic complication or compounding of the routinely ambiguous structure of language, the introduction of in-

formation that is misleading because it is superfluous.

a. The latter feature is a concomitant characteristic of the text's basic *écriture*, founded as it is on linguistic defamiliarization of a natural and trivial linguistic message. A prominent component of that defamiliarization is the use of the para-technical language of explanation such as is used in directions for mechanical assembly or any other routine context involving constituent combination and utilization like recipes or household chemicals. But let us consider carefully what such a language register involves with reference to both colloquial and literary expression. Technical and para-technical language is an automatized level of expression only within a pragmatic context appropriate to it. That is, while automatized levels of language structure are the expected norm (the unmarked register), it is necessary to establish a well-defined context in order for technical language—jargon—to be used without being foregrounded. In such a context, which is marked because it is not the norm, the jargon remains foregrounded. Yet, it is foregrounded neither by its internal features (which are automatic) nor by the nature of its users (the users of technical language seek automatized expression, while those of literary language aspire to complex forms of foregrounding) but by the pragmatic context in which it is deployed. Technical jargon, like colloquial expression and unlike truly foregrounded literary expression, is ruled by precise constraints on the types of lexical items and syntactic patterns that may be used.

Thus, technical jargon (including both lexical items, syntactic structures, and discourse structure: the types of logical coordination that rule the succession of constituents in the explanation) would be automatized were we dealing with instructions in a handicraftsman's manual on how to lay a carpet up the stairway. However, this same register becomes a part of the overall process of literary foregrounding (and one recalls the use of "mechanical" language in some futurist poetry) in Cortázar's text not only by the simple virtue of appearing in a "literary" context, but more specifically because it is used to describe a process that, pragmatically, neither calls for explanation in the first place nor could conceivably require a technical one anyway.

Let us give just one example of the patterns of para-technical jargon used in Cortázar's text. (It is interesting to note that the author eschews the infinitive imperative that is a clear marker of impersonal instructions in favor of the equally frequent formal imperative that is, however, not restricted to instructions. Curiously, in other texts—"Instrucciones para matar hormigas en Roma"—he uses an imperative form that is not normally found in instructions, the future imperative.) The second sentence of the first paragraph, beginning with the participial "Agachándose . . . " and continuing in the main clause with the impersonal "se está es posesión momentánea . . . ," is typical of the language of instructions. It is impersonal semantically because reference is avoided, via markers provided by the syntax of Spanish like the *se* pseùdo-subject, to any specific subject in the pragmatic context. In terms of the rules for constituent coordination, it can also be called a "situational preface" in that it describes a situation necessary for the actual instruction itself. Later, in the second paragraph, the instruction is given, once again making use of impersonal subject markers: "Para subir [= para que *se* suba] una escalera se comienza por levantar. . . . " The use of *se comienza*, the polite indicative imperative that also opens the final sentence of the text, "Se sale de ella . . . ," is another syntactic trait of the language of technical instructions without being exclusive to it.

In summary, Cortázar heightens the foregrounding of the language of this set of instructions by using a register that is, when employed in the proper pragmatic context, nonliterary and, with reference to an appropriately technical subject, automatized. The foregrounded automatized jargon becomes, therefore, a major element in the text's *écriture* of defamiliarization.

b. The retardation of lexical utilization—the "refusal" to use the right item in the right place and its postponement by inserting a diversionary, gratuitous ecphrasis[17]—is most noticeable midway through the directions on stair utilization in the second paragraph: the text delays, avoids as though a euphemism were in order, the use of the word *pie*: " . . . se comienza por levantar esa parte del cuerpo situada a la derecha abajo, [and so forth]." Only after a description of the foot that is clumsy both in the manner of describing it—compare a precise dictionary definition of *pie*—and in the constituent with which that description is joined ("envuelta [*sic*] casi siempre en cuero o gamuza") does the author resort gratuitously to the proper lexical item: "que para abreviar llamaremos pie. . . . " It is as though he were describing an unfamiliar device or component, only then to give it its equally unfamiliar technical term. This is a particularly ingenious ploy for defamiliarization, and the clumsiness of the explanation only contributes to its ridiculous effectiveness.

Another less involved example of gratuitous information that retards the explanation at hand is the reference in the beginning of

17. Retardation is another of Shklovsky's basic concepts concerning literary structure. See his "The Connection Between Devices of *Syuzhet* Construction and General Stylistic Devices," in Stephen Bann and John E. Bowlt, *Russian Formalism* (New York: Barnes and Noble, 1973), pp. 48–72.

the second paragraph to incorrect body positions for climbing stairs. Or, later in the following sentence, the comment concerning eye level. These examples clearly are part of the *écriture* of defamiliarization not only because retardation is an important feature of textual elaboration but also because they contribute to the general sense that the text is dealing with an unfamiliar phenomenon. It is only when the reader correlates these textual features with their underlying semantic structure and with the real world to which the latter, because it is comprehensible, has reference that we are able to gauge the exaggerated degree of retardation and gratuitous ecphrasis involved.

c. The "definition" of *pie* provides the opportunity for exploitation of ambiguous or, more properly, under-differentiated structures in Spanish. Despite what we sense to be the clear differences between phenomena in the real world, our languages do not always embody them in their lexical and syntactic structures.[18] If necessary, we may explicitly distinguish between *A* and *B*, which are not routinely differentiated structurally, by the addition of restrictive words or phrases. Thus, *planta* covers both "garden plant" and "sole of the foot" in Spanish; *planta de jardín* and *planta del pie* are attempts at overcoming under-differentiation. Although English differentiates between fingers and toes, Spanish does not, although both languages differentiate hands and feet. However, no Western language at least differentiates between left and right limbs: *pie/foot*, *mano/hand* may belong to either side of the body. Differentiation, of course, is achieved, when and where necessary (otherwise it is considered redundant and stylistically inelegant), by the use of left-side versus right-side adjectives, which come in various registers: *left/southpaw*, *izquierdo/zurdo*.

Cortázar plays with the universal feature of linguistic under-differentiation and the Spanish-language mechanisms to overcome it in his handling of the interaction of the two feet in the process of climbing a set of stairs. Although he distinguishes right from left, noting implicitly that most people begin to climb with their right foot, he goes on to ignore the concepts for the purpose of distinguishing between the two feet. Hence, the wackiness of the parenthetical expression beginning "(también llamada pie . . .)." And later in a further parenthetical observation, he uses this maximization of an integral under-differentiation in the language to deny, in effect, the economy of this technical explanation: "La coincidencia

18. Several sections of Geoffrey Leech's *Semantics* (Harmonsworth: Penguin Books, 1974) discuss this sort of semantic phenomena. See in particular chapter 3 entitled " 'Bony-Structured Concepts.' " See also Robert J. Di Pietro, *Language Structures in Contrast* (Rowley, Mass.: Newbury House, 1971), especially chapter 6 entitled "The Structure of Lexicon."

de nombres entre el pie y el pie hace difícil la explicación." What is more, by violating an obligatory rule for the fusion to two repeated nouns into one plural noun (*el pie y el pie* must, colloquially, be expressed as *los (dos) pies*), Cortázar only foregrounds more his defamiliarization of language. To put it in forthright terms, the text has created a semantic problem for itself—the difficulty of distinguishing between the two feet—by refusing to take advantage of normal devices in the language, the lexical pair *izquierdo/derecho* that have already been used. The use of *el pie y el pie* without these restrictive adjectives, therefore, becomes an added anomaly; *el pie izquierdo y el pie derecho* is, of course, not an anomalous construction.

But there is even more. After insisting on the under-differentiation of *pie* and *pie* and the difficulties created thereby for the presumably carefully wrought explanation, Cortázar goes on to caution: "Cuídese especialmente de no levantar al mismo tiempo el pie y el pie." In an explanation in which the realization of the process is questionable and the physical safety of the individual who undertakes it, the concept of *pie* is crucial. By insisting on the alleged difficulty in distinguishing between the members of the pair of limbs involved, Cortázar in a real sense denies the efficacy of his own "technical" explanation and instructions. This denial constitutes, in turn, a rupture with the system that the text sets up: precise technical description→ denial of necessary precision→ denial of efficacy of description. The text itself and the privileged register that inscribes it have been effectively placed *sous rature*.

IV

Although we have dealt with only two highly selective examples of Cortázar's texts, and two concentrated in only one of four sections of *Historias de cronopios y famas*, the sort of extended analysis that has been provided can serve as the starting point for an examination of the processes of rupture and language subversion that are operant in his writings as a whole. It is only possible to undertake such an examination and to perceive the processes at work if we have a clearly detailed characterization of how some of them work. It is for this reason that the highly selective analysis of this essay is appropriate. At the same time, if we accept the challenge to delve seriously into the language processes that characterize a particular textual *écriture*, we can only do it effectively with the sort of microscopic scrutiny brought to bear in the preceding pages, a scrutiny that recognizes the pressing need, if it is to be both precise and explicit, to make use of the full array of concepts concerning language structure that we currently have at our disposal. It is only in this fashion that the critic may specify with any degree of acceptable accuracy the clever jousts with everyday language that so strike the fancy of Cortázar's readers.

Chapter VII.

Cortázar's "Las armas secretas" and Structurally Anomalous Narratives

"No puede ser que todo sea tan absurdo . . . " (p. 189)
. . . todo tiene una explicación si se la busca. . . . (p. 208)[1]

I

A reading of the body of Cortázar's short fiction, including both the short stories and the "microtexts" of *Historias de cronopios y famas*, leaves one with the impression, above all, of a world in which things are not as they are "supposed to be." What is involved is not exactly fantasy, for this mode or genre of fiction implies the systematic substitution of the known by the unknown, usually with the implication that the former is far more profound or "richer" in meaning than our pedestrian minds had assumed, or that the latter is in some way a more valid image of experience than what we routinely call reality. True, in the case of some of Cortázar's fiction or in the case of some of the ways in which it may be focused, fantasy may seem like a viable denomination, particularly if we accept Todorov's suggestion that fantastic literature is a corollary of a creative and critical poetics that refuses to reduce texts—or the events and experiences on which they are ostensibly based—to discrete and single-minded interpretations.[2]

1. Julio Cortázar, "Las armas secretas," in *Las armas secretas*, 5th ed. (Buenos Aires: Editorial Sudamericana, 1966 [original 1964]), pp. 185–222. Also in his *Relatos* (Buenos Aires: Editorial Sudamericana, 1970), pp. 488–519.
2. Although there are subsequent studies that take exception to its premises and conclusions, the major point of departure for a structuralist investigation of the fantastic remains Tzvetan Todorov's *The Fantastic: A Structural Approach to a Literary Genre* (Ithaca, N.Y.: Cornell University Press, 1975 [original published in French in 1970]). See, for example, Roberto Reis, "Para uma definição do fantástico," *Chasqui* 6:3 (1977):37–43. There is no comprehensive, systematic study of fantasy in Cortázar's writings, although there are many references to it in the abundant criticism now

To be sure, Cortázar's stories deal insistently with the texture of daily events, often within the context of the Argentine middle class in which he lived or the constellations of Latin-American emigrés in Paris among which he has moved during most of his later life.[3] Indeed, the humorous note that is so pervasive in his stories, running parallel to or abetting the sense of horror over a secure world gone awry, derives directly from a degree of caricature and mockery at the expense of these two contexts. In the literature of fantasy, typically the structure of the known is displaced, replaced by the structure of the unknown, a structure that has its own "higher" meaning that we are obliged to accept, if we want the sequence of events to possess any sense. Literature characteristically depends upon such a desire, as somehow superior to the initial postulates of reality. In Cortázar's stories, however, such a mechanism of displacement is rarely carried out completely. Although some of the texts in *Historias de cronopios y famas* are based directly on an "unreal," that is, unfamiliar, premise (typically, those texts dealing with *cronopios* and *famas*) and some of the short stories proper do, in fact, conclude by substituting an extensively revised order of the known (those in which the unknown intrudes violently on the known, such as "Cartas de mamá" or "Carta a una señorita en París"), some of the best examples of Cortázar's short fiction cannot really be described as fantasy in the sense that has been stipulated: "El perseguidor," "Las babas diablo," "La salud de los enfermos," "Final del juego," "Las puertas del cielo." If these stories are not examples of fantasy, of the systematic displacement of the structure of the known by that of the unknown, how might we describe them so as to capture the particular nature of their narrative?

Structural anomaly, which will be used to manifest the particular nature of Cortázar's narratives, is a term taken from contemporary linguistics because it concerns the proper description of syntactic structure, semantic structure, and their interrelationship.[4] Dealing with utterances that are less than categorically ungrammatical (ut-

---

available on the writer. Categorizing all of Cortázar's stories under a single denomination such as the "fantastic" is typical of the many superficial commentaries on his work. See, for example, Roberto Escamilla Molina, *Julio Cortázar: visión de conjunto* (México, D.F.: Editorial Novaro, 1970). His chapter 2 entitled "La invención fantástica . . . ," does little more than summarize plots under the poorly defined term *fantastic*. See also Rosa Boldori, "La irrealidad en la narrativa de Cortázar," *Boletín de literaturas hispánicas* No. 6 (1966):13–27.

3. On the social context of Cortázar's fiction, see Joaquín Roy, *Julio Cortázar ante su sociedad* (Barcelona: Ediciones Península, 1974).

4. The theoretical aspects of the concept may be pursued in Janet Dean Fodor, *Semantics: Theories of Meaning in Generative Grammar* (New York: Thomas Y. Crowell, 1977). See particularly pp. 194–97.

terances that possess no semantic meaning and/or no syntactic coherence), the work on anomaly involves structures that appear to be only partially defective. Meaning and conventional syntactic cohesion are recoverable to varying degrees, and what may be fundamentally wrong with the anomalous sentence is that, because it does not seem to be "just right," we are uncertain as to which of a number of well-formed possibilities we should choose. For example, *The boys is here* is neither ungrammatical or meaningless; it is simply structurally deficient or anomalous. But which is the "correct" reading: *The boys are* or *The boy is*? Save from surrounding context, the utterance itself does not indicate the normalization to be selected (unless, of course, we base ourselves on statistical principles: there are more errors of incorrect verb agreement in normal English usage than of incorrect noun agreement; thus, the first normalization is to be chosen). One is aware of the dangers of translating linguistic concepts into putatively corresponding ones in literary theory. Yet, if there is any validity in the hypothesis that discourse analysis (and the structural description of literary texts is discourse analysis of verbal texts that serve artistic rather than communicational ends; however, "artistic" is defined) involves the linguistic issues of individual utterances as the latter combine themselves into more complex sequences, the concept of "structural anomaly" may, at least, serve as a workable starting point for approaching a literary text characterized by traits seemingly analogous to those of anomalous utterances. The concept, thus, becomes not a tool for analysis but a conceptual vehicle for undertaking the careful analysis of a complex literary text.

To the best of my knowledge, no one has attempted a typological classification of Cortázar's texts (although Cortázar himself uses a tripartite distribution of texts in his *Relatos*); thus, it is difficult to refer to them as a body with any sort of analytical rigor. What this means is that, until a proper classification is available, it would be risky to suggest which texts are best characterized as indicative of structural anomaly. For the purposes of this essay, "Las armas secretas," the title story of a 1966 collection that is recognized as one of Cortázar's best, may serve as a paradigmatic example.

II

"Las armas secretas" is an appropriate text for a study of narrative structural anomaly, for, unlike stories like "Casa tomada" or "Axolotl," there is no clear-cut movement toward a domain of events or circumstance that is in opposition to what we can roughly call the reader's normal world. Contemporary narrative analysis recognizes that all literature, particularly fiction, depends on reader reference to a vaguely defined referential code or code of the probable and the possible. This code embodies the received knowledge of a sociocultural community.[5] Although it is relative to the extent that it may change from generation to generation, from social class to social class, and even from one reader to another in accordance with what is tacitly accepted as "real," the referential code is, from a structural and semiological point of view, the touchstone for the identification of the marvelous or the fantastic. We may define such literature as exemplified by a text that implicitly juxtaposes the semantic postulates of its narrative to what the referential code of the implied reader of the text accepts as semantically permissible. Of course, actual readers change from generation to generation and even from society to society, and it is for this reason that we restrict the point of reference to the implied reader of the text, the reader that on the basis of a number of principles of identification we can propose as the reasonable addressee of the text. Gerald Prince has studied this aspect of narrative structure in detail, and it is to his separation between implied and actual reader that we may distinguish between the actual readers at different times and in different places of a text and a "kernel" reader that, because the text is structurally stable, remains equally stable over a range of the most diverse of readings.[6]

In the case of stories like "Casa tomada" and "Axolotl," there is an undeniable movement from the known to the unknown, from what is acceptable as real by the referential code of the implied reader (that is, that a brother and sister inhabit an old, rambling mansion in downtown Buenos Aires) to what goes beyond the domain of the accepted (that they are forced out of their house by unknown invaders and that, moreover, the pair passively allows themselves to be evicted from various sectors of the house and then from the house itself.) We might also add that there is an inherent contradiction or, at least, a fundamental implausibility in the fact that the brother would so passively accept the eviction and then narrate a statement concerning it in which his own passiveness remains patently clear. Of course, we must recognize that much literature that strains the postulates of the referential code of the implied reader depends less on overtly contradicting them (although texts from surrealistic literature or the theater of the absurd do, in fact, depend on such blatant contradictions) and more on the exploitation of internal weaknesses

5. See Roland Barthes's discussion of reader codes in his *S/Z* (New York: Hill and Wang, 1974 [original published in French in 1970]), pp. 18–20 in particular.
6. Gerald Prince, "Introduction a l'étude du narrataire," *Poétique* 14 (1973):178–96.

and ambiguities of that code. For example, in "Axolotl" the symbiosis of the narrator and the glass-enclosed animals may be read by a particular type of reader as less a case of fantastic metempsychosis than as a case of acute psychosis. That the narration is in the first person would support such a "normalizing" view of the narrative, which is thereby brought into line with what is recognized as actually or potentially possible by an accepted standard of modern psychology. Science fiction depends for its impact not on the proposition of the totally unknown or impossible (although, to be sure, such elements do figure prominently) but on speculation that exploits the fringes of the accepted referential code. It is for this reason that both science fiction and fantastic literature generally seem to come tantalizingly close to prophesying what will, in due course, become accepted by the received referential code (for example, space travel or human-organ transplants).

What all this means is that the critic must be exceedingly careful in making distinctions between different texts and the sorts of semantic postulates that they involve. In the case of Latin-American literature, two decades or more of dealing with the literature of Borges and other authors that were first grouped under the umbrella term *magical realism* have sharpened the ability to make such distinctions, assisted by some of the hypotheses of contemporary narrative analysis.[7] Neither Borges nor Cortázar can be conveniently classified—and then dismissed—as writers of fantasy. While it is true that their literature challenges the reader's referential code on various fronts, few would dismiss their stories as, therefore, frivolous. What we need, instead, are models of narrative reading that will enable us to appreciate the particular challenging complexity that these texts represent. What we do not need, it would seem, is a model for the routine "naturalization" of the unsettling texts of literature. Jonathan Culler[8] has spoken pointedly of the inherently unresolvable tension in literature. Because it is literature it is somehow different from both "life" and daily language, but because it does impinge upon life and makes use of what we recognize to be the structures of normal verbal communication we want it to be of use to us. In short, we want both to "monumentalize" literature (thereby justifying its difference) and to "naturalize" it (investing it with an existential usefulness):

Thus, the distinction between speech and writing becomes

7. See the distinction that Emir Rodríguez Monegal makes in "Borges: una teoría de la literatura fantástica," *Revista iberoamericana* No. 95 (1976):177–89.

8. Jonathan Culler, *Structuralist Poetics: Structuralism, Linguistics, and the Study of Literature*, p. 134.

the source of the fundamental paradox of literature: we are attracted to literature because it is obviously something other than ordinary communication; its formal and fictional qualities bespeak a strangeness, a power, an organization, a permanence which is foreign to ordinary speech. Yet the urge to assimilate that power and permanence or to let that formal organization work upon us requires us to make literature into a communication, to reduce its strangeness, and to draw upon supplementary conventions which enable it, as we say, to speak to us. The difference which seemed the source of value becomes a distance to be bridged by the activity of reading and interpretation. The strange, the formal, the fictional, must be recuperated or naturalized, brought within our ken, if we do not want to remain gaping before monumental inscriptions. (p. 134)

Allegorical literature may contain structurally the keys to its own hermeneutic code; contemporary literature in Latin America that is casually—and often carelessly—called fantastic or *mágicorrealista* does not. Naturalization, therefore, is a process of reading that attempts to resolve the conflicts between the semantic postulates of the text and the broad referential code. As such, it is essentially a reductionist process, one that we may see vividly at work in sociopolitical readings of Latin-American texts that oblige the textual complexities to render up a reading that fits into recognized sociopolitical schemes. For one sort of criticism, such a process may be legitimate. But for a criticism that accepts as its primary axiom the need to preserve a sense of the textual complexity of a work, it should be clear that reductionist readings are inappropriate. A reductionist reading of "Casa tomada" or "Axolotl" may safely align their meanings with accepted knowledge—the former is a parable of the assault on the Argentine oligarchy by *cabecitas negras* led by Juan Domingo and Eva Perón, the latter is a fictional treatment of a type of psychotic disturbance. But many sectors of modern criticism would acknowledge that somehow the particular fascination of the text gets lost in the process of applying such a reading.

III

With these principles in mind, we may return to "Las armas secretas" and begin to see how the text does and does not lend itself to the category of fantastic narratives and to reductionist or naturalized readings.

The story is quite simple: Pierre is in love with Michèle, a sensitive and somewhat remote girl who appears to be the particular concern of some older friends, Babette and Roland. Pierre is particularly anxious to consummate his love and, in the face of her seemingly inexplicable reluctance, he experiences a series of feelings of insecurities, speculations concerning how little we really know about even those with whom we are intimate, and, suddenly, a series of obsessive recollections that concerns Michèle but does not fit his own relationship with her. He means to take advantage of her invitation to her parents' chalet outside Paris to press his case with Michèle, who is both willing and reluctant, a circumstance that alternately bewilders Pierre and wounds his masculine pride. In the final section of the story, as the obsessive recollections become more insistent, Pierre "overwhelms" Michèle—it is not clear if he has just won her submission or if he is determined to force her. But Michèle has made a desperate appeal to her friends, who will arrive at the chalet during or just after Pierre's hard-won sexual triumph. This change of events would not be particularly outstanding if it were not for the integration of Pierre's obsessive recollections with their own role: it emerges that during the war (the story must, therefore, be set in the early fifties) Michèle was brutally raped by a German officer at a hunting lodge in Enghien. Babette and Roland were able to catch up with the rapist and to kill him with a shotgun. Subsequently, Michèle becomes unable to accept normal sexual relations with a man; her friends have hoped that Pierre and the affection between them would have helped to overcome that psychological hurdle. But in the final stages of his seduction of the girl, he appears to her to be the German rapist—hence, Michèle's desperate call to her friends (at a moment when Pierre storms from the house, only to return determined to possess her) and their flight to her aid. The story concludes on an appropriately ambiguous note, one that is even banal, given the circumstances just related. Yet, it is a significant departure for a structured reading of the story in terms of the semantic possibilities it postulates:

> —Ser valiente es siempre más fácil que ser hombre—dice Babette—. Abusar de una criatura que . . . Cuando pienso en lo que tuve que luchar para que Michèle no se matara. Esas primeras noches . . . No me extraña que ahora vuelva a sentirse la de antes, es casi natural.
> El auto entra a toda velocidad en la calle que lleva al pabellón.
> —Sí, era un cochino—dice Roland—. El ario puro, como lo entendían ellos en ese tiempo. Pidió un cigarrillo, naturalmente, la ceremonia completa. También quiso saber por qué íbamos a liquidarlo, y se lo explicamos, vaya si se lo explicamos. Cuando sueño con él es sobre todo en ese momento, su aire de sorpresa desdeñosa, su manera casi elegante de tartamudear. Me acuerdo de cómo cayó, con la cara hecha pedazos entre las hojas secas.
> —No sigas, por favor—dice Babette.
> —Se lo merecía, aparte de que no teníamos otras armas. Un cartucho de caza bien usado . . . ¿Es a la izquierda, allá en el fondo?

—Sí, a la izquierda.

—Espero que haya coñac—dice Roland, empezando a frenar. (pp. 221–22)

What should a "proper" reading of "Las armas secretas" be?[9] That is, what sort of reader does the narrative structure of the text imply? For many readers, the temptation to naturalize or normalize the story in psychological terms will be great, and it is undeniable that the relationship between Pierre and Michèle can, at least on an immediate level, be defined in these terms (as can the story, "Verano" in Cortázar's latest collection, *Octaedro*; what is involved here is the frigidity of female sexuality within a context of a tranquil but stultifying domestic routine). Michèle's frightening initiation into sexuality has understandably left her with deep psychological scars that jeopardize her intimacy with Pierre; the latter, unfamiliar with the girl's past, is equally and understandably bewildered and even aggressive in his determination to force the issue in order to put their relations on what should be a normal level. (Clearly, the story involves the reader's accepting, as part of his referential code, the normalcy of complete sexual relations between the two young adults. It also involves, but only to a circumstantial degree, the acceptability of Babette's and Roland's execution of the rapist be-

9. There are virtually no analyses of "Las armas secretas," although passing references abound. Alain Bosqueti's review of the French translation of the collection that contains the eponymic text is included in *La vuelta a Cortázar en nueve ensayos* (Buenos Aires: Carlos Pérez Editor, 1968), pp. 51–54. In "La intuición y la muerte en *Las armas secretas*, de Julio Cortázar," *Hispania* 52 (1969):846–51, Saúl Sosnowski does not give a convincing explanation of why Pierre is the victim of a "desdoblamiento involuntario"— that is, to what conclusions, fantastic or otherwise, does the rhetoric of the text's structure lead us. Lanin A. Gyurko, "Man as Victim in Two Stories by Cortázar," *Kentucky Romance Quarterly* 19 (1972):317–35, is more detailed in tracing the structure of an event seen as essentially fantastic. Gyurko also discusses "Las armas secretas" in the wider context of fantasy in Cortázar's fiction: "Destructive and Ironically Redemptive Fantasy in Cortázar," *Hispania* 56 (1973):988–99. The story is most often mentioned in the context of the *topos* of the Doppelgänger in Cortázar's works. Yet, these refrences do not represent an actual analysis of the structure of the story. See Malva E. Filer, "Las transformaciones del yo," in Helmy F. Giacoman, *Homenaje a Julio Cortázar: variaciones interpretativas en torno a su obra* (Long Island City, N.Y.: Las Américas-Anaya, 1972), pp. 260–76 (pp. 260–68 specifically); Marta Morello-Frosch, "El personaje y su doble en las ficciones de Cortázar," in Giacoman, *Homenaje a Julio Cortázar*, pp. 329–38; and Frances Wyers Weber, "Cortázar: Doubles, Figures, and Others," in Juan Bautista Avalle-Arce, *Narradores hispanoamericanos de hoy* (Chapel Hill, N.C.: University of North Carolina), pp. 21–31.

cause of the arrogant violence of his crime against a young innocent girl).

However, such a reading invites many obstacles. The possibility of viewing "Las armas secretas" in psychological terms has been raised by Graciela de Sola, although she does not pursue the implication of her suggestion[10]:

> El cuento objetiva una experiencia psicologica llevada a un grado de plena y estremecedora realización. Pierre tiene extraños anuncios. Oye un lied de Schumann cuyas palabras no comprende. Piensa en una casa en Enghien, con una bola de vidrio en el pasamanos, siente las hojas secas en la cara. Pero en el Pont Neuf no hay hojas secas. Una nueva personalidad desconocida parece aflorar a intervalos, y aunque Cortázar no lo señala en forma explícita en ningún momento queda abierta la posibilidad de un extraño caso de "posesión." (p. 60)

If we assume that the plot of a literary text has an internal logic and that the reader will apply the logic of his referential code to that text in an attempt to encompass the latter by the former—in more pedestrian terms, in order to oblige the story to "make sense"—there is a fundamental mismatch between a psychological reading of "Las armas secretas" and its narrative syntax. Psychologically, we can accept the likelihood of Michèle's sexual trauma; psychologically we can also accept a mechanism whereby part of that trauma is transferred unconsciously to Pierre: although he does not know the details of Michèle's dreadful experience or even that it occurred, his behavior could be seen as an unconscious reaction to abnormal or, at least, unexpected aspects of Michèle's behavior. For example, his decision to act aggressively could be "explained" as the result of his intuition that the girl suffers from some sort of "sexual block" that needs to be overcome through an appropriate affirmation of masculine sexuality. The opening of the story, which involves Pierre's stream-of-consciousness preoccupation over Michèle's sexual reserve, is an obvious example of a psychological reaction—one involving a sense of insecurity and confusion over what seems to be so natural—generated in one person by the preoccupations of another:

> Una escopeta de doble caño no tiene nada de raro, pero qué puede hacer a esa hora y en su pieza la idea de una escopeta de doble caño, y esa sensación como de extrañamiento. No le gusta esa hora en que todo vira al lila, al gris. Estira indolentemente el brazo

10. Graciela de Sola, *Julio Cortázar y el hombre nuevo* (Buenos Aires: Editorial Sudamericana, 1968). For a study of psychological conflicts in Cortázar's fiction, see Antoni, "Struttura psico-simbolica e rappresentazione di conflitti in alcuni racconti di Julio Cortázar," *Studi mediolatini e volgari* 22 (1974):7–33.

para encender la lámpara de la mesa. ¿Por qué no llega Michèle? Ya no vendrá, es inútil seguir esperando. Habrá que pensar que realmente no quiere venir a su cuarto. En fin, en fin. Nada de tomarlo a lo trágico; otro coñac, la novela empezada, bajar a comer algo al bistró de León. Las mujeres serán siempre las mismas, en Enghien o en París, jóvenes o maduras. Su teoría de los casos excepcionales empieza a venirse al suelo, la ratita retrocede antes de entrar en la ratonera. ¿Pero qué ratonera? Un día u otro, antes o después . . . La ha estado esperando desde las cinco, aunque ella debía llegar a las seis; ha alisado especialmente para ella el cobertor azul, se ha trepado como un idiota a una silla, plumero en mano, para desprender una insignificante tela de araña que no hacía mal a nadie. Y sería tan natural que en ese mismo momento ella bajara el autobús en Saint-Suplice y se acercara a su casa, deteniéndose ante las vitrinas o mirando las palomas de la plaza. No hay ninguna razón para que quiera subir a su cuarto. Claro que tampoco hay ninguna razón para pensar en una escopeta de doble caño, o decidir que en este momento Michaux sería mejor lectura que Graham Greene. La elección instantánea preocupa siempre a Pierre. No puede ser que todo sea gratuito, que un mero azar decida Greene contra Michaux, Michaux contra Enghien, es decir, contra Greene. Incluso confundir una localidad como Enghien con un escritor como Greene. . . "No puede ser que todo sea tan absurdo", piensa Pierre tirando el cigarrillo. "Yo si no viene es porque le ha pasado algo; no tiene nada que ver con nosotros dos." (pp. 188–89)

In addition, Pierre's musing concerning the difficulty of knowing another person would seem to be but a further specification of the psychological bases of their relationship:

[. . .] En esa remota vida que lleva, la única certidumbre es haber estado lo más cerca posible de Michèle, esperando y dándose cuenta de que no basta con eso, que todo es vagamente asombroso, que no sabe nada de Michèle, absolutamente nada en realidad (tiene ojos grises, tiene cinco dedos en cada mano, es soltera, se peina como una chiquilla), absolutamente nada en realidad. Entonces si uno no sabe nada de Michèle, basta dejar de verla un momento para que el hueco se vuelva una maraña espesa y amarga; te tiene miedo, te tiene asco, a veces te rechaza en lo más hondo de un beso, no se quiere acostar contigo, tiene horror de algo, esta misma mañana te ha rechazado con violencia (y qué encantadora estaba, y cómo se ha pegado contra ti en el momento de despedirse, y cómo lo ha preparado todo para reunirse contigo mañana e ir juntos a su casa de Enghien) y tú le has dejado la marca de los dientes en la boca, la estabas besando y la has mordido y ella se ha quejado, se ha pasado los dedos por la boca y se ha quejado sin enojo, un poco asombrada solamente, als alle Knospen sprangen, tú cantabas por dentro Schumann, pedazo de

bruto, cantabas mientras la mordías en la boca y ahora te acuer-
das, además subías una escalera, sí, la subías, rozabas con la mano
la bola de vidrio donde nace el pasamanos, pero después Michèle
ha dicho que en su casa no hay ninguna bola de vidrio. (p. 196)

Yet, these musings are read ironically by the reader, especially the
reader who, on the basis of elements of foreshadowing, senses that
Michèle's story is even less expected than Pierre believes or the
reader who reads the text a second time with its overall narrative
structure in mind. Pierre's thoughts are ironic to the extent that they
involve not just a degree of routine psychological introspection, but
that they bespeak his acquisition, in a way that we are basically
unable to explain, of a recollection of the specific details of Michèle's
traumatic sexual history. To be mundane about it, Pierre begins to
recall details of the circumstances of Michèle's rape that he cannot
reasonably have had any access to. She has not told him about her
rape by the German officer, nor have her friends. Moreover, as
Babette and Roland make clear at the end of the story, Michèle does
not know the circumstances surrounding the rapist's death and,
hence, could not have told Pierre how the officer fell forward into a
pile of dead leaves, his face blown off by Roland's shotgun. What is
more, Pierre sings, in a language he does not know (and with a
native accent?), parts of a Schumann song sung by the German
officer; and, in the chalet, he stutters as did the rapist, and he even
seems to speak with the same inflections of voice, despite the fact
that the two are speaking French and not German, languages that
are radically different phonologically.

Finally, how are we to take the closing scene of the story in the
context of such a reading: are Ronald and Babette on their way to try
to convince Michèle that it is time she overcame her traumatic
experience of the past and assumed a normal sex life? Or will they
attempt to prevent a new trauma by telling Pierre what he should
have been told by either Michèle or her protectors before events got
out of hand? A psychological reading of the story, moreover, would
expect, in addition to further information on these points, a clarifica-
tion of the effect Pierre's behavior had on Michèle. All we have is her
hysteria and her appeal to Babette and Ronald. But, since the story is
narrated from Pierre's point of view, we do not have any significant
depiction of psychological impact, only external signs of it. That the
story is related from Pierre's standpoint (there are only three brief
passages in which perspective is shifted away from Pierre to Babette
and Ronald) is somewhat odd, since we have neither a satisfactorily
complete representation of his psychological development regarding Michèle's problem nor anything approaching an adequate representation of his perception of that problem from her viewpoint;

and, were Michèle's trauma the point of the story, we would expect it to be narrated with greater focus on her perception of events, which is hardly the case.

In sum, then, we cannot naturalize "Las armas secretas" by a psychological reading, and I doubt if many readers have really attempted it—at least, not those readers who are familiar with the overall sense of Cortázar's writings. Yet, I think it is necessary to dwell in some detail on the psychological aspects of the story, since it unquestionably concerns a chain of events related directly to a circumstance of paramount psychological significance: the sexual traumatization of a young girl. Cortázar's fiction often deals with aspects of sex, especially within the context of trauma or frustration: the story from *Octaedro* already mentioned, La Maga's childhood as recounted in *Rayuela*, the "black widow" fiancée in "Circe," homosexual seduction in "Las babas del diablo," and sexual hypocrisy in "La señorita Cora." Furthermore, sexual mores are directly related to Cortázar's concern with the self-delusions of the Argentine middle class and with sex as a liberating force (compare *El libro de Manuel*). It is natural for a reader to want to relate direct and passing references to sex to the concerns over the subject, from both a psychological and a sociopolitical frame of reference, in the contemporary Argentine and European societies that figure in Cortázar's fiction. Nevertheless, it would be clear from an attempt to fit together a casebook understanding of sexual preoccupations in Cortázar's writings that they do not conform in detail or in logical development to what we understand as customary psychological narrative. Thus, we must either reject a story like "Las armas secretas" as psychological or we must find an acceptable alternate definition for psychological narrative.

IV

An alternate reading of "Las armas secretas" would seek such a modified definition and could presumably base itself on the potential of the story for a fantastic reading. Read from the perspective of fantastic fiction, where the semantic postulates of the text need not conform to the referential code and where they are obliged in fact to set themselves in opposition to it as a higher order of "logical" comprehension, the psychological problem of "Las armas secretas" may presumably be seen as internally coherent even when it seems to be unsatisfactory from the perspective of customary psychological narrative. The key or "trigger" to such a reading (in addition to the reader's general acceptance of the unusual and the unknown in Cortázar's fiction) is also to be found in the opening passage of the text.

Curioso que la gente crea que tender una cama es exactamente lo mismo que tender una cama, que dar la mano es siempre lo mismo que dar la mano, que abrir una lata de sardinas es abrir al infinito la misma lata de sardinas. "Pero si todo es excepcional", piensa Pierre alisando torpemente el gastado cobertor azul. "Ayer llovía, hoy hubo sol, ayer estaba triste, hoy va a venir Michèle. Lo único invariable es que jamás conseguiré que esta cama tenga un aspecto presentable." No importa, a las mujeres les gusta el desorden de un cuarto de soltero, pueden sonreir (la madre asoma en todos sus dientes) y arreglar las cortinas, cambiar de sitio un florero o una silla, decir sólo a ti se te podía ocurrir poner esa mesa donde no hay luz. Michèle dirá probablemente cosas así, andará tocando y moviendo libros y lámparas, y él la dejará hacer mirándola todo el tiempo, tirando en la cama o hundido en el viejo sofá, mirándola a través del humo de una Gauloise y deseándola. (p. 185)

Characteristic of the sort of ambiguities associated with Cortázar's "writerly" texts—works that demand exceptional effort on the part of the reader, who must collaborate with the writer, as it were, in the structural construction of the text[11]—this opening passage is fundamentally disorienting in that it is not immediately clear to whom we should attribute the first sentence. Since there is a formal distinction between the first and the second sentences—the former is not enclosed in quotation marks and the latter is; the former is not explicitly attributed to a source, while the latter is, to Pierre—it would be natural to assume that both observations do not belong to the same source. For example, the opening sentence could well be attributed to the narrator whom we discover to be omniscient in his reporting of Pierre's thoughts and events beyond Pierre's own range of knowledge. In this sense, the first and second sentence form an ironic counterpoint: one is attributable to a limited consciousness (Pierre's explicitly identified thought) and one is assigned to an omniscient narrator. Such a possible irony is supported by the fact that the parenthetical assignment of source in the second sentence ("piensa Pierre alisando *torpemente* el *gastado* corbertor azul") contains at least one lexical item and possibly a second one that, because they are subjective assessments, underline the superior and ironic perspective of the narrator.

Nevertheless, setting aside formal considerations, we see that there are reasons of a semantic order for attributing both observa-

11. The concept of *lector cómplice* in Cortázar's works has become a major critical premise and is related to the emphasis of contemporary structuralist theory on reader competence. The term was given currency by Mario Benedetti's early review, "Julio Cortázar, un narrador para los lectores cómplices," *Tiempos modernos* 1:2 (1965):16–19.

tions to Pierre, with the omniscient and, therefore, ironic narrator not appearing until the tag to the second sentence that explicitly identifies the character thinking to himself. That the second sentence begins with *pero* is an essential point in linking the two utterances: the concessive particle implies that what follows it is related to a preceding proposition: A, but (no, yet, then, therefore) B. The member "but B" cannot occur without at least implying that there is an accompanying A member. Language has a number of such patterns that systematically link utterances together into a coherent discourse beyond the level of the individual sentence, and to speak of the internal logic or sense or "flow" of a discourse is to acknowledge the functional presence of such patterns. Thus, in short, despite the superficial differences between the two sentences that open the text, we can see that we must attribute them both to the logical flow of Pierre's interior monologue as he waits in vain for Michèle to visit his humble bachelor quarters.

Why, then, might there even be a problem in making such an identification? If both utterances are Pierre's, why distinguish between them orthographically (quotation marks versus no quotation marks) and in terms of reported performance (explicit attribution to Pierre versus no attribution)? One might say that it is simply a question of making the narrative mise-en-scène mildly confusing or complicated enough to engage the writerly participation of the reader. One notes that the opening of "Las babas del diablo," in the same collection and one of Cortázar's major metatexts on the problems of art and literature, also involves a certain amount of confusing complexity, both in syntax and discourse coherency. Nevertheless, on a broader level, it is possible to relate the seemingly insignificant problem of the structural relationship between the two opening sentences of the story to the issue of structural anomaly and to whether or not the text involves a clear-cut—or, at the very least, an adequately convincing—case of the supplantation of the known by the fantastic unknown. The ambivalence of the textual inauguration may be taken as either (1) to signal the narrator's ironic foreshadowing of the eventual imposition of the unknown on the unassuming existence of the hopeless Pierre, or (2) a signal—itself a sort of foregrounding on the level of the metatext rather than on that of the events narrated—that no straightforward characterization of the meaning or implication for a "theory" of experiential reality will be forthcoming in the narrative logic of the text.

The foregoing is an important point. Although "Las armas secretas" deals in the shadowy side of what at first glance seems to be transparent human nature and its associated happenings, does the actual *récit* of the text provide anything in the way of a coherent

postulation of the fashion in which the unknown comes unsuspect-
edly to control modest human destinies? I would venture to say that
it does not. This is, in my opinion, no more a defect of the story than
is the fact that "Las armas secretas" does not provide anything
approaching a valid psychological analysis of the human behavior it
relates. This refusal, which we identify on the level of the metatext,
on the level on which we formally characterized the goals of the
narrative and the implications for its discourse structure of those
goals, is precisely what we have identified as the principle of structural anomaly. As a principle for text production, it becomes a
positive mechanism that identifies a certain range of narrative structures.

But before I pursue further the presence of structural anomaly in
"Las armas secretas," it is necessary to identify some of the motifs of
the imposition of fantasy on accepted reality and the ways in which
they do not coalesce into a clear-cut pattern. Clearly, the most
important elements in the story are those that suggest that Pierre is
reenacting, without realizing it, Michèle's brutal rape by the Nazi
officer. These elements are the details of the setting and circumstances of that event. Throughout the text and in ascending
frequency there are over forty references to approximately six major
allusions: the lodge at Enghien, the song in German, the double-
barreled shotgun that kills the officer, the dry leaves, the crystal ball
at the bottom end of the banister, the key to Michèle's room, plus a
few references that occur with lesser frequency, like Pierre's unexplained coolness to Ronald or his sudden fit of stuttering in the
face of what is for him the girl's sexual reticence. Moreover, these
references, which are, of course, functional motifs that underline
with growing frequency how something unusual is happening to
Pierre's prosaic existence and aspirations, are embodied in tran-
scriptions of his interior monologues and stream of consciousness,
which are, in turn, commented on ironically, both directly and
indirectly by the narrator. These comments come within the context
of Pierre's struggle to account rationally for what he only vaguely
senses as occurring (see the beginning extract of this chapter; both
are attributed to Pierre):

> La delicia de estar ahí, de sentirse tan bien en ese instante, de
> cerrar los ojos, [. . .] de pasarse la mano por el pelo, una, dos
> veces, sintiendo la mano que anda por el pelo casi como si no fuera
> suya, la leve cosquilla al llegar a la nuca, el reposo. Cuando abre
> los ojos ve la cara de Michèle, su boca entreabierta, la expresión
> como si de golpe se hubiera quedado sin una gota de sangre. La
> mira sin entender, un vaso de coñac rueda por la alfombra. Pierre
> está de pie frente al espejo; casi le hace gracia ver que tiene el pelo
> partido al medio, como los galanes del cine mudo. ¿Por qué tiene

que llorar Michèle? No está llorando, pero una carta entre las manos es siempre alguien que llora. Se las aparta bruscamente, la besa en el cuello, busca su boca. Nacen las palabras, las suyas, las de ella, como bestezuelas buscándose, un encuentro que se demora en caricias, un olor a siesta, a casa sola, a escalera esperando con la bola de vidrio en el nacimiento del pasamanos. Pierre quisiera alzar en vilo a Michèle, subir a la carrera, tiene la llave en el bolsillo, entrará en el dormitorio, se tenderá contra ella, la sentirá estremecerse, empezará torpemente a buscar cintas, botones, pero no hay una bola de vidrio en el nacimiento del pasamanos, todo es lejano y horrible, Michèle ahí a su lado está tan lejos y llorando, su cara llorando entre los dedos mojados, su cuerpo que respira y tiene miedo y lo rechaza. (pp. 210–11, see also pp. 218–20)

Yet, if we see the juxtaposition of Pierre's increasing uneasiness, framed by the narrator's ironic commentaries, as the clear representation of the imposition of the fantastic, of the shibboleth "There are more things on earth than man has dreamed of," the structure of such a narrative discourse is not carried out and we are left with a sense of incompleteness. For example, we have a straightforward postulation of such a discourse in the opening references (narrator *cum* Pierre) to how things are not always as easy or as consistently identical as they seem to be. Then we have the introduction of the first motif that does not fit the verisimilar context established; that is, Pierre's first recollection of a detail that belongs to the circumstances of Michèle's rape seven years ago: "Le parece verla, y a la vez se da cuenta de que está imaginando una escopeta de doble caño, justamente cuando traga el humo del cigarrillo y se siente como perdonado de su tontería. Una escopeta de doble caño no tiene nada de raro, pero qué puede hacer a esa hora y en su pieza la idea de una escopeta de doble caño, y esa sensación como de extrañamiento" (pp. 187–88). As has already been noted, these references increase in number and become obsessively insistent in Pierre's subsequent relations with Michèle. Moreover, they cluster themselves into a clear network of references to circumstances Pierre has had no possible knowledge of. Finally, the reader is presented with what should be the resolution of the pattern established by the narrative discourse or formula. This resolution should involve his attempts at sexual relations with Michèle and the definitive, triumphant imposition of the fantastic circumstance—the reenactment in a different time and place through the medium of a different agent of a past and horrible event (how many cheap Gothic thrillers can be summarized with that formula?). But what we have instead of the unequivocal representation of this prototypic resolution is a series of oblique references: does Pierre in fact carry Michèle up to her bedroom?

Does he in fact possess her by force? Does he in fact "become" literally (metempsychosis) or functionally (psychological role assignment) the arrogant defiler of a subjected individual? Do Ronald and Babette in fact return to the scene of the crime to carry out once again the brutal vengeance against the Nazi rapist? Indeed, as I have already mentioned, the text closes not with a taut, suspenseful denouement of the reenacted tragedy, but with a comically and banal exchange between the two putative avengers. Perhaps their conversation is meant ironically to suggest that they are once again to become unsuspecting participants in the terrible assault on Michèle. But, I think not, for what we still miss is the implication of a satisfactory answer to the other questions raised above, questions that are surely reasonable in terms of plot expectations.

To what extent does the situation I have described constitute structural anomaly? Perhaps, the use of the term is a somewhat pretentious extension of a linguistic concept. Yet, no other phrase comes immediately to mind to describe what happens in "Las armas secretas." Although we do not demand literature to be semantically transparent—and, indeed, this study has as one of its axioms that a criticism based on such an assumption is misguided—we nevertheless approach a text with a set of expectations as to what happens in the real world of meaning. When a text, linguistic or literary, deviates from that expectation, we are faced with a delicate choice. We can reject the text as unfortunately ungrammatical, which is what is often done in the case of colloquial discourse. But, in literature, by virtue of the special conventions that control our reading of literary discourse,[12] our choice would more likely be to accept the apparently anomalous as an expansion of an elaboration on accepted versions of reality in meaning. To this extent, anomaly in a literary text becomes crucial not as simply one aspect of its meaning but as the very validation of the way in which we are willing, by virtue of the discourse conventions that control the reading of literature, to accept such anomaly as an appropriate, albeit a perplexingly difficult, feature of literary texts. By foregrounding the fundamental conflict between possible ways of understanding what happens in "Las armas secretas," Cortázar stresses the inevitable semantic opacity of literature and the phenomena that, in his view, it deals with.

All narrative, then, depends on the workings of plot expectations: the reader demands that stories "make sense" in terms of either a Proppian universal plot scheme or in terms of a typology of potential narrative structures. The writer constructs his tale with the confi-

---

12. Concerning discourse structure, see Jonathan Culler's chapters on the novel, and Robert E. Scholes, *Structuralism in Literature: An Introduction*, chapter 5 entitled "The Structuralist Analysis of Literary Texts."

dence that such a demand is, in point of fact, the competence or ability of the reader to follow and impose discourse structure on his tale. [13] Naturally, we expect discourse structure in all serious literature to put the reader's competence to extreme, demanding tests, which is why attempts like Propp's to describe an ideal discourse structure in sufficient detail so as to be considered universal to a vast number of potential structural variants have been disappointing: there is always some narrative that makes complex sense but that does not seem to have been taken into account by the universal typology. But, it is in terms of what we expect, however we define that expectation in terms of narrative typologies, that one may say that the conclusion of Cortázar's story does not provide an adequate characterization of the ultimate triumph of the unknown over pedestrian reality. In other stories by Cortázar, such a triumph is indeed definitive, as in "Casa tomada" (there is no question that the undefined/undefinable strangers have taken over the house); in "Carta a una señorita en París" (there is no question that the protagonist vomits furry bunnies and commits suicide in desperation over his uncontrollable aberration); or in "La noche boca arriba" (there is no question over the complete fusion of the motorcycle accident victim with the victim of Aztec sacrificial rites). Note that in the last example, we have the sort of cyclical reenactment defined as a narrative resolution, an uncompromising definition that is lacking in "Las armas secretas." In sum, unexplained elements seem on the verge of controlling events in the story, but a plotting of the narrative discourse based on their functional presence reveals that, unlike other stories by Cortázar, this text is marked by a truncated resolution of the postulates concerning the necessary, definitive triumph of the unknown or the fantastic in our humble, unsuspecting lives. Rather than resolution, we are left with only an ambiguous suggestion, which may be richer in meanings but which may also confuse the reader.

V

Given the recognized quality of Cortázar's fiction, the critic can only reasonably propose that reader confusion is the goal of the narrative structure of "Las armas secretas." And perhaps such a "confusion" (if one may continue to use, without prejudice, what is nevertheless an essentially negative denomination) is part of the challenge to the competence of a reader of writerly texts that cannot, by virtue of the literary act, offer unambiguous meanings and pre-

13. Concerning the discourse conventions of literature, see Mary Louise Pratt, *Toward a Speech Act Theory of Literary Discourse.*

programmed interpretations—hence, the recourse to a narrative structure predicated on structural anomaly. We sense the potential for untroubled coherence, but the anomalous structure, by failing to conform to what our codes of competence would predict (in the case of "Las armas secretas" *either* a range of psychological interpretations *or* a range of transcendent and fantastic higher orders of experiential reality), we are left with a structure that cannot be resolved adequately in terms of what we perceive to be the potentially "proper" configuration. And it is not a question of ambiguity, which involves nonanomalous but polysemous structures. Ambiguity is what is involved in "Verano": the text is not anomalous, for the intrusion of the unknown appears to be consistently postulated as a fact with which the protagonist must contend. Rather, the story is ambiguous to the extent that there are a number of discrete and reasonable interpretations that a hermeneutic reading of the text could put forth.

In this sense, the problems for an adequate reading that arise with regard to "Las armas secretas" are not really matters of ambiguity. Whether the concept of structural anomaly is, in the final analysis, the best theoretical frame of reference to use in the description of the particular complexities of this one text is of secondary importance. What does stand out as of primary importance is the need to postulate some reasonable point of departure that will identify categorically those particular complexities and invest them with meaning within the context of contemporary models for narrative analysis.

Chapter VIII.

The *Écriture* of Social Protest in Mario Benedetti's "El cambiazo"

Despite the acknowledged importance of Mario Benedetti in the contemporary Latin-American narrative, one is surprised by the relative lack of studies devoted to the Uruguayan's works, particularly his short stories. Aside from those articles that do not go beyond a brief journalistic review, essays based on analytic criteria and theoretical precision are indeed rare, as can be determined from the collection of papers on his writings: *Mario Benedetti, variaciones críticas*.[1] Perhaps this lack of a sustained criticism, which is all the more perturbing if we remember that the new narrators have often received disproportionate critical attention in recent Latin-American literary scholarship, is due to the fact that Benedetti has been somewhat eclipsed by his fellow countryman, Juan Carlos Onetti, truly a forefather of the new narrative. It is possible that it is due also in part to Uruguay's present socio-intellectual situation, where Benedetti's political commitment (he has worked for a number of years with Cuba's official cultural agency, the Casa de las Américas) unquestionably makes him a pariah. Whatever the exact reason for this relative neglect, it is time that the situation be remedied, and this chapter, which deals with one of the stories from *La muerte y otras sorpresas* (1968; the collection has so far received only brief reviews[2]) is the attempt to demonstrate how the Uruguayan's narrative *écriture* places him in the mainstream of the contemporary short story in Latin America.

The story that is to be examined here is "El cambiazo." Like several of the texts in *La muerte*, this story concerns modern technology and its ability to produce in the populace—the mass of people to whom it is offered as a phenomenon for increasing the quality of

---

1. Jorge Ruffinelli, ed., *Mario Benedetti, variaciones críticas* (Montevideo: Libros del Astillero, 1973). This collection has a fairly complete bibliography.

2. Among these reviews is my own, the only one in English: "Mario Benedetti: *La muerte y otras sorpresas*," *Books Abroad* 43 (1969):565. Ruffinelli also comments on this collection, although not always in favorable terms, in his study cited in footnote 1.

their lives and, therefore, the level of their civilization as dignified human beings—an alienation that can assume truly psychotic proportions. This technology, whether nationally developed or imported as part of the country's participation in the international capitalist marketplace, comes to constitute a form of impersonal control over human beings, a control that in turn is nothing more nor less than one more manifestation of the oppression and repression that frames life in Latin America. In "El cambiazo," television is the technological "value" at issue; nevertheless, as I shall demonstrate, this foreign invention, which transmits foreign shows (or local imitations of them that are often worse than the originals) in order to sell foreign products, is touted as an instrument that can be transformed from a stupefying agent of the passive masses into a galvanizing force for revolutionary uprising. In Benedetti's other stories in *La muerte*, we find an assortment of similar technological advances. In "El fin de la disnea," it is medical technology (which may cure asthma, but in so doing destroys the human confraternity of commiserating sufferers). In "Musak," piped-in music triggers psychic disintegration: the music is so neutral that it becomes a maddening "civilized" heir to Chinese water torture. In "Acaso irreparable," it is aeronautics as represented by commercial aviation, which is so efficient it takes everything into account but the chaos of real life. And in "Ganas de embromar," the telephone is a metonymic instrument of how modern technology can be made to serve the ends of mindless political oppression.

"El cambiazo" is one of those stories in which two separate events seem to be unfolding at the same time and along parallel tracks. Two series of plot segments alternate: in one series Coronel Corrales, heading the operations of the Secret Police, converses with himself, with his colleagues and with the political prisoners he has hauled in about the country's problems and the value of the strong hand he knows how to wield so well in the campaign against the enemies of the fatherland; in another series we see the progressive stages of a television contest for young people, a contest in which Corrales's daughter participates and in which the contestants have to come up with changes for different parts of a song sung by Lito Suárez, a young crooner who is the idol of the program and its viewers. The last segment, after the successive stages in the change-game (hence, the story's title), we realize that the winning verses make up what is in fact the call for an uprising, and the young viewers take to the streets, invade Corrales's headquarters, and, screaming hysterically, shoot him to death. Thus, a paradigmatic figure of sociopolitical oppression is brought to (admittedly violent, lynch-law) justice by adolescents inflamed by the song of a callow idol of the teenybopper set.

To give the narrative form, a narrative that in the end addresses itself brutally to certain aspects of sociopolitical life in Latin America, the story marshals on the level of its *écriture* a series of thematic-semantic oppositions. These oppositions shape the text of the story as it evokes linearly, and our discovery or perception of them is what makes an approach to the sense of the narrative possible. To be sure, the fact that the text involves the interplay of two series of alternating segments reflects on the level of text composition the fact that what is fundamentally at issue is a network of oppositions. These oppositions, in turn, manifest themselves directly in the way the story is to be read in terms of two sequences of events that come together only in the closing scene. This network of oppositions cluster around three basic conflicts: (1) the police versus innocent youth (in the end there is an inversion with regard to the question of innocence); (2) sociopolitical reality versus the popular, gratuitous culture of the masses (a modification also takes place as concerns the issue of gratuitousness); and (3) machismo sex versus asexuality (innocent sexuality or at least the fear that is the antithesis of the swashbuckling dominance of the macho).

The first controlling opposition underlies the movement back and forth between scenes that give a faithful portrayal of police cynicism, especially the cynicism of the Secret Police, and scenes that present carefree youths, untroubled by social preoccupation and innocent of the reality that surrounds them, totally absorbed in the innocuous diversions served up by Lito Suárez's scandalously popular television program. What this means is that there is, on the one hand, a tragic social truth and, on the other, the maddening mindlessness of a subculture that is totally divorced from what should be the legitimate concern of the people. That this subculture belongs to the youth, to the future citizens of the Republic, serves all the more to underline how that subculture is supported by an officialdom that finds it immensely preferable to authentic civic and mass sentiment: "Las nuevas canciones son una idiotez. Pero ¿qué hay de malo en eso? La verdad es que la muchachada se entretiene, se pone juvenilmente histérica, pide autógrafos, besa fotografías, y mientras tanto no piensa. [. . .] Siempre es mejor que canten eso y no la Internacional" (p. 85, Coronel Corrales is speaking).[3] From the good Coronel's point of view, that is exactly how things should be: people, especially young people, do not think and, as long as they do not think, the defenders of the fatherland are able to pursue their job of ridding the country of enemies and the opposition cynically and peacefully:

3. All quotes are from *La muerte y otras sorpresas*, 2d ed. (México, D.F.: Siglo XXI Editores, 1969).

Y al final resultaba que ser soldado de la patria no era precisamente defender el suelo, las fronteras, la famosa dignidad nacional, de los fueros civiles el goce defendamos el código fiel, no, ser soldado de la patria, mejor dicho coronel de la patria, era joder a los muchachos, visitar al embajador, joder a los obreros, recibir la visita del subsecretario del secretario del embajador, joder a uno que otro cabecilla, dejar que los estimados colaboradores de esta Jefatura den rienda suelta a su sadismo en vías de desarrollo, insultar, agraviar, joder, siempre joder, y en el fondo también joderse a sí mismo. (p. 86)

The second opposition concerns the relationship between life and art: the latter is obliged to function only as a means for keeping intact the innocence and the passiveness of the young. In this sense "art"—subculture television—is diametrically opposed to the texture of life itself, which is reflected so faithfully in the words that have just been quoted from Corrales's stream of consciousness in another of the segments assigned to him. By way of contrast, the Coronel's daughter is completely swept away by the insane fluff of the tinsel world of her favorite television program:

hipnotizada frente al televisor, Julita no se atreve ni a papadear. No es para menos. Lito Suárez, con su rostro angelical y sus puñitos cerrados, ha cantado Siembra de Luz en seguida Mi Corazón Tiene un Remiendo. Gritos semejantes a los de la juvenil teleaudiencia salen también de la boca de Julita, quien para una mejor vocalización acomoda el bombón de menta al costado de la muela. Pero ahora Lito se pone solemne: "Hoy tengo una novedad y se llama El Cambiazo. Es una canción y también es un juego. Un juego que jugaremos al nivel de masas, al nivel de pueblo, al nivel de juventud . . .". (p. 82)

Yet, and herein lies the genius of Benedetti's story, the two oppositions described so far both undergo the process of rupture, a modification-inversion that alters their meaning completely while pointing at the same time to the possibility for a change in the structures to which they refer. In this way, the innocence attributable to the young television audience emerges as the real basis for potent revolution that is portentous in its implications. In exchange, the cynicism of the police is shown to mask a self-destructive naiveté as concerns the nature of mass persuasion. The manifestations of a cheap and trivial subculture end up suggesting their use as instruments for bringing about authentic communication among the masses, one that will effectively channel consciousness raising and positive responses. All of this is brought about via the game involving changes in the lyrics of a song as described by Lito Suárez at the end of the preceding quote. The change in lyrics involves a contest: the singer will provide the audience with the text of a song in the form of a quartet. Each week one of the lines will be replaced by the best verse chosen from among those submitted by the audience. As the text progresses, the reader witnesses along with Julita and her father (who, as we have seen, discusses the game with one of his subalterns) the gradual modification of the quartet, line by line. Only at the end do we realize what has happened: the quartet is no longer just another stupid modern song:

"Paraquená dieeeeee loimpida, paraquetuá mooooooor despierte, paravosmí voooooooooz rendida, paramisó looooooooo quererte". (p. 83)

Instead, it has become the battle cry of an insurrection:

"Paraqueseá braaaaa laherida, paraqueusé moooooooooos lasuerte, paranosó troooooooooos lavida, paracorrá leeeeeeees lamuerte". (p. 89)

Rupture, therefore, takes place not only in the reader's understanding of what has happened, but in the Coronel's as well. It is a rupture that directly concerns innocence: whereas the young are innocent in their apparent failure to participate in the tragedy of their country's sociopolitical reality, the policy and the entire system of oppression, particularly insofar as the police are cynical toward the value of the people, are innocent on another level because they are incapable of conceiving of an insurrection invited by mass communications and the subculture that they believe serves only to distract the people and to turn their attention away from the oppression that has become their lot. The game ceases to be a game when it becomes political action and when the hypnosis of the youth ceases to be the result of a stupefying subculture and to become the instrument for mobilizing the masses against one of the focal points of their oppression.

Sex-related topics are also one of the bases of the story's *écriture*, for they also point up the opposition between oppressive power and the masses and because they likewise undergo an inversion. Coronel Corrales is an expert in torture techniques. He is also the paradigmatic military macho and his machismo is in effect part of his exercise of power, part of his image, and his professional persona:

decime, podridito, ¿vos te crees que me chupo el dedo? Ustedes querían provocar el apagón, ¿no es cierto? Seguro que al buenazo de Ibarra se la hubiera hecho. Pero yo soy un jefe de policía, no un maricón. Conviene que lo aprendas. ¿Tenés miedo, eh? No te culpo. Yo no sólo tendría miedo sino pánico frente al coronel Corrales. Pero resulta que el coronel Corrales soy yo, y el gran

revolucionario Menéndez sos vos. Y el que se caga de miedo
también sos vos. Y el que se agarra la barriga de risa es otra vez el
coronel Corrales. ¿Te parece bien? Decímelo con franqueza, porque si no te parece bien volvemos a la electricidad. Sucede que a
mí no me gustan los apagones. A mí me gustan los toquecitos
eléctricos. Me imagino que todavía te quedarán güevos. Claro que
un poco disminuidos, ¿verdad? ¿Quién te iba a decir que los
güevos de avestruz se podían convertir en güevos de paloma?
(. . .) ¿te comieron la lengua los ratones, tesoro? (pp. 83–84)

What we have is a dual set of oppositions: *yo/vos, macho/marica*. As
a result, there is a degradation of the prisoner based on verbal abuse,
stressing his alleged "feminity," and based on the use of the electric
probe directed against his sexual organs by an individual who derives his power from his machismo and his position with the military
police. This opposition is defined principally in the segments assigned to Corrales, rather than being distributed between the two
parallel series of narrative segments like the first two oppositions
discussed. Nevertheless, Corrales sees young people in general and
Lito Suárez in particular as something having to do with homosexu-
als. As such, he is confident that he and his men can handle them
and that they represent no real threat to the security of the nation.
This is what Corrales believes (see the quote from p. 85) and this is
the impression that narrative itself gives in the manner in which
certain aspects of Lito Suárez and the behavior of his fans are
presented: "Lito Suárez, con su rostro angelical y sus puñitos cerrados . . . " (p. 82), "por fin ha conseguido una imagen de Lito. Un
ángel, eso es. Besa la foto con furia, con ternura . . . " (p. 85).
Moments before he is shot, Corrales converses with a subaltern:

"El [acto público autorizado] del cantante." "Bah." "Vengo de la
Plaza. Eran miles y miles de chiquilines y sobre todo de
muchachitas. Verdaderamente impresionate. Decían que allí él
iba a completar la canción, que allí iba a elegir el cuarto verso.
Usted diría que yo soy demasiado aprensivo, mi coronel, pero
¿usted no cree que habría que vigilarlos más?" "Créame, Fres-
nado, son taraditos. Los conozco bien, ¿sabe?, porque des-
graciadamente mi hija Julita es uno de ellos. Son inofensivos, son
cretinos, empezando por ese Lito. ¿Usted no cree que es un débil
mental?" (p. 89)

In summary, what I have been maintaining is that "El cambiazo"
from the outset is predicated on a fundamental opposition: the
young versus oppression in the hands of adults—Julita versus her
father, Coronel Corrales. This opposition in turn bases itself for the
generation of the linear narrative on three more immediate opposition that exemplify the central one. In each case we are presented

first with a dichotomy that is reinforced by the distribution of the narrative along two alternating but parallel axes that are well delineated. However, there is also in each case a modification and an inversion that take place: innocence becomes Corrales's guilty trait, television becomes a powerful instrument of the call to rebellion, and the "kids" end up assassinating Corrales, the macho par excellence. Seen in these terms, the distribution of the text in terms of two narrative sequences is only a parenthesis for the purpose of stressing the distance between the two realms, that of blind power and that of the innocent young. Yet, these two sequences—and the realms they seem to differentiate—end up by coming together or overlapping when the latter attacks the former and executes the symbol that incarnates its meaning. Thus, the oppositions that stressed a sociopolitical dichotomy have been nullified and, to a certain extent, overcome.

This structural study of the semantic bases of Benedetti's story, of the principles of *écriture* that give coherence to the linear text, could be accused of reducing the human commitment of "El cambiazo" to formalist schematics. Nevertheless, the semiological and structural analysis of a text cannot avoid dealing with what is being said via the structures of the text. This is because such an analysis is based as it is on the demand to provide not a reductionist interpretation, but guidelines for an adequate reading in the sense that it elucidates the principles of *écriture* on which the text has been constructed. It is not so much a question of "message," expressed in heavy-handed extraliterary terms, as it is of that segment of human experience given meaning through the signifying medium of the text. Far from ignoring the meaning of a literary text, structuralism studies the possibilities for dealing with it, always basing itself on an approach to reading that takes into account how we set about understanding linguistic messages (on which the text is based in its character as a form of linguistic discourse), how we come to see an abstract relationship between the flow of the text, barely divided into fragments by the conventions of orthography, and the underlying semantic denominators that give it meaning. There is, one must insist, a dialectical relationship between the flow of the text and these common denominators that I have called the principles of a text's *écriture*, and an adequate reading of any literary text involves the perception and the evaluation of this dialectic.[4] In "El cambiazo,"

4. From the point of view of the structural study of a work, it is possible to see how questions of "style" become a subcategory of *écriture*. This is why the present study and the one by Oscar Fernández are so different in their critical premises: "Mario Benedetti: Four Stories, Four Styles," *Studies in Short Fiction* 11 (1974):283–90.

where the "artistry" of Lito Suárez's song and the story itself become homologous as a text capable of awakening an impulse for rebellion in their respective audiences (and no one will deny that Benedetti sees art as an instrument of consciousness raising and of activist mobilization), the ability to grasp the underlying principles of *écriture* that give structural shape to the story means the concomitant ability to convert the reading of a story that would otherwise seem to be a confusing example of clever new narrative writing into an appreciation of the essential semantic oppositions that it evokes.

Chapter IX.

Guillermo Cabrera Infante's
Vista del amanecer en el trópico
and the Generic Ambiguity
of Narrative

> *El general preguntó la hora y un edecán se acercó rápido a*
> *musitar: "La que usted quiera, señor Presidente". (p. 99)[1]*

I

While it may be true that *Vista del amanecer en el trópico* owes its title as well as many of its narrative segments to material left over from the author's *Tres tristes tigres* (1967), it is undeniable that the distance separating the two works is great and that Cabrera Infante's most recent work of fiction represents a marked change in his writings.[2] The following points constitute basic features of *Vista* that any adequate characterization of the work—whether seen as a fragmentary novel or as a loosely connected series of stories[3]—must account for:

1. Narrative texture is the most noteworthy feature. We claim that the texture of a work is the direct manifestation of underlying structures, of its *écriture* as text. Yet, these considerations aside and to focus on only the verbal substance of the text, it is surprising to observe how Cabrera Infante has left behind the norm-breaking linguistic experimentation that distinguishes his *Tres tristes tigres*,

1. Guillermo Cabrera Infante, *Vista del amanecer en el trópico* (Barcelona: Editorial Seix Barral, 1974). I know of only two review articles: Eloy González Arguelles, "Guillermo Cabrera Infante: *Vista del amanecer en el trópico*," *Caribe* 1:2 (1976):121–23; Matías Montes Huidobro, "Review of *Vista del amanecer en el trópico* and *O*," *Chasqui* 5:2 (1976):81–84.
2. For a representative collection of essays on Cabrera Infante's fiction prior to *Vista*, see Julio Ortega, ed., *Guillermo Cabrera Infante* (Madrid: Ed. Fundamentos, 1974).
3. For what the datum is worth, Editorial Seix Barral published *Vista* in its *Relatos* series.

José Lezama Lima's *Paradiso*, and Sarduy's *Cobra*—all of which are eminent examples of what Barthes called reader challenging (if not reader defying) *scriptible/writerly* texts. The result is a work that seems to be above all *lectible/writerly*, at least regarding its immediate linguistic expression, which gives the impression of document whose meaning is decidedly transparent. Meaning in the aforementioned novels, of course, is not transparent: whatever meaning that can be purported to underlie the textual *enoncé* is maddeningly elusive. Since the new Latin-American novel is known for its insistence on the nontransparent text whose play of signifiers impedes access to a realm of text-independent meanings, in order to create—to suggest or to insinuate—meanings dependent on the unstable structures of the textual *parole*, Cabrera Infante's shift to a form of pseudo-journalistic expression that seems more document than narrative hopscotch is significant.

2. In *Vista*, we encounter a series of fragments whose interrelationship is tenuous. All extensive narratives (save those that suppress any internal division) are made up of fragments, whether the traditional division into chapters or "scenes" or the more experimental division into blocks of narration that are short as such but are tightly interrelated. *Vista* follows the pattern of Julio Cortázar's *Rayuela* (1963) rather than that of Augusto Roa Bastos's *Yo el Supremo* (1975), which means a narrative made up of a string of fragments that appear to be autonomous in the sense that, rather than following each other in a continuum, each fragment is isolated graphically to the extent that it begins on a separate page and, if it is especially short, is followed by blank space at the bottom of the page and even by a blank overleaf. Moreover, each fragment appears in the index with its opening words by way of a title. Since there are 101 fragments in *Vista*, the index belongs more to a collection of untitled poems than to a work of fiction. What is particularly significant about this fragmentation—and what sets *Vista* off from *Rayuela*, where we can speak of a novel in at least a skeletal fashion, with characters and action-plot trajectory—is that it bespeaks a fundamental ambiguity of genre on Cabrera Infante's part. In other words, it is not clear whether we should speak of an organically structural novel or of a series of short stories, or whether we should speak of fragments that are scenes which, in turn, refer kaleidoscopically to a miscellany of narrative possibilities: an event, an impersonal circumstance, an outstanding individual, even a song or a news item that is spread by word of mouth.

Since the fragments take on the character of autonomous scenes, even when grouped together on the basis of the constant of the *trópico* in the title, the book stands in the end outside the genre of the novel to which *Tres tristes tigres,* when all is said and done, does belong, no matter how hard it may be on occasion to know what is happening in the latter in terms of a unified *fable*. To this extent, *Vista* cannot be studied in terms of novel-reading conventions but insists instead on a reading of independent vignettes. Yet, at the same time and due to the organization of the fragments under an umbrella title and our natural desire to seek organic structures where there seems to be only chaos and disorder, the reader discovers common denominators among the fragments in order to bring them together into a homogeneous text, one without gaps on the level of its abstract meaning. By departing from the patterns of easily recognized genres, especially the novel that is based on a trajectory of events and the short story that stands apart from the other stories with which it appears in a collection, the author forces us with unusual emphasis to think about such conventions. We undertake to see how they are applicable to the text at hand, to what extent; and, if they are not applicable, what the conventions are that should be brought to bear in order to achieve a coherent reading of the text.

3. As a result of the foregoing generic ambiguity, *Vista* brings into focus the question of extratextual versus intratextual unity.[4] It would be impossible not to notice how the fragments are unified not by the trajectory of persons or events described by the inner action, but by the sweep of Cuban history. This point is made explicitly by the back of the book. But it is also made clear by the internal references of the fragments themselves, where chronological movement and allusions to certain happenings and key figures of Cuba's history are obvious to even the reader who lacks a complete knowledge of the history of the island. It is true that Cabrera Infante can count on a more perfect knowledge on the part of the average reader than would be the case, let us say, if he were dealing with the trajectory of Bolivian history, a country that has not been in the public eye to the same extent as Cuba has been in the last twenty years. It is undeniable that Cabrera Infante's text allows one to read it on various levels, from an approach that what is related is understood as a series of key references to men and events that are part of common knowledge (to which is added "historical fact" in this reading), to a reading where we know that the basis is in history but also that what is narrated is to be taken as history without our having to identify documentarily the points of historical reference. It is probable that an intermediary reading is the most normal or appropriate one, the one that Cabrera Infante counted on implicitly in

4. Concerning intertextuality, see Julia Kristeva, *El texto de la novela* (Barcelona: Editorial Lumen, 1974).

structuring his stories so as to place emphasis on first what are historically verifiable data and then on what are really fictional elaborations but with a remote and more mythic historical quality.

The end result is a text in which specific extratextual and intratextual knowledge enriches one's reading, but also one in which this knowledge remains more the possibility of concrete historical knowledge and not an obligation imposed on the reader by the author. The effect is at times one of ambiguity or the hint of ambiguity: the reader has the impression that more is going on than he can handle because he has only an imperfect acquaintanceship with Cuban history. Yet, it is an ambiguity that emerges more from the lack of preciseness in the presentation of many of the data, or from a certain obliqueness in the elaboration of the text itself than from the absence of sufficient historical learning on the author's part. One could go so far as to say that such an ambiguity is operant even for the reader who is extensively familiar with Cuban history, since it is an ambiguity that arises functionally from the mode of narration rather than from the formation of the average reader of the text. In this sense, any question concerning Cuban history in *Vista* concerns more a trap for an adequate reading of the text and not an inherent feature that necessarily defines as such the nature of that text.

4. The use of the principles of intertextuality—references that are both explicit and oblique to other works of history and literature—as well as the fragmentariness that gives *Vista* its particular character contribute to a situation in which the narrative voice, in addition to being multifaceted like that of *Tres tristes tigres*, where we have a text that seems to be self-generating (and self-destructive), depends on the intrinsic nature of each segment, rather than functioning as a "presence" that unites the text as a whole. One could refer to the idea of a pseudo-mythic voice that replaces the perspective of a narrator circumscribed by his limitations as the source of data and opinions (that is, the unreliable narrators of new novel texts that suggest the problem of the inaccessibility of knowledge, such as we have in many of the narrators of Borges's stories). Such a mythic voice insists on a gnosiological primacy based on its being the center whence flow the structures of linguistic expression. It controls expression because it encompasses it as the spokesman of an absolute knowledge as regards the phenomena to be portrayed through the agency of the mythic tale. In primitive, "innocent" contexts, we have myths that lack self-awareness and in which self-contemplation is impossible: they stand as witnesses to an absolute faith in the expressive power of the word. In the new narrative, the need to achieve distance between the narrator (as the maker of fictions) and the narrative material, as well as to permit the latter to "speak itself,"

as the cliché goes, or to vanish as a non-meaning that cannot be independent from the narration that articulates it, gives new life to the possibilities of mythic expression whereby the text exists only as the product of *énonciation* by an explicit narrative voice. But, at the same time, in a modern context, where innocence is impossible, where metaliterature—literature that turns in upon itself to engage in self-commentary and self-criticism—becomes an imperative, mythic expression demands dialectics in which the structures of expression embody not only a meaning with an absolute value (the "truth" about something or some experience—in this case, the intrahistorical trajectory of Cuba)—but also an often cutting irony that exposes all of our uncertainties concerning actions, characters, and values that intrahistory represents. In this latter sense, the text can be the expression of a myth while at the same time it bespeaks the strain on myth by modern human ineptness.

Thus, *Vista* may be using the anonymity of historical facts and figures to create, on the one hand, a mythic setting in which values are what is most important, but also, on the other, to achieve a demythification of a certain canon of received Cuban history by relating it via a fragmentary narration lacking in one controlling voice as though it were unimportant as a specific story, as if anonymity were a reference to relativity, if not to the cyclical and perennial nature, of the national *gesta*. In this sense, the narration that functions more in terms of the individual fragments than with references to a cohesive voice serves to delineate, rather than a mythic expression that is self-narrating (which is what we associated with epic or mythic texts, characterized by unobtrusive—and, therefore, nonironic—narrators), an ironic and self-challenging text.

II

The foregoing are the features that most distinguish *Vista*'s *écriture* and that set it off from Cabrera Infante's other writings, despite whatever similarity it may have to them on the basis of the constants that underlie any writer's works. To characterize the fragments' specificity as texts, the following passage will be examined:

[segmento 4]
Al llegar a una aldea grande, los conquistadores encontraron reunidos en la plaza central a unos dos mil indios, que los espera-ban con regalos, mucho pescado y casabe, sentados todos en cuclillas y algunos fumando. Empezaron los indios a repartir la comida cuando un soldado sacó su espada y se lanzó sobre uno de ellos cercenándole la cabeza de un solo tajo. Otros soldados imita-ron la acción del primero y sin ninguna provocación empezaron a tirar sablazos a diestra y siniestra. La carnicería se hizo mayor

cuando varios soldados entraron en un batey, que era una casa muy grande en la que había reunidos más de quinientos indios, "de los cuales muy pocos tuvieron oportunidad de huir". Cuenta el padre Las Casas: "Iba el arroyo de sangre como si hubieran muerto muchas vacas". Cuando se ordenó una investigación sobre el sangriento incidente, se supo que al ser recibidos los conquistadores con tal amistosidad "pensaron que tanta cortesía era por les matar de seguro". (p. 17)

In addition to the seemingly cold or detached narrative voice, this segment, which belongs to the first group of texts that deal with the colonization of the island by the Spaniards and the "hosts" of civilization, lends itself to considerations on the point of reference in any code of knowledge and value. In general, *Vista* concerns a series of events that satirizes or attacks through satire the official commonplaces of Cuban history (and one will recall that Cabrera Infante's political position is both anti-Batista and anti-Castro). Although some of these segments are marked by a truly tragic-pathetic note, Cabrera Infante prefers to focus on his material from a satirical angle where officially propounded pretensions, the kitsch of school texts on Cuban history, and the lachrymose literature of mass taste make up a textual point of reference for the elaboration of his own writing. (For examples of segments of truly tragic-pathetic note, see segment [98], "Primero me quitaron el taller," which deals with the injustices of a social and liberating revolution; and segment [21], "Habian estado jugando," which concerns the Spanish reprisals against independence movements.) What this means is that Cabrera Infante's text degrades another canonical text, either because it forms part of the written elitist tradition or because it is a part of an oral tradition: both cry out for submission into the critical rewriting of iconoclastic literature. Only in this way can the lies, distortions, and mistakes come to surface.

In the segment quoted, we see very well how the process of constructing a text on the degradation of other texts works. On the one hand, we have a story told with all the stylistic flourishes of public-school textbooks: the slightly journalistic tone, made weightier due to more balanced periods. This tone, worthy of an elevated rhetorical standard, is not used to portray the deliberations of a constitutional convention or some other event where such a standard would be an appropriate vehicle of expression, but to report an episode of startling barbarity and military perversion. It is as though this register were being used in a contemporary context to describe police torture, for the values that justify the style or register are in irresolvable conflict with the meaning they convey, and herein lies the deployment of satire for textual degradation. Moreover, this segment contains a reference to Padre de las Casas's chronicle of the Conquest. This reference does not contribute to the neutral journalistic tone, but constitutes rather a rupture with it, to the extent that it is the only sentence in the fragment that establishes the sense most appropriate to the scene in its use of the simile equating the massacre of the Indians with the slaughter of cattle. This play of language is what defines most categorically the essense of the textually elaborated "view" of the tropics put forth by Cabrera Infante's writing.

Another segment that makes a specific issue out of its own textuality is [12], "Dice la historia . . . ," in which there is a hierarchy of references to a slave conspiracy. The segment is made up of four paragraphs. The first one begins with: "Dice la historia . . . " and is followed by a sentence in quotes. The second paragraph opens with "Cuenta la leyenda que . . . " and is followed by the complement introduced by *que*, without quotation marks. The third paragraph, on the other hand, closes the matter with the statement that "En realidad . . . " And the fourth one consists of the single sentence: "Todos los conspiradores fueron ahorcados." In this way, the segment juggles a series of versions, so to speak, on a single matter. History and legend are marked by a single quality that allows them to avoid the central issue: the execution of the conspirators. The proposition of "reality" serves in exchange to put that fact forth, which in the end is the most important one. Thus, it is unquestionable that the text bases its *écriture* on the problematic question of multiple versions of events, versions that disagree with each other, less because truth is relative and unstable, but rather because each version originates in a different understanding of what is important and how it should be presented. The literary text thus defines its own space as a story opposing all other versions and possible texts. See also, in this regard, segment [18], which addresses itself to patriotic poetry: "Los insurrectos lograron tomar. . . ."

One other fragment also suggests the question of fiction and reality in the facts it relates. But here, the text occupies a space in which the distinction is no longer valid or is meaningless:

[segmento 43]
Los obreros haitianos y jamaiquinos enviaron una delegación a hablar con el hacendado. Decidieron terminar la huelga si recibían el aumento. Todo pareció ir de lo mejor y el hacendado propuso hacer una foto del grupo para conmemorar el acuerdo. Los delegados haitianos y jamaiquinos se colocaron en fila enfrente de la máquina, cubierta con una tela negra. El hacendado salió del grupo para dar una orden a su mayoral. El mayoral destapó la máquina y tranquilamente fusiló con la ametralladora al grupo de delgados. No hubo más quejas de los cortadores de caña en esa

zafra y en muchas más por venir.
  La historia puede ser real o falsa. Pero los tiempos la hicieron creíble. (p. 97)

What is most characteristic about this segment is the fact that it discusses in general terms an event of undeniable injustice and moral irresponsibility, this time one that occurred after independence. And one feature that deserves detailed comment is the rhythm of the text between segments that portray the same type of happening but at different moments and in different times in history (the Colonial Period, independence, right-wing dictatorships, socialist government) that are nevertheless homologous in their implications. That is, to say, the segment at hand describes a strike by slaves and Negro workers, and as such is a repetition of an event that is described in segment [12], "Dice la historia . . . ," where the *clases de color* set out to imitate their Haitian counterparts by rising up against Spanish slave owners. This time around it is the Haitian and Jamaican workers who request better working conditions not by demanding a black republic as part of their revolt (an eighteenth-century Enlightenment solution), but a salary increase as part of strike demands (a twentieth-century remedy). The former are hanged, the latter, shot by a machine gun disguised as a camera, which is a brilliant touch and one that symbolizes perfectly the newly dawned age of technology. And, finally, where history, legend, and reality were categorized, in segment [43] we are given a circumstance that is ambivalent as to whether it is fiction or history. What is, thus, at issue is a certain parallelism between the two segments in not only their sociocultural meanings—they are accurate vignettes of an emerging people—but also in their *écriture*, where the tone and essential facts are told as something that is more potentially true than documentarily historic.

This type of segment brings up another question concerning *Vista's écriture*: how the fragmentation of events and the ambiguity of documentary history result in the participation of figures that are more outlines of a certain form of human conduct than they are independent individuals. It is for this reason that, alongside the ambiguity of historical data, we have the anonymity of historical protagonists. The result is that the personages who appear in Cabrera Infante's stories or texts, many of whom could be easily identified as historical or public names by one type of reader (one certainly in the minority outside of Cuba or a Cuban exile community), do not differ markedly from the sort of character we are accustomed to finding in the *nueva narrativa*.

In a study on how the character-hero of the literature of the last century has given way to the character-*actant* (A. J. Greimas's term) of the contemporary narrative, Jitrik identifies nine key processes. The character-*actant* who exists only to the extent that he intervenes in a fictional text that is not necessarily verisimilar and in a fashion such that we assign him specific structural roles in terms of the overall pattern of the narrative stems from the interest on the part of contemporary fiction in speaking of the world as a structure of circumstances and not as the drama of extravagant personalities. Thus, the character-*actant* is antithetical to the character-hero, who enjoys a well-defined biographical and psychological verisimilitude that gives him the impression of possessing an extratextual autonomy. Undoubtedly, features of this character-*actant*, of this nonexistent cavalier, define the role that Cabrera Infante assigns to the great (but often infamous) figures of Cuban history that parade through his texts:

> 1°) *Procedimiento de la "grupalización"*. [. . .] un personaje que sea un grupo: es la tentativa de romper la "psicología" radicada en lo individual y proponer una figura más amplia en el interior de la cual se pueden producir desplazamientos—que no se explicitan—y que apelan a un nivel más profundo de psiquismo; en el fondo, se trata de volver al momento del mito, más allá del coro que, de todos modos, actuaba como un solo cuerpo aunque de él se desprendieran los personajes. [. . .]: la conjetura se constituye no sólo en cuanto a la "identidad" de los encargados de encarnar la conciencia del grupo, sino en cuanto a la consistencia del grupo mismo, es decir a su posibilidad de ser aprehendido o pensado por lectores acostumbrados a hacer del singular el punto de toda relación con el mundo y del plural una noción que sirve para descripciones de orden general. . . . (p. 82)[5]

There is no doubt that this procedure of categorization (along with those of levelling, metonymy, and disjunction, which is what leads to a kaleidoscopic effect) defines perfectly both the role of individuals and that of events themselves in *Vista*: participants as well as facts typify metonymically and synecdochically a plural generalness where one has traditionally spoken of a singular trajectory of historically outstanding men and events.

To close this characterization of the texts that make up *Vista* and the salient features of their *écriture*, let us examine a segment that exemplifies how Cabrera Infante sees the participation of the character-*actant* within a context shown to be eternal and inalterable. It is in the juxtaposition between the human being as type and his equally paradigmatic circumstance wherein we can see the writer's undeniable humanistic preoccupation, despite his conception of

---

5. Noé Jitrik, *El no existente caballero, la idea de personaje y su evolución en la narrative latinoamericana* (Buenos Aires: Ediciones Megápolis, 1975).

the depersonalized role of the individuals in his texts:

[segmento 72]
¿Es cierto que ningún arado se detiene por un moribundo? Los autos pasaron de largo toda la noche mientras el hombre moría a un lado de la carretera. Deben haberlo sacado de la cárcel a medianoche y vinieron y lo mataron aquí. O tal vez ya estaba muerto, torturado, y un carro lo trajo de madrugada y lo dejó junto al laguito. O [tal vez] lo tiraron, al anochecer, de una perseguidora. Le dieron por muerto y el hombre estaba vivo todavía y se estuvo muriendo la noche entera.

Amaneció como siempre. La luna se ocultó temprano y Venus se fue haciendo primero más brillante y después pálida, tenue. Dejó de soplar el viento de tierra, pero había más fresco que al atardecer. Varios gallos cantaron o un solo gallo cantó muchas veces. Los pájaros empezaron a silbar o a piar o a gorjear sin moverse de los árboles. El cielo se hizo azul y luego regresó al violeta, al púrpuro, al rojo, al rosa y más tarde fue naranja y amarillo y blanco al salir el sol. Las nubes llegaron desde la costa. Ahora olía a café. Alguien abrió una cancela. El tráfico se hizo mayor.

El muerto siguió en la cuneta hasta que a media mañana lo levantó el forense. (p. 163)

Beyond the division of the segment into three parts or "movements," what stands out is the correlation between the first two: the opening paragraph refers to the cruel lot of a political prisoner, while the second alludes to a gorgeous tropical morning. The third paragraph rounds out the juxtaposition with the impersonal journalistic information concerning what happens subsequently to what is now human garbage. What underlies the interfacing of the first two segments is the transition from the personal (the dead man's lot) to the impersonal (the verbal sketch describing the dawn), from an erotesis (the series of rhetorical questions that serve to mark the stages of the first movement) to a lyrical evocation (the use of allusions, a certain type of "emotive" adjective, the references to pleasurable and simple natural phenomena, the use of polysyndeton to reinforce the latter). This rhetorical procedure involving the juxtaposition of two so different verbal subtexts can be identified as the major stylistic feature of segment [72] for inscribing the underlying *écriture*, which in turn concerns the need to structure a portrayal of the violent conflict between the human individual and his socionatural environment.

In the first movement, although there is only one rhetorical question overtly marked with question marks, the subsequent sentences possess an identical interrogative value, as though they were dominated by the abstract clause, "¿Será que . . . ?" Thus, we can identify a series of dubitative structures that stress, on the one hand, the ambiguity of this event lost in the night and unknown to the world of the living, while, on the other hand, it calls our attention to how this fact is ambiguous to the extent that it is paradigmatic, typical of this island (not "vale") of tears: "Es cierto . . . ?" "Deben [that is, deben de] haberlo sacado . . . ," "O tal vez ya estaba muerto . . . ," "O [tal vez] lo tiraron, al anochecer, de una perseguidora." These four sentences (of the six that make up the paragraph) convey a markedly reserved tone. It is as though it were difficult to establish with any certainty the nature of the events, as though there were too many possible explanations for how a prisoner who has been tortured and is now slowly dying has come to spend the night of his extended agony in a ditch alongside the road.

By way of contrast, the opening sentence of the second movement sets forth, with the authority of a narrator accustomed to executing such verbal portraits, a delightful and eternal scene: "Amaneció como siempre." The extent to which this text is based on an *écriture* of juxtaposition is evident: a movement that dwells on a pathetic and ambiguous human circumstance is correlated with one that places that circumstance within the lush context of a tropical morning. Thus, one could say that, if there is one text in *Vista* that synthesizes Cabrera Infante's perspective, his "view" of non-transcendent Cuban history, it is unquestionably this one.

III

Vista is an important collection of texts both for the form adopted for the presentation of Cuba's sociohistorical experience and for its particularly unique *écriture*. This *écriture* is based on a series of principles that substitute for the cohesive novel and the organic collection of autonomous short stories a textuality based on narrative fragments that are neither completely interdependent nor completely autonomous. There are no characters, no "cavaliers," and a documentary precision is lacking that would give the reader facile entrance into extratextual meaning. Thus, he is obliged to maintain his distance and to experience the play of allusions and references as dynamic but nontransparent signifiers. *Vista* is, in sum, a collection of texts whose nature is synthesized by a phrase from one of the segments quoted above [43]: "La historia puede ser real o falsa. Pero los tiempos la hicieron creíble".

Conclusions

As opposed to a chronological registry of contemporary practitioners of the short story in Spanish America, a country-by-country survey of prizewinning names and titles, or an index of sociopolitical and philosophical motifs to be found in the major collections, I have chosen instead to emphasize a highly selective inventory of structural issues associated with an equally, highly selective choice of individual texts.

Virtually all of the stories discussed have been translated into English and other languages, and there is no doubting the pivotal role played by Borges, Cortázar, García Márquez, Rulfo, and, to only a slightly lesser extent, by Benedetti and Cabrera Infante in what we call the "new Latin-American fiction."

By the same token, topics like "fictional *narrataire*," "reader complicity," "structural or pattern rupture," aside from being issues associated with universal literature by virtue of the inherent nature of verbal discourse, enjoy particular prominence in contemporary fiction, especially in Latin America, where they can be related to the acknowledged sociopolitical objectives of the literature of these writers. Thus, while I have foregrounded the analysis of the discrete structural and textual markers of the theoretical processes identified in the title of each chapter, attention has been paid, if only obliquely or implicitly, to how a process is the extension of the overall significance of the text being studied: Cabrera Infante's intertextuality, which derives to a great measure from his blending fictional and nonfictional modes of discourse, novelistic and short-story procedures, stresses the mythical nature of official Cuban history; linguistic rupture in Cortázar is a striking reflex of how his fiction breaks with conventional views of reality, partly because we have come to believe that a secure reality is cameoed by stable linguistic structures. Reader complicity in García Márquez's fictions has less a patronizing attitude toward the material he is describing than the imperative that the "objective" addressee be drawn into and assume responsibility for a seriously awry social order.

I do not maintain that these observations or that this sort of textual analysis blends easily with accepted sociological analyses of Latin-American literature. I do, however, claim that the appropriate structural analysis of verbal discourse must view the text as part of a larger structural context in which the former alludes to and incorporates the latter in a systematic fashion. Thus, the *écriture* of literary texts does, as I insisted in my opening programmatic chapter, in-

121

volve implicitly an answer to the metaliterary question as to why write literature at all. This study has not rehearsed the many and complex debates that have surrounded the new Latin-American narrative and its sociocultural role. Gordon Brotherston's recent work entitled *The Emergence of the Latin American Novel* (London: Cambridge University Press, 1977) is one excellent study in which to pursue this subject. Nevertheless, the theoretical underpinning of the textual analyses contained in this study has led naturally to the goals inherent in processes like structural rupture and reader complicity.

From one point of view, this study is necessarily fragmentary: the decision to examine individual short-story texts in depth means that, in practical terms, only a handful of works can be studied. Yet, the distinguishing characteristics of the *nuevo cuento hispanoamericano* should have emerged nonetheless: the insistence on a dialectical relationship between a perception of the sociopolitical reality of Latin American and its semiological representation in the narrative; the challenge to colloquial and literary dialects of Spanish to rid themselves of rhetorical clichés and to convey with greater fidelity the unstable nature of Latin-American man's contemporary experience; the need to experiment with received literary forms and to enrich the literary tradition by fashioning new ones (specifically, the *microtexto* and varieties of nonfiction narrative); the imperative that literary discourse recognize in its structural markers the nonprivileged status of narrator, *narrataire*, and text, and that it incorporate features to demonstrate explicitly the problems of verbal art in a culture degraded by the inescapable facts of political life. To this extent, the structural issues discussed and the consequences of the demand that particular verbal and technical features be dealt with in terms of the larger context of discourse *écriture* do, in the final analysis, involve the most general concerns of fictional writing in Latin America today.

Selected Bibliography

Primary References

Barthes, Roland. *Le Degré zéro de l'écriture*. Paris: Seuil, 1972.
————. *S/Z*. Paris: Seuil, 1970.
————. "To Write: An Intransitive Verb." In R. Macksey and E. Donato, *The Languages of Criticism and the Sciences of Man*, pp. 134–45. Baltimore: The Johns Hopkins University Press, 1970.
Culler, Jonathan. *Structuralist Poetics: Structuralism, Linguistics, and the Study of Literature*. Ithaca, N.Y.: Cornell University Press, 1975.
Jameson, Frederic. *The Prison-House of Language: A Critical Account of Structuralism and Russian Formalism*. Princeton, N.J.: Princeton University Press, 1972.
Kristeva, Julia. *Le Texte du roman*. 's-Gravenhage: Mouton, 1970.
Pratt, Mary Louise. *Toward a Speech Act Theory of Literary Discourse*. Bloomington, Ind.: Indiana University Press, 1977.
Scholes, Robert E. *Structuralism in Literature: An Introduction*. New Haven: Yale University Press, 1974.
Todorov, Tzvetan. *Poétique de la prose*. Paris: Seuil, 1971.

Secondary References

Barthes, Roland. *Le Plaisir du texte*. Paris: Seuil, 1973.
Bremond, Claude. *Logique du récit*. Paris: Seuil, 1973.
Derrida, Jacques. *De la Grammatologie*. Paris: Minuit, 1967.
————. *L'Écriture et la différence*. Paris: Seuil, 1967.
Eco, Umberto. *La struttura assente*. Milano: Bompiani, 1968.
Genette, Gérard. *Figures*. 4 vols. Paris: Seuil, 1966–1972.
Goldmann, Lucien. *Pour une sociologie du roman*. Paris: Gallimard, 1964.
Greimas, A. J. *Sémantique structurale*. Paris: Larousse, 1966.
Hendricks, William O. *Essays on Semiolinguistics and Verbal Art*. The Hague: Mouton. 1973.
Jameson, Frederic. *Marxism and Form*. Princeton, N.J.: Princeton University Press, 1971.
————. "Metacommentary." *PMLA* 86 (1971):9–18.
Jitrik, Noé. *Producción literaria y producción social*. Buenos Aires: Editorial Sudamericana, 1975.
Lima, Luíz Costa. *Estruturalismo e teoria da literatura, introdução às problemáticas estética e sistêmica*. Petrópolis: Editora Vozes, 1973.
Maldavsky, David. *Teoría literaria general*. Buenos Aires: Editorial Paidós, 1974.
Mounin, Georges. *Introducción a la semiología*. Barcelona: Editorial Anagrama, 1970.

Portella, Eduardo. *Teoria da comunicação literária*. 3d ed. Rio de Janeiro: Tempo Brasileiro, 1976. Original volume published in 1970.

Silva, Vítor Manuel de Aguiar. *Teoría de la literatura*. Madrid: Editorial Gredos, 1972. Versión española de Valentin García Yerba.

Todorov, Tzvetan. *Grammaire du Décaméron*. 's-Gravenhage: Mouton, 1969.

———. *Introduction a la littérature fantastique*. Paris: Seuil, 1970.

———. *Poétique de la prose*. Paris: Seuil, 1971.

Index

125